Rhetoric: Discovery and Change

Rhetoric:
Discovery and Change

Richard E. Young *University of Michigan*
Alton L. Becker *University of Michigan*
Kenneth L. Pike *University of Michigan*

HARCOURT, BRACE & WORLD, INC.

New York Chicago San Francisco Atlanta

ISBN: 0-15-576895-6

LIBRARY OF CONGRESS CATALOG CARD NUMBER: 70-13712

PRINTED IN THE UNITED STATES OF AMERICA

Copyrights and Acknowledgments

For permission to use the selections reprinted in this book, the authors
are grateful to the following publishers and copyright holders:

GEORGE ALLEN & UNWIN LTD. For an excerpt from *The Romance of Tristan and
Iseult* by Joseph Bédier, translated by Hilaire Belloc.

AMERICAN PHILOSOPHICAL SOCIETY. For excerpts from "The Architecture of
Complexity" by Herbert A. Simon from *Proceedings of the American
Philosophical Society*, Vol. 106, No. 6 (1962).

AMERICAN PSYCHOLOGICAL ASSOCIATION. For "They Saw a Game: A Case
Study" by Albert H. Hastorf and Hadley Cantril from *The Journal of
Abnormal and Social Psychology*, Vol. 49 (1954), pp. 129–34. Copyright
1954 by the American Psychological Association and reproduced by
permission.

AMERICAN SCIENTIST. For "Life Can Be *So* Nonlinear" by Ladis D. Kovach
from *American Scientist* (June, 1960).

ANN ARBOR NEWS. For a selection from the *Ann Arbor News* (June 8, 1965).

ASSOCIATION FOR COMPUTING MACHINERY. For "Contextual Understanding by
Computers" by Joseph Weizenbaum in *Communications of the ACM*,
Vol. 10, No. 8 (August, 1967). Copyright © 1967, Association for Com-
puting Machinery, Inc.

BANTAM BOOKS, INC. For an excerpt from *The Medium Is the Massage* by
Marshall McLuhan and Quentin Fiore. Copyright © 1967 by Marshall
McLuhan, Quentin Fiore, and Jerome Agel. By permission of Bantam
Books, Inc. All rights reserved.

BEACON PRESS. For "Stranger in the Village" from *Notes of a Native Son* by
James Baldwin. Reprinted by permission of the Beacon Press, copyright
© 1953, 1955 by James Baldwin.

BELKNAP PRESS OF HARVARD UNIVERSITY PRESS. For excerpts from "The Art of
Discovery" from *On Knowing* by Jerome Bruner.

BLACKWELL & MOTT LTD. For an excerpt from *The Nature of the Universe* by
Fred Hoyle.

CAMBRIDGE UNIVERSITY PRESS. For excerpts from *The Stars and Their Courses* by Sir James Jeans; from *Studies in Words* by C. S. Lewis; from *The Discarded Image* by C. S. Lewis; from *An Enquiry Concerning the Principles of Natural Knowledge* by Alfred North Whitehead; and from *Process and Reality* by Alfred North Whitehead.

CHAPMAN AND HALL LTD. For "Biotic Communities" from *The Nature of Natural History* by Marston Bates. Published in Great Britain by Chapman and Hall Ltd., London.

CHATTO & WINDUS LTD. For an excerpt from *Queen Victoria* by Lytton Strachey. Reprinted by permission of Mrs. A. S. Strachey and Chatto & Windus Ltd.

NOAM CHOMSKY. For an excerpt from *Syntactic Structures* by Noam Chomsky.

CLARENDON PRESS. For excerpts from *The Dialogues of Plato*, translated by Benjamin Jowett, 4th ed., 1953, and by permission of the Clarendon Press, Oxford.

JAMES CLARKE & COMPANY, LTD. For "An Effective Substitute for War" from *The Power of Nonviolence* by Richard B. Gregg.

COLUMBIA UNIVERSITY PRESS. For an excerpt from *The Columbia-Viking Desk Encyclopedia*.

CORNELL UNIVERSITY PRESS. For excerpts reprinted from Karl von Frisch, *Bees: Their Vision, Chemical Senses, and Language*. Copyright 1950 by Cornell University. Used by permission of Cornell University Press.

JOHN CUSHMAN ASSOCIATES, INC. For an excerpt from *What Is Mother* by Lee Parr McGrath and Joan Scobey. Reprinted by permission of John Cushman Associates, Inc. Copyright © 1968 by Lee Parr McGrath and Joan Scobey.

EDGAR DALE. For an excerpt from "Clear Only If Known" by Edgar Dale from *The News Letter* (Bureau of Educational Research, Ohio State University).

JOAN DAVES. For "Letter from Birmingham Jail" from *Why We Can't Wait* by Martin Luther King, Jr. Reprinted by permission of Joan Daves. Copyright © 1963 by Martin Luther King, Jr.

DOUBLEDAY & COMPANY, INC. For an excerpt from *The Silent Language* by Edward T. Hall. Copyright © 1959 by Edward T. Hall. Reprinted by permission of Doubleday & Company, Inc.

DOVER PUBLICATIONS, INC. For an excerpt from *Creative Power* by Hughes Mearns. Dover Publications, Inc., New York, N. Y. Reprinted through permission of the publisher.

ESTATE OF ALBERT EINSTEIN. For "The Laws of Science and the Laws of Ethics" from *Out of My Later Years* by Albert Einstein.

LOREN EISELEY. For an excerpt from *Man, Time, and Prophecy* by Loren Eiseley.

FABER AND FABER LTD. For "The Thought-Fox" from *The Hawk in the Rain* by Ted Hughes. Reprinted by permission of Faber and Faber Ltd. from *The Hawk in the Rain*.

JOHN FARQUHARSON LTD. For "Stranger in the Village" from *Notes of a Native Son* by James Baldwin.

FARRAR, STRAUS & GIROUX, INC. For an excerpt from *Listening with the Third Ear* by Theodor Reik. Copyright © 1954 by Farrar, Straus & Giroux, Inc.

HARCOURT, BRACE & WORLD, INC. For excerpts from *Abinger Harvest* by E. M. Forster; and from *Queen Victoria* by Lytton Strachey.

THE OPEN COURT PUBLISHING COMPANY, LA SALLE, ILLINOIS. For an excerpt from *An Analysis of Knowledge and Valuation* by C. I. Lewis.

PETER OWEN LTD. For excerpts from *Let Us Now Praise Famous Men* by James Agee and Walker Evans, published by Peter Owen.

OXFORD UNIVERSITY PRESS, INC. For "Thinking like a Mountain" from *A Sand County Almanac* by Aldo Leopold, copyright 1949 by Oxford University Press, Inc.; and for an excerpt from *Power, Politics, and People* by C. Wright Mills. Both are reprinted by permission.

PANTHEON BOOKS, INC. For an excerpt from *The Romance of Tristan and Iseult* by Joseph Bédier, translated by Hilaire Belloc and Paul Rosenfeld. Copyright 1945 by Pantheon Books, Inc., a Division of Random House, Inc. Reprinted by permission of the publisher.

PATHFINDER PRESS, INC. For an excerpt from *Malcom X Speaks*. Copyright © 1965 by Merit Publishers and Betty Shabazz.

PENDLE HILL PUBLICATIONS. For excerpts from "The Journal of a College Student" by Joseph Havens from Pendle Hill Pamphlet No. 141 (June, 1965).

S. G. PHILLIPS, INC. For "Crossing into Poland" by Isaac Babel from *The Collected Stories* of Isaac Babel. Copyright © 1929 by S. G. Phillips, Inc. Reprinted by permission of S. G. Phillips, Inc.

EUNICE PIKE. For permission to reprint a letter to Kenneth L. Pike.

PITMAN PUBLISHING CORPORATION. For an excerpt from the book *How Children Fail* by John Holt. Copyright 1964 by the Pitman Publishing Corporation. Reprinted by permission of the publisher.

PRINCETON UNIVERSITY PRESS. For an excerpt from *Logic and Rhetoric in England 1500–1700* by Wilbur Samuel Howell. Copyright © 1956 by Princeton University Press.

HENRY REGNERY COMPANY. For an excerpt from *The World of Silence* by Max Picard.

ROUTLEDGE & KEGAN PAUL LTD. For excerpts from *The Poems of Andrew Marvell*, edited by Hugh MacDonald; from *Personal Knowledge* by Michael Polanyi; and from *The Conditions of Knowing* by Angus Sinclair.

SCHOCKEN BOOKS, INC. For "An Effective Substitute for War" from *The Power of Nonviolence* by Richard B. Gregg. Copyright © 1959 by Richard B. Gregg. Reprinted by permission of Schocken Books, Inc.

CHARLES SCRIBNER'S SONS. For an excerpt from *I and Thou* by Martin Buber, translated by Ronald Gregor Smith. "Biotic Communities" is reprinted with the permission of Charles Scribner's Sons from *The Nature of Natural History* by Marston Bates. Copyright 1950 Marston Bates.

HERBERT A. SIMON. For an excerpt from "The Architecture of Complexity" by Herbert A. Simon from *Proceedings of the American Philosophical Society*, Vol. 106, No. 6 (1962).

SIMON & SCHUSTER, INC. For an excerpt from *What Is Mother* by Lee Parr McGrath and Joan Scobey.

SUMMER INSTITUTE OF LINGUISTICS. For excerpts from *Laboratory Manual for Morphology and Syntax* by William R. Merrifield and others.

THAMES AND HUDSON LTD. For an excerpt from *The Informed Heart* by Bruno Bettelheim. Published in the United Kingdom by Thames and Hudson Ltd.

Preface

THIS book can be seen as a solution to two related but quite different problems that the authors faced prior to their collaboration. Pike, a linguistic scholar, had sought to determine whether linguistics could provide the basis for a method of improving competence in writing. Many linguists and composition teachers had assumed that it could, yet the actual contributions of linguistics had not borne out the assumption. New methods of grammatical analysis and pattern practice, and sophisticated approaches to punctuation and usage — to name some of the more significant contributions — came nowhere near providing the basis for a coherent and comprehensive method. Pike suggested that one particular linguistic theory, tagmemics, could make a much more extensive and fundamental contribution by supplying the theoretical principles and problem-solving procedures necessary for a distinctly new approach to rhetoric. Becker and Young, for several years teachers of freshman rhetoric, were convinced that rhetoric was potentially an important part, perhaps the most important part, of a college student's education; yet they were dismayed by the intellectual emptiness and practical ineffectiveness of conventional courses. The solution Pike proposed to his problem seemed also to offer a solution to their own. This book is thus drawn from linguistic theory, but it does not aim to teach that — indeed no knowledge of linguistics is required of either teacher or student. The aim, rather, is to teach the student to solve and see, and share what he has seen.

We laid the groundwork for the book by defining rhetoric much more broadly than it had been defined for many years. Rhetoric, we argued, is concerned primarily with a creative process that includes all the choices a writer makes from his earliest tentative explorations of a problem in what has been called the "prewriting" stage of the writing process, through choices in arrangement and strategy for a particular audience, to the final editing of the final draft.

This concept of rhetoric is reflected in the arrangement of the chapters and in the wording of the chapter titles. Chapters 2–7, which follow a brief historical introduction to rhetoric, are concerned with prewriting, or "invention" — discovering information, forming concepts, seeing relationships, and analyzing and solving problems prior to the act of communicating. Chapters 8–12 deal with the relationship of writer and reader. They show the student how to discover his reader's values and interests and what his reader knows about his topic; they discuss prerequisites for interaction between writer and reader, such as allaying the reader's sense of threat; and they illustrate how the writer can accomplish his goal of informing the reader, strengthening his convictions, or changing his mind. Chapters 13–15 are devoted to language and editing — to the linguistic choices the writer can make as he revises his draft. These three chapters are concerned not so much with what is said as with how it is said — with the common writing problems of structure, coherence, focus, and loading. The final, summary chapter concerns style. This chapter focuses on the characteristics of the process of writing rather than on the characteristics of the finished product, as style is usually defined. An intelligent style is an efficient and effective way of solving the sequence of problems that the process of writing presents. We have rejected the two popular notions that practice alone is sufficient to develop an intelligent style and that natural talent for writing is essential. We believe, rather, that an intelligent style can be taught. This book provides the tools to form an intelligent style or reform an unintelligent one.

In planning this book we sought to isolate and describe the choice-points in the writing process — the points between first discovery and finished work at which the writer has a major choice to make. To make appropriate choices the student must understand the process of writing and must have procedures for controlling it. The contributions of tagmemics to understanding and controlling this process are presented in a series of six maxims; these constitute the theoretical core of the book. Maxim 3, for example, explains that a person can adequately understand a unit of experience (another person, an object, an abstract concept) only if he knows three aspects of the unit: (1) its contrastive features, (2) its range of variation, and (3) its distributions. That is, he needs to know what features of the unit make it different from similar units, in what ways it may vary without losing its identity, and in what contexts it is normally found. Maxim 3 offers the student a procedure for analyzing and defining a unit of experience: the maxim gives him a way of systematically exploring and understanding the unit, and a way of determining when he has adequately defined it. The book provides other procedures for controlling the process of writing—procedures for stating problems, for discovering ordering generalizations, for testing the adequacy of generalizations, for isolating relevant characteristics of the audience, for developing a discourse, and so on.

Any theory, our own included, provides criteria for determining what must be attended to and what can be minimized or ignored. Thus we have not treated thoroughly all the subjects that have been considered at one time or another a part of rhetoric. Such subjects as grammar, spelling, punctuation, and usage we treat only briefly, usually in exercises, for we assume that the student has already mastered them or is able to solve his remaining problems without extensive instruction. Other subjects, such as use of the library and bibliographical conventions, we consider relatively peripheral to rhetoric and so omit entirely. Still others, most notably formal logic, we treat in more detail but without any effort at completeness. For the student who needs extensive work in any of these subjects, specialized textbooks are readily available.

We consider the exercises an integral part of each chapter. Carefully arranged, they generally progress from relatively simple tasks based directly on the discussion in the chapter to complex tasks demanding original and imaginative thought. Problems that are suggested at the end of one exercise are often considered in detail in a subsequent exercise. The readings included in many of the exercises serve a quite different function from readings in more conventional rhetoric textbooks. They were not selected as masterpieces of English prose, although some of them are; rather, they were selected either because they provide further discussion of the principles presented in the chapter or because they illustrate these principles.

The book can be used in a one-semester course or a two-semester course. We do not mean to imply, however, that the art of rhetoric can be mastered in one or two semesters. The formal study of rhetoric is only an aid in developing one of the most complex and difficult of human skills, a skill that can be acquired only through practice over several years. What we have sought to do is to prepare the student to continue his training independent of a teacher.

Perhaps the most succinct summary of our concept of rhetoric is the one St. Augustine made of his own rhetoric over 1500 years ago: "There are two things necessary . . . a way of discovering those things which are to be understood, and a way of teaching what we have learned." Despite significant differences between our concept of rhetoric and Augustine's, we share his views that the *process of discovering knowledge* must be yoked with the process of communicating it and that, of the two, the first demands greater attention. And we believe, as he did, that *psychological change* in the audience, rather than elegant prose, is the immediate and proper goal of the writer. Above all, we share his belief that training in rhetoric should provide the writer with a means of both improving the quality of his intellectual life and entering the struggle for a more civilized community.

Many have given us aid and encouragement, and to them we are grateful. We would like in particular to thank Ronald Campbell and Patricia Stoltz of Harcourt, Brace & World for their patience and good advice; Thomas Sawyer, George McEwen, and Sharon Curtis of the Department of Humanities, University of Michigan, for their help in preparing the manuscript; Warner Rice of the Department of English, University of Michigan, for the opportunity to test our ideas on teachers of composition; Frank Koen of the Department of Psychology, University of Michigan, for helping us test our ideas formally; Harlan Lane and Ian Catford of the Center for Research on Language and Language Behavior, University of Michigan, for time to think and write; and finally those to whom this book is dedicated, our rhetoric students at the University of Michigan, from whom we learned even as we taught.

Richard E. Young
Alton L. Becker
Kenneth L. Pike

Contents

Rhetoric: Discovery and Change

Rhetoric is concerned with the state of Babel
after the Fall.
KENNETH BURKE, *A Rhetoric of Motives*

1 The domain of rhetoric

THE word *rhetoric* can be traced back ultimately to the simple assertion *I say* (*eirō* in Greek). Almost anything related to the act of saying something to someone—in speech or in writing—can conceivably fall within the domain of rhetoric as a field of study: phonetics, grammar, the process of cognition, language acquisition, perception, penmanship, social relations, persuasive strategies, stylistics, logic, and so on. Obviously no one book can discuss adequately every aspect of rhetoric. From the time of the Greek rhetoricians who developed the art over two thousand years ago, men have successively defined and redefined rhetoric, at times narrowing it to little more than the art of dazzling an opponent in an argument by verbal elaboration (hence the pejorative phrase "mere rhetoric"), at times broadening it to include discovering truth through the art of dialectic, that is, through the exchange of rigorously logical arguments. This chapter is the beginning of an attempt to define this domain of study once again, first by examining some earlier conceptions of rhetoric and then by suggesting how the conditions and insights of our own times seem to demand a new rhetoric.

The classical tradition

GREEK THEORIES OF RHETORIC

In 399 B.C. when Socrates appeared before the Athenian court that later sentenced him to death, he began his defense with these words:

> How you, O Athenians, have been affected by my accusers, I cannot tell; but I know that they almost made me forget who I was — so persuasively did they speak; and yet they have hardly uttered a word of truth. But of the many falsehoods told by them, there was one which quite amazed me — I mean when they said that you should be upon your guard and not allow yourselves to be deceived by the force of my eloquence. To say this, when they were certain to be detected as soon as I opened my lips and proved myself to be anything but a great speaker, did indeed appear to me most shameless — unless by the force of eloquence they mean the force of truth; for if such is their meaning, I admit that I am eloquent. But in how different a way from theirs! Well, as I was saying, they have scarcely spoken the truth at all; from me you shall hear the whole truth, but not delivered after their manner in a set oration duly ornamented with fine words and phrases. No, by heaven! I shall use the words and arguments which occur to me at the moment, for I am confident in the justice of my cause . . . .
>
> PLATO, *Apology*, trans. Benjamin Jowett

The passage from Plato's *Apology* is particularly interesting because it reveals two extremes between which the art of rhetoric fluctuated during its development. At times rhetorical theory emphasized thought, truth, wisdom — the content of the discourse and the character of the man. At other times it emphasized eloquence and form — that is, language and the techniques of effective presentation.

For Plato, rhetoric was not mere verbal expertise, the art of linguistic cosmetology; it was the expression of truth, which had power because it appealed to man's rationality. Rhetoric, for him, was closely related to philosophy. In Plato's *Phaedrus* Socrates remarks, after giving a speech on the subject of love, that although the speech was "playful," it illustrated two processes essential to both philosophy and rhetoric.

> PHAEDRUS   What are they?
> SOCRATES   First, the survey of scattered particulars, leading to the comprehension in one idea; as in our definition of love, which

whether true or false certainly gave clearness and consistency to the
discourse, the speaker should define his several notions and so make
his meaning clear.

PHAEDRUS   What is the other principle, Socrates?

SOCRATES   The second principle is that of division into species according to the natural formation, where the joint is, not breaking any
part as a bad carver might.

.   .   .

I am myself a great lover of these processes of division and generalization; they help me to speak and to think.

PLATO, *Phaedrus*, trans. Benjamin Jowett

As this passage suggests, Plato regarded rhetoric as the art of rational
discourse rather than the art of eloquent expression. Clarity, consistency, and "naturalness" were the only features necessary for the
effective presentation of ideas.

But men disagree—and none more so than those who argue
questions of philosophy and rhetoric. Aristotle insisted in his *Rhetoric* that even though, ideally, rational discourse alone should suffice to persuade men, experience shows us that it often fails: "It is
not sufficient to know what one ought to say, but one must also
know how to say it." For Aristotle, rhetoric was "the faculty of discovering the possible means of persuasion in reference to any subject whatever."

The rhetorical tradition has a moral as well as a theoretical
dimension. Plato's insistence that genuine eloquence derives its
force from truth and spontaneity was in part a reaction to the use of
rhetorical artifice by the Sophists as a means of deceiving and manipulating people. Aristotle, on the other hand, considered rhetoric
a tool, like a knife, morally neutral and capable of being used for
good or ill. He would have agreed with Ralph Waldo Emerson's
remark, "All things have two handles: beware of the wrong one."
What made someone a Sophist was not his mastery of the arts of
persuasion but his lack of moral purpose.

Thus Greek rhetoric was not a single, homogeneous theory.
Aristotle's formulation of the art, however, became the nucleus of
the theory that dominated the tradition of rhetoric. The influence of
his theory is no doubt attributable, at least in part, to its being the
most fully developed of all theories of rhetoric; but its influence
may also be the result of its ability to reconcile the apparently rival
claims of truth and eloquence.

ROMAN DEVELOPMENTS

It was Aristotle's conception of rhetoric, modified and developed by the Roman rhetoricians Cicero and Quintilian, that shaped

the great tradition of Western rhetoric. This tradition treated rhetoric as the art of popular (as opposed to scientific and philosophical) argument. Primarily a spoken rather than a written art, it was designed for use in law courts, political meetings, and ceremonies, such as funerals and religious services. It was concerned not with questions that could be answered conclusively but with questions that were open to debate; that is, it dealt with the probable rather than the demonstrably true. At the heart of the theory, as it was elaborated by the Romans, were the five arts of invention, arrangement, style, memory, and delivery.

"Invention," wrote Cicero, "is the discovery of valid or seemingly valid arguments to render one's cause probable." Discovering arguments was a systematic activity guided by a set of questions, or *topics*, an elaborate checklist of mental acts — for example, comparison, contrast, definition, and cause and effect — to be used when investigating and developing a subject. Today journalists often use a simplified set of topics when developing a newspaper report — the familiar who, what, when, where, how, and why. Three kinds of arguments were associated with the art of invention: appeals to the emotions, appeals to the character of the speaker, and appeals to reason (considered superior to the first two). A method was also developed for identifying the relevant characteristics of the audience, for without this knowledge it was impossible to determine which arguments would be most effective. It is not surprising that some of the earliest contributions to psychology were made by rhetoricians.

Arrangement, the second of the five arts, was the art of organizing a discourse by means of flexible systems of slots (or stages in a discourse) into which appropriate categories of subject matter were fitted. One such system had six slots: the exordium (or opening), the narrative (or exposition of the background of the subject), the proposition, the argument supporting it, the refutation of alternative positions, and the close. Arrangement consisted of distributing within this basic pattern the subject matter gathered in the invention stage and of modifying the pattern to meet the needs of the subject and the audience by expanding, omitting, or reorganizing its parts. The heart of the system was the proposition and argument; the other parts were designed to make them more effective.

Style, the third of the arts, was largely a method for framing effective sentences. Its function was to give clarity, force, and beauty to the argument. Such familiar devices as metaphor, simile, allegory, and hyperbole, along with a considerable number of less familiar ones, such as hyperbaton, metalepsis, and catachresis, added power to the argument, rendering it more persuasive.

Memory, the art of committing the speech to memory by various mnemonic devices, and delivery, an art akin to acting, were essential to rhetoric as a spoken art. As the importance of the written word increased (Gutenberg's discovery of movable type contributed greatly to this change), the importance of memory and delivery as rhetorical disciplines diminished.

The decline of the classical tradition

Our purpose here is not to give a detailed account of the classical tradition; it is merely to suggest the complexity and completeness of the theory that dominated rhetoric from antiquity until the beginning of the nineteenth century, when forces that had been operating within it and within society finally made it appear irrelevant to the times. In addition to the increasingly mechanical approach to the teaching of rhetoric and the tendency to complicate the theory unnecessarily, changes in philosophy and in the social system created pressures for a new theory of rhetoric. The growth of science and technology, for example, brought an increased interest in expository prose — prose designed to convey information rather than to persuade. In addition, as the discovery of new truths through the direct examination of the physical world began to preempt the deductive method of reasoning from prior beliefs to new applications, the art of invention lost its importance. With the rise to power of the middle class, the elaborate art of style, so appropriate to an aristocratic audience, became unsuitable. And the emergence of numerous Protestant sects in northern Europe also contributed to the decline of traditional rhetoric, for the extensive schooling of the public speaker and the elegance of the spoken word that had characterized the tradition seemed unnecessary to preachers, often unsophisticated men with little training, who spoke to the common man in terms he could understand. For them and their followers, traditional rhetoric was part of the Establishment, hence suspect.

During the nineteenth century a much less systematic and sophisticated approach to rhetoric was developed, which is still being taught in many American schools today. Its chief emphasis is on language rather than content — on such matters as clarity of statement, emphasis, coherence, and correct usage. This approach is in part the result of the increasing dominance of the middle class, unsure of its linguistic competence and eager to establish a school system open to all. With few exceptions, the classical tradition survives today only in the training of formal debaters.

Rhetorical strategies and images of man

Assumptions about rhetoric have also been shaped by people's changing notions of what men are like. Underlying the classical tradition is the notion that although men are often swayed by passions, their basic and distinguishing characteristic is their ability to reason. Aristotle emphasized this characteristic when he defined man as a *rational animal*. The essential appeal of the classical rhetorician was to reason: Logical argument — deductive reasoning in particular — was the heart of persuasive discourse.

THE PAVLOVIAN STRATEGY

During the past hundred years, the image of man as a rational animal has been questioned. Pavlovian psychology, for example, represents man as a bundle of habits that can be shaped and controlled by a skilled manipulator. Modern advertisers clearly have adopted Pavlovian techniques and the attendant image of man as a conditioned animal: We all salivate when the right bell is rung. Discoveries in Pavlovian psychology have led some educators to consider education largely human engineering. One product of this view is the teaching machine, a device that trains the learner to respond properly to a given stimulus. Brainwashing represents a more sinister application of the principles of Pavlovian psychology.

THE FREUDIAN STRATEGY

Another image of man has grown out of Freudian psychoanalysis. A man's delusions and the acts based on them are seen as caused in part by experiences in his early years that he has suppressed in his unconscious mind. The analyst's task is to uncover these hidden memories and, by revealing them, to loosen the patient's hold on his delusions. The assumption is that once a person sees the real reasons for his beliefs he will give them up. An effective rhetorical strategy can be developed from this theory, as Anatol Rapoport shows in these two illustrations from his classroom experiences:

> Once when teaching elementary physics, I was impressed with the resistance of mature intelligent students to some fundamental facts and concepts. For example, when a man falling in a parachute has reached constant velocity, the forces acting on him add up to zero. Beginners almost invariably resist this conclusion. "If there is no resultant force acting on a falling body," they ask, "why does it fall?" Proof by appeal to the fundamental equation of motion is of little

avail. They "believe" the equation, but they *believe* their preconceptions.

Getting to the core of the matter usually helps. One must point out *where the preconceptions come from*. They come from an inner conviction (based on direct experience!) that it takes a force to move a body. The force in the muscles is felt directly, but the opposing force, say of friction or air resistance (which must be equal and opposite if the body is moved with constant velocity) is not directly felt and therefore ignored. Hence the false notion that an unbalanced force is acting on a body moving with constant velocity.

Another idea difficult to put across was that underlying the operation of a Venturi tube. As the stream of air passes through the constriction in this device, the velocity of the flow increases, and the pressure decreases. The prevailing image resists these facts. Most students believe that pressure is greater in the narrower portions and the velocity of flow is smaller. When the probable origin of this notion is pointed out ("You are thinking of squeezing tooth paste and of traffic jams") the mental resistance usually collapses.

ANATOL RAPOPORT, *Fights, Games, and Debates*

In both instances the faulty ideas are based on prior experiences, inadequately understood or inappropriately applied. Once these origins are revealed, the ideas are rejected. Notice that the students' ideas are not refuted logically; the teacher merely shows what motivated the students to hold them.

The strategy of classical rhetoric rests on the assumption that humans are reasonable and can be swayed by reasonable means, particularly by the processes of logic. The strategy of what might be called Pavlovian persuasion or training rests on the assumption that humans are conditioned and can be swayed by regulated punishments and rewards. The strategy of Freudian persuasion, or explaining away, rests on the assumption that men are motivated by unconscious memories that lead to delusions from which they can be freed once the irrational origins of their delusions are revealed. Different as they are, all three strategies share a common goal—the control of one human being by another.

THE ROGERIAN STRATEGY

There is another strategy, however, derived from the work of the psychotherapist Carl Rogers, which is based on quite different assumptions about men and which has quite different goals. It rests on the assumption that a man holds to his beliefs about who he is and what the world is like because other beliefs threaten his identity and integrity. Hence, the first requirement for changing beliefs is the elimination of this sense of threat. If this assumption is true, then the weaknesses of the other strategies are apparent. A strong

sense of threat may render a person immune to even the most carefully reasoned and well developed argument. Likewise, attempts to
condition him or to explain away his beliefs become very threatening once he discovers what is happening to him. From the Rogerian
point of view, man has free will, but his ability to consider alternative positions is limited if he feels threatened. The primary goal of
this rhetorical strategy is to reduce the reader's sense of threat so
that he is *able* to consider alternatives to his own beliefs. The goal is
thus not to work one's will on others but to establish and maintain
communication *as an end in itself.*

The need for a new rhetoric

Each of these rhetorical strategies reveals something undoubtedly
true about people: All of us are at times rational, often manipulated,
often deluded, and increasingly threatened. But many other forces
are also at work to shape new conceptions of rhetoric. Profound
changes are taking place in the system of Western values that has
for centuries guided conduct and provided social stability and continuity between generations. Thus it becomes more and more difficult to reason from ethical assumptions that are generally accepted.
Truth has become increasingly elusive and men are driven to embrace conflicting ideologies. Ours is an age of isms. As a result of
rapid and mass means of communication and transportation, our
world is becoming smaller, and all of us are learning to become citizens of the world, confronting people whose beliefs are radically
different from our own and with whom we must learn to live. It has
become imperative to develop a rhetoric that has as its goal not
skillful verbal coercion but discussion and exchange of ideas.

　　Furthermore, forms of communication themselves are rapidly
changing. The ubiquity of radio and television, of tape recorders,
records, and films presents a challenge to the primacy of the written
word. The familiar essay, which was the basic concern of courses in
rhetoric in past years, has come to seem less relevant as a means of
communication than, for instance, serious popular songs, group
discussions, or articles written as tentative contributions to a continuing discussion within a large community of scholars.

Rhetoric as process

What, then, is the domain of rhetoric? What is its purpose as a field
of study? At the moment these questions are difficult to answer.
The present state of rhetoric might be characterized as a need in
search of a discipline. Perhaps never before in our history has there
been such a need for effective communication, but the old formula-

tions of rhetoric seem inadequate to the times. The outlines of a
modern discipline appear to be emerging, however. This book can
be taken as one effort to redefine the nature of the discipline. The
features of the book are, in part, the result of our concern with the
social changes we have been discussing. We have sought to develop
a rhetoric that implies that we are all citizens of an extraordinarily
diverse and disturbed world, that the "truths" we live by are tentative and subject to change, that we must be discoverers of new
truths as well as preservers and transmitters of the old, and that enlightened cooperation is the preeminent ethical goal of communication.

The book's structure is a consequence of our belief that the
discipline of rhetoric is primarily concerned with the control of a
process. Mastering rhetoric means not only mastering a theory of
how and why one communicates but mastering the process of
communication as well.

As a process, rhetoric clearly begins with a person's impulse to
communicate, to share some experience with others—although this
is a somewhat arbitrary starting point since he often has explored
his experiences and formulated ordering principles before he feels a
desire to communicate. At some stage in the process he must identify his audience and decide what strategy he can use to present his
ideas. If he chooses to write rather than speak, he must at some
stage begin to write and rewrite what he wants to say. However, the
process is not strictly linear, with clearly defined stages; they often
overlap—the writing stage, for example, frequently serves as an
opportunity to explore and clarify the experience in his own mind.
But in spite of this blurring and merging of stages, the writer does
at various times shift his attention from his experience and his own
resources to his audience and to the written work itself; these shifts
of attention and activity constitute the rhetorical process for the
writer.

In each of the following chapters we study some stage in the
process of writing, although much that we say is relevant to speaking and to other means of communication as well. Writing is a
lonely and difficult process; the purpose of a theory of rhetoric is to
make it less lonely and less difficult, to help the writer take his part
in establishing and maintaining a community of intelligent seekers,
in Babel, after the Fall.

EXERCISES

1   Explain what Kenneth Burke means when he says that "rhetoric is concerned with the state of Babel after the Fall." For a
start see Genesis 9—11.

2 Search out or invent some definitions of man other than the ones suggested in Chapter 1. (Example: symbol-using animal, selfish angel, self-reproducing machine.) What rhetorical strategy might be appropriate to each definition?

3 What major event or change has made your generation different from previous generations? How might this event affect modern conceptions of rhetoric? (Examples: atomic bomb, computers, material abundance.)

4 Read carefully the following letter by Martin Luther King, Jr. What immediate problem prompted the letter? What other problems is King trying to solve? Be specific. To whom is he writing? In what ways, specifically, does this audience affect what King says? What is King's purpose in writing the letter? Of the various theories and strategies we have discussed, which seems to explain best what King is doing? Which do not seem relevant? Why?

*Letter from Birmingham Jail**
MARTIN LUTHER KING, JR.

April 16, 1963

MY DEAR FELLOW CLERGYMEN:

While confined here in the Birmingham city jail, I came across your recent statement calling my present activities "unwise and untimely." Seldom do I pause to answer criticism of my work and ideas. If I sought to answer all the criticisms that cross my desk, my secretaries would have little time for anything other than such correspondence in the course of the day, and I would have no time for constructive work. But since I feel that you are men of genuine good will and that your criticisms are sincerely set forth, I want to try to answer your statement in what I hope will be patient and reasonable terms.

*AUTHOR'S NOTE: This response to a published statement by eight fellow clergymen from Alabama (Bishop C. C. J. Carpenter, Bishop Joseph A. Durick, Rabbi Hilton L. Grafman, Bishop Paul Hardin, Bishop Holan B. Harmon, the Reverend George M. Murray, the Reverend Edward V. Ramage and the Reverend Earl Stallings) was composed under somewhat constricting circumstances. Begun on the margins of the newspaper in which the statement appeared while I was in jail, the letter was continued on scraps of writing paper supplied by a friendly Negro trusty, and concluded on a pad my attorneys were eventually permitted to leave me. Although the text remains in substance unaltered, I have indulged in the author's prerogative of polishing it for publication.

I think I should indicate why I am here in Birmingham, since you have been influenced by the view which argues against "outsiders coming in." I have the honor of serving as president of the Southern Christian Leadership Conference, an organization operating in every southern state, with headquarters in Atlanta, Georgia. We have some eighty-five affiliated organizations across the South, and one of them is the Alabama Christian Movement for Human Rights. Frequently we share staff, educational and financial resources with our affiliates. Several months ago the affiliate here in Birmingham asked us to be on call to engage in a nonviolent direct-action program if such were deemed necessary. We readily consented, and when the hour came we lived up to our promise. So I, along with several members of my staff, am here because I was invited here. I am here because I have organizational ties here.

But more basically, I am in Birmingham because injustice is here. Just as the prophets of the eighth century B.C. left their villages and carried their "thus saith the Lord" far beyond the boundaries of their home towns, and just as the Apostle Paul left his village of Tarsus and carried the gospel of Jesus Christ to the far corners of the Greco-Roman world, so am I compelled to carry the gospel of freedom beyond my own home town. Like Paul, I must constantly respond to the Macedonian call for aid.

Moreover, I am cognizant of the interrelatedness of all communities and states. I cannot sit idly by in Atlanta and not be concerned about what happens in Birmingham. Injustice anywhere is a threat to justice everywhere. We are caught in an inescapable network of mutuality, tied in a single garment of destiny. Whatever affects one directly, affects all indirectly. Never again can we afford to live with the narrow, provincial "outside agitator" idea. Anyone who lives inside the United States can never be considered an outsider anywhere within its bounds.

You deplore the demonstrations taking place in Birmingham. But your statement, I am sorry to say, fails to express a similar concern for the conditions that brought about the demonstrations. I am sure that none of you would want to rest content with the superficial kind of social analysis that deals merely with effects and does not grapple with underlying causes. It is unfortunate that demonstrations are taking place in Birmingham, but it is even more unfortunate that the city's white power structure left the Negro community with no alternative.

In any nonviolent campaign there are four basic steps: collection of the facts to determine whether injustices exist; negotiation; self-purification; and direct action. We have gone through all these steps in Birmingham. There can be no gainsaying the fact that racial injustice engulfs this community. Birmingham is probably the most thoroughly segregated city in the United States. Its ugly record of brutality is widely known. Negroes have experienced grossly unjust treatment in the courts. There have been more unsolved bombings of

Negro homes and churches in Birmingham than in any other city in the nation. These are the hard, brutal facts of the case. On the basis of these conditions, Negro leaders sought to negotiate with the city fathers. But the latter consistently refused to engage in good-faith negotiation.

Then, last September, came the opportunity to talk with leaders of Birmingham's economic community. In the course of the negotiations, certain promises were made by the merchants — for example, to remove the stores' humiliating racial signs. On the basis of these promises, the Reverend Fred Shuttlesworth and the leaders of the Alabama Christian Movement for Human Rights agreed to a moratorium on all demonstrations. As the weeks and months went by, we realized that we were the victims of a broken promise. A few signs, briefly removed, returned; the others remained.

As in so many past experiences, our hopes had been blasted, and the shadow of deep disappointment settled upon us. We had no alternative except to prepare for direct action, whereby we would present our very bodies as a means of laying our case before the conscience of the local and the national community. Mindful of the difficulties involved, we decided to undertake a process of self-purification. We began a series of workshops on nonviolence, and we repeatedly asked ourselves: "Are you able to accept blows without retaliating?" "Are you able to endure the ordeal of jail?" We decided to schedule our direct-action program for the Easter season, realizing that except for Christmas, this is the main shopping period of the year. Knowing that a strong economic-withdrawal program would be the by-product of direct action, we felt that this would be the best time to bring pressure to bear on the merchants for the needed change.

Then it occured to us that Birmingham's mayoral election was coming up in March, and we speedily decided to postpone action until after election day. When we discovered that the Commissioner of Public Safety, Eugene "Bull" Connor, had piled up enough votes to be in the run-off, we decided again to postpone action until the day after the run-off so that the demonstrations could not be used to cloud the issues. Like many others, we waited to see Mr. Connor defeated, and to this end we endured postponement after postponement. Having aided in this community need, we felt that our direct-action program could be delayed no longer.

You may well ask: "Why direct action? Why sit-ins, marches and so forth? Isn't negotiation a better path?" You are quite right in calling for negotiation. Indeed, this is the very purpose of direct action. Nonviolent direct action seeks to create such a crisis and foster such a tension that a community which has constantly refused to negotiate is forced to confront the issue. It seeks so to dramatize the issue that it can no longer be ignored. My citing the creation of tension as part of the work of the nonviolent-resister may sound rather shocking. But I must confess that I am not afraid of the word "tension." I have earnestly opposed violent tension, but there is a type of constructive, nonviolent tension which is necessary for growth. Just as Socrates felt that it was necessary to create a tension in the mind so that individuals could rise from the bondage of myths and half-truths to the unfettered realm of creative analysis and objective appraisal, so must we see the need for nonviolent gadflies to create the kind of tension in society that will help men rise from the dark depths of prejudice and racism to the majestic heights of understanding and brotherhood.

The purpose of our direct-action program is to create a situation so crisis-packed that it will inevitably open the door to negotiation. I therefore concur with you in your call for negotiation. Too long has our beloved Southland been bogged down in a tragic effort to live in monologue rather than dialogue.

One of the basic points in your statement is that the action that I and my associates have taken in Birmingham is untimely. Some have asked: "Why didn't you give the new city administration time to act?" The only answer that I can give to this query is that the new Birmingham administration must be prodded about as much as the outgoing one, before it will act. We are sadly mistaken if we feel that the election of Albert Boutwell as mayor will bring the millennium to Birmingham. While Mr. Boutwell is a much more gentle person than Mr. Connor, they are both segregationists, dedicated to maintenance of the status quo. I have hope that Mr. Boutwell will be reasonable enough to see the futility of massive resistance to desegregation. But he will not see this without pressure from devotees of civil rights. My friends, I must say to you that we have not made a single gain in civil rights without determined legal and nonviolent pressure. Lamentably, it is an historical fact that privileged groups seldom give up their privileges voluntarily. Individuals may see the moral light and voluntarily give up their unjust posture; but, as Reinhold Niebuhr has reminded us, groups tend to be more immoral than individuals.

We know through painful experience that freedom is never voluntarily given by the oppressor; it must be demanded by the oppressed. Frankly, I have yet to engage in a direct-action campaign that was "well timed" in the view of those who have not suffered unduly from the disease of segregation. For years now I have heard the word "Wait!" It rings in the ear of every Negro with piercing familiarity. This "Wait" has almost always meant "Never." We must come to see, with one of our distinguished jurists, that "justice too long delayed is justice denied."

We have waited for more than 340 years for our constitutional and God-given rights. The nations of Asia and Africa are moving with jetlike speed toward gaining political independence, but we still creep at horse-and-buggy pace toward gaining a cup of coffee at a lunch counter. Perhaps it is easy for those who have never felt the stinging darts of segregation to say, "Wait." But when you have seen vicious mobs lynch your mothers and fathers at will and drown your sisters and brothers at whim; when you have seen hate-filled policemen curse, kick and even kill your black brothers and sisters; when you see the vast majority of your twenty million Negro brothers smothering in an airtight cage of poverty in the midst of an affluent society; when you suddenly find your tongue twisted and your speech stammering as you seek to explain to your six-year-old daughter why she can't go to the public amusement park that has just been advertised on television, and see tears welling up in her eyes when she is told that Funtown is closed to colored children, and see ominous clouds of inferiority beginning to form in her little mental sky, and see her beginning to distort her personality by developing an unconscious bitterness toward white people; when you have to concoct an answer for a five-year-old son who is asking: "Daddy, why do white people treat colored people so mean?"; when you take a cross-country drive and find it necessary to sleep night after night in the uncomfortable corners of your automobile because no motel will accept you; when you are humiliated day in and day out by nagging signs reading "white" and "colored"; when your first name becomes "nigger," your middle name becomes "boy" (however old you are) and your last name becomes "John," and your wife and mother are never given the respected title "Mrs."; when you are harried by day and haunted by night by the fact that you are a Negro, living constantly at tiptoe stance, never quite knowing what to expect next, and are plagued with inner fears and outer resentments; when you are forever fighting a degenerating sense of "nobodiness" — then you will understand why we find it difficult to wait. There comes a time when the cup of endurance runs over, and men are no longer willing to be plunged into the abyss of despair. I hope, sirs, you can understand our legitimate and unavoidable impatience.

You express a great deal of anxiety over our willingness to break laws. This is certainly a legitimate concern. Since we so diligently urge people to obey the Supreme Court's decision of 1954 outlawing segregation in the public schools, at first glance it may seem rather paradoxical for us consciously to break laws. One may well ask: "How can you advocate breaking some laws and obeying others?" The answer lies in the fact that there are two types of laws: just and unjust. I would be the first to advocate obeying just laws. One has not only a legal but a moral responsibility to obey just laws. Conversely, one has a moral responsibility to disobey unjust laws. I would agree with St. Augustine that "an unjust law is no law at all."

Now, what is the difference between the two? How does one determine whether a law is just or unjust? A just law is a man-made code that squares with the moral law or the law of God. An unjust law is a code that is out of harmony with the moral law. To put it in the terms of St. Thomas Aquinas: An unjust law is a human law that is not rooted in eternal law and natural law. Any law that uplifts human personality is just. Any law that degrades human personality is unjust. All segregation statutes are unjust because segregation distorts the soul and damages the personality. It gives the segregator a false sense of superiority and the segregated a false sense of inferiority. Segregation, to use the terminology of the Jewish philosopher Martin Buber, substitutes an "I-it" relationship for an "I-thou" relationship and ends up relegating persons to the status of things. Hence segregation is not only politically, economically and sociologically unsound, it is morally wrong and sinful. Paul Tillich has said that sin is separation. Is not segregation an existential expression of man's tragic separation, his awful estrangement, his terrible sinfulness? Thus it is that I can urge men to obey the 1954 decision of the Supreme Court, for it is morally right; and I can urge them to disobey segregation ordinances, for they are morally wrong.

Let us consider a more concrete example of just and unjust laws. An unjust law is a code that a numerical or power majority group compels a minority group to obey but does not make binding on itself. This is *difference* made legal. By the same token, a just law is a code that a majority compels a minority to follow and that it is willing to follow itself. This is *sameness* made legal.

Let me give another explanation. A law is unjust if it is inflicted on a minority that, as a result of being denied the right to vote, had no part in enacting or devising the law. Who can say that the legislature of Alabama which set up that state's segregation laws was democratically elected? Throughout Alabama all sorts of devious methods are used to prevent Negroes from becoming registered voters, and there are some counties in which, even though Negroes constitute a majority of the population, not a single Negro is registered. Can any law enacted under such circumstances be considered democratically structured?

Sometimes a law is just on its face and unjust in its application. For instance, I have been arrested on a charge of parading without a permit. Now, there is nothing wrong in having an ordinance which requires a permit for a parade. But such an ordinance becomes unjust when it is used to maintain segregation and to deny citizens the First-Amendment privilege of peaceful assembly and protest.

I hope you are able to see the distinction I am trying to point out. In no sense do I advocate evading or defying the law, as would the rabid segregationist. That would lead to anarchy. One who breaks an unjust law must do so openly, lovingly, and with a willingness to accept the penalty. I submit that an individual who breaks a law that conscience tells him is unjust, and who willingly accepts the penalty of imprisonment in order to arouse the conscience of the community over its injustice, is in reality expressing the highest respect for law.

Of course, there is nothing new about this kind of civil disobedience. It was evidenced sublimely in the refusal of Shadrach, Meshach and Abednego to obey the laws of Nebuchadnezzar, on the ground that a higher moral law was at stake. It was practiced superbly by the early Christians, who were willing to face hungry lions and the excruciating pain of chopping blocks rather than submit to certain unjust laws of the Roman Empire. To a degree, academic freedom is a reality today because Socrates practiced civil disobedience. In our own nation, the Boston Tea Party represented a massive act of civil disobedience.

We should never forget that everything Adolf Hitler did in Germany was "legal" and everything the Hungarian freedom fighters did in Hungary was "illegal." It was "illegal" to aid and comfort a Jew in Hitler's Germany. Even so, I am sure that, had I lived in Germany at the time, I would have aided and comforted my Jewish brothers. If today I lived in a Communist country where certain principles dear to the Christian faith are suppressed, I would openly advocate disobeying that country's antireligious laws.

I must make two honest confessions to you, my Christian and Jewish brothers. First, I must confess that over the past few years I have been gravely disappointed with the white moderate. I have almost reached the regrettable conclusion that the Negro's great stumbling block in his stride toward freedom is not the White Citizen's Counciler or the Ku Klux Klanner, but the white moderate, who is more devoted to "order" than to justice; who prefers a negative peace which is the absence of tension to a positive peace which is the presence of justice; who constantly says: "I agree with you in the goal you seek, but I cannot agree with your methods of direct action"; who paternalistically believes he can set the timetable for another man's freedom; who lives by a mythical concept of time and who constantly advises the Negro to wait for a "more convenient season." Shallow understanding from people of good will is more frustrating than absolute misunderstanding from people of ill will. Lukewarm acceptance is much more bewildering than outright rejection.

I had hoped that the white moderate would understand that law and order exist for the purpose of establishing justice and that when they fail in this purpose they become the dangerously structured dams that block the flow of social progress. I had hoped that the white moderate would understand that the present tension in the South is a necessary phase of the transition from an obnoxious negative peace, in which the Negro passively accepted his unjust plight, to a substantive and positive peace, in which all men will respect the dignity and worth of human personality. Actually, we who engage in nonviolent direct action are not the creators of tension. We merely bring to the surface the hidden tension that is already alive. We bring it out in the open, where it can be seen and dealt with. Like a boil that can never be cured so long as it is covered up but must be opened with all its ugliness to the natural medicines of air and light, injustice must be exposed, with all the tension its exposure creates, to the light of human conscience and the air of national opinion before it can be cured.

In your statement you assert that our actions, even though peaceful, must be condemned because they precipitate violence. But is this a logical assertion? Isn't this like condemning a robbed man because his possession of money precipitated the evil act of robbery?

Isn't this like condemning Socrates because his unswerving commitment to truth and his philosophical inquiries precipitated the act by
the misguided populace in which they made him drink hemlock?
Isn't this like condemning Jesus because his unique God-conscious-
ness and never-ceasing devotion to God's will precipitated the evil
act of crucifixion? We must come to see that, as the federal courts
have consistently affirmed, it is wrong to urge an individual to cease
his efforts to gain his basic constitutional rights because the quest
may precipitate violence. Society must protect the robbed and punish
the robber.

I had also hoped that the white moderate would reject the myth
concerning time in relation to the struggle for freedom. I have just
received a letter from a white brother in Texas. He writes: "All Christians know that the colored people will receive equal rights eventually, but it is possible that you are in too great a religious hurry. It has
taken Christianity almost two thousand years to accomplish what it
has. The teachings of Christ take time to come to earth." Such an attitude stems from a tragic misconception of time, from the strangely
irrational notion that there is something in the very flow of time that
will inevitably cure all ills. Actually, time itself is neutral; it can be
used either destructively or constructively. More and more I feel that
the people of ill will have used time much more effectively than have
the people of good will. We will have to repent in this generation not
merely for the hateful words and actions of the bad people but for the
appalling silence of the good people. Human progress never rolls in
on wheels of inevitability; it comes through the tireless efforts of men
willing to be co-workers with God, and without this hard work, time
itself becomes an ally of the forces of social stagnation. We must use
time creatively, in the knowledge that the time is always ripe to do
right. Now is the time to make real the promise of democracy and
transform our pending national elegy into a creative psalm of brotherhood. Now is the time to lift our national policy from the quicksand
of racial injustice to the solid rock of human dignity.

You speak of our activity in Birmingham as extreme. At first I
was rather disappointed that fellow clergymen would see my nonviolent efforts as those of an extremist. I began thinking about the fact
that I stand in the middle of two opposing forces in the Negro community. One is a force of complacency, made up in part of Negroes
who, as a result of long years of oppression, are so drained of self-
respect and a sense of "somebodiness" that they have adjusted to
segregation; and in part of a few middle-class Negroes who, because
of a degree of academic and economic security and because in some
ways they profit by segregation, have become insensitive to the problems of the masses. The other force is one of bitterness and hatred,
and it comes perilously close to advocating violence. It is expressed in
the various black nationalist groups that are springing up across the
nation, the largest and best-known being Elijah Muhammad's Mus-
lim movement. Nourished by the Negro's frustration over the contin-

ued existence of racial discrimination, this movement is made up of people who have lost faith in America, who have absolutely repudiated Christianity, and who have concluded that the white man is an incorrigible "devil."

I have tried to stand between these two forces, saying that we need emulate neither the "do-nothingism" of the complacent nor the hatred and despair of the black nationalist. For there is the more excellent way of love and nonviolent protest. I am grateful to God that, through the influence of the Negro church, the way of nonviolence became an integral part of our struggle.

If this philosophy had not emerged, by now many streets of the South would, I am convinced, be flowing with blood. And I am further convinced that if our white brothers dismiss as "rabble-rousers" and "outside agitators" those of us who employ nonviolent direct action, and if they refuse to support our nonviolent efforts, millions of Negroes will, out of frustration and despair, seek solace and security in black-nationalist ideologies—a development that would inevitably lead to a frightening racial nightmare.

Oppressed people cannot remain oppressed forever. The yearning for freedom eventually manifests itself, and that is what has happened to the American Negro. Something within has reminded him of his birthright of freedom, and something without has reminded him that it can be gained. Consciously or unconsciously, he has been caught up by the *Zeitgeist*, and with his black brothers of Africa and his brown and yellow brothers of Asia, South America and the Caribbean, the United States Negro is moving with a sense of great urgency toward the promised land of racial justice. If one recognizes this vital urge that has engulfed the Negro community, one should readily understand why public demonstrations are taking place. The Negro has many pent-up resentments and latent frustrations, and he must release them. So let him march; let him make prayer pilgrimages to the city hall; let him go on freedom rides—and try to understand why he must do so. If his repressed emotions are not released in nonviolent ways, they will seek expression through violence; this is not a threat but a fact of history. So I have not said to my people: "Get rid of your discontent." Rather, I have tried to say that this normal and healthy discontent can be channeled into the creative outlet of nonviolent direct action. And now this approach is being termed extremist.

But though I was initially disappointed at being categorized as an extremist, as I continued to think about the matter I gradually gained a measure of satisfaction from the label. Was not Jesus an extremist for love: "Love your enemies, bless them that curse you, do good to them that hate you, and pray for them which despitefully use you, and persecute you." Was not Amos an extremist for justice: "Let justice roll down like waters and righteousness like an ever-flowing stream." Was not Paul an extremist for the Christian gospel: "I bear in my body the marks of the Lord Jesus." Was not Martin Luther an extremist: "Here I stand; I cannot do otherwise, so help me God." And John Bunyan: "I will stay in jail to the end of my days before I make a butchery of my conscience." And Abraham Lincoln: "This nation cannot survive half slave and half free." And Thomas Jefferson: "We hold these truths to be self-evident, that all men are created equal . . ." So the question is not whether we will be extremists, but what kind of extremists we will be. Will we be extremists for hate or for love? Will we be extremists for the preservation of injustice or for the extension of justice? In that dramatic scene on Calvary's hill three men were crucified. We must never forget that all three were crucified for the same crime — the crime of extremism. Two were extremists for immorality, and thus fell below their environment. The other, Jesus Christ, was an extremist for love, truth and goodness, and thereby rose above his environment. Perhaps the South, the nation and the world are in dire need of creative extremists.

I had hoped that the white moderate would see this need. Perhaps I was too optimistic; perhaps I expected too much. I suppose I should have realized that few members of the oppressor race can understand the deep groans and passionate yearnings of the oppressed race, and still fewer have the vision to see that injustice must be rooted out by strong, persistent and determined action. I am thankful, however, that some of our white brothers in the South have grasped the meaning of this social revolution and committed themselves to it. They are still all too few in quantity, but they are big in quality. Some — such as Ralph McGill, Lillian Smith, Harry Golden, James McBride Dabbs, Ann Braden and Sarah Patton Boyle — have written about our struggle in eloquent and prophetic terms. Others have marched with us down nameless streets of the South. They have languished in filthy, roach-infested jails, suffering the abuse and brutality of policemen who view them as "dirty nigger-lovers." Unlike so many of their moderate brothers and sisters, they have recognized the urgency of the moment and sensed the need for powerful "action" antidotes to combat the disease of segregation.

Let me take note of my other major disappointment. I have been so greatly disappointed with the white church and its leadership. Of course, there are some notable exceptions. I am not unmindful of the fact that each of you has taken some significant stands on this issue. I commend you, Reverend Stallings, for your Christian stand on this past Sunday, in welcoming Negroes to your worship service on a nonsegregated basis. I commend the Catholic leaders of this state for integrating Spring Hill College several years ago.

But despite these notable exceptions, I must honestly reiterate that I have been disappointed with the church. I do not say this as one of those negative critics who can always find something wrong with the church. I say this as a minister of the gospel, who loves the church; who was nurtured in its bosom; who has been sustained by its spiritual blessings and who will remain true to it as long as the cord of life shall lengthen.

When I was suddenly catapulted into the leadership of the bus protest in Montgomery, Alabama, a few years ago, I felt we would be supported by the white church. I felt that the white ministers, priests and rabbis of the South would be among our strongest allies. Instead, some have been outright opponents, refusing to understand the freedom movement and misrepresenting its leaders; all too many others have been more cautious than courageous and have remained silent behind the anesthetizing security of stained-glass windows.

In spite of my shattered dreams, I came to Birmingham with the hope that the white religious leadership of this community would see the justice of our cause and, with deep moral concern, would serve as the channel through which our just grievances could reach the power structure. I had hoped that each of you would understand. But again I have been disappointed.

I have heard numerous southern religious leaders admonish their worshipers to comply with a desegregation decision because it is the law, but I have longed to hear white ministers declare: "Follow this decree because integration is morally right and because the Negro is your brother." In the midst of blatant injustices inflicted upon the Negro, I have watched white churchmen stand on the sideline and mouth pious irrelevancies and sanctimonious trivialities. In the midst of a mighty struggle to rid our nation of racial and economic injustice, I have heard many ministers say: "Those are social issues, with which the gospel has no real concern." And I have watched many churches commit themselves to a completely otherworldly religion which makes a strange, un-Biblical distinction between body and soul, between the sacred and the secular.

I have traveled the length and breadth of Alabama, Mississippi and all the other southern states. On sweltering summer days and crisp autumn mornings I have looked at the South's beautiful churches with their lofty spires pointing heavenward. I have beheld the impressive outlines of her massive religious-education buildings. Over and over I have found myself asking: "What kind of people worship here? Who is their God? Where were their voices when the lips of Governor Barnett dripped with words of interposition and nullification? Where were they when Governor Wallace gave a clarion call for defiance and hatred? Where were their voices of support when bruised and weary Negro men and women decided to rise from the dark dungeons of complacency to the bright hills of creative protest?"

Yes, these questions are still in my mind. In deep disappointment I have wept over the laxity of the church. But be assured that my tears have been tears of love. There can be no deep disappointment where there is not deep love. Yes, I love the church. How could I do otherwise? I am in the rather unique position of being the son, the grandson and the great-grandson of preachers. Yes, I see the church as the body of Christ. But, oh! How we have blemished and scarred that body through social neglect and through fear of being nonconformists.

There was a time when the church was very powerful—in the time when the early Christians rejoiced at being deemed worthy to suffer for what they believed. In those days the church was not merely a thermometer that recorded the ideas and principles of popular opinion; it was a thermostat that transformed the mores of society. Whenever the early Christians entered a town, the people in power became disturbed and immediately sought to convict the Christians for being "disturbers of the peace" and "outside agitators." But the Christians pressed on, in the conviction that they were "a colony of heaven," called to obey God rather than man. Small in number, they were big in commitment. They were too God-intoxicated to be "astronomically intimidated." By their effort and example they brought an end to such ancient evils as infanticide and gladiatorial contests.

Things are different now. So often the contemporary church is a weak, ineffectual voice with an uncertain sound. So often it is an archdefender of the status quo. Far from being disturbed by the presence of the church, the power structure of the average community is consoled by the church's silent—and often even vocal—sanction of things as they are.

But the judgment of God is upon the church as never before. If today's church does not recapture the sacrificial spirit of the early church, it will lose its authenticity, forfeit the loyalty of millions, and be dismissed as an irrelevant social club with no meaning for the twentieth century. Every day I meet young people whose disappointment with the church has turned into outright disgust.

Perhaps I have once again been too optimistic. Is organized religion too inextricably bound to the status quo to save our nation and the world? Perhaps I must turn my faith to the inner spiritual church, the church within the church, as the true *ekklesia* and the hope of the world. But again I am thankful to God that some noble souls from the ranks of organized religion have broken loose from the paralyzing chains of conformity and joined us as active partners in the struggle for freedom. They have left their secure congregations and walked the streets of Albany, Georgia, with us. They have gone down the highways of the South on tortuous rides for freedom. Yes, they have gone to jail with us. Some have been dismissed from their churches, have lost the support of their bishops and fellow ministers. But they have acted in the faith that right defeated is stronger than evil triumphant. Their witness has been the spiritual salt that has preserved the true meaning of the gospel in these troubled times. They have carved a tunnel of hope through the dark mountain of disappointment.

I hope the church as a whole will meet the challenge of this decisive hour. But even if the church does not come to the aid of justice, I have no despair about the future. I have no fear about the outcome of our struggle in Birmingham, even if our motives are at present misunderstood. We will reach the goal of freedom in Birmingham and all over the nation, because the goal of America is freedom. Abused and scorned though we may be, our destiny is tied up with America's destiny. Before the pilgrims landed at Plymouth, we were here. Before the pen of Jefferson etched the majestic words of the Declaration of Independence across the pages of history, we were here. For more than two centuries our forebears labored in this country without wages; they made cotton king; they built the homes of their masters while suffering gross injustice and shameful humiliation—and yet out of a bottomless vitality they continued to thrive and develop. If the inexpressible cruelties of slavery could not stop us, the opposition we now face will surely fail. We will win our freedom because the sacred heritage of our nation and the eternal will of God are embodied in our echoing demands.

Before closing I feel impelled to mention one other point in your statement that has troubled me profoundly. You warmly commended the Birmingham police force for keeping "order" and "preventing violence." I doubt that you would have so warmly commended the police force if you had seen its dogs sinking their teeth into unarmed, nonviolent Negroes. I doubt that you would so quickly commend the policemen if you were to observe their ugly and inhumane treatment of Negroes here in the city jail; if you were to watch them push and curse old Negro women and young Negro girls; if you were to see them slap and kick old Negro men and young boys; if you were to observe them, as they did on two occasions, refuse to give us food because we wanted to sing our grace together. I cannot join you in your praise of the Birmingham police department.

It is true that the police have exercised a degree of discipline in handling the demonstrators. In this sense they have conducted themselves rather "nonviolently" in public. But for what purpose? To preserve the evil system of segregation. Over the past few years I have consistently preached that nonviolence demands that the means we use must be as pure as the ends we seek. I have tried to make clear that it is wrong to use immoral means to attain moral ends. But now I must affirm that it is just as wrong, or perhaps even more so, to use moral means to preserve immoral ends. Perhaps Mr. Connor and his policemen have been rather nonviolent in public, as was Chief Pritchett in Albany, Georgia, but they have used the moral means of nonviolence to maintain the immoral end of racial injustice. As T. S. Eliot has said: "The last temptation is the greatest treason: To do the right deed for the wrong reason."

I wish you had commended the Negro sit-inners and demonstrators of Birmingham for their sublime courage, their willingness to suffer and their amazing discipline in the midst of great provocation. One day the South will recognize its real heroes. They will be the James Merediths, with the noble sense of purpose that enables them to face jeering and hostile mobs, and with the agonizing loneliness that characterizes the life of the pioneer. They will be old, oppressed, battered Negro women, symbolized in a seventy-two-year-old woman in Montgomery, Alabama, who rose up with a sense of dignity and with her people decided not to ride segregated buses, and who responded with ungrammatical profundity to one who inquired about her weariness: "My feets is tired, but my soul is at rest." They will be the young high school and college students, the young ministers of the gospel and a host of their elders, courageously and nonviolently sitting in at lunch counters and willingly going to jail for conscience' sake. One day the South will know that when these disinherited children of God sat down at lunch counters, they were in reality standing up for what is best in the American dream and for the most sacred values in our Judaeo-Christian heritage, thereby bringing our nation back to those great wells of democracy which were dug deep by the founding fathers in their formulation of the Constitution and the Declaration of Independence.

Never before have I written so long a letter. I'm afraid it is much too long to take your precious time. I can assure you that it would have been much shorter if I had been writing from a comfortable desk, but what else can one do when he is alone in a narrow jail cell, other than write long letters, think long thoughts and pray long prayers?

If I have said anything in this letter that overstates the truth and indicates an unreasonable impatience, I beg you to forgive me. If I have said anything that understates the truth and indicates my having a patience that allows me to settle for anything less than brotherhood, I beg God to forgive me.

I hope this letter finds you strong in the faith. I also hope that circumstances will soon make it possible for me to meet each of you, not as an integrationist or a civil-rights leader but as a fellow clergyman and a Christian brother. Let us all hope that the dark clouds of racial prejudice will soon pass away and the deep fog of misunderstanding will be lifted from our fear-drenched communities, and in some not too distant tomorrow the radiant stars of love and brotherhood will shine over our great nation with all their scintillating beauty.

Yours for the cause of Peace and Brotherhood,

MARTIN LUTHER KING, JR.

5   The following poem describes the process of writing, emphasizing several points made in this chapter. It stresses in particular the complex interrelationship of discovery and writing — truth and word.

The Thought-Fox
TED HUGHES

I imagine this midnight moment's forest:
Something else is alive
Beside the clock's loneliness
And this blank page where my fingers move.

Through the window I see no star:
Something more near
Though deeper within darkness
Is entering the loneliness:

Cold, delicately as the dark snow,
A fox's nose touches twig, leaf;
Two eyes serve a movement, that now
And again now, and now, and now

Sets neat prints into the snow
Between trees, and warily a lame
Shadow lags by stump and in hollow
Of a body that is bold to come

Across clearings, an eye,
A widening deepening greenness,
Brilliantly, concentratedly,
Coming about its own business

Till, with a sudden sharp hot stink of fox
It enters the dark hole of the head.
The window is starless still; the clock ticks,
The page is printed.

The only excuse a man has for writing is to write himself—
to reveal to others the kind of world reflected
in his individual mirror.

RÉMY DE GOURMONT, Preface to *Le Livre des masques*

2 The writer as interpreter of experience

THE world mirrored in each man's mind is unique. Constantly changing, bafflingly complex, the external world is not a neat, well-ordered place replete with meaning, but an enigma requiring interpretation. This interpretation is the result of a transaction between events in the external world and the mind of the individual—between the world "out there" and the individual's previous experience, knowledge, values, attitudes, and desires. Thus the mirrored world is not just the sum total of eardrum rattles, retinal excitations, and so on; it is a creation that reflects the peculiarities of the perceiver as well as the peculiarities of what is perceived. In a very real sense there are as many interpretations of the world as there are people in it, since no two people are precisely alike. Whatever purposes writing and speaking may have, and there are several, one of the most important is to reveal to others one's own image of the world.

The observer and experience

People are seldom aware of their uniqueness because those they talk to and write for have usually had experiences similar to their own and as a result interpret the world in similar ways. At times, however, differences do become apparent, even among members of the same family. The older son never sees the world in quite the same way as the younger, nor does the parent see it in the same way as his child does. Differences in age, sex, and social role may lead to different interpretations of the "same thing." You can easily find illustrations from your own experience.

Differences in interpretation become even more evident when people from different cultures confront each other; the same event may have strikingly different meanings for them. Once while conducting a lesson in the Thai language for a group of Peace Corps volunteers, one of the authors noticed a rather pretty Thai girl gesturing at him through an open doorway. She was waving at him — palm outward — in a way that means "hello" to an American. He smiled, waved back, and went on with the lesson. She continued to wave. Thinking that she had not seen him return her greeting, he smiled and waved again. But she persisted in her waving with increasing vigor, and he became confused and embarrassed. Finally she went away, obviously annoyed. This teacher had failed to learn the Thai language of gestures; to a Thai the girl's wave meant "Come here!" The meaning of an event, then, depends in large part on who the observer is.

How can we overcome such differences of interpretation and eliminate the misunderstandings they can create? The goal of rhetoric is the resolution of these differences. Throughout this book we will present a number of assumptions about human behavior (based on the observations of linguists and anthropologists about different languages and cultures) that suggest means of resolving these differences. These assumptions can help the writer understand his own interpretations of the world, develop them, and present them to others.

The first assumption may be stated as Maxim 1: *People conceive of the world in terms of repeatable units.* In the continuously changing, dynamic flow of events, there are always recognizable, namable, recurring "sames" — discrete units of experience. Although every instant in life is different from all previous instants, people act as if things were constant, as if situations or events could occur repeatedly. We may never be able to step into the same river twice, but we act as if we can. Men themselves can be seen as dynamic processes, ever changing in time, space, and function — from children to adults, from sons to fathers, from students to teachers, and from followers to leaders. But each recognizes himself, and others recognize him, as being somehow the same, as an individual (a discrete unit) who maintains an identity throughout these changes. Otherwise no one would try to get a date a week in advance, or expect to collect a debt, or bring a criminal to trial.

One way to study how people conceive of the world in terms of recurring units is to examine language, which reflects differences in segmenting the world into units and differences in focusing on these units.

Language and experience

Language provides a way of unitizing experience: a set of symbols that label recurring chunks of experience. Space and time are divided into namable parts: towns, states, nations; seconds, minutes, hours, and epochs. Although the label *chair* is applied to many quite different things (e.g., rockers, sling chairs, reclining chairs) and although the meaning of *chair* is constantly changing as people use the term in new situations, each individual chair is seen as a special instance of a recurring unit. If we all applied separate labels to each and every chair we experienced, language would become unmanageable and past experience would have no relevance to the present and future. Not only would each person's vocabulary become unwieldy, but because everyone's experiences are slightly different, everyone would have an individual vocabulary, and communication would become nearly impossible. Language depends on our seeing certain experiences as constant or repeatable. And seeing the world as repeatable depends, in part at least, on language. A language is, in a sense, a theory of the universe, a way of selecting and grouping experiences in a fairly consistent and predictable way.

Our way of segmenting the color spectrum is another example of labeling chunks of experience. The color spectrum is a continuum, and what we call red is a particular section of the spectrum that includes a wide range of wave lengths. Within this range, many of us—art students, for example—learn to make increasingly fine distinctions; red is not red but vermilion, cerise, scarlet, and so on.

Speech sounds are also areas on a continuum, as you will discover if you hold the vowel sound in the word *he* and then slowly lower your tongue. This vowel sound is, in fact, a range of sounds treated as instances of the same sound, just as *red* is a range of colors regarded as one color.

Different languages provide somewhat different theories of the

universe, thus dividing men into groups who have difficulty understanding each other's ways of seeing and responding to the world.
An English speaker and a speaker of Burmese segment the color
spectrum a bit differently: What the English speaker calls orange the
Burman regards as an instance of red; what the English speaker calls
gray he labels a shade of blue. In each case, Burmese provides a
single term where English provides two. Similarly, the distinction
an English speaker makes between the vowel in *sheep* and the
vowel in *ship* is difficult for the Spanish speaker learning English
because in Spanish these are variations of the same sound. The
Spanish speaker hears nothing unusual in the statement "I came to
this country on a sheep." The two sounds are no more different to
him than the two *t* sounds in *tatter* are to the English speaker. Under special experimental conditions the Burman can perceive a
difference between red and orange and the Spanish speaker can
distinguish between *ship* and *sheep*. But ordinarily these distinctions are simply not significant for them.

Because language is involved in the way people understand
the world, learning a new language is more than learning new
words for things; it is also, in a sense, learning new "things," learning to interpret the world somewhat differently. Some people
resist learning a new language because they seem to sense that the
process is a threat to their identity.

Just how deeply language is involved in the ways people understand the world and just how different two languages may be in
the ways they categorize the world are questions open to speculation. No one can get inside the head of another person to see the
world as he sees it. But we know that everyone has individual
biases, more or less personal ways of segmenting and ordering the
world, and that he reveals these biases subtly in his use of language. Every man is an outsider when he attempts to understand
another's interpretation of the world; he is somewhat less of an outsider when he shares his culture and language with someone else —
but he is still an outsider.

Experience and the observer's focus

Besides segmenting and organizing the world differently and recognizing different chunks of experience as significant units, people
also focus on these units in different ways. For example, a baseball
game can be seen as an identifiable chunk of experience, that is, a
repeatable unit with a name. Within the game, however, there are
smaller units such as innings, plays, individual pitches, signals. In
addition to the activity on the field, there are announcements over

the public-address system, shouts from the spectators, conversations, and so on. All of these can be seen as parts of the larger unit, the baseball game; each can also be seen as a unit in itself. Any unit of experience can be seen as a complex system composed of interrelated parts, or subsystems, each of which is in turn composed of still smaller systems, and so on until some elementary subsystem is reached. Furthermore, the unit is itself a part of a larger system. Thus Maxim 2: _Units of experience are hierarchically structured systems._

When a person enters a ball park, he may shift his focus from the spectacle as a whole to one particular part, such as the team on the field, and then perhaps to a still smaller part, such as the pitcher warming up. He may even focus on the way the pitcher moves his leg as he throws. Someone else will focus on different things during the game and form a different interpretation. Picture a knowledgeable fan, his less knowledgeable wife, and a foreign visitor all describing the "same" game. A person who knows nothing about baseball may focus on all the "wrong" things, missing, for example, a brilliant putout at second base because he was watching the first-base coach waving his arms. Many people become angry when the game is not interpreted "properly"—that is, their way. But the game becomes many games when mirrored in the minds of the spectators. Thus an objective account of the game, one unaffected by the particular biases of the observer, simply does not exist. Nor does a single, proper interpretation.

There are at least three different ways of focusing on the same event:

1) A person can focus on different parts of a whole at different times. He may watch the batter, then shift his focus to the pitcher.

2) A person can have two different parts of the whole in focus simultaneously, one in central or _nuclear_ focus and the other in subsidiary or _marginal_ focus. He may watch the batter and at the same time watch the pitcher out of the corner of his eye. A unit in nuclear focus is more distinct than one in marginal focus, but the border between the two is blurred and shifts from time to time. Often when a person is excited or deeply moved, his area of nuclear focus may enlarge greatly to include many objects, ideas, and sensations; at other times, when he is ill or depressed, it may contract to, say, a throbbing head or a particularly painful memory. Great pain or embarrassment may even drive all other thoughts from his mind.

3) A person can focus on a unit at different levels of magnification. He may focus on the infield during a double play,

seeing three or four players related to each other in a particular way, but with this broad a focus he loses sight of details, such as the movements of a particular player. He may focus on the arm movements of the shortstop, but with this narrow a focus he misses the larger pattern: A double play cannot be seen in the arm movements of one player. An extremely narrow focus, with accompanying magnifications, would be even more limiting: If a fan went down to the field and focused a microscope on the tip of the batter's nose, he might not even recognize the face of his favorite!

Overcoming differences of interpretation

We can now begin to formulate the process for reducing differences of interpretation. The writer must first understand the nature of his own interpretation and how it differs from the interpretations of others. Since each man segments experience into discrete, repeatable units, the writer can begin by asking how his way of segmenting and ordering experience differs from his reader's. How do units of time, space, the visible world, social organization, and so on differ? Second, he can ask how their focuses differ. Are they focusing on different parts of the same whole? Are the same units nuclear for them? Marginal? Are they both using the same level of magnification?

As he discovers how others differ from him, the writer begins to see what he has to write about that is original, interesting, and even important. His message emerges from the unique features of his image of the world. If everyone saw the world in more or less the same way, communication would be relatively unimportant; there would be little news and no surprises, no jokes and no disputes. Human differences are the raw material of writing — differences in experiences and ways of segmenting them, differences in values, purposes, and goals. They are our reason for wishing to communicate. Through communication we create community, the basic value underlying rhetoric. To do so, we must overcome the barriers to communication that are, paradoxically, the motive for communication.

EXERCISES

1 Read the following essay by Albert H. Hastorf and Hadley Cantril. How do they explain the differences in the responses

of people who saw the game? How are such differences traditionally explained? Can you explain what is wrong with the
traditional distinction between *objective* and *subjective* knowledge?

They Saw a Game: A Case Study

ALBERT H. HASTORF AND HADLEY CANTRIL

On a brisk Saturday afternoon, November 23, 1951, the Dartmouth
football team played Princeton in Princeton's Palmer Stadium. It
was the last game of the season for both teams and of rather special
significance because the Princeton team had won all its games so far
and one of its players, Kazmaier, was receiving All-American mention and had just appeared as the cover man on *Time* magazine, and
was playing his last game.

A few minutes after the opening kick-off, it became apparent
that the game was going to be a rough one. The referees were kept
busy blowing their whistles and penalizing both sides. In the second quarter, Princeton's star left the game with a broken nose. In
the third quarter, a Dartmouth player was taken off the field with a
broken leg. Tempers flared both during and after the game. The official statistics of the game, which Princeton won, showed that
Dartmouth was penalized 70 yards, Princeton 25, not counting more
than a few plays in which both sides were penalized.

Needless to say, accusations soon began to fly. The game immediately became a matter of concern to players, students, coaches,
and the administrative officials of the two institutions, as well as to
alumni and the general public who had not seen the game but had
become sensitive to the problem of big-time football through the
recent exposures of subsidized players, commercialism, etc. Discussion of the game continued for several weeks.

One of the contributing factors to the extended discussion of
the game was the extensive space given to it by both campus and
metropolitan newspapers. An indication of the fervor with which
the discussions were carried on is shown by a few excerpts from the
campus dailies.

For example, on November 27 (four days after the game), the
Daily Princetonian (Princeton's student newspaper) said:

This observer has never seen quite such a disgusting exhibition of so-called
"sport." Both teams were guilty but the blame must be laid primarily on
Dartmouth's doorstep. Princeton, obviously the better team, had no reason
to rough up Dartmouth. Looking at the situation rationally, we don't see why
the Indians should make a deliberate attempt to cripple Dick Kazmaier or any
other Princeton player. The Dartmouth psychology, however, is not rational
itself.

The November 30th edition of the *Princeton Alumni Weekly* said:

But certain memories of what occurred will not be easily erased. Into the record books will go in indelible fashion the fact that the last game of Dick

Kazmaier's career was cut short by more than half when he was forced out with a broken nose and a mild concussion, sustained from a tackle that came well after he had thrown a pass.

This second-period development was followed by a third quarter outbreak of roughness that was climaxed when a Dartmouth player deliberately kicked Brad Glass in the ribs while the latter was on his back. Throughout the often unpleasant afternoon, there was undeniable evidence that the losers' tactics were the result of an actual style of play, and reports on other games they have played this season substantiate this.

Dartmouth students were "seeing" an entirely different version of the game through the editorial eyes of the *Dartmouth* (Dartmouth's undergraduate newspaper). For example, on November 27 the *Dartmouth* said:

However, the Dartmouth-Princeton game set the stage for the other type of dirty football. A type which may be termed as an unjustifiable accusation.

Dick Kazmaier was injured early in the game. Kazmaier was the star, an All-American. Other stars have been injured before, but Kazmaier had been built to represent a Princeton idol. When an idol is hurt there is only one recourse—the tag of dirty football. So what did the Tiger Coach Charley Caldwell do? He announced to the world that the Big Green had been out to extinguish the Princeton star. His purpose was achieved.

After this incident, Caldwell instilled the old see-what-they-did-go-get-them attitude into his players. His talk got results. Gene Howard and Jim Miller were both injured. Both had dropped back to pass, had passed, and were standing unprotected in the backfield. Result: one bad leg and one leg broken.

The game was rough and did get a bit out of hand in the third quarter. Yet most of the roughing penalties were called against Princeton while Dartmouth received more of the illegal-use-of-the-hands variety.

On November 28 the *Dartmouth* said:

Dick Kazmaier of Princeton admittedly is an unusually able football player. Many Dartmouth men traveled to Princeton, not expecting to win—only hoping to see an All-American in action. Dick Kazmaier was hurt in the second period, and played only a token part in the remainder of the game. For this, spectators were sorry.

But there were no such feelings for Dick Kazmaier's health. Medical authorities have confirmed that as a relatively unprotected passing and running star in a contact sport, he is quite liable to injury. Also, his particular injuries—a broken nose and slight concussion—were no more serious than is experienced almost any day in any football practice, where there is no more serious stake than playing the following Saturday. Up to the Princeton game, Dartmouth players suffered about 10 known nose fractures and face injuries, not to mention several slight concussions.

Did Princeton players feel so badly about losing their star? They shouldn't have. During the past undefeated campaign they stopped several individual stars by a concentrated effort, including such mainstays as Frank Hauff of Navy, Glenn Adams of Pennsylvania and Rocco Calvo of Cornell.

In other words, the same brand of football condemned by the *Prince*—that of stopping the big man—is practiced quite successfully by the Tigers.

Basically, then, there was disagreement as to what had happened during the "game." Hence we took the opportunity presented by the occasion to make a "real life" study of a perceptual problem.[1]

PROCEDURE

Two steps were involved in gathering data. The first consisted of answers to a questionnaire designed to get reactions to the game and to learn something of the climate of opinion in each institution. This questionnaire was administered a week after the game to both Dartmouth and Princeton undergraduates who were taking introductory and intermediate psychology courses.

The second step consisted of showing the same motion picture of the game to a sample of undergraduates in each school and having them check on another questionnaire, as they watched the film, any infraction of the rules they saw and whether these infractions were "mild" or "flagrant."[2] At Dartmouth, members of two fraternities were asked to view the film on December 7; at Princeton, members of two undergraduate clubs saw the film early in January.

The answers to both questionnaires were carefully coded and transferred to punch cards.[3]

RESULTS

Table 1 shows the questions which received different replies from the two student populations on the first questionnaire.

Questions asking if the students had friends on the team, if they had ever played football themselves, if they felt they knew the rules of the game well, etc. showed no differences in either school and no relation to answers given to other questions. This is not surprising since the students in both schools come from essentially the same type of educational, economic, and ethnic background.

Summarizing the data of Tables 1 and 2, we find a marked contrast between the two student groups.

Nearly all *Princeton* students judged the game as "rough and dirty"—not one of them thought it "clean and fair." And almost nine-tenths of them thought the other side started the rough play. By and large they felt that the charges they understood were being

[1] We are not concerned here with the problem of guilt or responsibility for infractions, and nothing here implies any judgment as to who was to blame.

[2] The film shown was kindly loaned for the purpose of the experiment by the Dartmouth College Athletic Council. It should be pointed out that a movie of a football game follows the ball, is thus selective, and omits a good deal of the total action on the field. And of course, in viewing only a film of a game, the possibilities of participation as specatator are greatly limited.

[3] We gratefully acknowledge the assistance of Virginia Zerega, Office of Public Opinion Research and J. L. McCandless, Princeton University, and E. S. Horton, Dartmouth College, in the gathering and collation of the data.

TABLE 1 Data from First Questionnaire

Question	Dartmouth Students (N = 163) %	Princeton Students (N = 161) %
1. Did you happen to see the actual game between Dartmouth and Princeton in Palmer Stadium this year?		
Yes	33	71
No	67	29
2. Have you seen a movie of the game or seen it on television?		
Yes, movie	33	2
Yes, television	0	1
No, neither	67	97
3. (Asked of those who answered "yes" to either or both of above questions.) From your observations of what went on at the game, do you believe the game was clean and fairly played, or that it was unnecessarily rough and dirty?		
Clean and fair	6	0
Rough and dirty	24	69
Rough and fair*	25	2
No answer	45	29
4. (Asked of those who answered "no" on both of the first questions.) From what you have heard and read about the game, do you feel it was clean and fairly played, or that it was unnecessarily rough and dirty?		
Clean and fair	7	0
Rough and dirty	18	24
Rough and fair*	14	1
Don't know	6	4
No answer	55	71
(Combined answers to questions 3 and 4 above)		
Clean and fair	13	0
Rough and dirty	42	93
Rough and fair*	39	3
Don't know	6	4

TABLE 1 Data from First Questionnaire — *(Continued)*

Question	Dartmouth Students (N = 163) %	Princeton Students (N = 161) %
5. From what you saw in the game or the movies, or from what you have read, which team do you feel started the rough play?		
Dartmouth started it	36	86
Princeton started it	2	0
Both started it	53	11
Neither	6	1
No answer	3	2
6. What is your understanding of the charges being made?**		
Dartmouth tried to get Kazmaier	71	47
Dartmouth intentionally dirty	52	44
Dartmouth unnecessarily rough	8	35
7. Do you feel there is any truth to these charges?		
Yes	10	55
No	57	4
Partly	29	35
Don't know	4	6
8. Why do you think the charges were made?		
Injury to Princeton star	70	23
To prevent repetition	2	46
No answer	28	31

* This answer was not included on the checklist but was written in by the percentage of students indicated.
** Replies do not add to 100% since more than one charge could be given.

made were true; most of them felt the charges were made in order to avoid similar situations in the future.

When Princeton students looked at the movie of the game, they saw the Dartmouth team make over twice as many infractions as their own team made. And they saw the Dartmouth team make over twice as many infractions as were seen by Dartmouth students. When Princeton students judged these infractions as "flagrant" or "mild,"

TABLE 2 Data from Second Questionnaire Checked While Seeing Film

Group	N	Total Number of Infractions Checked Against			
		Dartmouth Team		Princeton Team	
		Mean	SD	Mean	SD
Dartmouth students	48	4.3*	2.7	4.4	2.8
Princeton students	49	9.8*	5.7	4.2	3.5

* Significant at the .01 level.

the ratio was about two "flagrant" to one "mild" on the Dartmouth team, and about one "flagrant" to three "mild" on the Princeton team.

As for the *Dartmouth* students, while the plurality of answers fell in the "rough and dirty" category, over one-tenth thought the game was "clean and fair" and over a third introduced their own category of "rough and fair" to describe the action. Although a third of the Dartmouth students felt that Dartmouth was to blame for starting the rough play, the majority of Dartmouth students thought both sides were to blame. By and large, Dartmouth men felt that the charges they understood were being made were not true, and most of them thought the reason for the charges was Princeton's concern for its football star.

When Dartmouth students looked at the movie of the game they saw both teams make about the same number of infractions. And they saw their own team make only half the number of infractions the Princeton students saw them make. The ratio of "flagrant" to "mild" infractions was about one to one when Dartmouth students judged the Dartmouth team, and about one "flagrant" to two "mild" when Dartmouth students judged infractions made by the Princeton team.

It should be noted that Dartmouth and Princeton students were thinking of different charges in judging their validity and in assigning reasons as to why the charges were made. It should also be noted that whether or not students were spectators of the game in the stadium made little difference in their responses.

INTERPRETATION: THE NATURE OF A SOCIAL EVENT[4]

It seems clear that the "game" actually was many different games and that each version of the events that transpired was just as "real" to a

[4] The interpretation of the nature of a social event sketched here is in part based on discussions with Adelbert Ames, Jr., and is being elaborated in more detail elsewhere.

particular person as other versions were to other people. A consideration of the experiential phenomena that constitute a "football game"
for the spectator may help us both to account for the results obtained
and illustrate something of the nature of any social event.

Like any other complex social occurrence, a "football game"
consists of a whole host of happenings. Many different events are
occurring simultaneously. Furthermore, each happening is a link in a
chain of happenings, so that one follows another in sequence. The
"football game," as well as other complex social situations, consists of
a whole matrix of events. In the game situation, this matrix of events
consists of the actions of all the players, together with the behavior of
the referees and linesmen, the action on the sidelines, in the grand-
stands, over the loud-speaker, etc.

Of crucial importance is the fact that an "occurrence" on the
football field or in any other social situation does not become an experiential "event" unless and until some significance is given to it: an
"occurrence" becomes an "*event*" only when the happening has significance. And a happening generally has significance only if it reac
tivates learned significances already registered in what we have
called a person's assumptive form-world (1) .

Hence the particular occurrences that different people experienced in the football game were a limited series of events from the
total matrix of events *potentially* available to them. People experienced those occurrences that reactivated significances they brought
to the occasion; they failed to experience those occurrences which did
not reactivate past significances. We do not need to introduce "attention" as an "intervening third" (to paraphrase James on memory) to
account for the selectivity of the experiential process.

In this particular study, one of the most interesting examples of
this phenomenon was a telegram sent to an officer of Dartmouth College by a member of a Dartmouth alumni group in the Midwest. He
had viewed the film which had been shipped to his alumni group
from Princeton after its use with Princeton students, who saw, as we
noted, an average of over nine infractions by Dartmouth players during the game. The alumnus, who couldn't see the infractions he had
heard publicized, wired:

Preview of Princeton movies indicates considerable cutting of important part
please wire explanation and possibly air mail missing part before showing
scheduled for January 25 we have splicing equipment.

The "same" sensory impingements emanating from the football
field, transmitted through the visual mechanism to the brain, also
obviously gave rise to different experiences in different people. The
significances assumed by different happenings for different people
depend in large part on the purposes people bring to the occasion
and the assumptions they have of the purposes and probable behavior of other people involved. This was amusingly pointed out by
the New York *Herald Tribune's* sports columnist, Red Smith, in de-

scribing a prize fight between Chico Vejar and Carmine Fiore in his column of December 21, 1951. Among other things, he wrote:

You see, Steve Ellis is the proprietor of Chico Vejar, who is a highly desirable tract of Stamford, Conn., welterweight. Steve is also a radio announcer. Ordinarily there is no conflict between Ellis the Brain and Ellis the Voice because Steve is an uncommonly substantial lump of meat who can support both halves of a split personality and give away weight on each end without missing it.

This time, though, the two Ellises met head-on, with a sickening, rending crash. Steve the Manager sat at ringside in the guise of Steve the Announcer broadcasting a dispassionate, unbiased, objective report of Chico's adventures in the ring. . . .

Clear as mountain water, his words came through, winning big for Chico. Winning? Hell, Steve was slaughtering poor Fiore.

Watching and listening, you could see what a valiant effort the reporter was making to remain cool and detached. At the same time you had an illustration of the old, established truth that when anybody with a preference watches a fight, he sees only what he prefers to see.

That is always so. That is why, after any fight that doesn't end in a clean knockout, there always are at least a few hoots when the decision is announced. A guy from, say, Billy Graham's neighborhood goes to see Billy fight and he watches Graham all the time. He sees all the punches Billy throws, and hardly any of the punches Billy catches. So it was with Steve.

"Fiore feints with a left," he would say, honestly believing that Fiore hadn't caught Chico full on the chops. "Fiore's knees buckle," he said, "and Chico backs away." Steve didn't see the hook that had driven Chico back. . . .

In brief, the data here indicate that there is no such "thing" as a "game" existing "out there" in its own right which people merely "observe." The "game" "exists" for a person and is experienced by him only in so far as certain happenings have significances in terms of his purpose. Out of all the occurrences going on in the environment, a person selects those that have some significance for him from his own egocentric position in the total matrix.

Obviously in the case of a football game, the value of the experience of watching the game is enhanced if the purpose of "your" team is accomplished, that is, if the happening of the desired consequence is experienced—i.e., if your team wins. But the value attribute of the experience can, of course, be spoiled if the desire to win crowds out behavior we value and have come to call sportsmanlike.

The sharing of significances provides the links except for which a "social" event would not be experienced and would not exist for anyone.

A "football game" would be impossible except for the rules of the game which we bring to the situation and which enable us to share with others the significances of various happenings. These rules make possible a certain repeatability of events such as first downs, touchdowns, etc. If a person is unfamiliar with the rules of the game, the behavior he sees lacks repeatability and consistent significance and hence "doesn't make sense."

And only because there is the possibility of repetition is there the possibility that a happening has a significance. For example, the

balls used in games are designed to give a high degree of repeatability. While a football is about the only ball used in games which is not
a sphere, the shape of the modern football has apparently evolved in
order to achieve a higher degree of accuracy and speed in forward
passing than would be obtained with a spherical ball, thus increasing
the repeatability of an important phase of the game.

The rules of a football game, like laws, rituals, customs, and
mores, are registered and preserved forms of sequential significances
enabling people to share the significances of occurrences. The sharing
of sequential significances which have value for us provides the links
that operationally make social events possible. They are analogous
to the forces of attraction that hold parts of an atom together, keeping
each part from following its individual, independent course.

From this point of view it is inaccurate and misleading to say
that different people have different "attitudes" concerning the same
"thing." For the "thing" simply is *not* the same for different people
whether the "thing" is a football game, a presidential candidate,
Communism, or spinach. We do not simply "react to" a happening or
to some impingement from the environment in a determined way
(except in behavior that has become reflexive or habitual). We behave according to what we bring to the occasion, and what each of us
brings to the occasion is more or less unique. And except for these
significances which we bring to the occasion, the happenings around
us would be meaningless occurrences, would be "inconsequential."

From the transactional view, an attitude is not a predisposition
to react in a certain way to an occurrence or stimulus "out there" that
exists in its own right with certain fixed characteristics which we
"color" according to our predisposition (2). That is, a subject does not
simply "react to" and "object." An attitude would rather seem to be a
complex of registered significances reactivated by some stimulus
which assumes its own particular significance for us in terms of our
purposes. That is, the object as experienced would not exist for us
except for the reactivated aspects of the form-world which provide
particular significance to the hieroglyphics of sensory impingements.

References

1. CANTRIL, H. *The "why" of man's experience.* New York: Macmillan, 1950.
2. KILPATRICK, F. P. (Ed.) *Human behavior from the transactional point of view.*
   Hanover, N. H.: Institute for Associated Research, 1952.

2 Read the following excerpt from *Flatland* by Edwin A. Abbott.
In this book the mathematician-author presents two imaginary
worlds: Flatland, a two-dimensional world, and Lineland,
a one-dimensional world in which "women" exist as points
and "men" as segments along a single line. The hero is a
square from Flatland; in this excerpt he is trying to explain to
the King of Lineland what it means to move sideways, to the
right or left.

Notice that the two characters are talking about the differences in their experience: The personal factor in knowledge provides the basic reason for wanting to communicate. These differences are also the barriers to communication, the causes of misinterpretation. Why do both characters in the episode get angry?

Would it be possible to convince the King that other dimensions exist without moving him out of his world (i.e., the line)? Using your answer to this question, state generally the major problems that arise when one person tries to convince another of something.

Can you think of a possible situation—with yourself as one of the participants—that would be analogous to the situation in the excerpt from *Flatland?* (If you find an interesting answer to this question, it might make a good essay.)

from

Flatland

EDWIN A. ABBOTT

KING   Exhibit to me, if you please, this motion from left to right.

I   Nay, that I cannot do, unless you could step out of your Line altogether.

KING   Out of my Line? Do you mean out of the world? Out of Space?

I   Well, yes. Out of *your* World. Out of *your* Space. For your Space is not the true Space. True Space is a Plane; but your Space is only a Line.

KING   If you cannot indicate this motion from left to right by yourself moving in it, then I beg you to describe it to me in words.

I   If you cannot tell your right side from your left, I fear that no words of mine can make my meaning clear to you. But surely you cannot be ignorant of so simple a distinction.

KING   I do not in the least understand you.

I   Alas! How shall I make it clear? When you move straight on, does it not sometimes occur to you that you *could* move in some other way, turning your eye round so as to look in the direction towards which your side is now fronting? In other words, instead of always moving in the direction of one of your extremities, do you never feel a desire to move in the direction, so to speak, of your side?

KING   Never. And what do you mean? How can a man's inside "front" in any direction? Or how can a man move in the direction of his inside?

I   Well then, since words cannot explain the matter, I will try deeds, and will move gradually out of Lineland in the direction which I desire to indicate to you.

At the word I began to move my body out of Lineland. As long as any part of me remained in his dominion and in his view, the King kept exclaiming, "I see you, I see you still; you are not moving."

Lineland →   My body just before I disappeared   The King

But when I had at last moved myself out of his Line, he cried in his shrillest voice, "She is vanished; she is dead." "I am not dead," replied I; "I am simply out of Lineland, that is to say, out of the Straight Line which you call Space, and in the true Space, where I can see things as they are. And at this moment I can see your Line, or side — or inside as you are pleased to call it; and I can see also the Men and Women on the North and South of you, whom I will now enumerate, describing their order, their size, and the interval between each."

When I had done this at great length, I cried triumphantly, "Does that at last convince you?" And, with that, I once more entered Lineland, taking up the same position as before.

But the Monarch replied, "If you were a Man of sense — though, as you appear to have only one voice I have little doubt you are not a Man but a Woman — but, if you had a particle of sense, you would listen to reason. You ask me to believe that there is another Line besides that which my senses indicate, and another motion besides that of which I am daily conscious. I, in return, ask you to describe in words or indicate by motion that other Line of which you speak. Instead of moving, you merely exercise some magic art of vanishing and returning to sight; and instead of any lucid description of your new World, you simply tell me the numbers and sizes of some forty of my retinue, facts known to any child in my capital. Can anything be more irrational or audacious? Acknowledge your folly or depart from my dominions."

Furious at his perversity, and especially indignant that he professed to be ignorant of my sex, I retorted in no measured terms, "Besotted Being! You think yourself the perfection of existence, while you are in reality the most imperfect and imbecile. You profess to see, whereas you can see nothing but a point! You plume yourself on inferring the existence of a Straight Line; but I *can see* Straight Lines, and infer the existence of Angles, Triangles, Squares, Pentagons, Hexagons, and even Circles. Why waste more words? Suffice it that I am the completion of your incomplete self. You are a Line, but I am a Line of Lines, called in my country a Square: and even I, infinitely superior though I am to you, am of little account among the great nobles of Flatland, whence I have come to visit you, in the hope of enlightening your ignorance."

Hearing these words the King advanced towards me with a menacing cry as if to pierce me through the diagonal; and in that same moment there arose from myriads of his subjects a multitudinous war-cry, increasing in vehemence till at last methought it rivalled the roar of an army of a hundred thousand Isosceles, and the artillery of a thousand Pentagons. Spell-bound and motionless, I could neither speak nor move to avert the impending destruction; and still the noise grew louder, and the King came closer, when I awoke to find the breakfast-bell recalling me to the realities of Flatland.

3 Discuss how the following continua might be segmented. There are no right or wrong answers, so speculate freely. How is each continuum conventionally segmented? Can you think of alternatives that are unconventional but at the same time useful?

1) A day in your life.
2) Your life as a whole.
3) The town where you live. (Remember that it has a temporal as well as a spatial dimension.)
4) A particular class period. (Its function as well as its spatial and temporal features might be considered.)

Illustrate the three different ways of focusing, using one of the topics above. For example, once you have segmented a day, what focuses are possible? What parts are seen in nuclear focus? What marginal? What levels of magnification are possible? What focuses are unconventional but useful?

Select one idea that emerges from this speculation and discuss it in a brief, informal essay directed toward the other members of the class.

4 Contrast the way you segmented any continuum listed in Exercise 3 with the way someone else might segment it. For example, consider how you segmented a day in your life and how your mother or father or best friend might segment it. What differences in focus are apparent?

5 Read the following excerpt from an essay by Herbert A. Simon. Although difficult and technical in places, it is provocative and rewarding to the reader who takes the time necessary to understand it. Many of the points Simon raises are important to subsequent discussions in this book.

Simon's argument has clear application to the process of writing. For example, if we consider an essay to be a complex system that has evolved through time, we should be able to imagine two writers who parallel Hora and Tempus. How would their writing procedures differ? If we consider writing a highly complex problem-solving process, what other applications of Simon's argument are apparent?

from
The Architecture of Complexity*
HERBERT A. SIMON

A number of proposals have been advanced in recent years for the development of "general systems theory" which, abstracting from properties peculiar to physical, biological, or social systems, would be applicable to all of them.[1] We might well feel that, while the goal is laudable, systems of such diverse kinds could hardly be expected to have any nontrivial properties in common. Metaphor and analogy can be helpful, or they can be misleading. All depends on whether the similarities the metaphor captures are significant or superficial.

It may not be entirely vain, however, to search for common properties among diverse kinds of complex systems. The ideas that go by the name of cybernetics constitute, if not a theory, at least a point of view that has been proving fruitful over a wide range of applications.[2] It has been useful to look at the behavior of adaptive systems in terms of the concepts of feedback and homeostasis, and to analyze adaptiveness in terms of the theory of selective information.[3] The ideas of feedback and information provide a frame of reference for viewing a wide range of situations, just as do the ideas of evolution, of relativism, of axiomatic method, and of operationalism.

In this paper I should like to report on some things we have been learning about particular kinds of complex systems encountered in the behavioral sciences. The developments I shall discuss arose in the context of specific phenomena, but the theoretical formulations

* EDITORS' NOTE: This essay was first presented as a speech at a meeting of the American Philosophical Society on April 26, 1962.

[1] See especially the yearbooks of the Society for General Systems Research. Prominent among the exponents of general systems theory are L. von Bertalanffy, K. Boulding, R. W. Gerard, and J. G. Miller. For a more skeptical view — perhaps too skeptical in the light of the present discussion — see H. A. Simon and A. Newell, Models: their uses and limitations, *in* L. D. White, ed., *The state of the social sciences*, 66-83, Chicago, Univ. of Chicago Press, 1956.

[2] N. Wiener, *Cybernetics*, New York, John Wiley & Sons, 1948. For an imaginative forerunner, see A. J. Lotka, *Elements of mathematical biology*, New York, Dover Publications, 1951, first published in 1924 as *Elements of physical biology*.

[3] C. Shannon and W. Weaver, *The mathematical theory of communication*, Urbana, Univ. of Illinois Press, 1949; W. R. Ashby, *Design for a brain*, New York, John Wiley & Sons, 1952.

themselves make little reference to details of structure. Instead they refer primarily to the complexity of the systems under view without specifying the exact content of that complexity. Because of their abstractness, the theories may have relevance — application would be too strong a term — to other kinds of complex systems that are observed in the social, biological, and physical sciences.

In recounting these developments, I shall avoid technical detail, which can generally be found elsewhere. I shall describe each theory in the particular context in which it arose. Then, I shall cite some examples of complex systems, from areas of science other than the initial application, to which the theoretical framework appears relevant. In doing so, I shall make reference to areas of knowledge where I am not expert — perhaps not even literate. I feel quite comfortable in doing so before the members of this society, representing as it does the whole span of the scientific and scholarly endeavor. Collectively you will have little difficulty, I am sure, in distinguishing instances based on idle fancy or sheer ignorance from instances that cast some light on the ways in which complexity exhibits itself wherever it is found in nature. I shall leave to you the final judgment of relevance in your respective fields.

I shall not undertake a formal definition of "complex systems."[4] Roughly, by a complex system I mean one made up of a large number of parts that interact in a nonsimple way. In such systems, the whole is more than the sum of the parts, not in an ultimate, metaphysical sense, but in the important pragmatic sense that, given the properties of the parts and the laws of their interaction, it is not a trivial matter to infer the properties of the whole. In the face of complexity, an in-principle reductionist may be at the same time a pragmatic holist.[5]

.   .   .

The central theme that runs through my remarks is that complexity frequently takes the form of hierarchy, and that hierarchic systems have some common properties that are independent of their specific content. Hierarchy, I shall argue, is one of the central structural schemes that the architect of complexity uses.

[4] W. Weaver, in: Science and complexity, *American Scientist* 36: 536, 1948, has distinguished two kinds of complexity, disorganized and organized. We shall be primarily concerned with organized complexity.

[5] See also John R. Platt, Properties of large molecules that go beyond the properties of their chemical sub-groups, *Jour. Theoret. Biol.* 1: 342–358, 1961. Since the reductionism-holism issue is a major *cause de guerre* between scientists and humanists, perhaps we might even hope that peace could be negotiated between the two cultures along the lines of the compromise just suggested. As I go along, I shall have a little to say about complexity in the arts as well as in the natural sciences. I must emphasize the pragmatism of my holism to distinguish it sharply from the position taken by W. M. Elsasser in *The physical foundation of biology*, New York, Pergamon Press, 1958.

HIERARCHIC SYSTEMS

By a *hierarchic system,* or hierarchy, I mean a system that is composed of interrelated subsystems, each of the latter being, in turn, hierarchic in structure until we reach some lowest level of elementary subsystem. In most systems in nature, it is somewhat arbitrary as to where we leave off the partitioning, and what subsystems we take as elementary. Physics makes much use of the concept of "elementary particle" although particles have a disconcerting tendency not to remain elementary very long. Only a couple of generations ago, the atoms themselves were elementary particles; today, to the nuclear physicist they are complex systems. For certain purposes of astronomy, whole stars, or even galaxies, can be regarded as elementary subsystems. In one kind of biological research, a cell may be treated as an elementary subsystem; in another, a protein molecule; in still another, an amino acid residue.

Just why a scientist has a right to treat as elementary a subsystem that is in fact exceedingly complex is one of the questions we shall take up. For the moment, we shall accept the fact that scientists do this all the time, and that if they are careful scientists they usually get away with it.

Etymologically, the word "hierarchy" has had a narrower meaning than I am giving it here. The term has generally been used to refer to a complex system in which each of the subsystems is subordinated by an authority relation to the system it belongs to. More exactly, in a hierarchic formal organization, each system consists of a "boss" and a set of subordinate subsystems. Each of the subsystems has a "boss" who is the immediate subordinate of the boss of the system. We shall want to consider systems in which the relations among subsystems are more complex than in the formal organizational hierarchy just described. We shall want to include systems in which there is no relation of subordination among subsystems. (In fact, even in human organizations, the formal hierarchy exists only on paper; the real flesh-and-blood organization has many inter-part relations other than the lines of formal authority.) For lack of a better term, I shall use hierarchy in the broader sense introduced in the previous paragraphs, to refer to all complex systems analyzable into successive sets of subsystems, and speak of "formal hierarchy" when I want to refer to the more specialized concept.[6]

---

[6] The mathematical term "partitioning" will not do for what I call here a hierarchy; for the set of subsystems, and the successive subsets in each of these defines the partitioning, independently of any systems of relations among the subsets. By hierarchy I mean the partitioning in conjunction with the relations that hold among its parts.

Social systems

I have already given an example of one kind of hierarchy that is frequently encountered in the social sciences: a formal organization. Business firms, governments, universities all have a clearly visible parts-within-parts structure. But formal organizations are not the only, or even the most common, kind of social hierarchy. Almost all societies have elementary units called families, which may be grouped into villages or tribes, and these into larger groupings, and so on. If we make a chart of social interactions, of who talks to whom, the clusters of dense interaction in the chart will identify a rather well-defined hierarchic structure. The groupings in this structure may be defined operationally by some measure of frequency of interaction in this sociometric matrix.

Biological and physical systems

The hierarchical structure of biological systems is a familiar fact. Taking the cell as the building block, we find cells organized into tissues, tissues into organs, organs into systems. Moving downward from the cell, well-defined subsystems—for example, nucleus, cell membrane, microsomes, mitochondria, and so on—have been identified in animal cells.

The hierarchic structure of many physical systems is equally clear-cut. I have already mentioned the two main series. At the microscopic level we have elementary particles, atoms, molecules, macromolecules. At the macroscopic level we have satellite systems, planetary systems, galaxies. Matter is distributed throughout space in a strikingly non-uniform fashion. The most nearly random distributions we find, gases, are not random distributions of elementary particles but random distributions of complex systems, i.e. molecules.

A considerable range of structural types is subsumed under the term hierarchy as I have defined it. By this definition, a diamond is hierarchic, for it is a crystal structure of carbon atoms that can be further decomposed into protons, neutrons, and electrons. However, it is a very "flat" hierarchy, in which the number of first-order subsystems belonging to the crystal can be indefinitely large. A volume of molecular gas is a flat hierarchy in the same sense. In ordinary usage, we tend to reserve the word hierarchy for a system that is divided into a *small or moderate number* of subsystems, each of which may be further subdivided. Hence, we do not ordinarily think of or refer to a diamond or a gas as a hierarchic structure. Similarly, a linear polymer is simply a chain, which may be very long, of identical subparts, the monomers. At the molecular level it is a very flat hierarchy.

In discussing formal organizations, the number of subordinates who report directly to a single boss is called his *span of control*. I will speak analogously of the *span* of a system, by which I shall mean the number of subsystems into which it is partitioned. Thus, a hierarchic system is flat at a given level if it has a wide span at that level. A diamond has a wide span at the crystal level, but not at the next level down, the molecular level.

In most of our theory construction in the following sections we shall focus our attention on hierarchies of moderate span, but from time to time I shall comment on the extent to which the theories might or might not be expected to apply to very flat hierarchies.

There is one important difference between the physical and biological hierarchies, on the one hand, and social hierarchies, on the other. Most physical and biological hierarchies are described in spatial terms. We detect the organelles in a cell in the way we detect the raisins in a cake—they are "visibly" differentiated substructures localized spatially in the larger structure. On the other hand, we propose to identify social hierarchies not by observing who lives close to whom but by observing who interacts with whom. These two points of view can be reconciled by defining hierarchy in terms of intensity of interaction, but observing that in most biological and physical systems relatively intense interaction implies relative spatial propinquity. One of the interesting characteristics of nerve cells and telephone wires is that they permit very specific strong interactions at great distances. To the extent that interactions are channeled through specialized communications and transportation systems, spatial propinquity becomes less determinative of structure.

Symbolic systems

One very important class of systems has been omitted from my examples thus far: systems of human symbolic production. A book is a hierarchy in the sense in which I am using that term. It is generally divided into chapters, the chapters into sections, the sections into paragraphs, the paragraphs into sentences, the sentences into clauses and phrases, the clauses and phrases into words. We may take the words as our elementary units, or further subdivide them, as the linguist often does, into smaller units. If the book is narrative in character, it may divide into "episodes" instead of sections, but divisions there will be.

The hierarchic structure of music, based on such units as movements, parts, themes, phrases, is well known. The hierarchic structure of products of the pictorial arts is more difficult to characterize. . . .

THE EVOLUTION OF COMPLEX SYSTEMS

Let me introduce the topic of evolution with a parable. There once were two watchmakers, named Hora and Tempus, who manufactured very fine watches. Both of them were highly regarded, and the phones in their workshops rang frequently—new customers were constantly calling them. However, Hora prospered, while Tempus became poorer and poorer and finally lost his shop. What was the reason?

The watches the men made consisted of about 1,000 parts each.

Tempus had so constructed his that if he had one partly assembled and had to put it down—to answer the phone say—it immediately fell to pieces and had to be reassembled from the elements. The better the customers liked his watches, the more they phoned him, the more difficult it became for him to find enough uninterrupted time to finish a watch.

The watches that Hora made were no less complex than those of Tempus. But he had designed them so that he could put together subassemblies of about ten elements each. Ten of these subassemblies again, could be put together into a larger subassembly; and a system of ten of the latter subassemblies constituted the whole watch. Hence, when Hora had to put down a partly assembled watch in order to answer the phone, he lost only a small part of his work, and he assembled his watches in only a fraction of the man-hours it took Tempus.

It is rather easy to make a quantitative analysis of the relative difficulty of the tasks of Tempus and Hora: Suppose the probability that an interruption will occur while a part is being added to an incomplete assembly is p. Then the probability that Tempus can complete a watch he has started without interruption is $(1-p)^{1000}$—a very small number unless p is .001 or less. Each interruption will cost, on the average, the time to assemble $1/p$ parts (the expected number assembled before interruption). On the other hand, Hora has to complete one hundred eleven subassemblies of ten parts each. The probability that he will not be interrupted while completing any one of these is $(1-p)^{10}$, and each interruption will cost only about the time required to assemble five parts.[7]

Now if p is about .01—that is, there is one chance in a hundred that either watchmaker will be interrupted while adding any one part to an assembly—then a straightforward calculation shows that it will

[7] The speculations on speed of evolution were first suggested by H. Jacobson's application of information theory to estimating the time required for biological evolution. See his paper, Information, reproduction, and the origin of life, in *American Scientist* 43: 119–127, January, 1955. From thermodynamic considerations it is possible to estimate the amount of increase in entropy that occurs when a complex system decomposes into its elements. (See, for example, R. B. Setlow and E. C. Pollard, *Molecular biophysics*, 63–65, Reading, Mass., Addison-Wesley Publishing Co., 1962, and references cited there.) But entropy is the logarithm of a probability, hence information, the negative of entropy, can be interpreted as the logarithm of the reciprocal of the probability—the "improbability," so to speak. The essential idea in Jacobson's model is that the expected time required for the system to reach a particular state is inversely proportional to the probability of the state—hence increases exponentially with the amount of information (negentropy) of the state.

Following this line of argument, but not introducing the notion of levels and stable subassemblies, Jacobson arrived at estimates of the time required for evolution so large as to make the event rather improbable. Our analysis, carried through in the same way, but with attention to the stable intermediate forms, produces very much smaller estimates.

take Tempus, on the average, about four thousand times as long to assemble a watch as Hora.

We arrive at the estimate as follows:

1. Hora must make 111 times as many complete assemblies per watch as Tempus; but,
2. Tempus will lose on the average 20 times as much work for each interrupted assembly as Hora [100 parts, on the average, as against 5]; and,
3. Tempus will complete an assembly only 44 times per million attempts ($.99^{1000} = 44 \times 10^{-6}$), while Hora will complete nine out of ten ($.99^{10} = 9 \times 10^{-1}$). Hence Tempus will have to make 20,000 as many attempts per completed assembly as Hora. $(9 \times 10^{-1})/(44 \times 10^{-6}) = 2 \times 10^4$. Multiplying these three ratios, we get:

$$1/111 \times 100/5 \times .99^{10}/.99^{1000} = 1/111 \times 20 \times 20,000 \sim 4,000.$$

.   .   .

Problem solving as natural selection

Let us turn now to . . . human problem-solving processes. Consider, for example, the task of discovering the proof for a difficult theorem. The process can be—and often has been—described as a search through a maze. Starting with the axioms and previously proved theorems, various transformations allowed by the rules of the mathematical systems are attempted, to obtain new expressions. These are modified in turn until, with persistence and good fortune, a sequence or path of transformations is discovered that leads to the goal.

The process usually involves a great deal of trial and error. Various paths are tried; some are abandoned, others are pushed further. Before a solution is found, a great many paths of the maze may be explored. The more difficult and novel the problem, the greater is likely to be the amount of trial and error required to find a solution. At the same time, the trial and error is not completely random or blind; it is, in fact, rather highly selective. The new expressions that are obtained by transforming given ones are examined to see whether they represent progress toward the goal. Indications of progress spur further search in the same direction; lack of progress signals the abandonment of a line of search. Problem solving requires *selective* trial and error.[12]

A little reflection reveals that cues signaling progress play the same role in the problem-solving process that stable intermediate

---

[12] See A. Newell, J. C. Shaw, and H. A. Simon, Empirical explorations of the logic theory machine, *Proceedings of the 1957 Western Joint Computer Conference*, February, 1957, New York: Institute of Radio Engineers; Chess-playing programs and the problem of complexity, *IBM Journal of Research and Development* 2: 320–335, October, 1958; and for a similar view of problem solving, W. R. Ashby, Design for an intelligence amplifier, 215–233 in C. E. Shannon and J. McCarthy, *Automata studies*, Princeton, Princeton Univ. Press, 1956.

forms play in the biological evolutionary process. In fact, we can take over the watchmaker parable and apply it also to problem solving. In problem solving, a partial result that represents recognizable progress toward the goal plays the role of a stable subassembly.

Suppose that the task is to open a safe whose lock has ten dials, each with one hundred possible settings, numbered from 0 to 99. How long will it take to open the safe by a blind trial-and-error search for the correct setting? Since there are 100^{10} possible settings, we may expect to examine about one-half of these, on the average, before finding the correct one—that is, fifty billion billion settings. Suppose, however, that the safe is defective, so that a click can be heard when any one dial is turned to the correct setting. Now each dial can be adjusted independently, and does not need to be touched again while the others are being set. The total number of settings that has to be tried is only 10×50, or five hundred. The task of opening the safe has been altered, by the cues the clicks provide, from a practically impossible one to a trivial one.[13]

A considerable amount has been learned in the past five years about the nature of the mazes that represent common human problem-solving tasks—proving theorems, solving puzzles, playing chess, making investments, balancing assembly lines, to mention a few. All that we have learned about these mazes points to the same conclusion: that human problem solving, from the most blundering to the most insightful, involves nothing more than varying mixtures of trial and error and selectivity. The selectivity derives from various rules of thumb, or heuristics, that suggest which paths should be tried first and which leads are promising. We do not need to postulate processes more sophisticated than those involved in organic evolution to explain how enormous problem mazes are cut down to quite reasonable size.[14]

The sources of selectivity

When we examine the sources from which the problem-solving system, or the evolving system, as the case may be, derives its selec-

[13] The clicking safe example was supplied by D. P. Simon. Ashby, *op. cit.*, 230, has called the selectivity involved in situations of this kind "selection by components." The even greater reduction in time produced by hierarchization in the clicking safe example, as compared with the watchmaker's metaphor, is due to the fact that a random *search* for the correct combination is involved in the former case, while in the latter the parts come together in the right order. It is not clear which of these metaphors provides the better model for biological evolution, but we may be sure that the watchmaker's metaphor gives an exceedingly conservative estimate of the savings due to hierarchization. The safe may give an excessively high estimate because it assumes all possible arrangements of the elements to be equally probable.

[14] A. Newell and H. A. Simon, Computer simulation of human thinking, *Science* 134: 2011–2017, December 22, 1961.

tivity, we discover that selectivity can always be equated with some kind of feedback of information from the environment.

Let us consider the case of problem solving first. There are two basic kinds of selectivity. One we have already noted: various paths are tried out, the consequences of following them are noted, and this information is used to guide further search. In the same way, in organic evolution, various complexes come into being, at least evanescently, and those that are stable provide new building blocks for further construction. It is this information about stable configurations, and not free energy or negentropy from the sun, that guides the process of evolution and provides the selectivity that is essential to account for its rapidity.

The second source of selectivity in problem solving is previous experience. We see this particularly clearly when the problem to be solved is similar to one that has been solved before. Then, by simply trying again the paths that led to the earlier solution, or their analogues, trial-and-error search is greatly reduced or altogether eliminated.

What corresponds to this latter kind of information in organic evolution? The closest analogue is reproduction. Once we reach the level of self-reproducing systems, a complex system, when it has once been achieved, can be multiplied indefinitely. Reproduction in fact allows the inheritance of acquired characteristics, but at the level of genetic material, of course; i.e., only characteristics acquired by the genes can be inherited. . . .

On empires and empire-building

We have not exhausted the categories of complex systems to which the watchmaker argument can reasonably be applied. Philip assembled his Macedonian empire and gave it to his son, to be later combined with the Persian subassembly and others into Alexander's greater system. On Alexander's death, his empire did not crumble to dust, but fragmented into some of the major subsystems that had composed it.

The watchmaker argument implies that if one would be Alexander, one should be born into a world where large stable political systems already exist. Where this condition was not fulfilled, as on the Scythian and Indian frontiers, Alexander found empire building a slippery business. So too, T. E. Lawrence's organizing of the Arabian revolt against the Turks was limited by the character of his largest stable building blocks, the separate, suspicious desert tribes.

The profession of history places a greater value upon the validated particular fact than upon tendentious generalization. I shall not elaborate upon my fancy, therefore, but will leave it to historians to decide whether anything can be learned for the interpretation of history from an abstract theory of hierarchic complex systems.

Conclusion: The evolutionary explanation of hierarchy

We have shown thus far that complex systems will evolve from simple systems much more rapidly if there are stable intermediate forms than if there are not. The resulting complex forms in the former case will be hierarchic. We have only to turn the argument around to explain the observed predominance of hierarchies among the complex systems nature presents to us. Among possible complex forms, hierarchies are the ones that have the time to evolve. The hypothesis that complexity will be hierarchic makes no distinction among very flat hierarchies, like crystals, and tissues, and polymers, and the intermediate forms. Indeed, in the complex systems we encounter in nature, examples of both forms are prominent. A more complete theory than the one we have developed here would presumably have something to say about the determinants of width of span in these systems.

*George Gudger is a man, et cetera. But obviously, in the effort
to tell of him (by example) as truthfully as I can,
I am limited. I know him only so far as I know him,
and only in those terms in which I know him;
and all of that depends as fully on who I am
as on who he is.*

JAMES AGEE, *Let Us Now Praise Famous Men*

3 Toward understanding and sharing experience

As James Agee suggests, there are limitations on what a writer can say about any particular experience, be it a man like George Gudger, an episode in his own life, a place, or an idea. George Gudger was, for Agee, a complex experience, a series of interactions by which Agee came to know certain things about the man. Someone else who knew George Gudger undoubtedly experienced him differently and probably selected different features of this experience to label "George Gudger." Both Agee and this second observer, in their conceptions of the man, identified George Gudger as a recurring unit in a continuum of interactions. They would probably agree about some of the things they *know* about George Gudger and disagree about others. And each, in telling what he knows about the man, must select certain details about him and reject others. How do they decide which details are relevant and interesting?

This is a question everyone faces when he chooses to write about an experience, and the answer is not easy, nor can it be complete. Chapters 4–12, which include discussions of various constraints on selection, show you how to make these choices more consciously and thus bring them under control. Learning the craft of writing is learning how to control the multitude of choices that confront you between the initial inspiration and the final, polished product.

One way to approach a difficult question is to restate it. If you examine the question above carefully, you will see that it includes at least two questions:

1) What kinds of details are relevant to understanding an experience?
2) What kinds of details are likely to be sufficiently interesting to a reader to warrant sharing them with him?

Discovering details relevant to understanding

The difficulty in answering this first question arises in part because the word *relevant* is hard to define. When is information relevant? A summary answer is that information is relevant when it allows an outsider to think and act like an insider in relation to the experience being described, for only then has the outsider understood the experience. This definition needs some explanation.

When an outsider first begins to live among people who speak and act in ways that are new and strange to him, his initial impression is one of overwhelming difference. Ways of dressing, eating, and interacting with other people appear on the surface to be totally outside his experience. He is an intruder in an alien world, like the square in Lineland. He must quickly learn to experience this world as an insider, for shared experience is prerequisite to communication. Otherwise he will remain alone, a stranger in a strange world.

How can a well-intentioned outsider learn to think and act in a new way, as an insider? Let's consider a particular case. In a Southeast Asian village a visiting American notices that some people bow low as they pass others and that children bend almost to the ground when they pass in front of adults. To him such behavior may seem undignified, servile, and even humiliating. If he is thoughtful, however, he will remind himself that he sees through alien eyes and will try to understand the villagers' behavior in their terms. If he knows the language, he may ask people why they bow, and he will probably be told that people bow because it is polite and proper: It would be rude not to. (Ask yourself how you would respond if a foreigner asked, "Why do you Americans shake hands with each other?") Unless he wishes to remain an outsider, he must learn by observation how to bow and when to bow. The information that enables him to know how and when to bow is what we will call *relevant detail*. The details that allow him to act as an insider are the same details that are relevant to understanding and describing the experience.

CONTRASTIVE FEATURES

What must the outsider know about bowing so that he can begin to act as an insider? First, he must know what features of this act make it a bow and not something else. He observes that certain movements must be performed in a certain way: The head must be inclined below the level of the other person's head, the eyes must be lowered, these actions must be executed slowly. All these features make a bow different from an act of greeting, in which the head is not lowered and the eyes meet those of the other person, and from an act of worship, during which the hands are placed palm to palm before the body. These are the *contrastive features* of the act of bowing—features that make it different from similar acts and that allow an insider to recognize instances of bowing.

RANGE OF VARIATION

Second, the outsider must know how this act can vary and remain a bow and what the variations mean. He observes that no two bows are exactly alike. Some people bow lower than others. Why? Does this variation show different degrees of respect or is it unimportant? What is the range within which bowing may vary and still be polite and proper? He learns, for instance, that bowing from the waist is more respectful than bowing from the neck. In other words, he learns to recognize a wide *range of variation* in this act, some of it meaningful and some not.

DISTRIBUTION

Third, the outsider must know the context in which people bow. Where do they bow? When do they bow? To whom do they bow? What response can be expected from the person bowed to? He learns that one does not approach within about five feet of an elder, a teacher, or a monk without lowering his head and eyes. Thus he begins to see that conventional behavior is patterned and that there are places, or *slots*, in the pattern where certain acts are appropriate and inappropriate. He soon finds that examining the rules for bowing leads him to a study of the status of different people in the village. He also learns, if he pursues his observations, that lowering the head is related to a conceptual hierarchy in which various parts of the body are assigned specific values and functions, the head having the highest value. In short, he learns the *distribution* of this act in time and space and in larger social and conceptual contexts, including religion and myth.

Notice that the alien observer, by beginning with the apparently simple task of learning how and when to bow, finds himself learning a new interpretation of the world, a new way of unitizing experience. He begins to see the world of the village as insiders see it, starting with a single unit of behavior and learning its contrastive features, its range of variation, and its distribution in larger contexts. These, then, are the details relevant to an adequate understanding of any experience. They can be restated in general terms as Maxim 3: *A unit, at any level of focus, can be adequately understood only if three aspects of the unit are known: (1) its contrastive features, (2) its range of variation, and (3) its distribution in larger contexts.*

Suppose that the American in the Southeast Asian village (or in any other strange environment) wishes to describe this bowing behavior (or any equally unfamiliar behavior) to friends back home. His readers are now in the position that he was in: They are outsiders and he wants to share with them what he has experienced. The questions implied by Maxim 3 help him discover the relevant details he must pass on to his friends. What he had to understand, they also must understand. Likewise, if he wants to describe some experience of his own to the people of the village, Maxim 3 is a useful guide.

USING MAXIM 3

A student of one of the authors considered teaching handicapped children to swim a unique and important experience in his life and decided to use the experience as the subject of an essay. He began to try to understand the process by asking himself the questions implied by Maxim 3.

> 1) What are the *contrastive features* of this unit? What makes teaching handicapped children different from teaching other children? Is teaching them to swim different from teaching them other things? How was this experience unique for me? What makes it stand out in my memory as a significant experience?

The writer should rephrase his questions in several different ways, for different phrasings of a basic question often prompt different answers by isolating various facets of the experience. For example, some of the questions above seek to identify the contrastive features of the experience for the children involved; others seek to isolate what made it different for the writer. Each rephrasing highlights a different facet of the experience.

2) What is the unit's *range of variation?* Conceived of as a unit, the experience of teaching handicapped children to swim is a recurring experience—it can be done more than once. Nevertheless, each instance of the unit is somewhat different. How did the experience change from day to day? What different sorts of situations did I encounter? How did different kinds of handicaps alter the experience? What particular experiences with particular children illustrate the sorts of problems I encountered and the different results I achieved? How did I myself change from day to day or from the beginning to the end of the summer?

Notice that each particular experience the writer had in teaching these children is thought of as a variant of the total experience or unit, teaching handicapped children to swim. The unit as a whole is an abstract conception in the writer's mind; the variants are observable physical events or particular manifestations of the unit, just as each actual, physical bow in the earlier illustration was a variant or particular manifestation of a conceptual unit, bowing in a Southeast Asian village. No human act ever recurs in all its physical details; experience is repeatable only when someone conceives of it as a unit.

3) What is the unit's *distribution* in larger contexts? That is, what place, or slot, does it occupy in a larger pattern or system? Where and when did this teaching take place? What was the physical setting? What was the larger program of which swimming lessons were a part? What was the function or purpose of swimming in this program? How did this experience fit into my life? What other experiences preceded it? Followed it? What other experiences were similar for me? Can I conceive of it as one of a class of experiences that all share some feature?

Questions of context are limitless, bounded only by the writer's imagination, persistence, and perspective. Everything in the universe, now or in the past, is conceivably the context for any single experience. Each unit of experience can be seen as part of a larger unit, and the writer can shift his focus from level to level; the writer himself will have to decide at what point to stop speculating about context.

Discovering interesting details for sharing

Use of the maxim provided the student with more than enough raw material for an essay. He then needed to sort out the details and choose which ones to include. One guide to making his selection was a comparison of what he knew about the experience being described with what his readers could be presumed to know. As we pointed out at the end of Chapter 2, the pressure to communicate, particularly in writing, is usually the result of the writer's wish or need to share with the reader some unshared experience. The heart of his message will be this unshared experience. It follows that the writer must know who his reader is, for the notion of sharing implies sharing with someone.

The student could assume that his readers knew many of the details; they probably knew, for example, that handicapped children have a difficult time learning to swim, that different sorts of handicaps lead to different difficulties, that it can be a rewarding experience to teach someone less fortunate than oneself. Such details as these are already understood, and the writer need not stress them, although he may mention them. The student could further assume that his readers knew something about learning to swim, something about what swimming pools look like, and something about the importance of exercise. The good writer avoids dwelling on the obvious, for such writing is uninteresting.

Details that are likely to interest the reader are those that he does not share with the writer. If the reader has little or no knowledge of the event, its basic features (i.e., its contrastive features, its range of variation, and its distributions) will be the heart of the communication. What would you want to know if you were reading about fronton, a game played by the Basques? If, on the other hand, the reader is familiar with the event, then special details and circumstances should be focused on. Since most people have learned to swim, the student who chose to write about teaching handicapped children to swim decided to focus his attention on the details of teaching a blind boy.

Curiously, we often read a report of an event more avidly when we have seen and understood the "same" event that the writer witnessed. Did the reviewer of a play react to it in the same way that we did? Did the sports writer notice the crucial, split-second actions that we noticed? In such cases, we read for the writer's perspective rather than for information necessary for understanding.

In general, then, the nucleus of the writer's message is an unshared experience. The writer is the insider speaking to outsiders; enabling them to become insiders is his goal. In his effort to describe a man, a place, an act, a thought, or any other experience as truthfully as he can, the writer is limited. He is limited by the subject, by his own knowledge and desires, and by the knowledge and desires of his readers. Within these limits, Maxim 3 is a guide for discovering relevant details. By asking which details are unknown to his readers, the writer has a basis for selecting those that will interest his readers when they are shared.

Obviously Maxim 3 does not guide the writer unerringly from an experience to a good essay. There is no automatic and infallible procedure that will do this. All the maxims discussed in this book demand intelligent and imaginative application. However, Maxim 3 offers one way to begin the complex process of translating personal experience into effective writing.[1]

Postscript

You will recall that the last part of Maxim 3 affirms that no unit of experience can be understood out of context. Part of what a unit *is* is its relationship to other units; this, we believe, is true of all human experience. When a baby is born, he does not learn first about, say, logic and then about mother, feeding, and so on. Rather he learns, no matter how vaguely, about a number of things concurrently. Gradually these become clearer and more distinct in his mind; he learns to distinguish recurrent units, their variants and distributions. But the important point to be grasped is that he learns to deal with units of experience in a dynamic context. And so with this book.

Our assumption about the importance of context to understanding places certain strains on the organization of the book; units of the book are not, and cannot be, presented "logically" in a strictly linear order. None of the units can be understood adequately by itself; each is fully understandable only in relation to the others. The first three chapters of the book provide an introduction to aspects of rhetorical theory and practice that will be given more

[1] The problems inherent in this process are examined in greater detail in later chapters: the problem of invention, or gathering relevant information, in Chapters 4–7 and the problem of selection in Chapters 8–12.

detailed attention in the following chapters. Thus the book has a cyclical structure: It is deliberately, and from our point of view necessarily, redundant.

EXERCISES

1 In each of the following passages, the writer is attempting to describe to his readers a significant unit of experience. Each writer is, in a sense, an insider—the unit he is describing is a significant part of his interpretation of the world—whereas the reader is in some respect an outsider. For each passage, answer the following questions:

1) What unit of experience is being described?
2) Does the passage include the unit's contrastive features (C), its range of variation (V), and its distribution in larger contexts (D)? Identify the portion (or portions) of the passage in which each of these three aspects is described.
3) If any aspect (C/V/D) of the unit is omitted, could the description be improved by including it? How?
4) Does the writer include enough information so that the reader ceases to be an outsider and can *act* as an insider? If not, what aspects (C/V/D) of the unit must be described further?
5) What does the writer assume that the reader already knows about the unit he is describing? Has he assumed correctly in your case?

a **American Redstart.** *Setophaga ruticilla.*
Field marks:—4 1/2–5 1/2. The Redstart is one of the most butterfly-like of birds. It is constantly flitting about, drooping its wings and spreading fanwise its tail. *Male:*—Largely black with *bright orange patches on the wings and tail;* belly white. *Female:*—Chiefly olive-brown above, white below, with large *yellow* flash-patches on wings and tail. *Immature male:*—Considerable variation; much like the female; yellow often tinged with orange. The Redstart pattern is obvious in any plumage.
Similar species:—The only other small bird similarly colored is the male Blackburnian Warbler, which, however, has the orange confined to the head, throat, and upper breast.
Voice:—Three commonest songs *tsee tsee tsee tsee tseet* (last note higher), *tsee tsee tsee tsee tsee-o* (with drop on last syllable), and *teetsa teetsa teetsa teetsa teet* (double-noted). The songs are often alternated, an excellent field aid.

Range: — Breeds in medium deciduous forest growth (second growth saplings, etc.) from Gulf of St. Lawrence and cent. Manitoba s. to North Carolina, n. Georgia, s. Alabama, Louisiana, and Oklahoma; winters in West Indies and Central and South America.

ROGER TORY PETERSON, *A Field Guide to the Birds*

b **Sonnet.** Poem of 14 lines, usually in iambic pentameter, in definite rhyme scheme. The main types are the Italian (Petrarchan) sonnet, an octave and sestet rhyming abbaabba cdecde, and the Elizabethan (Shakespearian) sonnet, three quatrains and a couplet rhyming abab cdcd efef gg. Essence of sonnet is unity of thought or idea.

The Columbia-Viking Desk Encyclopedia

c A **speech-community** is a group of people who interact by means of speech. All the so-called higher activities of man — our specifically human activities — spring from the close adjustment among individuals which we call society, and this adjustment, in turn, is based upon language; the speech-community, therefore, is the most important kind of social group. Other phases of social cohesion, such as economic, political, or cultural groupings, bear some relation to the grouping by speech-communities, but do not usually coincide with it; cultural features, especially, are almost always more widespread than any one language. Before the coming of the white man, an independent Indian tribe which spoke a language of its own formed both a speech-community and a political and economic unit; as to religion and general culture, however, it resembled neighboring tribes. Under more complex conditions there is less correlation between language and the other groupings. The speech-community which consists of all English-speaking people is divided into two political communities: the United States and the British Empire, and each of these is in turn sub-divided; economically, the United States and Canada are more closely united than politically; culturally, we are part of a great area which radiates from western Europe. On the other hand, even the narrowest of these groups, the political United States, includes persons who do not speak English: American Indians, Spanish-speakers in the Southwest, and linguistically unassimilated immigrants. Colonial occupation, as in the Philippines or India, puts a speech-community into political and economic dependence upon a foreign speech-community. In some countries the population is divided into several speech-communities that exist together without local division: a town in Poland consists of Polish-speaking and German-speaking people; by religion, the former are Catholics, the latter Jews, and, until quite recently, very few persons in either group troubled themselves to understand the other group's language.

LEONARD BLOOMFIELD, *Language*

d [**Outfit**] This Western term is used to designate a group of relatives (larger than the extended family) who regularly cooperate for certain purposes. Two or more extended families, or one or more extended families linked with one or more independent biological families, may habitually pool their resources on some occasions—say, planting and harvesting, or the giving of any major ceremonial for an individual member. The differentiae of "outfit" and extended family are two-fold: the members of the true Navaho extended family always live at least within shouting distance of each other, whereas the various families in an "outfit" may be scattered over a good many square miles; an extended family has its focus in the families of sisters or of brothers and/or parents and their married children, whereas the families in an "outfit," while always related, include a wider circle of kin. Participation in cooperative work is not absolutely regular, and indeed membership in an "outfit" is somewhat fluid. But the solidarity of an "outfit" will always be recognized, however vaguely, by the white trader who knows the region; he will take this unit into account in extending credit and the like.

The variations in the size and composition of "outfits" are in-finite. Commonly, one biological or extended family is a kind of nucleus for the whole group, and the "outfit" will be referred to col-loquially by using the name of the principal man in the nuclear family. Careful analysis shows, however, that when the traders or Navahos speak of "So-and-so's folks," this does *not* include *all* his relatives within certain degrees. Geographical distance and other factors may have the effect of excluding some relatives actually closer by blood than others embraced within the "outfit." The test is always the intensity and regularity of the economic and other reciprocities involved. The size of an "outfit" tends to depend on the wealth of its leader or, more exactly, of the leader and/or his wife or wives. Wealthy Navahos who control thousands of sheep are often the focal points of "outfits" which include a hundred or more individuals in a ramified system of dependence. Sometimes the members of an "out-fit" live on lands that have unbroken geographical contiguity. In this case the "outfit" constitutes a "land-use community" which may occupy from 12,000 to 80,000 acres and include from fifty to two hun-dred persons.

One can usually see best who actually belongs to an "outfit" when communal ploughing is taking place in the spring or sheep dipping in the summer. Some data from the Dennehotso area in the north and from the Klagetoh area in the south give a specific picture of how individuals split up into these various units. In the Dennehotso Valley in 1934 the 669 people lived in 131 hogans. Eighteen of these were isolated; the remainder made up 37 distinct extended family groups, each of which had from two to six hogans. Nine different "outfits" could be recognized, but 108 persons could not be said to belong to any "outfit." At Klagetoh in 1939 there were 233 people living in 29 hogans. All but four of these families combined in vari-ous ways to make up eight or nine extended families. There was some coöperative work between any two or more of these extended family groups at the busy seasons.

CLYDE KLUCKHOHN AND DOROTHEA LEIGHTON, *The Navaho*

e A **pulse** is one of a series of regularly recurring, precisely equivalent stimuli. Like the ticks of a metronome or a watch, pulses mark
off equal units in the temporal continuum. Though generally established and supported by objective stimuli (sounds), the sense of
pulse may exist subjectively. A sense of regular pulses, once established, tends to be continued in the mind and musculature of the
listener, even though the sound has stopped. For instance, objective
pulses may cease or may fail for a time to coincide with the
previously established pulse series. When this occurs, the human
need for the security of an actual stimulus or for simplicity of response generally makes such passages seem to point toward the re-
establishment of objective pulses or to a return to pulse coincidence.

All pulses in a series are by definition exactly alike. However,
preferring clear and definite patterns to such an unorganized and
potentially infinite series, the human mind tends to impose some sort
of organization upon such equal pulses. As we listen to the ticks of a
clock or the clicks of a railroad car passing over the tracks, we tend to
arrange the equal pulses into intelligible units of finite duration or
into even more obviously structured groups. Thus, although pulse
can theoretically exist without either meter or rhythm, the nature of
the human mind is such that this is a rare occurrence in music.

While pulse is seldom heard in a pure state (as a series of undif-
ferentiated stimuli), this does not mean that it is not an important
aspect of musical experience. Not only is pulse necessary for the existence of meter, but it generally, though not always, underlies and
reinforces rhythmic experience.

GROSVENOR COOPER AND LEONARD B. MEYER,
The Rhythmic Structure of Music

2 Attend any of the following activities and then describe the
pattern that orders the events: a sports match, a church service,
a symphony concert, a protest demonstration, a committee
meeting. Where are there slots, or choice points, in the pattern;
that is, where can substitutions be made? At the beginning of
certain activities, programs are customarily distributed that
reveal the pattern, at least partially (e.g., a program for a concert, an agenda for a committee meeting). Such outlines indicate the choice points in the pattern (different musical works
could be substituted for those on the program, different items
for those on the agenda). Note appropriate and inappropriate
substitutions in various slots. Is it possible to leave any slots
unfilled?

3 The following letter to one of the authors is from Eunice
Pike, a linguist engaged in field work in Mexico. As a review,
discuss the details of the letter in terms of the ideas presented
in this chapter.

Instituto Linguistico
Apartado 22067
Mexico 22, D. F.
Dec. 24, 1966

Hi:

Those of us here at workshop decided that we'd have a party while the visiting linguists were here (two from Univ. of Calif. at Los Angeles, and one from Univ. of Calif. at Berkeley). We decided on a special menu so that some of the Otomi Indians of the region could be caterers and we and our visitors would enjoy watching as well as eating. So, we bargained with an Otomi family to barbeque two goats for us. We asked for two goats, rather than one, so that everybody, including informants, informants' families, and Otomi maids could have plenty.

Saturday morning they walked the goats over, slaughtered and dressed them. In our back yard they dug a pit, filled it with wood, and put stones on top. Everything was ready. The Otomi family stayed over night so that at four the next morning they could start the fire to heat the rocks. The wood burned, the rocks sank into the hole; on top of the rocks they put a big big bowl of vegetables, then the goats, then maguey leaves, then dirt. Thus it cooked. Otomi women set up an outdoor kitchen and cooked rice, beans, chile, and all the fixings.

It was a happy time. Four little boys got a goat's eye apiece. The linguists took pictures of each stage. At two P.M. the Otomi chef swept off the dirt, and carefully raised the maguey leaves. We were all watching. The informants were as interested as we were. (Not all tribes know how to barbeque and they were watching each step.)

When the chef started to lift out the meat and salt it, one informant held each piece for him, another held a succession of bowls as the chef filled them with broth and delicious looking vegetables.

We had set up tables out on the front lawn, each family bringing dishes enough for themselves and their informants and informants' families. It takes a while to move a crowd like that—always somebody wants one last picture. But at last we had gathered and the blessing was asked—but there were lots of empty places at the tables. People began to ask each other, "Where is your informant? I wonder if ours could be with him?"

One of the translators asked me, "Have you seen our informant? I wonder why he doesn't come?"

I answered, "Did you invite him?"

"No, but he eats with us all the time! Three meals a day!"

"This is a party; a party is different; it requires a special invitation."

Another translator spoke up. "I *did* invite mine, and he is not here either!"

We went ahead. Some of the translators decided that their informant didn't like goat and so had slipped away. Some went looking for their informant families, and found and brought back the wife and children but the man of the family had "gone for a walk."

A couple of poorly dressed Otomi men drifted in from the road and stood at a distance watching us. When we were about finished, Ann (she was sort of hostess) went over, invited them to a table and gave them a big bowl of food.

"Who are they?" I asked her.

"Just beggars. They stand at a distance hoping we will see them and invite them to have something. It's the Indian who is an invited guest who stays out of sight so that you have to go after him."

That was the missing bit of information that was needed to explain our troubled party. The informants had been eating happily with the translators inside the house three times a day, and the translators had not guessed that an outdoor party demanded not only a special invitation but an escort. For at least some of the tribes the difference between a beggar and an honored guest is that the beggar stands around hoping to be motioned over, whereas the guest deliberately stays out of sight. A hostess seeks out her guest and urges him to the table.

(Ann told us that one time in her tribe she had been asked to be godparent at a wedding. The host and hostess came after her with a band and walked with her across the center of town while the band tooted loudly all the way. When the occasion was over her hosts and the band walked her back again.)

The party was breaking up. I started for my house carrying a stack of dirty dishes. On the way I met one of the Otomi maids; "Aren't you going to eat?" I asked her. She giggled some kind of an answer. By that time I was beginning to suspect trouble and the reason for it, so I asked, "Shall I go with you?" and I started to put the dishes down right there on the ground.

"Oh no, take your dishes home; I'll go." Her intonation spelled truth so I went ahead.

The Otomi maids have been working here at the center long enough so that they are beginning to understand that things which people of their own culture might do because of arrogance, we do because of different customs, so they adjust accordingly. As far as I know none of the Otomi were angry, but some translators had a hard time with their informants from other tribes. Some of them were furious; several threatened to go home; one refused to eat the goat when it was served as leftovers the next day.

Ann had two informants here. One was 72 years old; he had been chief of his village more than 30 years. When she finally found him she asked, "Why didn't you come and eat?"

"Nobody came for me," he answered. He is a nice old man; he wasn't angry, but he went hungry rather than walk to the table alone.

The other informant, 32 years old, ranted and raved at the way she had insulted them. "That's the way jacket-people are. Whenever they have a party they want it all to themselves. They don't want the rest of us around." (Footnote: That's a little signpost that shows that Mexico is progressing. A few years ago the poor distinguished themselves from the rich by "those who wear shoes." Now it has become "the jacket-people.")

Well, things eventually settled down. As an instrument of joy our barbeque was an absolute failure, but as an educational device it was excellent. Sort of made me feel sorry for Uncle Sam. I suspect that many times our help goes sour for some cultural reason that we don't even suspect.

4   Read the following excerpts from James Agee's *Let Us Now Praise Famous Men*. What obvious details has Agee taken for granted in his descriptions? What new experience is he attempting to share? What inferences about the writer and his intended readers can you draw from the description?

Odors and the use of space are characteristic (i.e., contrastive) features that distinguish the sharecroppers' houses as a group from other houses. But odors and space vary in these houses; the Gudger's house, for example, does not smell quite like the Woods'. What, specifically, are these variations? Note that features identifying all sharecroppers' houses have variations that serve to distinguish one particular sharecropper's house from another; thus at a different level of focus these variations are contrastive features.

Describe a specific person or place, attempting to avoid obvious details; try to find details that uniquely characterize the experience.

from

Let Us Now Praise Famous Men
JAMES AGEE

ODORS

BARENESS AND SPACE

The Gudgers' house, being young, only eight years old, smells a little dryer and cleaner, and more distinctly of its wood, than an average white tenant house, and it has also a certain odor I have never found in other such houses: aside from these sharp yet slight subtleties, it has the odor or odors which are classical in every thoroughly poor white southern country house, and by which such a house could be identified blindfold in any part of the world, among no matter what other odors. It is compacted of many odors and made into one, which is very thin and light on the air, and more subtle than it can seem in analysis, yet very sharply and constantly noticeable. These are its ingredients. The odor of pine lumber, wide thin cards of it, heated in the sun, in no way doubled or insulated, in closed and darkened air. The odor of woodsmoke, the fuel being again mainly pine, but in part also, hickory, oak, and cedar. The odors of cooking. Among these, most strongly, the odors of fried salt pork and of fried and boiled pork lard, and second, the odor of cooked corn. The odors of sweat in many stages of age and freshness, this sweat being a distillation of pork, lard, corn, woodsmoke, pine, and ammonia. The odors of sleep, of bedding and of breathing, for the ventilation is poor. The odors of all the dirt that in the course of time can accumulate in a quilt and mattress. Odors of staleness from clothes hung or stored away, not washed. I should further describe the odor of corn: in sweat, or on the teeth, and breath, when it is eaten as much as they eat it, it is of a particular sweet stuffy fetor, to which the nearest parallel is the odor of the yellow excrement of a baby. All these odors as I have said are so combined into one that they are all and always present in balance, not at all heavy, yet so searching that all fabrics of bedding and clothes are saturated with them, and so clinging that they stand softly out of the fibers of newly laundered clothes. Some of their components are extremely 'pleasant,' some are 'unpleasant'; their sum total has great nostalgic power. When they are in an old house, darkened, and moist, and sucked into all the wood, and stacked down on top of years of a moldering and old basis of themselves, as at the Ricketts', they are hard to get used to or even hard to bear. At the Woods', they are blowsy and somewhat moist and dirty. At the Gudgers', as I have mentioned, they are younger, lighter, and cleaner-smelling. There too, there is another and special odor, very dry and edged: it is somewhere between the odor of very old newsprint and of a victorian bedroom in which, after long illness, and many medicines, someone has died and the room has been fumigated, yet the odor of dark brown medicines, dry-bodied sickness, and staring death, still is strong in the stained wallpaper and in the mattress.

Bareness and space (and spacing) are so difficult and seem to me of such greatness that I shall not even try to write seriously or fully of them. But a little, applying mainly to the two bedrooms.

The floors are made of wide planks, between some of which the daylighted earth is visible, and are naked of any kind of paint or cloth or linoleum covering whatever, and paths have been smoothed on them by bare feet, in a subtly uneven surface on which the polished knots are particularly beautiful. A perfectly bare floor of broad boards makes a room seem larger than it can if the floor is covered, and the furniture too, stands on it in a different and much cleaner sort of relationship. The walls as I have said are skeleton; so is the ceiling in one of these rooms; the rooms are twelve feet square and are meagerly furnished, and they are so great and final a whole of bareness and complete simplicity that even the objects on a crowded shelf seem set far apart from each other, and each to have a particularly sharp entity of its own. Moreover, all really simple and naïve people[1] incline strongly toward exact symmetries, and have some sort of instinctive dislike that any one thing shall touch any other save what it rests on, so that chairs, beds, bureaus, trunks, vases, trinkets, general odds and ends, are set very plainly and squarely discrete from one another and from walls, at exact centers or as near them as possible, and this kind of spacing gives each object a full strength it would not otherwise have, and gives their several relationships, as they stand on shelves or facing, in a room, the purest power such a relationship can have. This is still more sharply true with such people as the Gudgers, who still have a little yet earnest wish that everything shall be as pleasant and proper to live with as possible, than with others such as the Woods and Ricketts, who are disheveled and wearied out of any such hope or care.

[1]And many of the most complex, and not many between.

5 Write a description of a significant unit in your experience that you feel your readers probably do not share with you at present. This might be a technical unit from an area in which you have special competence (e.g., from meteorology, archeology, music), a unit of activity in which you have taken part and that you consider significant (e.g., teaching handicapped children to swim, spelunking, flying a glider, deciphering codes), or an unusual concept from a foreign culture with which you are familiar (e.g., the meaning of *shibui* to a Japanese, of *ennui* to a Frenchman, of *dharma* to a Hindu).

Describe all three aspects (C/V/D) of the unit in the following order: contrastive features, range of variation (giving examples of some of its variants), and distribution in several contexts. Note that the arrangement of the details in the essay may differ from the sequence in which you discovered them.

Specify your audience and make a list of the things that they already know about the unit you are describing.

6 Read the following story by Isaac Babel. It concerns two strikingly different interpretations of the world, that of an army officer and that of a poor woman. The miracle of the story is that communication does occur, that the officer does get an insight into the alien world of the peasant woman.

List the differences between the two principal characters and consider how each difference affects their views of the world. How, for example, does the Russian officer regard Jews? Red army troops? How are these attitudes revealed in the details of the story? Do his views change by the end of the story? Can you explain what happens in the story in terms of Maxims 1 and 3? You might begin by speculating whether the story concerns the officer's discovery of a basis for reordering his experiences or his discovery of the possibility that widely different variant forms exist among members of a single class.

How many changes of focus can you find in this story? Identify them as

1) changes from part to part in some larger whole,
2) changes from nuclear to marginal focus (or vice versa), or
3) changes in level of magnification.

Note that such changes may occur simultaneously.

What makes communication possible between two so very different people in this story when it is not possible between the square and the King of Lineland without heat and anger on both sides? As a guide, ask what they share.

Awareness of another person's view of the world sometimes comes suddenly and dramatically, as it does in this story. If you have had such an experience, use it as the subject of an essay.

Crossing into Poland
ISAAC BABEL

The Commander of the VI Division reported: Novograd-Volynsk was taken at dawn today. The Staff had left Krapivno, and our baggage train was spread out in a noisy rearguard over the highroad from Brest to Warsaw built by Nicholas I upon the bones of peasants.

Fields flowered around us, crimson with poppies; a noontide breeze played in the yellowing rye; on the horizon virginal buckwheat rose like the wall of a distant monastery. The Volyn's peaceful stream moved away from us in sinuous curves and was lost in the pearly haze of the birch groves; crawling between flowery slopes, it wound weary arms through a wilderness of hops. The orange sun rolled down the sky like a lopped-off head, and mild light glowed from the cloud gorges. The standards of the sunset flew above our heads. Into the cool of evening dripped the smell of yesterday's blood, of slaughtered horses. The blackened Zbruch roared, twisting itself into foamy knots at the falls. The bridges were down, and we waded across the river. On the waves rested a majestic moon. The horses were in to the cruppers, and the noisy torrent gurgled among hundreds of horses' legs. Somebody sank, loudly defaming the Mother of God. The river was dotted with the square black patches of the wagons, and was full of confused sounds, of whistling and singing, that rose above the gleaming hollows, the serpentine trails of the moon.

Far on in the night we reached Novograd. In the house where I was billeted I found a pregnant woman and two red-haired, scraggy-necked Jews. A third, huddled to the wall with his head covered up, was already asleep. In the room I was given I discovered turned-out wardrobes, scraps of women's fur coats on the floor, human filth, fragments of the occult crockery the Jews use only once a year, at Eastertime.

"Clear this up," I said to the woman. "What a filthy way to live!" The two Jews rose from their places and, hopping on their felt soles, cleared the mess from the floor. They skipped about noiselessly, monkey-fashion, like Japs in a circus act, their necks swelling and twisting. They put down for me a feather bed that had been disemboweled, and I lay down by the wall next to the third Jew, the one who was asleep. Faint-hearted poverty closed in over my couch.

Silence overcame all. Only the moon, clasping in her blue hands her round, bright, carefree face, wandered like a vagrant outside the window.

I kneaded my numbed legs and, lying on the ripped-open mattress, fell asleep. And in my sleep the Commander of the VI Division appeared to me; he was pursuing the Brigade Commander on a heavy stallion, fired at him twice between the eyes. The bullets pierced the Brigade Commander's head, and both his eyes dropped to the ground. "Why did you turn back the brigade?" shouted Savitsky, the Divisional Commander, to the wounded man—and here I woke up, for the pregnant woman was groping over my face with her fingers.

"Good sir," she said, "you're calling out in your sleep and you're tossing to and fro. I'll make you a bed in another corner, for you're pushing my father about."

She raised her thin legs and rounded belly from the floor and removed the blanket from the sleeper. Lying on his back was an old man, a dead old man. His throat had been torn out and his face cleft in two; in his beard blue blood was clotted like a lump of lead.

"Good sir," said the Jewess, shaking up the feather bed, "the Poles cut his throat, and he begging them: 'Kill me in the yard so that my daughter shan't see me die.' But they did as suited them. He passed away in this room, thinking of me. —And now I should wish to know," cried the woman with sudden and terrible violence, "I should wish to know where in the whole world you could find another father like my father?"

The true method of discovery
is like the flight of an aeroplane.
It starts from the ground of particular observation;
it makes a flight into the thin air
of imaginative generalization;
and it again lands for renewed observation
rendered acute by rational interpretation.
ALFRED NORTH WHITEHEAD, *Process and Reality*

Trains of thought run through dark tunnels.
THEODOR REIK, *Listening with the Third Ear*

4 The process of inquiry

PEOPLE usually experience the world as orderly and meaningful—but not always. At times we are all puzzled or disturbed by our experiences, and if they seem sufficiently important to us we try to find out what bothers us. In the preceding chapter we discussed both kinds of experience: the readily understandable and the puzzling. The student teaching handicapped children to swim had no trouble understanding what he was doing; his difficulties occurred only when he sought to explain it to others. But the person experiencing for the first time the custom of bowing was confronted with an event he did not adequately understand. Before he could tell others about it he had to understand it himself. In this chapter and the three that follow, we will discuss in detail what a person can do when he is confronted with problematic experiences.

Problems arise when one becomes aware of inconsistencies in his own image of the world. James Agee's discussion of the wretched houses of the Alabama sharecroppers provides an illustration of such an experience. An intensely sensitive and moral man, Agee sees in the houses a beauty that is usually neglected, and begins to sense a moral problem involved in evaluating this beauty.

> The houses are built in the 'stinginess,' carelessness, and traditions of an unpersonal agency; they are of the order of 'company' houses. They are furnished, decorated and used in the starved needs, traditions and naiveties of profoundly simple individuals. Thus there are conveyed here two kinds of classicism, essentially different yet related and beautifully euphonious. These classicisms are created of economic need, of local availability, and of local-primitive tradition: and in their purity they are the exclusive property and privilege of the people at the bottom of that world. To those who own and create it this 'beauty' is, however, irrelevant and undiscernible.
>
> JAMES AGEE, *Let Us Now Praise Famous Men*

Outsiders, with their educational and economic advantages, are able to discern the beauty of the houses, but they usually respond with "non-perception, or apologetic perception, or contempt for those who perceive and value" the beauty apparent to Agee. Such a response, however, reveals as much about the perceiver as about what is perceived. Those who respond with apology or contempt seem to Agee to have "only shameful and thief's right" to the beauty.

> . . . It seems to me necessary to insist that the beauty of a house, inextricably shaped as it is in an economic and human abomination, is at least as important a part of the fact as the abomination itself: but that one is qualified to insist on this only in proportion as one faces the brunt of his own 'sin' in so doing and the brunt of the meanings, against human beings, of the abomination itself.

The incongruous beauty of the houses is difficult to explain in terms of his customary assumptions. He struggles to formulate and solve the problem but gives up:

> . . . Consider this merely as a question raised: for I am in pain and uncertainty as to the answers, and can write no more of it here.

The raw material of Agee's sketch is not a clear and distinct segment of experience, but rather the tension within the writer himself. Tensions like this one have a number of causes: a paradoxical "fact" that doesn't make sense, a situation that is incompatible with a person's values, an apparent opposition of two respected authorities on an important issue, the seeming inadequacy of a strongly held theory, a clash of two sets of values to which a person is deeply committed.

If the uneasiness that grows out of one of these inconsistencies is insistent enough, a person seeks an explicit, conscious under-standing of the problem and a reconciliation of the uneasiness. We will call the movement from this feeling of uneasiness to some ade-quate solution of the problem *the process of inquiry*. There are many accounts of this process by mathematicians, scientists, poets, artists, and philosophers, all of whom agree about its general outlines. It begins with a troubled feeling about something perceived. This uneasiness is followed by conscious probing of the problem, then withdrawal in frustration over a failure to solve it, sudden intuition of a solution, and, finally, careful testing to determine whether the problem has in fact been solved. Although the process may be seg-mented in numerous ways, there is a considerable agreement on the location of what Plato would have called the "joints" of the process. Carving at the joints, we will segment it into four stages: preparation, incubation, illumination, and verification.

The four stages of inquiry

PREPARATION

The preparation stage of the process of inquiry includes (1) initial awareness of a difficulty, (2) formulation of the difficulty as a problem, and (3) exploration of the problem. The general movement at this stage is from feeling to conscious analysis as the problem is put into language and explored. Language is not only a means of communicating with others; it is also an instrument for communi-cating with one's self, which is of crucial importance in the process of inquiry. Part of the process is the articulation of the difficulty by means of a system of symbols that can be manipulated more effi-ciently and more subtly than the data. For many scientific problems the language chosen is mathematical. But whatever language the investigator uses to code the data, he explores the problem by stat-ing it in different ways, isolating its distinctive features, trying out various solutions, and so on, often without moving from his chair.

Careful exploration of the problem is an essential part of this stage. It is also the part that most beginners hurry over in their eager-ness to find a solution. Exploration helps the investigator grasp all the subtleties of the problem and foresee the characteristics that a solution must have if it is to solve the problem.

INCUBATION

The preparation stage is followed by a period of subconscious activity that is somewhat mysterious and hard to discuss explicitly. People tend to ignore its importance, placing undue emphasis on the conscious analytical procedures as if these alone were sufficient for solving problems. But each of us has a subconscious intelligence, a strong and vital force in our mental life that seems to have a greater capacity than reason for dealing with the complex and the unfamiliar. Poets have called it their muse; others, their imagination or creative ability. In the incubation period this subconscious intelligence is brought to bear on the problem.

If it has been adequately instructed, a person's subconscious mind continues to work even after that person has shifted his attention to other matters. For example, each of us has had the experience of not being able to recall a familiar name and then having it come to mind after our attention has moved on to something else. This is a simple illustration of continuing subconscious activity that leads to the sudden appearance of an idea in the conscious mind. The alternation of conscious and subconscious activity is as natural and necessary in our mental life as breathing in and out or waking and sleeping are in our physical life.

ILLUMINATION

In the third stage, illumination, there is an imaginative leap to a possible solution, a hypothesis. Since this hypothesis is the result of subconscious activity, one can never be sure just when it will come or exactly why. Here is the way Charles Darwin describes his discovery of a hypothesis explaining the dynamics of evolution:

> In October 1838, that is, fifteen months after I had begun my systematic enquiry, I happened to read for amusement 'Malthus on Population,' and being well prepared to appreciate the struggle for existence . . . it at once struck me that under these circumstances favourable variations would tend to be preserved, and unfavourable ones to be destroyed. The result of this would be the formation of new species. Here then I had at last got a theory by which to work.
>
> *The Life and Letters of Charles Darwin,* ed. Francis Darwin

The French mathematician Henri Poincaré suddenly intuited the solution to a mathematical problem as he boarded a bus. Isaac Newton, it is said, discovered the law of universal gravitation as he watched an apple fall. According to the great Roman architect Vitruvius, Archimedes deduced his principle of floating bodies while he was taking a bath. Apparently insignificant or chance circumstances can trigger significant insights.

It should be noted, however, that each of these men possessed considerable knowledge of his subject and had studied the problem for some time before intuiting its solution. Furthermore, these men were fortunate: Not all such insights are sound. The brilliant hypothesis of 3:00 A.M. may prove disappointing in the clear light of day. The conscious mind has its role, too.

VERIFICATION

In all careful inquiry the last stage consists of some sort of test of the hypothesis. Does the hypothesis in fact provide an adequate solution to the initial problem? Kinds of tests range from an informal check against the investigator's own experience to formal laboratory investigation. In some fields of inquiry, particularly the more rigorous of the sciences, the verification stage may be highly involved and time-consuming. Often an attempt at verification reveals an inadequacy in the hypothesis, and the process of inquiry begins again.

The process of inquiry is clearly undulatory; it progresses toward a solution through recurring periods of conscious and subconscious activity. "Often when one works at a hard question," remarks Henri Poincaré,

> nothing good is accomplished at the first attack. Then one takes a rest, longer or shorter, and sits down anew to the work. During the first half-hour, as before, nothing is found, and then all of a sudden the decisive idea presents itself to the mind. It might be said that the conscious work has been more fruitful because it has been interrupted and the rest has given back to the mind its force and freshness. But it is more probable that this rest has been filled out with unconscious work and that the result of this work has afterward revealed itself to the geometer just as in the cases I have cited; only the revelation, instead of coming during a walk or a journey, has happened during a period of conscious work, but independently of this work which plays at most a rôle of excitant, as if it were the goad stimulating the results already reached during the rest, but remaining unconscious, to assume the conscious form.
>
> HENRI POINCARÉ, "Mathematical Creation," *Science and Method*,
> trans. George B. Holsted

Having recognized the importance of subconscious activity, Poincaré goes on to describe the role of the conscious mind:

> There is another remark to be made about the conditions of this unconscious work: it is possible, and of a certainty it is only fruitful, if it is on the one hand preceded and on the other hand followed by a period of conscious work. These sudden inspirations . . . never happen except after some days of voluntary effort which has appeared absolutely fruitless and whence nothing good seems to have come, where the way taken seems totally astray. These efforts then have not been as sterile as one thinks; they have set agoing the unconscious machine and without them it would not have moved and would have produced nothing.

The need for the second period of conscious work, after the inspiration, is still easier to understand. It is necessary to put in shape the results of this inspiration, to deduce from them the immediate consequences, to arrange them, to work the demonstrations, but above all is verification necessary. I have spoken of the feeling of absolute certitude accompanying the inspiration; in the cases cited this feeling was no deceiver, nor is it usually. But do not think this is a rule without exception; often this feeling deceives us without being any the less vivid, and we only find it out when we seek to put on foot the demonstration.

Poincaré's description of the process of inquiry shows the human intellect working as a kind of dialogue between reason and intuition. It also points out something else that is extremely important for the investigator to understand and accept: the necessity of making mistakes. "These sudden inspirations," warns Poincaré, "never happen except after some days of voluntary effort which has appeared absolutely fruitless and whence nothing good seems to have come, where the way taken seems totally astray." We are all reluctant to make errors, but without a willingness to make them, original inquiry is impossible. Inquiry normally proceeds by a succession of increasingly intelligent mistakes; we learn from them and move ever closer to a solution. If your inquiry is to be independent and original, you must accept the risks involved.

The process in practice: variant forms

The highly abstract view of the process of inquiry as a sequence of clearly defined stages does not provide an entirely adequate account of what occurs as a person moves toward a resolution of a problem, for this movement is extremely complex, fluid, and deeply personal. Its stages often telescope: With simple, familiar problems a solution may come almost simultaneously with the awareness of a difficulty. At other times the incubation period leads to several hypotheses that must be checked against each other. Often the process is cyclical: For example, an artist may make several sketches, each of which suggests an idea for a better one. Each sketch is a kind of test of an intuition, serving to clarify the artistic problem further and to bring the artist closer to a solution. Finally, even the treatment of similar problems differs from person to person: Mozart frequently composed his music in his head and then wrote it out brilliantly at one sitting; Beethoven, on the other hand, wrote and rewrote continually through a long series of drafts.

In the chapters that follow, the various stages of the process of inquiry are investigated in detail. As you come to understand this process, you will learn the necessity for using both your reason and your intuition in speculating and in probing your speculations, and for resisting the impulse to commit yourself to a solution too quickly. We hope that a knowledge of the process will also lead you to recognize the importance of failure in moving toward a successful communication. Such an awareness can help you develop the patience necessary to see your work through to the end. Like the artist with his series of sketches, a writer normally proceeds toward a finished essay through a series of approximations, each of which brings him closer to an effective statement of his conception.

EXERCISES

1 John Dewey divides the process of inquiry into five stages: "(1) a felt difficulty; (2) its location and definition; (3) a suggestion of a possible solution; (4) development by reasoning of the bearings of the suggestion; and (5) further observation and experiment leading to its acceptance or rejection." Alfred North Whitehead, in one of the epigraphs to this chapter, divides it into three stages: (1) a particular observation, (2) an imaginative generalization, and (3) further observation controlled by rational analysis. Henri Poincaré also divides it into three stages: (1) a period of conscious struggle, (2) a period of unconscious work, and (3) a second period of conscious work that leads to verification or rejection of one's hypothesis. In our discussion you have been presented with still another division. Can you supply other possibilities? What are the strengths and weaknesses of each description of the process? Which descriptions seem to you to be most useful to the writer? Why? What we have are different systems that constitute analyses of the same psychological process. How is this possible? Which is "correct"? Recall the discussions in the preceding chapters.

2 Read the following essay by Charles Nicholle and analyze it in terms of the process of inquiry outlined in this chapter. What is his problem? What clue triggers his hypothesis? What does he do after intuiting the hypothesis? After reading Nicholle's essay can you outline one effective way of structuring an essay that reports on a discovery?

The Mechanism of the Transmission of Typhus
CHARLES NICHOLLE

It is in this way that the mode of transmission of exanthematic typhus was revealed to me. Like all those who for many years fre-
quented the Moslem hospital of Tunis, I could daily observe typhus
patients bedded next to patients suffering from the most diverse
complaints. Like those before me, I was the daily and unhappy witness of the strange fact that this lack of segregation, although inexcus-
able in the case of so contagious a disease, was nevertheless not followed by infection. Those next to the bed of a typhus patient did not
contract the disease, while, almost daily, during epidemic outbreaks,
I would diagnose contagion in the *douars* (the Arab quarters of the
town), and amongst hospital staff dealing with the reception of patients. Doctors and nurses became contaminated in the country in
Tunis, but never in the hospital wards.

One day, just like any other, immersed no doubt in the puzzle
of the process of contagion in typhus, in any case not thinking of it
consciously (of this I am quite sure), I entered the doors of the hospital,
when a body at the bottom of the passage arrested my attention.

It was a customary spectacle to see poor natives, suffering from
typhus, delirious and febrile as they were, gain the landing and collapse on the last steps. As always I strode over the prostrate body. It
was at this very moment that the light struck me. When, a moment
later, I entered the hospital, I had solved the problem. I knew beyond
all possible doubt that this was it. This prostrate body, and the door
in front of which he had fallen, had suddenly shown me the barrier
by which typhus had been arrested. For it to have been arrested, and,
contagious as it was in entire regions of the country and in Tunis, for
it to have remained harmless once the patient had passed the Reception Office, the agent of infection must have been arrested at this
point. Now, what passed through this point? The patient had already
been stripped of his clothing and of his underwear; he had been
shaved and washed. It was therefore something outside himself,
something that he carried on himself, in his underwear, or on his
skin, which caused the infection. This could be nothing but a louse.
Indeed, it was a louse. The fact that I had ignored this point, that all
those who had been observing typhus from the beginnings of history
(for it belongs to the most ancient ages of humanity) had failed to
notice the incontrovertible and immediately fruitful solution of the
method of transmission, had suddenly been revealed to me. I feel
somewhat embarrassed about thus putting myself into the picture. If
I do so, nevertheless it is because I believe what happened to me is a
very edifying and clear example, such as I have failed to find in the
case of others. I developed my observation with less timidity. At the
time it still had many shortcomings. These, too, appear instructive to
me.

If this solution had come home to me with an intuition so sharp that it was almost foreign to me, or at least to my mind, my reason nevertheless told me that it required an experimental demonstration.

Typhus is too serious a disease for experiments on human subjects. Fortunately, however, I knew of the sensitivity of monkeys. Experiments were therefore possible. Had this not been the case I should have published my discoveries without delay, since it was of such immediate benefit to everybody. However, because I could support the discovery with a demonstration, I guarded my secret for some weeks even from those close to me, and made the necessary attempts to verify it. This work neither excited nor surprised me, and was brought to its conclusion within two months.

In the course of this very brief period I experienced what many other discoverers must undoubtedly have experienced also, viz. strange sentiments of the pointlessness of any demonstration, of complete detachment of the mind and of wearisome boredom. The evidence was so strong, that it was impossible for me to take any interest in the experiments. Had it been of no concern to anybody but myself, I will believe that I should not have pursued this course. It was because of vanity and self-love that I continued. Other thoughts occupied me as well. I confess a failing. It did not arrest my research work. The latter, as I have recounted, led easily and without single day's delay to the confirmation of the truth, which I had known ever since that revealing event, of which I have spoken.

3   The biblical story of Solomon's Wise Judgment offers another example of the process of inquiry. Read it, then answer the following questions: What clashes in his mind (what does he desire, and what is he confronted with)? What must be discovered? What is his hypothesis and how does he test it? Is Nicholle's test likely to be more reliable than Solomon's? Why?

Two harlots came to the king, and stood before him. The one woman said, "Oh, my lord, this woman and I dwell in the same house; and I gave birth to a child while she was in the house. Then on the third day after I was delivered, this woman also gave birth; and we were alone; there was no one else with us in the house, only we two were in the house. And this woman's son died in the night, because she lay on it. And she arose at midnight and took my son from beside me, while your maidservant slept, and laid it in her bosom, and laid her dead son in my bosom. When I rose in the morning to nurse my child, behold, it was dead; but when I looked at it closely in the morning, behold, it was not the child that I had borne." But the other woman said, "No, the living child is mine, and the dead child is yours." The first said, "No, the dead child is yours, and the living child is mine." Thus they spoke before the king.

Then the king said, "The one says, 'This is my son that is alive, and your son is dead'; and the other says, 'No; but your son is dead, and my son is the living one.' " And the king said, "Bring me a sword." So a sword was brought before the king. And the king said, "Divide the living child in two, and give half to the one, and half to the other." Then the woman whose son was alive said to the king because her heart yearned for her son, "Oh, my lord, give her the living child, and by no means slay it." But the other said, "It shall be neither mine nor yours; divide it." Then the king answered and said, "Give the living child to the first woman, and by no means slay it; she is its mother."

I Kings 3:16–27

4 Read the following essay by Ray Bradbury. Can you infer from the essay Bradbury's assumptions about the stages of the process of inquiry? Are there any ways in which this process might differ for science and art? What methods does Bradbury recommend for keeping and feeding a muse? Relate each of these methods to some stage of the process of inquiry.

How to Keep and Feed a Muse

RAY BRADBURY

It isn't easy. Nobody has ever done it consistently. Those who try hardest, scare it off into the woods. Those who turn their backs and saunter along, whistling softly between their teeth, hear it treading quietly behind them, lured by a carefully acquired disdain.

We are of course speaking of The Muse.

The term has fallen out of the language in our time. More often than not when we hear it now we smile and summon up images of some fragile Greek goddess, dressed in ferns, harp in hand, stroking the brow of your perspiring Scribe.

The Muse, then, is that most terrified of all the virgins. She starts if she hears a sound, pales if you ask her questions, spins and vanishes if you disturb her dress.

What ails her? you ask. Why does she flinch at the stare? Where does she come from and where go? How can we get her to visit for longer periods of time? What temperature pleasures her? Does she like loud voices, or soft? Where do you buy food for her, and of what quality and quantity, and what hours for dining?

We might start off by paraphrasing Oscar Wilde's poem, substituting the word "Art" for "Love."

> Art will fly if held too lightly,
> Art will die if held too tightly,
> Lightly, tightly, how do I know
> Whether I'm holding or letting Art go?

For "Art" substitute, if you wish, "Creativity" or "The Subconscious" or "Heat" or whatever your own word is for what happens when you spin like a firewheel and a story "happens."

Another way of describing The Muse might be to reassess those little specks of light, those airy bubbles which float across everyone's vision, minute flaws in the lens or the outer, transparent skin of the eye. Unnoticed for years, when you first focus your attention on them, they can become unbearable nuisances, ruptures in one's attention at all hours of the day. They spoil what you are looking at, by getting in the way. People have gone to psychiatrists with the problem of "specks." The inevitable advice: ignore them, and they'll go away. The fact is, they don't go away; they remain, but we focus out beyond them, on the world and the world's ever-changing objects, as we should.

So, too, with our Muse. If we focus beyond her, she regains her poise, and stands out of the way.

It is my contention that in order to Keep a Muse, you must first offer food. How you can feed something that isn't there yet is a little hard to explain. But we live surrounded by paradox. One more shouldn't hurt us.

The fact is simple enough. Through a lifetime, by ingesting food and water, we build cells, we grow, we become larger and more substantial. That which was not, *is*. The process is undetectable. It can be viewed only at intervals along the way. We know it is happening, but we don't know quite how or why.

Similarly, in a lifetime, we stuff ourselves with sounds, sights, smells, tastes, and textures of people, animals, landscapes, events, large and small. We stuff ourselves with these impressions and experiences and our reaction to them. Into our subconscious goes not only factual data but reactive data, our movement toward or away from the sensed events.

These are the stuffs, the foods, on which The Muse grows. This is the storehouse, the file, to which we must return every waking hour to check reality against memory, and in sleep to check memory against memory, which means ghost against ghost, in order to exorcise them, if necessary.

What is the subconscious to every other man, in its creative aspect becomes, for writers, The Muse. They are two names for one thing. But no matter what we call it, here is the core of the individual we pretend to extol, to whom we build shrines and hold lip services in our democratic society. Here is the stuff of originality. For it is in the totality of experience reckoned with, filed, and forgotten, that each man is truly different from all others in the world. For no man sees the same events in the same order, in his life. One man sees death younger than another, one man knows love more quickly than another. Two men, as we know, seeing the same accident, file it with different cross-references, in another part of their own alien alphabet. There are no 100 elements, but two billion elements in the world. All would assay differently in the spectroscopes and scales.

We know how fresh and original is each man, even the slowest and dullest. If we come at him right, talk him along, and give him his head, and at last say, What do you want? (Or if the man is very old,

What *did* you want?) every man will speak his dream. And when a man talks from his heart, in his moment of truth, he speaks poetry.

I have had this happen not once but a thousand times in my life. My father and I were really not great friends, until very late. His language, his thought, from day to day, were not remarkable, but whenever I said, "Dad, tell me about Tombstone when you were seventeen," or "the wheatfields, Minnesota, when you were twenty," Dad would begin to speak about running away from home when he was sixteen, heading west in the early part of this century, before the last boundaries were fixed—when there were no highways, only horse paths, and train tracks, and the Gold Rush was on in Nevada.

Not in the first minute, or the second, or the third minute, no, did the thing happen to Dad's voice, did the right cadence come, or the right words. But after he had talked five or six minutes and got his pipe going, quite suddenly the old passion was back, the old days, the old tunes, the weather, the look of the sun, the sound of the voices, the boxcars traveling late at night, the jails, the tracks narrowing to golden dust behind, as the West opened up before—all, all of it, and the cadence there, the moment, the many moments of truth, and, therefore, poetry.

The Muse was suddenly there for Dad.

The Truth lay easy in his mind.

The Subconscious lay saying its say, untouched, and flowing off his tongue.

As we must learn to do in our writing.

As we can learn from every man or woman or child around us when, touched and moved, they tell of something they loved or hated this day, yesterday, or some other day long past. At a given moment, the fuse, after sputtering wetly, flares, and the fireworks begin.

Oh, it's limping crude hard work for many, with language in their way. But I have heard farmers tell about their very first wheat crop on their first farm after moving from another state, and if it wasn't Robert Frost talking, it was his cousin, five times removed. I have heard locomotive engineers talk about America in the tones of Tom Wolfe who rode our country with his style as they ride it in their steel. I have heard mothers tell of the long night with their first born when they were afraid that they and the baby might die. And I have heard my grandmother speak of her first ball when she was seventeen. And they were all, when their souls grew warm, poets.

If it seems I've come the long way around, perhaps I have. But I wanted to show what we all have in us, that it has always been there, and so few of us bother to notice. When people ask me where I get my ideas, I laugh. How strange—we're so busy looking out, to find ways and means, we forget to look *in*.

The Muse, to belabor the point then, is there, a fantastic storehouse, our complete being. All that is most original lies waiting for us to summon it forth. And yet we know it is not as easy as that. We know how fragile is the pattern woven by our fathers or uncles or friends, who can have their moment destroyed by a wrong word, a slammed door, or a passing fire-wagon. So, too, embarrassment, self-consciousness, remembered criticisms, can stifle the average person so that less and less in his lifetime can he open himself out.

Let's say that each of us has fed himself on life, first, and later, on books and magazines. The difference is that one set of events happened to us, and the other was forced feeding.

If we are going to diet our subconscious, how prepare the menu?

Well, we might start our list like this:

Read poetry every day of your life. Poetry is good because it flexes muscles you don't use often enough. Poetry expands the senses and keeps them in prime condition. It keeps you aware of your nose, your eye, your ear, your tongue, your hand. And, above all, poetry is compacted metaphor or simile. Such metaphors, like Japanese paper flowers, may expand outward into gigantic shapes. Ideas lie everywhere through the poetry books, yet how rarely have I heard short story teachers recommending them for browsing.

My story "The Shoreline at Sunset" is a direct result of reading Robert Hillyer's lovely poem about finding a mermaid near Plymouth Rock. My story "There Will Come Soft Rains" is based on the poem of that title by Sara Teasdale, and the body of the story encompasses the theme of her poem. From Byron's "And the Moon Be Still as Bright" came a chapter for my novel *The Martian Chronicles,* which speaks for a dead race of Martians who will no longer prowl empty seas late at night. In these cases, and dozens of others, I have had a metaphor jump at me, give me a spin, and run me off to do a story.

What poetry? Any poetry that makes your hair stand up along your arms. Don't force yourself too hard. Take it easy. Over the years you may catch up to, move even with, and pass T. S. Eliot on your way to other pastures. You say you don't understand Dylan Thomas? Yes, but your ganglion does, and your secret wits, and all your un-born children. Read him, as you can read a horse with your eyes, set free and charging over an endless green meadow on a windy day.

What else fits in our diet?

Books of essays. Here again, pick and choose, amble along the centuries. You'll have much to pick over from the days before the es-say became less popular. You can never tell when you might want to know the finer points of being a pedestrian, keeping bees, carving headstones, or rolling hoops. Here is where you play the dilettante, and where it pays to do so. You are, in effect, dropping stones down a well. Every time you hear an echo from your subconscious, you know yourself a little better. A small echo may start an idea. A big echo may result in a story.

In your reading, find books to improve your color sense, your sense of shape and size in the world. Why not learn about the senses of smell and hearing? Your characters must sometimes use their noses and ears or they may miss half the smells and sounds of the city, and all of the sounds of the wilderness still loose in the trees and on the lawns of the city.

Why all this insistence on the senses? Because in order to convince your reader that he is *there,* you must assault each of his senses, in turn, with color, sound, taste, and texture. If your reader feels the sun on his flesh, the wind fluttering his shirt sleeves, half your fight is won. The most improbable tales can be made believable, if your reader, through his senses, feels certain that he stands at the middle of events. He cannot refuse, then, to participate. The logic of events always gives way to the logic of the senses. Unless, of course, you do something really unforgivable to wrench the reader out of context, such as having the American Revolution won with machine guns, or introducing dinosaurs and cave men into the same scene (they lived millions of years apart). Even with this last, a well-described, technically perfect Time Machine can suspend disbelief again.

Poetry, essays. What about short stories, novels? Of course. Read those authors who write the way you hope to write, those who think the way you would like to think. But also read those who do not think as you think or write as you want to write, and so be stimulated in directions you might not take for many years. Here again, don't let the snobbery of others prevent you from reading Kipling, say, while no one else is reading him.

Ours is a culture and a time immensely rich in trash as it is in treasures. Sometimes it is a little hard to tell the trash from the treasure, so we hold back, afraid to declare ourselves. But since we are out to give ourselves texture, to collect truths on many levels, and in many ways, to test ourselves against life, and the truths of others, offered us in comic strips, TV shows, books, magazines, newspapers, plays, and films, we should not fear to be seen in strange companies. I have always felt on good terms with Al Capp's "Lil Abner." I think there is much to be learned about child psychology from "Peanuts." A whole world of romantic adventure has existed, beautifully drawn by Hal Foster in his "Prince Valiant." As a boy I collected and was perhaps influenced in my later books by the wonderful middle-class American daily strip "Out Our Way" by J. C. Williams. I am as much Charlie Chaplin in "Modern Times" in 1935 as I am Aldous Huxley's reader-friend in 1961. I am not one thing. I am many things that America has been in my time. I had enough sense to keep moving, learning, growing. And I have never reviled or turned my back on the things I grew out of. I learned from Tom Swift, and I learned from George Orwell. I delighted in Edgar Rice Burroughs' *Tarzan* (and still respect that old delight and will not be brainwashed from it) as today I delight in C. S. Lewis' *Screwtape Letters.* I have known Bertrand Russell and I have known Tom Mix, and my Muse has grown out of the mulch of good, bad, and indifferent. I am such a creature as can remember with love not only Michelangelo's Vatican ceilings but the long-gone sounds of the radio show *Vic and Sade.*

What is the pattern that holds all this together? If I have fed my Muse on equal parts of trash and treasure, how have I come out at the farther end of life with what some people take to be acceptable stories?

I believe one thing holds it all together. Everything I've ever done was done with excitement, because I wanted to do it, because I loved doing it. The greatest man in the world for me, one day, was Lon Chaney, was Orson Welles in "Citizen Kane," was Laurence Olivier in *Richard III*. The men change, but one thing remains always the same: the fever, the ardor, the delight. Because I wanted to do, I did. Where I wanted to feed, I fed. I remember wandering, stunned, off a stage in my home town, holding a live rabbit given to me by Blackstone the Magician in the greatest performance ever! I remember wandering, stunned, in the papier-mâché streets of the Century of Progress Exhibition in Chicago in 1933; in the halls of the Venetian doges in Italy in 1954. The quality of each event was immensely different, but my ability to drink it in, the same.

This does not mean to say that one's reaction to everything at a given time should be similar. First off, it cannot be. At ten, Jules Verne is accepted, Huxley rejected. At eighteen, Tom Wolfe accepted, and Buck Rogers left behind. At thirty, Melville discovered, and Tom Wolfe lost.

The constant remains: the search, the finding, the admiration, the love, the honest response to materials at hand, no matter how shabby they one day seem, when looked back on. I sent away for a statue of an African gorilla made of the cheapest ceramics when I was ten, said statue a reward for enclosing the wrapper from a package of Fould's Macaroni. The gorilla, arriving by mail, got a reception as large as that given the Boy David at his first unveiling.

The Feeding of the Muse then, which we have spent most of our time on here, seems to me to be the continual running after loves, the checking of these loves against one's present and future needs, the moving on from simple textures to more complex ones, from naïve ones to more informed ones, from nonintellectual to intellectual ones. Nothing is ever lost. If you have moved over vast territories and dared to love silly things, you will have learned even from the most primitive items collected and put aside in your life. From an ever-roaming curiosity in all the arts, from bad radio to good theatre, from nursery rhyme to symphony, from jungle compound to Kafka's *Castle*, there is basic excellence to be winnowed out, truths found, kept, savored, and used on some later day. To be a child of one's time is to do all these things.

Do not, for money, turn away from all the stuff you have collected in a lifetime.

Do not, for the vanity of intellectual publications, turn away from what you are—the material within you which makes you individual, and therefore indispensable to others.

To feed your Muse, then, you should always have been hungry about life since you were a child. If not, it is a little late to start. Better late than never, of course. Do you feel up to it?

It means you must still take long walks at night around your city or town, or walks in the country by day. And long walks, at any time, through bookstores and libraries.

And while feeding, How to *Keep* Your Muse is our final problem.

The Muse must have shape. You will write a thousand words a day for ten or twenty years in order to try to give it shape, to learn enough about grammar and story construction so that these become part of the subconscious, without restraining or distorting the Muse.

By living well, by observing as you live, by reading well and observing as you read, you have fed Your Most Original Self. By training yourself in writing, by repetitious exercise, imitation, good example, you have made a clean, well-lighted place to keep the Muse. You have given her, him, it, or whatever, room to turn around in. And through training, you have relaxed yourself enough not to stare discourteously when inspiration comes into the room.

You have learned to go immediately to the typewriter and preserve the inspiration for all time by putting it on paper.

And you have learned the answer to the question asked earlier: Does creativity like loud or soft voices?

The loud, the passionate voice seems to please most. The voice upraised in conflict, the comparison of opposites. Sit at your typewriter, pick characters of various sorts, let them fly together in a great clang. In no time at all, your secret self is roused. We all like decision, declaration; anyone loudly for, anyone loudly against.

This is not to say the quiet story is excluded. One can be as excited and passionate about a quiet story as any. There is excitement in the calm still beauty of a Venus de Milo. The spectator, here, becomes as important as the thing viewed.

Be certain of this: When honest love speaks, when true admiration begins, when excitement rises, when hate curls like smoke, you need never doubt that creativity will stay with you for a lifetime. The core of your creativity should be the same as the core of your story and of the main character in your story. What does your character want, what is his dream, what shape has it, and how expressed? Given expression, this is the dynamo of his life, and your life, then, as Creator. At the exact moment when truth erupts, the subconscious changes from wastebasket file to angel writing in a book of gold.

Look at yourself then. Consider everything you have fed yourself over the years. Was it a banquet or a starvation diet?

Who are your friends? Do they believe in you? Or do they stunt your growth with ridicule and disbelief? If the latter, you have no friends. Go find some.

And finally, have you trained well enough so you can say what you want to say without getting hamstrung? Have you written enough so that you are relaxed and can allow the truth to get out without being ruined by self-conscious posturings or changed by a desire to become rich?

To feed well is to grow. To work well and constantly is to keep what you have learned and know in prime condition. Experience. Labor. These are the twin sides of the coin which when spun is neither experience nor labor, but the moment of revelation. The coin, by optical illusion, becomes a round, bright, whirling globe of life. It is the moment when the porch swing creaks gentle and a voice speaks. All hold their breath. The voice rises and falls. Dad tells of other years. A ghost rises off his lips. The subconscious stirs and rubs its eyes. The Muse ventures in the ferns below the porch, where the summer boys, strewn on the lawn, listen. The words become poetry that no one minds, because no one has thought to call it that. Time is there. Love is there. Story is there. A well-fed man keeps and calmly gives forth his infinitesimal portion of eternity. It sounds big in the summer night. And it is, as it always was down the ages, when there was a man with something to tell, and ones, quiet and wise, to listen.

5 The following sentences may make you feel uneasy; each seems to us to be inappropriate for inclusion in a formal essay. Can you rewrite each to produce a more appropriate sentence? (If a particular sentence does not bother you, go on to the next.)

1) He jumps as frequently as six feet.
2) The long-awaited furnishing of the building has been done.
3) Democracy is where everybody elects his government.
4) Am I right in writing right now?

Next, using the concepts that we have discussed in this chapter, analyze briefly what you have just done to one of the sentences. To guide your analysis, answer the following questions. Did you make any false starts, that is, try any unsatisfying versions? Did you produce several satisfying versions? Can you give an absolutely accurate description of what occurred in your mind? Why not? Can you construct a simple, abstract account of what occurred?

6 Make a short list of events that have made you uneasy: for example, social, political, or moral problems about which you have been thinking. Can you state your concerns as questions? Try phrasing them in several ways. Would some versions be easier to work with as essay topics than others? Why?

Even more useful to you as a writer than such a list is a journal in which you note the important events of your intellectual life: problems, observations, significant quotations from your reading. Such a journal, if it is kept for some time, can lead you to greater self-awareness and to knowledge of what problems are *for you* really crucial. It can also help you to retain information that may be useful in writing your essays: You are less likely to lose important ideas, and more likely to fix them in your mind, if you write them down.

7 Write a short story based on a personal experience.

*To recognize a problem which can be solved
and is worth solving is . . . a discovery in its own right.*
MICHAEL POLANYI, *Personal Knowledge*

*The most difficult portion of any inquiry
is its initiation.*
F. S. C. NORTHROP, *The Logic of the Sciences and the Humanities*

5 Preparation: identifying and stating the problem

W<small>HEN</small> you sense a difficulty, how can you get enough control over it to begin systematic investigation? Usually you cannot press your inquiry to a satisfactory conclusion without first having a clear idea of the problem you are trying to solve. The more novel or complex the problem, the more essential it is that you understand it as clearly as possible. A false start affects all subsequent stages of the inquiry; what begins poorly is likely to end the same way. "One may have the most rigorous of methods during the later stages of investigation," says F. S. C. Northrop,

> but if a false or superficial beginning has been made, rigor later on will never retrieve the situation. It is like a ship leaving port for a distant destination. A very slight erroneous deviation in taking one's bearings at the beginning may result in entirely missing one's mark

at the end regardless of the sturdiness of one's craft or the excellence of one's subsequent seamanship.

F. S. C. NORTHROP, *The Logic of the Sciences and the Humanities*

In order to develop skill in identifying and stating problems, you must come to understand the nature and origin of problems, and you must learn to explore sensitively the uneasiness that signals the existence of a problem.

The nature and origin of problems

Problems do not exist independent of men. There are no problems floating around in the world out there waiting to be discovered; there are only problems *for someone*. As we pointed out earlier, a person's image of the world is composed of attitudes, values, beliefs, and various kinds of information, all of which combine to form an exceedingly complex, more or less coherent system. Problems arise when features of the image are perceived to be inconsistent with one another, to clash in some way: when a person becomes aware that two beliefs to which he is deeply committed are incompatible, when he notices that his acts or the acts of others clash with his values, when he discovers something in the nature of the world that doesn't "fit" his conception of it, when he has a desire or a need that he finds he cannot fulfill, and so on. When a person becomes aware of such an inconsistency, he finds himself in what might be called a *problematic situation*. The uneasy feeling that accompanies this awareness is characteristic of the earliest stage of inquiry.

Because the image held by each of us is in some respects unique, our problems are frequently unique. The moral problem that James Agee sensed as he pondered the beauty of the sharecroppers' houses is highly personal; other people would probably not respond in the same way, and if they did, their response would indicate that they shared certain values with Agee. The man who says that he "can't see what you're getting all worked up about" is probably being honest; he really can't. The event to which you respond with so much agitation simply does not clash with anything in his image. Or if it does, the intensities of the clashes may differ, so that what is a very important problem to you is relatively inconsequential to him. Such differences suggest that you must be true to your own responses; your own problems are as real as anyone else's.

If, as some say, a man's image is his map of the world, it is a highly unusual map, for it is continuously readjusting itself, much as the lens of the eye changes its shape in response to variations in distance between it and what is seen. Within the image conservative forces are constantly operating to maintain its consistency and stability; when a person becomes aware of an inconsistency in his image, pressures develop to eliminate it.

Karl von Frisch, whose simple and elegant experiments with bees are models of scientific research, describes the inception of a forty-year investigation in this way:

> About 1910 a famous ophthalmologist, Professor C. von Hess, performed many experiments on fishes, insects, and other lower animals. He tested them while they were in a positively phototactic condition—that is, under circumstances where they moved into the brightest available light. He found that in a spectrum the animals always collected in the green and the yellow-green region, which is the brightest part of the spectrum for a color-blind human eye. Therefore, von Hess asserted, fishes and invertebrates, and in particular bees, are totally color-blind. If this were true, the colors of flowers would have no biological significance. But I could not believe it, and my skepticism was the first motive which led me to begin my studies of bees about forty years ago. I tried to find out whether bees have a color sense.
>
> KARL VON FRISCH, *Bees: Their Vision, Chemical Senses, and Language*

Von Frisch's skepticism resulted from the inconsistency between von Hess's conclusion and his own belief that the colors of flowers had biological significance. Here, then, was a problematic situation out of which grew a series of inquiries and discoveries about the perceptual and communicative abilities of bees.

To become an effective inquirer, it is essential that you develope sensitivity and receptivity to problematic situations. It is, of course, difficult to ignore some situations—air pollution, violence in the streets, and so on—but not all situations are so intrusive. Our reactions to a flawed theory or an imprecisely phrased statement may be more subtle: We may feel that something is not quite right but not be able to pinpoint the difficulty. Furthermore, because many of us have come to believe that having problems is evidence of a personal deficiency we may often be reluctant to acknowledge them, particularly intellectual problems in the classroom. Yet it is the perceptive and knowledgeable person who most often has problems; it is the best student who sees the limitations of human understanding and the need for inquiry in every aspect of human affairs. The existence of a problem does indicate inadequacies of some sort, but it is more profitably seen as an opportunity to be seized, as a state from which growth and productive change can come. Uneasiness is the seed from which subsequent investigation grows; ignore it and the process of inquiry may never begin.

Analyzing and stating the problem

One important component of a problem is apparent: the problematic situation. Clearly, this situation must be made explicit in any adequate statement of a problem. A description of the problematic situation does not in itself constitute a complete statement, however. You must also identify the *unknown*—that which will enable you to eliminate the problematic situation. Since the unknown describes the nature of the solution, which remains to be discovered, it is usually stated as a question. Although people ordinarily think of the unknown as the problem and the identifying question as the complete statement of that problem, our consideration of the nature and origin of problems reveals problems to be complex conceptual units with two basic components: a problematic situation and an unknown, both of which must be made explicit in a complete statement.

A statement of the unknown is actually a partial description of the solution. As such, it serves two functions: (1) It acts as a guide to inquiry, since it describes what you are looking for; and (2) it enables you to know when you have found your solution, since the solution will match the description. Riddles offer amusing, although somewhat unusual, examples of such statements: A riddle is a partial description of a solution, and it is phrased as a question. What's purple and lives at the bottom of the sea? (Solution: Moby Plum.) What goes on four feet, on two feet, and three; but the more feet it goes on, the weaker it be? Riddles, however, are designed to puzzle; a clearly stated unknown facilitates inquiry. Everyone has had the embarrassing experience of being momentarily unable to recall a name that he should know perfectly well. We are placed in a position—a problematic situation—in which we need a name that is not immediately available to us; we seem to have a peculiar gap in our consciousness where the word should be. Often, however, we can give a partial description of the word. For instance, we may know that the name has two syllables and that it begins with the letter *B*. This description guides our inquiry from the outset. We seek the solution in a subset of names with these two characteristics and ignore other subsets. The unknown, then, is not totally unknown; it is partially known, and our question will include this partial knowledge.

The procedure for stating problems can be better understood if it is seen in operation. Suppose someone said, "We talked from religion to politics."[1] Most of us would feel uneasy about this sentence. We have a firm enough grasp of English grammar to know immedi-

---

[1] For this example the authors are indebted to Kellogg W. Hunt, "Improving Sentence Structure," *The English Journal*, April, 1958.

ately that something is wrong — but what? Since intuition suggests that the phrase *from religion to politics* creates the difficulty, we can try eliminating the content words from the phrase to make the sentence read "We talked from _____ to _____." What *kind* of words do we expect to find in the blanks? *From eight to nine* would work; so would *from dawn to dusk*, but not *from dogs to cats* or *from ships to sealing wax*. We are troubled because the construction requires words referring to time; words like *religion* and *politics* don't fit. Certain features of this unknown are obvious: It must convey the same information as the original sentence, and it must not violate our sense of good grammar. This description, which specifies the essential features of an adequate solution to the problem, can be stated as a question: How can the sentence be rephrased so that it carries the same information and follows the rules of grammar?

We would all probably agree that these are necessary features of a solution, but they are not the only features that can be stated beforehand. For a description of an adequate solution is in part determined by characteristics of the observer. An adequate solution is always adequate *for somebody*. A teacher of English might insist that the solution have other features as well: for example, that it be clear, economical, and precise, and that it be appropriate to its verbal and social context. Such additional descriptive features add further constraints to the inquiry and reduce the number of solutions that can be considered acceptable, as every student of composition knows.

Not all problems are as simple as this one. More often than not, what appears to be a single problem is in fact a cluster of interdependent, subordinate problems, each of which must be solved before a solution to the larger one can be found. For an illustration, consider the act of communication itself, in particular the communication problem discussed in Chapter 3. To solve this problem the writer has to find out what he can say that will enable his friends at home to understand the custom of bowing in a Southeast Asian village. He has already solved one problem to his satisfaction: He has discovered the conventions of bowing and learned their meaning; the custom no longer puzzles him. But if he wants to teach others to understand the custom, too, he must solve a series of subordinate problems. He must discover what his readers are likely to know about the custom, or about similar customs; he must determine what it is they do not know that is essential to understanding. He must decide where the heart of his message lies, that is, what he must focus on for his particular audience. He must develop the discourse itself, choosing what seem to him the most effective divisions of his subject, finding illustrations, analogies, and so on. Finally, he must edit his rough copy, eliminating inappropriate and obscure statements, misspellings, and flaws in structure. He must solve, then, an extraordinarily large number of subordinate problems before he can solve his initial problem, that of developing a means of enabling his audience to understand the custom as he understands it. The number of problems that the writer must solve in preparing even this comparatively simple essay suggests why writing is so difficult — and why many people avoid it if they can.

AIDS IN STATING THE UNKNOWN

Discovering the unknown is often the most important and difficult task in problem analysis. A well-stated unknown greatly increases the efficiency of an inquiry, for it frequently carries with it hints of a solution and occasionally even suggests a hypothesis. Consider this simple example. Suppose you want to know how to build a house with southern exposures on all four sides. If the question is phrased in this way, you will probably see no answer. But if the question is *where* can a house be built with southern exposures on all four sides, the answer is easy: at the North Pole. The difference between the two questions is more than a mere difference in wording. *How* can the house be built implies that the unknown is a process, a set of operations; *where* implies that the unknown is a location. Thus the way an unknown is stated strongly influences the direction of the subsequent inquiry.

There are no rules for arriving at a well-stated unknown; the adequacy of the statement depends principally on a careful study of the problematic situation. There are, however, some techniques that can be helpful if they are used with a kind of speculative playfulness and a willingness to accept the mistakes that inevitably accompany original thought. The preceding example suggests one such technique for playing with the unknown: successively classifying and reclassifying it as a question of fact, of process, and of relationships.

1) A *question of fact* requires that the answer isolate and identify something (Who? What? When? Where?).
2) A *question of process* requires that the answer describe an activity or prescribe a set of operations (How did it happen? How can it be done?).
3) A *question of relationships* always involves systems or units in systems. Questions of relationships include:
    a) value questions, which ask about the relative positions of units in a value system (Which is better?);
    b) questions of causation and probability (What caused it? What is its probable effect? Which is more likely?);
    c) questions of consistency, such as questions of logic and

classification (Does the conclusion follow from the evidence? Do the units have enough in common to warrant being grouped in a single category?);

d) and questions of policy (What should be done?).

In your quest for the most appropriate category, you must accompany each successive reclassification with an actual restatement of the unknown as a question. Articulation of the question is necessary for complete understanding and control.

Another way of playing with a problem is to recall similar problems with which you are familiar and then to specify how the immediate problem differs from each. This method encourages you to bring past experience to bear on present problems. A new problem is seldom so unusual as to make all the problems with which you have dealt in the past completely irrelevant. Thus the familiar becomes the key to understanding the unfamiliar. Every problem, however, is to some extent unique — hence the importance of noting differences. This way of treating a problem is particularly useful when you are working with very complex problems, for it can give insight into numerous features of the problem rapidly.

CHARACTERISTICS OF WELL-STATED UNKNOWNS

As we have said, the way an unknown is stated establishes the direction of subsequent inquiry. This is true of well-stated unknowns but also, unfortunately, equally true of many poorly stated ones. The former make investigation efficient and productive; the latter lead us astray. For an illustration, suppose a student is disturbed by the antagonism between students and administration on his campus. There are at least two unknowns to be discovered here: What causes the conflict between students and administrators? And what can be done to eliminate it? Suppose now that he attempts to state the first of these unknowns by asking, "What's wrong with the administration?" The question does establish a direction for inquiry, but it assumes something that is not known, namely, that the administration is the principle source of the conflict. This may well be, but it may also be that the students are to blame, or a combination of the two. (The observer may also be at fault. The source of the problematic situation may be neither the students nor the administration, for it is possible that the conflict is normal and the observer's expectations unrealistic.) The question implies a knowledge of the cause when it is precisely this that the student is seeking to discover. Assuming to be true what one is attempting to find out is called begging the question. (Assuming that an unknown is a cause, a fact, or a process before careful investigation is also a form of question-begging.) It would be better to ask *what* the cause or causes of the conflict are. Although this question does indicate the kind of unknown that is sought, it does not commit the investigator beforehand to a particular cause, closing off other possibilities prematurely. At this point in the process of inquiry, a well-stated question ought to be data-oriented, not solution-oriented. It should be a guide to exploring the data, not an appeal for support for a particular solution.

A well-stated question also enables you to know when you have answered it. Suppose investigation reveals that certain policies of the administration are indeed the cause of the conflict. Someone might state the second unknown this way: "What can be done about our oppressive administration?" Nothing in this question will enable the inquirer to know when he has answered it, for the question lacks adequate clarity and precision. What is an oppressive administration? When does it cease to be oppressive? Avoiding such vague and emotion-laden terms and examining the data — in this case, the specific acts of the administration — may lead to a better statement; for instance, how can the administration be induced to keep the libraries open until midnight, to eliminate student driving restrictions, to abolish its requirement that all freshmen live in dormitories, and so on.

A well-asked question, then, serves as an instruction for effective investigation. It defines what is sought and guides but does not constrict inquiry.

Unsolvable and apparently unsolvable problems

You should avoid committing yourself to solving certain kinds of problems; for example, problems that demand more skill and knowledge than can be acquired in the time available to you, or that require special equipment not at your disposal, or that cost too much to solve. Other problems cannot be solved no matter what the conditions. Sigmund Freud gave an instance of such a problem when he remarked that it is pointless to ask whether people who lived at other times in history were happier than we are, for happiness is a subjective state and we have no means of measuring it in those long dead. Addressing yourself to such problems can lead nowhere but to frustration and failure.

Other problems only appear to be unsolvable. Since problems arise from clashing elements in our image of the world, they can be solved by our changing *either* or *both* of the elements. The physical and social worlds around us and the conceptual world within us are, of course, subject to change. We can solve many problems by deliberately producing changes in these worlds: We can build a dam to make barren land fertile, take medicine to relieve an ailment, recast a sentence to correct a stylistic flaw, or apologize to someone who is irritated with us. In doing so we eliminate the clash between our experiences in the world and our values, beliefs, and desires.

Some problems, however, do not lend themselves to this sort of solution. They require that the observer change himself — his values, desires, and so on. If we fail to see the changes that must be made in such a situation, or if we refuse for one reason or another to make them, we find ourselves trapped in an apparently unsolvable problem. The notion of an unsolvable problem frequently arises from a failure to understand that the observer contributes to the creation of problems. Many problems appear unsolvable because the observer insists on approaching the data with a particular set of values, attitudes, and habits. If he changes his approach, the problem may disappear, or the means to a satisfactory solution may become apparent. Many of our most pressing social problems are of this kind, for they are rooted in our cultural values and habits of behavior. In the following passage Edward T. Hall describes a problematic situation caused by the conflict of two conceptual systems.

> The Taos are a very independent people who carefully guard all their culture from the white man. They even make a secret of how to say "Thank you" in Taos. This makes it exceedingly difficult for the governmental representatives whose job it is to work with them. According to [the superintendent of the Northern Pueblo Agency, John] Evans, there had been some difficulty finding an agricultural extension agent who could work with the Taos. Finally a young man was chosen who liked the Taos and who was careful to approach them slowly. Everything went along very well, and it seemed that he was, indeed, the right man for a very ticklish job. When spring arrived, however, Evans was visited in Albuquerque by the agriculturist, who was wearing a very long face. Evans asked, "What's the matter? You look depressed." His visitor replied, "As a matter of fact, I am. I don't know what's wrong. The Indians don't like me any more. They won't do any of the things I tell them." Evans promised to find out what he could. The next time there was a council meeting at Taos he took one of the older Indians aside and asked him what was wrong between the tribe and the young man. His friend looked him in the eye and said, "John, he just doesn't know certain things! You know, John — *think*. . . ."
>
> Suddenly Evans understood. In the spring the Taos believe that Mother Earth is pregnant. To protect the surface of the earth they do

not drive their wagons to town, they take all the shoes off their horses, they refuse to wear hardsoled shoes themselves. Our agriculturist had been trying to institute a program of early-spring plowing!

EDWARD T. HALL, *The Silent Language*

Unless the agriculturist can persuade the Indians to abandon their beliefs (an unlikely prospect) or can change his own (a more likely eventuality), an impasse has been reached.

Whenever a person has a problem, his way of thinking about the world is automatically called into question. This world image may well be the principal source of the problem, and to change it may be the only way to initiate a solution. When some deep-rooted feature of the image stands in the way of an adequate solution, trying to find a solution consistent with the image is likely to be, at best, unproductive.

In some ways, problems that require a person to change his habitual way of thinking are more difficult to solve than those that require him to change something external, although these problems, too, are often formidable. When a person is called on literally to change his mind, to alter his values and beliefs, he often shrinks from the prospect, sometimes resisting violently. His sense of stability, perhaps even his sense of identity, is threatened. Many people would rather struggle with a dilemma or seek, although mistakenly, to change the world around them than venture to change themselves.

EXERCISES

1 In the selection that follows, Kenneth E. Boulding sketches various features of his own knowledge system. This is, of course, an incomplete statement; a complete statement would be extraordinarily long and probably impossible to make, since none of us is aware of *all* the values and beliefs that function in our images. Notice that we share some features of Boulding's image but do not share others.

Write a comparable essay in which you sketch features of your own image, paying particular attention to values, beliefs, and information that you do not share with Boulding.

As I sit at my desk, I know where I am. I see before me a window; beyond that some trees; beyond that the red roofs of the campus of Stanford University; beyond them the trees and the roof tops which mark the town of Palo Alto; beyond them the bare golden hills of the Hamilton Range. I know, however, more than I see. Behind me, although I am not looking in that direction, I know there is a window, and beyond that the little campus of the Center for the Advanced Study in the Behavioral Sciences; beyond that the Coast Range; beyond that the Pacific Ocean. Looking ahead of me again, I know that beyond the mountains that close my present horizon, there is a broad valley; beyond that a still higher range of mountains; beyond that other mountains, range upon range, until we come to the Rockies; beyond that the Great Plains and the Mississippi; beyond that the Alleghenies; beyond that the eastern seaboard; beyond that the Atlantic Ocean; beyond that is Europe; beyond that is Asia. I know, furthermore, that if I go far enough I will come back to where I am now. In other words, I have a picture of the earth as round. I visualize it as a globe. I am a little hazy on some of the details. I am not quite sure, for instance, whether Tanganyika is north or south of Nyasaland. I probably could not draw a very good map of Indonesia, but I have a fair idea where everything is located on the face of this globe. Looking further, I visualize the globe as a small speck circling around a bright star which is the sun, in the company of many other similar specks, the planets. Looking still further, I see our star the sun as a member of millions upon millions of others in the Galaxy. Looking still further, I visualize the Galaxy as one of millions upon millions of others in the universe.

I am not only located in space, I am located in time. I know that I came to California about a year ago, and I am leaving it in about three weeks. I know that I have lived in a number of different places at different times. I know that about ten years ago a great war came to an end, that about forty years ago another great war came to an end. Certain dates are meaningful: 1776, 1620, 1066. I have a picture in my mind of the formation of the earth, of the long history of geological time, of the brief history of man. The great civilizations pass before my mental screen. Many of the images are vague, but Greece follows Crete, Rome follows Assyria.

I am not only located in space and time, I am located in a field of personal relations. I not only know where and when I am, I know to some extent who I am. I am a professor at a great state university. This means that in September I shall go into a classroom and expect to find some students in it and begin to talk to them, and nobody will be surprised. I expect, what is perhaps even more agreeable, that regular salary checks will arrive from the universtiy. I expect that when I open my mouth on certain occasions people will listen. I know, furthermore, that I am a husband and a father, that there are people who will respond to me affectionately and to whom I will respond in like manner. I know, also, that I have friends, that there are houses here, there, and everywhere into which I may go and I will be welcomed and recognized and received as a guest. I belong to many societies. There are places into which I go, and it will be recognized that I am expected to behave in a certain manner. I may sit down to worship, I may make a speech, I may listen to a concert, I may do all sorts of things.

I am not only located in space and in time and in personal relationships, I am also located in the world of nature, in a world of how
things operate. I know that when I get into my car there are some
things I must do to start it; some things I must do to back out of the
parking lot; some things I must do to drive home. I know that if I
jump off a high place I will probably hurt myself. I know that there
are some things that would probably not be good for me to eat or
to drink. I know certain precautions that are advisable to take to
maintain good health. I know that if I lean too far backward in my
chair as I sit here at my desk, I will probably fall over. I live, in other
words, in a world of reasonably stable relationships, a world of "ifs"
and "thens," of "if I do this, then that will happen."

Finally, I am located in the midst of a world of subtle intimations and emotions. I am sometimes elated, sometimes a little depressed, sometimes happy, sometimes sad, sometimes inspired,
sometimes pedantic. I am open to subtle intimations of a presence
beyond the world of space and time and sense.

What I have been talking about is knowledge. Knowledge, perhaps, is not a good word for this. Perhaps one would rather say my
Image of the world. Knowledge has an implication of validity, of
truth. What I am talking about is what I believe to be true; my subjective knowledge. It is this Image that largely governs my behavior. In
about an hour I shall rise, leave my office, go to a car, drive down to
my home, play with the children, have supper, perhaps read a book,
go to bed. I can predict this behavior with a fair degree of accuracy
because of the knowledge which I have: the knowledge that I have a
home not far away, to which I am accustomed to go. The prediction,
of course, may not be fulfilled. There may be an earthquake, I may
have an accident with the car on the way home, I may get home to
find that my family has been suddenly called away. A hundred and
one things may happen. As each event occurs, however, it alters my
knowledge structure or my image. And as it alters my image, I behave accordingly.

KENNETH E. BOULDING, *The Image*

2   Spend the next fifteen minutes listing all the things in your
immediate surroundings that clash in some way with features
of your image; then state the problematic situations. Ask yourself why, if these situations are indeed problematic, you don't
set about eliminating all of them.

3   Read the following essay by Richard B. Gregg. What problems does he identify? What is the problematic situation?
The unknown? What features must the unknown solution
have? If the solution is to be effective, what changes must we
make in our values and beliefs?

An Effective Substitute for War
RICHARD B. GREGG

Despite the horrors, futilities and destructiveness of war, there are nevertheless certain virtues and truths associated with it which humanity cannot afford to lose. In any discussion of new ways of settling conflicts, these military virtues cannot safely be disregarded.

Before the First World War, the romance and glamor of war was an undoubted fact, especially for those who never had taken part in war. The two world wars have destroyed all the glamor. Yet there is in all hearts a desire to live a significant life, to serve a great idea and sacrifice oneself for a noble cause, to feel the thrill of spiritual unity with one's fellows and to act in accordance therewith. We all wish for strenuous action and the exercise of courage and fortitude, to be carried away by the enthusiasm of daring. We all love to undergo a common discipline and hardship for the sake of a fine ideal; to be in good effective order; to be strong, generous and self-reliant; to be physically fit, with body, mind and soul harmoniously working together for a great purpose, thus becoming a channel of immense energies. Under such conditions, the whole personality is alert, conscious, unified and living profoundly, richly and exaltedly. Then one can be truly and gloriously happy. Martial music suggests many of these elements and their consequent exhilaration and exaltation.

Probably war and conflict seem to promise such results partly because our ordinary life of alleged peace is so often dull, trivial, monotonous and devoid of fine purpose. It is so full of frustration, resentments, balked disposition, hidden violence, oppression, pettiness and meanness; so insipid, fragmentary, full of cross-purposes and evil.

"Such a hopeless snarl, Anything to be relieved of such a mess!" So cries the heart. Yet what a risk, to wrench ourselves from established life.

One reason why we take such deep delight in risk attending the search for this release is that such adventures may turn possibilities into accomplished facts. They are modes of creation, of "free activity of the soul," as Clausewitz says. Hence, after men have long been chained to an industrial routine, feeling themselves helpless cogs in a vast machine, the call of an immeasurable risk cannot easily be resisted. But war is attractive not merely for its orderly action and sense of unity for a great purpose; it also has solid elements of truth and virtue.

The most outstanding virtue of violence is that of courage. But violence is not the only occasion or test or proof of courage.

Another virtue is energy. All the deep emotions, especially fear and anger, are generators of tremendous energy. To be a channel of immense energy gives one a thrill and a satisfaction that can never be forgotten. Fear, anger and hatred are doubtless evil, but the energy that they arouse is, by itself, good; for as William Blake said, energy is divine.

Furthermore, the sincerity of many fighters and warriors is admirable. They live and work, sacrifice and die for their vision of the truth, even though they may be too inarticulate to express it in words. The militarist's vision of truth may be partial and cloudy, but he nevertheless lives, suffers and dies for the truth as he sees it. He may even be inspired by hatred, anger, and revenge, and may put his whole faith in material weapons, but he is true to himself and the faith that is in him. That much is fine and solid.

Another virtue of the militarists which deserves our admiration is discipline. Discipline establishes and maintains effective habits, creates solidarity and reliability, promotes self-respect and elicits respect from others.

The militarist is right when he says that conflict is an inevitable part of life. This world is inherently diverse and changing, and since human beings differ so much in the values they hold, in environment, inheritance, intelligence, tolerance and unselfishness, and are so bound by tradition and habit, the adjustments involved in change and growth necessarily result in conflicts. No strong or sensible person would want to abolish growth or change or the positive achievements that often issue from struggle. Struggle is a part of the very meaning of life.

These, then, seem to be the important virtues of the violent fighter: enterprise, courage, strenuous action, and endurance; sincerity, devotion and a sense of unity with one's own kind; order, training and discipline. His truth that conflict is inevitable is another element of his strength.

All these virtues and truths of war are given full scope and exercise in the nonviolent method of settling great disputes. If any nation or group adopts mass nonviolent resistance, no moral losses will result.

Walter Lippmann, in an excellent article on "The Political Equivalent of War," quotes from William James' essay, "The Moral Equivalent of War," and continues:

"It is not sufficient to propose an equivalent for the military virtues. It is even more important to work out an equivalent for the military methods and objectives. For the institution of war is not merely an expression of the military spirit. It is not a mere release of certain subjective impulses clamoring for expression. It is also — and, I think, primarily — one of the ways by which great human decisions are made. If that is true, then the abolition of war depends primarily upon inventing and organizing other ways of deciding those issues which hitherto have been decided by war. . . .

"Any real program of peace must rest on the premise that there will be causes of dispute as long as we can foresee, and that those disputes have to be decided, and that a way of deciding them must be found which is not war."

"A way of deciding them which is not war." Is that way nonviolent resistance? Closer examination shows that it satisfies Lipp-

mann's requirements. Nonviolent resistance not only utilizes the
military virtues; it uses also on a moral plane many of the military
methods and principles; it employs many of the same psychological
processes; and it even retains some of the military objectives, with
moral modifications. Military men know much about human nature,
but nonviolent resisters know still more. If war has been in the past a
practical method of making great human decisions, of settling great
disputes, this new method will be still more effective for such a purpose.

The very principles of military strategy operate in this new
mode of struggle.

Clausewitz's principles of war have been summarized by a British writer as follows:

"Retaining the initiative, using the defensive as the decisive form of action,
concentration of force at the decisive point, the determination of that point,
the superiority of the moral factor to purely material resources, the proper relation between attack and defense, and the will to victory."

Other authorities state them somewhat differently, Foch, for
instance, laying more stress on the offensive.

We have seen that the nonviolent resister begins an entirely
new line of conduct. He seizes and maintains the moral initiative. He
uses the principle of surprise most effectively. Clausewitz said: "Surprise plays a much greater part in strategy than in tactics; it is the
most powerful element of victory," and a long line of military authorities agree.

The surprise of nonviolent resistance is effective partly because
it is startling and partly because the opponent is so bound by his
violent habits that he is ill-prepared to utilize the new tactics himself.
He is like a wrestler using European methods pitted against a Japanese using jiu-jitsu. The surprise of nonviolent resistance, unlike that
of war, is not due to deceit or stratagem but simply to its novelty and
daring.

Napoleon stated,

"It is an approved maxim in war, never to do what the enemy wishes you to
do, for this reason alone, that he desires it. A field of battle, therefore, which
he has previously studied and reconnoitred, should be avoided, and double
care should be taken where he has had time to fortify and entrench. One
consequence deducible from this principle is, never to attack a position in
front which you can gain by turning."

Nonviolent resistance acts fully in accord with Napoleon's principle. Your violent opponent wants you to fight in the way to which he
is accustomed. If you utterly decline, and adopt a method wholly new
to him, you have thus gained an immediate tactical advantage.

In "using the defensive as the decisive form of action," the
peaceful resister in his external actions agrees with Clausewitz and
Liddell Hart, but in respect to his psychological energies he agrees
with Foch; he is constantly "attacking," that is, energetically seeking

the psychological road for a truly satisfactory solution of the conflict. His energy is not used so much in opposition as in trying to open new, adequate and wise channels for the energies of both his opponents and himself to unite in and flow on together, and in removing defects from his own position. Nonviolent resistance is not directed against the *energy* of the opponent's desires but merely against their immediate direction, form or method. It seeks to discover for him a new and wiser channel for his energy.

This does not mean reducing the conflict to a tame debating society. Although sometimes a safe and easy issue of the conflict may be found, the nonviolent resister may feel assured of a fair probability that he will sooner or later have to suffer hardships and perhaps wounds, imprisonment and even death. If the struggle is against a powerful group, a corporation, a government or an established system of socio-economic beliefs, and is prolonged, the resisters may have to suffer a great deal. "War is hell," and in a long struggle soldiers and police may abandon all restraints. We assume that the peaceful resister is really in earnest, really believes in his cause, is ready to sacrifice for it, and is no more a coward than any soldier is. He must take risks. This is a real adventure, no parlor make-believe for pretenders or boasters.

But psychologically, nonviolent resistance differs in one respect from war. The object is not to make the opponent believe that he is crushed, but to persuade him to realize that he can attain practical security, or whatever else his ultimate desire may be, by easier and surer means than he saw formerly. The effort is furthermore to help him work out such new means, not rigidly or on any *a priori* plan, but flexibly in accordance with the deepest growing truth of the entire situation in all its bearings. Nonviolence does not destroy the opponent's courage, but merely alters his belief that his will and desire must be satisfied only in *his* way. Thus he is led to see the situation in a broader, more fundamental and far-sighted way, so as to work out a solution which will more nearly satisfy both parties in the light of a new set of conditions.

Does the nonviolent resister "concentrate his force at the decisive point," and is he active in "the determination of that point"? He certainly is. He decides, with Marshal Saxe, that "the secret of victory lies in the hearts of human beings" — that is, that it is a matter of psychology. Therefore he concentrates upon the psychological forces in the situation, and deals with them as efficiently and powerfully as he possibly can. And in so far as concentration means bringing strength to bear against weakness, he does that also, for in this moral or psychological field he is far stronger and better prepared than his opponent.

We need not dilate further upon the belief and action of the nonviolent resister, in respect to the principle of the "superiority of the moral factor to purely material resources." He acts more consistently and completely upon that principle than any soldier could.

"The proper relation between attack and defense" has been

very searchingly considered by the peaceful resister. He knows that the best relation of all between these two energies is not one of opposition but of resolution, integration and sublimation. He thus enables both sides to win, and conquers both his own possible short-sightedness of aim and that of his enemy at the same time. The result is not a triumphant victor on the one side and a despondent, repressed vanquished on the other. Both sides are happy in the joint victory of their better selves and the common defeat of their mistakes.

Does the peaceful resister have the "will to conquer" which Foch calls "the first condition of victory"? He surely does. Indeed, he must have an indomitable will to victory in order to endure the suffering put upon him. Moreover, he has a stronger incentive to win than has the ordinary soldier in war, for by this new way the final result is *sure* and settled permanently, and with a great release of energy and happiness for all concerned. There is no aftermath of resentment, hatred, bitterness, or revenge, no necessity for further threats or force.

There are other principles of strategy which also find parallels here — such principles as the economy of forces, the importance of information, mobility, endurance, etc. — but we need not discuss all of these. The similarities to the principles of military strategy are clear.

But the similarities between war and nonviolent resistance are not merely an interesting set of analogies. This entire chapter up to this point answers two doubts: namely, whether this method of struggle is not utterly foreign and new and suited only to Oriental peoples, and therefore whether it could be adopted by people with the modern Western attitude of mind. The facts that the military virtues are used and needed in this new form of struggle, and that the principles of military strategy apply here too, show that if we adopt this new mode of settling conflicts we will not be entirely reversing our previous experience, nor abandoning whatever true principles and values the human race may have garnered from its age-long experience of war. It may be that, for its first great mass success, nonviolent resistance had to be used among a people who have much social awareness and who had been thoroughly inculcated and disciplined for many centuries with ideas of nonviolence, as the Indians with their Buddhist, Jain, and Hindu traditions have been. But after its first success, a desire to try it has risen in other countries, and its rationale is coming to be understood. For obvious reasons, their desire and understanding will increase. Given desire and understanding, the courage, organizing ability, and disciplinary capacity of other peoples, whether Asian, African or Western, is not less than that of Indians. Hence the use of the method may be expected to spread. The new method is an advance, an improvement in the art of deciding public disputes, but not so utterly foreign as to be unworkable by other peoples. By fully understanding these relationships between war and nonviolent resistance we may provide ourselves an assurance with which we may advance to this new procedure.

In cases where Asians and Africans have tried to relieve themselves of the economic and military pressure of European domination, they have complained that the West cannot understand any language but that of force. If that is true, it means that the West will be utterly unprepared and helpless in the face of well-disciplined, thoroughly organized and wisely led nonviolent resistance, especially if it is accompanied by an equally thorough temporary non-vindictive economic boycott. The strategic principle of surprise would operate most dramatically and effectively. To use nonviolent resistance against the West would be complying with Napoleon's Sixteenth Maxim of War quoted above. But I am inclined to think that the West will come to understand the new language fairly soon, once it is shown to be strong language. Already there is a partial understanding of the new language, and considerable worry to boot. The grant of freedom to Ghana by the British government is one instance of this.

If, in some future conflict, both sides should use nonviolent resistance, that side would win which most deeply understood and was best disciplined and prepared in this new method. That would be the side which achieved the most self-purification, which attained the most social truth and showed the finest love. It would thereby attain the greater inner unity and strength, the greater respect from its opponents and the public.

In summary, we see that nonviolent resistance resembles war in these eight ways:

(1) It has a psychological and moral aim and effect,
(2) It is a discipline of a parallel emotion and instinct,
(3) It operates against the morale of the opponents,
(4) It is similar in principles of strategy,
(5) It is a method of settling great disputes and conflicts,
(6) It requires courage, dynamic energy, capacity to endure fatigue and suffering, self-sacrifice, self-control, chivalry, action,
(7) It is positive and powerful,
(8) It affords an opportunity of service for a large idea, and for glory.

It does not avoid hardships, suffering, wounds or even death. In using it men and women may still risk their lives and fortunes and sacrifice all. Nevertheless the possibilities of casualties and death are greatly reduced under it, and they are all suffered voluntarily and not imposed by the nonviolent resisters.

In the Indian struggle for independence, though I know of no accurate statistics, hundreds of thousands of Indians went to jail, probably not more than five hundred received permanent physical injuries, and probably not over eight thousand were killed immediately or died later from wounds. No British, I believe, were killed or wounded. Considering the importance and size of the conflict and the many years it lasted, these numbers are much smaller than they would have been if the Indians had used violence toward the British.

Nonviolent resistance is more efficient than war because it costs far less in money as well as in lives and suffering. Also it usually permits a large part of the agricultural and industrial work of the people to go on, and hence the life of the country can be maintained during the struggle.

It is again more efficient than war because "the legitimate object of war is a more perfect peace." If the peace after the war is to be better than that which preceded it, the psychological processes of the conflict must be such as will create a more perfect peace. You can't climb a mountain by constantly going downhill. Mutual violence inevitably breeds hatred, revenge and bitterness—a poor foundation for a more perfect peace. The method of nonviolent resistance, where there really is resistance, so as to bring all the issues out into the open, and the working out of a really new settlement, as nearly as possible in accord with the full truth of the issues at stake—this method does not leave a sense of frustration and it brings a more perfect peace.

Considering the completeness of its effects, nonviolent resistance is as quick and probably quicker than war. It is a weapon that can be used equally well by small or large nations or groups, by the economically weak and by the apparently strong, and even by individuals. It compels both sides and neutrals to seek the truth, whereas war blinds both sides and neutrals to the truth.

As we have already seen and will show further, nonviolent resistance certainly produces less ill-effects, if any, than war does, and this decrease of ill-effects applies to the users of nonviolence, to the opposing side, and to society and the world at large.

It is interesting to note that in early 1958 there was published a book by a British naval officer (not a pacifist), Commander Sir Stephen King-Hall, in which he argues that nonviolent resistance is now the best and only possible successful mode of defense of Great Britain against armed attack. He argues the points in detail and cogently: "We must," he says, "ask ourselves this question: 'If the contribution of violence (*i.e.*, military operations) to the settlement of differences of opinion or conflicts (*werre*) between sovereign states has evolved to such intensity that it is totally destructive, has not violence outlived its usefulness in disputes between large states?' It looks to me as if this is the truth. Bearing in mind that in major disputes violence has become equated with nuclear energy violence, I am forced to consider what possibilities are open to us if we exclude violence from our defense plans on the grounds that violence has become our master instead of our slave." Many other keen thinkers all through the West agree that nuclear weapons have destroyed the effectiveness of war as a means to settle large disputes between nations.

May we not then fairly describe nonviolent resistance as an effective substitute for war?

It is realistic in that it does not eliminate or attempt to eliminate possibilities of conflict and differences of interest, and includes *all* factors in the situation—both material and imponderable, physical and psychological. A British psychologist argues that the fundamental reasons for war are sadism and masochism, and that, until these deep-seated urges are modified, war cannot be ended. In so far as sadism and masochism are perverted expressions of a desire for power, however, nonviolent resistance can control them by substituting its own method of securing a power that is much greater and more satisfying.

It does not require any nation to surrender any part of its real sovereignty or right of decision, as a world government might. It does not surrender the right of self-defense, although it radically alters the nature of the defense. It requires no expensive weapons or armament, no drill grounds or secrecy. It does not demoralize those who take part in it, but leaves them finer men and women than when the struggle began.

Moreover, the method does not require the machinery of a government or a large wealthy organization. It may be practiced and skill may be acquired in it in every situation of life, at home and abroad, by men and women of any and all races, nations, tribes, groups, classes or castes, young and old, rich and poor. That women take part in it is important. Indeed, they are more effective in it than most men.

Inasmuch as some of the elements involved are essentially the same as trust, they have the same energizing effect as financial credit, only more so. Thus it stimulates and mobilizes, during the conflict and for a long time thereafter, all the idealism and energy of all groups and parties.

It is much superior to William James' detailed suggestions in his essay on "The Moral Equivalent of War," in that it does not require state organization, direction or assistance; it is not used against the exterior forces and conditions of nature but against human wrongs and evils. It is therefore much more dramatic, interesting and alluring, both for young men and old, and for women, too. It has even more possibilities of high daring, adventure, risk, bravery, endurance, and truly fine and noble romance than any of the chivalrous violent fighting of bygone ages.

May we not therefore say of it in the words which Marshal Foch used in reference to a different occasion: "The new kind of war has begun, the hearts of soldiers have become a new weapon."

4   We have discussed two methods of playing with problems. Can you think of any others that might be useful? How, for example, might the technique of brainstorming (i.e., listing anything that happens to come to mind) be used?

One of our two methods requires that we classify and reclassify the unknown as a question of fact, of process, and of relationships. Can you develop other classification systems? For example, consider a system that distinguishes unknowns discoverable by rule-governed procedures (e.g., mathematical problems) from those discoverable by other kinds of procedures (e.g., problems in literary criticism or personal problems). Or consider a system in which the specificity of description of initial and terminal states is the principle for grouping. Suppose you want to make a silk purse out of a sow's ear; here both states—"before" and "after"—are clearly specified. But suppose you want to make a cheap, one-piece glue dispenser; in this case, the terminal state is clearly specified but the initial state is not. We can see these two manufacturing situations as two different categories of problems. Can you expand this system by adding comparable categories? Find problems to illustrate each category.

5   Isolate from your reading in newspapers and magazines a current social problem (e.g., drug addiction, race relations, abortion laws). Analyze it using the methods discussed in this chapter. (Don't worry about solving it.) In what ways have the values and beliefs of those responsible for dealing with the problem affected their formulation of it and the kinds of solutions they have sought? Have any of the formulations resulted in apparently unsolvable problems?

6   Examine the opening paragraphs of several essays included in this book. How many begin with a problem? What components of the problem are stated in each? What can you conclude about the uses of problem analysis in the writing process?

7   At times problems can become the subject of an entire discourse. For illustrations, read the following essays by Aldo Leopold and Ladis Kovach. Isolate and analyze the problem or problems in each essay, stating the problematic situations and the unknowns. Then isolate and state a significant problem in your own experience. Write an essay explaining it that will enable other members of the class not only to understand it but to appreciate its significance for you.

Thinking like a Mountain
ALDO LEOPOLD

A deep chesty bawl echoes from rimrock to rimrock, rolls down the mountain, and fades into the far blackness of the night. It is an outburst of wild defiant sorrow, and of contempt for all the adversities of the world.

Every living thing (and perhaps many a dead one as well) pays heed to that call. To the deer it is a reminder of the way of all flesh, to the pine a forecast of midnight scuffles and of blood upon the snow, to the coyote a promise of gleanings to come, to the cowman a threat of red ink at the bank, to the hunter a challenge of fang against bullet. Yet behind these obvious and immediate hopes and fears there lies a deeper meaning, known only to the mountain itself. Only the mountain has lived long enough to listen objectively to the howl of a wolf.

Those unable to decipher the hidden meaning know nevertheless that it is there, for it is felt in all wolf country, and distinguishes that country from all other land. It tingles in the spine of all who hear wolves by night, or who scan their tracks by day. Even without sight or sound of wolf, it is implicit in a hundred small events; the midnight whinny of a pack horse, the rattle of rolling rocks, the bound of a fleeing deer, the way shadows lie under the spruces. Only the ineducable tyro can fail to sense the presence or absence of wolves, or the fact that mountains have a secret opinion about them.

My own conviction on this score dates from the day I saw a wolf die. We were eating lunch on a high rimrock, at the foot of which a turbulent river elbowed its way. We saw what we thought was a doe fording the torrent, her breast awash in white water. When she climbed the bank toward us and shook out her tail, we realized our error: it was a wolf. A half-dozen others, evidently grown pups, sprang from the willows and all joined in a welcoming melee of wagging tails and playful muslings. What was literally a pile of wolves writhed and tumbled in the center of an open flat at the foot of our rimrock.

In those days we have never heard of passing up a chance to kill a wolf. In a second we were pumping lead into the pack, but with more excitement than accuracy: how to aim a steep downhill shot is always confusing. When our rifles were empty, the old wolf was down, and a pup was dragging a leg into impassable slide-rocks.

We reached the old wolf in time to watch a fierce green fire dying in her eyes. I realized then, and have known ever since, that there was something new to me in those eyes—something known only to her and to the mountain. I was young then, and full of trigger-itch; I thought that because fewer wolves meant more deer, that no wolves would mean hunter paradise. But after seeing the green fire die, I sensed that neither the wolf nor the mountain agreed with such a view.

. . .

Since then I have lived to see state after state extirpate its wolves. I have watched the face of many a newly wolfless mountain, and seen the south-facing slopes wrinkle with a maze of new deer trails. I have seen every edible bush and seedling browsed, first to anemic desuetude, and then to death. I have seen every edible tree defoliated to the height of a saddlehorn. Such a mountain looks as if someone had given God a new pruning shears, and forbidden Him all other exercise. In the end the starved bones of the hoped-for deer herd, dead of its own too-much, bleach with the bones of the dead sage, or molder under the high-lined junipers.

I now suspect that just as a deer herd lives in mortal fear of its wolves, so does a mountain live in mortal fear of its deer. And perhaps with better cause, for while a buck pulled down by wolves can be replaced in two or three years, a range pulled down by too many deer may fail replacement in as many decades.

So also with cows. The cowman who cleans his range of wolves does not realize that he is taking over the wolf's job of trimming the herd to fit the range. He has not learned to think like a mountain. Hence we have dustbowls, and rivers washing the future into the sea.

·   ·   ·

We all strive for safety, prosperity, comfort, long life, and dullness. The deer strives with his supple legs, the cowman with trap and poison, the statesman with pen, the most of us with machines, votes, and dollars, but it all comes to the same thing: peace in our time. A measure of success in this is all well enough, and perhaps is a requisite to objective thinking, but too much safety seems to yield only danger in the long run. Perhaps this is behind Thoreau's dictum: In wildness is the salvation of the world. Perhaps this is the hidden meaning in the howl of the wolf, long known among mountains but seldom perceived among men.

Life Can Be So Nonlinear
LADIS KOVACH

It was inevitable that the question would be asked. I've been working with nonlinear problems for a number of years and various books have found their way into our home. Books like *Nonlinear Problems in Random Theory* by Norbert Wiener and *Nonlinear Analysis* by Cunningham. One day my nine-year-old son asked, "What does non-lie-near (sic) mean?" Remembering that a parent should always answer questions about the facts of life, I pretended to ponder for a few minutes until my mind could get into high gear.

Here was a golden opportunity to take the advice of that Latin motto, *qui docet discit* — who teaches learns. Shall I tell him it means not linear? No, he would only ask what linear means. There isn't any use, either, to talk about transfer functions. The only transfers he knows about are the ones he gets on the bus. But confound it, there is no simple explanation that requires nothing beyond fourth grade arithmetic. That's it! He knows addition and multiplication. These operations can be considered analogous to linear and nonlinear processes. Look, son, I'm going to write down two sets of numbers like this:

$$1, 4, 7, 10, 13, 16, 19,$$
$$1, 4, 9, 16, 25, 36, 49.$$

Now look carefully at the first line and tell me what the next number after 19 should be. That's right, it's like counting by threes but starting with one. You say 22? Because you always add three to each number to get the next one? Correct! Now, how about the second row? You don't know what to add because it keeps changing? Why don't you try multiplying? How do you get 4? 9? 16? That's the idea, 7 times 7 is 49 so the next one will be 8 times 8 or 64. Very good! Well, the first line is like a linear problem and the second is like a nonlinear problem. No! Nonlinear problems are *not* just multiplication problems!

I had better forget about arithmetic and think of some other approach. Remember when the Cub Scouts had their camp fire and we put a large log on the fire? At first the log didn't burn, then it burned strongly and finally it burned down very gradually. But when you threw a piece of paper in the fire it started to burn immediately and in a short time it was gone. The paper burned in a steady, even manner which we call linear, while the log burned in an uneven way which we can call nonlinear. I can't help it, nonlinear means many things and I'm trying to give you enough examples so you'll understand.

If you were riding your bicycle in the neighborhood of Grandma's house and you pedalled in a steady, even manner, would you be going at the same speed? Your answer, "I think so," shows me that you are beginning to realize that steady pedalling together with level, smooth streets will give uniform or constant speed. You can think of this example as being a linear one. Now, if you pedalled in a steady manner in our own neighborhood would your bicycle go at the same speed? You say you couldn't pedal in a steady manner because of all the hills around here? Smart kid! Just *pretend* you could pedal evenly; would your speed be the same as you went up and down these hills? Of course it would not—downhill you would go very fast and uphill you would go very slowly. Your speed would be uneven or nonlinear. *How* uneven it would be depends on the shape of the hills. What's that? You just thought of something? What would happen if you changed gears? You would be throwing another nonlinearity into the problem and ruining my explanation at the same time.

Let's give an example that shows how nonlinear our own actions are. If you happened to touch a hot stove you would pull your hand back quickly. If the stove were twice as hot, would you pull your hand back *twice* as far or *twice* as fast? You would if your arm were longer? But it isn't, so you see your reaction cannot be linear. Twice the temperature cannot cause twice the action. That is what we mean when we say that something is nonlinear.

In order to show you how even the most common things in the world about us can be nonlinear, let me give you some examples. We've already talked about fire being nonlinear—it flares up now and then, flames shoot out in every direction, its heat and color change and its whole action and shape are uneven and ragged. This same situation can be found in another part of nature. Remember that river we saw when we went up to the mountains last year? In the middle the water flowed very swiftly but at the edges it did not. However, this wasn't the whole story either. Rocks and boulders caused the water to foam up, swirl around and flow in different directions at different speeds. In some places small pools were formed in which the water was perfectly still. We can think of the river as being nonlinear, you see. At the beach the waves and breakers behave in an uneven, unexpected way and can also be called nonlinear. Still another example of natural nonlinearity, while not as noticeable as fire and water, is the atmosphere, that is, the air around us. Its temperature is different at different places; its movement changes from stillness to slight breeze to blustering wind; it contains different amounts of moisture, smoke, dust, etc., at various times and in various localities. In short, the atmosphere appears to be an unexpectedly changing covering about the earth — a nonlinear part of nature.

Even a simple thing like how you feel about dogs is nonlinear. Sometimes you're afraid of them and at other times you want to pet them. Which one it is doesn't depend entirely on the dog either — it depends on where you are when you see the dog, what you're doing, and how you feel. These are things that cause your ears to hear the dog's bark as friendly or threatening. In this sense your hearing can be nonlinear, too. For instance, when you make a joking remark and someone says, "You crazy nut," your ears hear this as, "You funny, clever boy." Our eyes, too, are subject to this type of nonlinearity. We do not see the faults in those we love, but criticize those we do not know. These last examples are ones we might call "psychological nonlinearity" but this need not concern you just now.

That is the way I explained nonlinearity to my son. But, why was this so important that it had to be explained at all? The complete answer to this question cannot be given at present, but some people feel that the answer, if known, would shake the very foundations of mathematics and science. Let us examine in greater detail the broad implications of this little word, "nonlinear" — a word that cannot even be found in most dictionaries.

The rapid advancement of technology in the last ten or fifteen years has produced some unusual problems. One of these arises from the alteration of the relationship between science and engineering. The lead time, which had previously existed between scientific discovery and industrial application, is rapidly disappearing. This fact has been illustrated very dramatically by McEachron.[1] . . .

The basic laws of motor and generator behavior were discovered by Michael Faraday in the early part of the 19th century. It

---

[1] McEachron, Karl B.: Engineering Education Is Closing the Gap. *Case Alumnus*, April 1958, p. 18.

was not until late in that century that Thomas A. Edison made practical application of these to build a central station to supply power for his newly invented electric light. Thus, more than fifty years elapsed between discovery and application.

During the 1920's the basic principles of radar were discovered. But it was not until the late 30's, and particularly the war period, that any practical application was made of this discovery. About fifteen years went by before the scientific discovery was applied practically.

The discovery of the amplification effect of semiconductor materials by the Bell Telephone Laboratories in 1947 preceded by only five years the wide-spread practical application of transistors in telephony and communication circuits.

Finally, the discovery in the Research Laboratories of the General Electric Company of the principles underlying the manufacture of artificial diamonds resulted in a production line process within two years.

These illustrations show the trend and emphasize the point that engineering developments today are almost on top, in point of time, of the scientific discoveries preceding them.

The elapsed time between the conception of a practical way to create an earth satellite and the accomplishment has revealed in a spectacular fashion the closing of the "gap" between discovery and application. The engineer must now recognize that he has to pick up developments before the scientist has even completed his work of discovery.

Quite another situation exists in mathematics. Many branches of mathematics were developed because of the need to solve problems in physics. It is well-known, for example, that Sir Isaac Newton invented the calculus in 1680 to enable him to solve a certain gravitation problem. It is not so well-known, however, that scarcely ten years later a Frenchman, L'Hospital, was applying calculus to his problems.

As we approach the present we find that the time between discovery and application is *increasing* — exactly the opposite of the last situation. . . .

Again, a few specific examples will suffice to show the trend. The basic principles of group theory were set down by twenty-one-year-old Evariste Galois in 1832, the night before he was killed in a duel. Approximately sixty years later, in 1890, Fedorov, Schoenflies, and Barlow independently, applied these principles in crystallography and led the way to the classification of crystals according to their symmetry.

The value of the tensor calculus was not recognized until 1905 when Einstein stated his theory of special relativity, although Grassman had developed tensors in 1844. Thus, sixty-one years elapsed between discovery and application.

Finally, the theory of matrices was formulated by Cayley in 1858, but it did not come into general use until 1925 when Heisenberg used it in quantum mechanics. This represented an elapsed time of sixty-seven years.

The full impact of this "gap" between discovery and application in mathematics can be felt if one realizes that practically all of classical mathematical physics has evolved from the hypothesis of linearity. If it should be necessary to reject this hypothesis because of the refinements of modern experience, then our linear equations are at best a first and inadequate approximation. It was Einstein himself who suggested that the basic equations of physics must be non-linear, and that mathematical physics will have to be done over again. Should this be the case, the outcome may well be a mathematics totally different from any now known. The mathematical techniques that might be used to formulate a unified and general nonlinear theory have not been recognized. . . .

We have broken through the sonic barrier, we are well on our way to conquering the thermal barrier and we are now at the threshold of the nonlinear barrier. Of all three, this last seems the most insurmountable. Strange that these nonlinear phenomena that abound so widely in nature should be so intractable. It is almost as if Man is to be denied a complete knowledge of the universe unless he makes a superhuman effort to solve its nonlinearities.

Let us examine in some detail the attitudes we have taken in our calculations. Perhaps the most common procedure is to mention nonlinearities merely to dismiss them. This results in a host of phrases which can be found in any textbook and which give the general impression that we are living in a regular Shangri-La. For example, "assume that the pulley and rope are weightless" or "we will be dealing in this chapter with ideal fluids" or "given the perfect insulator . . ." or "neglect the friction of the pulleys" or "in isotropic media we can simplify the equations to . . ." and so on in every scientific field. In a way we have been lulled into the belief that everything is ideal, homogeneous, uniform, isotropic, perfect as well as frictionless, weightless, but withal infinitely rigid.

If it serves our purpose, we do not hesitate to make a transmission line infinitely long or the parallel plates of a condenser infinite in both directions. At the other extreme, in the study of the kinetic theory of gases, we assume that all gas molecules are alike, being infinitely small rigid spheres and that the time occupied in collisions of these molecules is zero.

For those whose sensibilities rebel at such goings-on, there is a more realistic approach. The magic phrases here are "for a sufficiently small displacement we can consider the equations to be linear and . . ." or "in a certain range the curve can be approximated by straight lines as shown" or "by changing variables we can convert to a linear equation whose solution . . ." . . . It should be quite apparent that this method is subject to errors and is of only limited utility.

Many other sorties have been made into nonlinear territory but they have been cautious attempts to extend linear theory. So far, our efforts to scale the nonlinear barrier have consisted of chiselling a few footholds which are low enough so that we can always keep one foot on linear ground. We have, so to speak, located a few nonlinear zippers in the blanket of nonlinearity that covers us. Opening these zippers has allowed us to put our hand through and try to fathom the vast unknown in this way.

There is no general theory for nonlinear problems, so that it is necessary to develop solutions by means of special techniques for each type. While solutions to linear problems can be called *prefabricated*, the solutions to nonlinear problems are *custom made*. The various implications of the term "custom made," such as, more expensive, requiring a longer time to fabricate, noninterchangeability of parts, tailored to fit individual needs, etc., seem to hold true in mathematics also. The situation is complex and special methods will have to be developed to resolve it.

What is required is a boldness such as was exhibited by certain 19th century mathematicians. The courage of a Lobachewsky, for example, who rejected the time-honored postulate of Euclid that through a point not on a given line only one line in the plane, determined by the point and line, could be drawn parallel to the given line. Or the audacity of a Hamilton who said that $a \times b$ does not always have to be the same as $b \times a$. The first of these departures from classical mathematics resulted in several important non-Euclidean geometries and the second in the development of the theory of quaternions which was the forerunner of much work in abstract algebra.

Some mathematicians feel that topology will make a major transition in mathematics possible.[2] Topology is concerned with certain qualitative properties of space and in particular with those properties which remain unchanged (invariant) under various transformations. It seems entirely plausible that the qualitative habit of thought will eventually supersede the present quantitative one in mathematics. There are certain indications in science and many in mathematics which point to the analysis of structure as the mathematics of the future. In simple language, it is not things that matter, but the relations between them. Thus topology with its spatial visualizations of intricate relations between abstract "objects" is making possible a basic but still difficult analysis of relations.

Whether it will be topology or some other branch of mathematics that will enable us to surmount the nonlinear barrier, it is certain that a considerable amount of basic research will be necessary. In today's descriptive language, "a major breakthrough of these proportions can result only from a tremendous know-how." In mathematics this "know-how" is attained by following many paths which suggest themselves to the mathematician engaged in pure research.

Scientists must be encouraged as much as possible to do basic

[2] Bell, E. T.: "The Development of Mathematics." First edition, McGraw-Hill Book Company, New York, 1940.

research. Dr. Albert R. Hibbs, Chief Research Analyst of the California Institute of Technology Jet Propulsion Laboratory, said recently,[3]
"We cannot indefinitely extend the structure of applied science without also strengthening and extending the foundation of pure science
on which it rests. . . . We have learned time and again that nature
cannot be ordered to give up her secrets. Nature has never been a
willing tool to be used for some human objective. To understand nature, she must be courted patiently and for herself alone." The nonlinear barrier appears to be one of nature's least vulnerable strong-
holds. Only vigorous attack from several directions can hope to prevail
against it.

[3] Hibbs, A. R.: Do We Care About Science?, talk at IRE meeting, Pasadena,
California, April 1959.

The method of our time is to use not a single but multiple models for exploration — the technique of the suspended judgment is the discovery of the twentieth century as the technique of invention was the discovery of the nineteenth.

MARSHALL MCLUHAN, *The Medium Is the Massage*

The Mind, that Ocean where each kind
Does streight its own resemblance find;
Yet it creates, transcending these,
Far other Worlds, and other Seas;
Annihilating all that's made
To a green thought in a green Shade.

ANDREW MARVELL, "The Garden"

6 Preparation: exploring the problem

ALL of us have groped blindly and wearily for solutions to problems, often for long periods of time, before we reached even a tentative one. The student in a rhetoric course is in a particularly difficult position, for within a short time he must write a number of essays, the most challenging of which grow out of the perception of a problem and the discovery of an original solution. If he is to write effective and original essays without failing to meet deadlines, he must find a way of making the process of inquiry less chancy and time-consuming, more systematic and efficient. Some people would argue that this is impossible, that the process is highly personal and that since it has its origins in the individual's subconscious mind, it is not subject to control. We believe, however, that although methods cannot be developed that infallibly lead the writer through the process to an adequate solution, we can develop methods that will be helpful in his search. As we pointed out earlier, the process of inquiry is undulatory; periods of subconscious activity alternate with periods of conscious activity. During the conscious periods a person can systematically ask questions or perform operations that speed up the process and encourage the intuition of provisional solutions, or hypotheses. A set of such questions or operations is called a *heuristic procedure.*

Heuristic

Heuristic, heuretic, and *invention* are all names for an art that was a part of rhetoric and the sciences from Aristotle's time into the Renaissance. It was the art of systematic inquiry and provided a method for gathering information about a problem and asking fruitful questions. Although the sciences today employ a well-developed heuristic procedure, the scientific method, rhetoric seldom makes explicit use of one. The art of inquiry in rhetoric has declined; the need for it, however, has not.

Heuristic procedures should not be confused with rule-governed procedures. A rule-governed procedure specifies a finite series of steps that can be carried out in mechanical fashion without the use of intuition or special ability and that infallibly results in a correct answer: for example, the procedure in arithmetic for finding the least common denominator of a number and the procedure in syllogistic reasoning for making valid inferences. If we all follow the same rules, we all get the same result. The procedure can be made entirely conscious, each step leading to the next in an unbroken sequence. The process is single-minded and rather simple-minded in the sense that it can be simulated by a machine.

A heuristic procedure, on the other hand, provides a series of questions or operations that guides inquiry and increases the chances of discovering a workable solution. More specifically, it serves three functions:

1) It aids the investigator in retrieving relevant information that he has stored in his mind. (When we have a problem, we generally know more that is relevant to it than we think we do, but we often have difficulty in retrieving the relevant information and bringing it to bear on the problem.)
2) It draws attention to important information that the investigator does not possess but can acquire by direct observation, reading, experimentation, and so on.
3) It prepares the investigator's mind for the intuition of an ordering principle, or hypothesis.

We all have at times employed the simple and powerful method of analogy, seeing the puzzling experience of the moment as only a variation of a familiar type of experience that we know how to deal with; we interpret the unfamiliar in terms of the familiar. There are also more formal and elaborate heuristic procedures, such as the set of questions used by journalists to gather information for a newspaper article—Who? What? When? Where? How? and Why? In Chapters 3 and 5 we introduced two others: the procedure for defining a unit by contrast, variation, and distribution; and the procedure for stating problems. Heuristic search, although systematic, is never a purely conscious, mechanical activity; intuition is indispensable and some trial and error inevitable.

Certain kinds of problems either do not lend themselves, or have not yet lent themselves, to solution by rule-governed procedures. We have algorithms for solving arithmetic problems but no rules for discovering the algorithms themselves; nor do we have rules for solving such loosely defined problems as "When is civil disobedience justified?" and "Why are there no green mammals?" Problems of this kind have several dimensions, some of which are not apparent; for this reason they are often described as *ill-defined*. In contrast to a *well-defined* problem, which has a single correct answer discoverable by a rule-governed procedure, an ill-defined problem may have several reasonable answers that are reached only by more or less random search or by heuristic procedures. Ill-defined problems constitute by far the largest number of problems that men must solve in their daily lives. And it is with this kind of problem that this chapter and this book are primarily concerned.

Exploration by varying perspectives

When a very young child finds something that to him is strange and interesting—a telephone, a transistor radio, or a watch—he sets about trying to understand it. He turns it over in his hands, shakes it, drops it, puts it in his mouth, takes it apart, and so on. Whatever adults may think of this, he is actually engaging in the very important activity of rendering the enigmatic world intelligible, and his initial efforts are devoted to accumulating as much relevant information as he can as quickly as possible.

An adult confronted with a problematic situation engages in comparable, if less sticky and destructive, activity; but his effort usually involves mental rather than physical exploration, although it may involve both. Such exploration brings into play at least two distinctively human abilities: the ability to use language and the ability to shift perspectives on a unit deliberately. These abilities enable him to explore problematic data, both tangible and intangible, with astonishing speed and thoroughness by manipulating lin-

guistic symbols and mental images rather than the objects themselves. Furthermore, intellectual manipulation can be far more subtle
and sophisticated than physical manipulation.

Involved in this activity are a perceiver, what is perceived, and
the symbolic system that the perceiver uses to encode his perceptions. In Chapters 2 and 3 we focused our attention primarily on the
last two, the unit and language. In this chapter our focus shifts to
the first, the activity of the perceiver. It should be noted, however,
that all three elements are present in any exploratory activity; it
makes no sense to speak of a perceiver without his perceiving
something, or of a unit without a perceiver, or of a unit without
some formulation of it in a mind. The difference in emphasis in this
chapter, though subtle, is significant. Units have contexts, variant
forms, contrastive features, and parts. But units can not take different
perspectives; only perceivers can do this.

ALTERNATIVE PERSPECTIVES:
PARTICLE, WAVE, AND FIELD

We have found three perspectives particularly useful in exploring a unit of experience. These three perspectives are identified in
Maxim 4: *A unit of experience can be viewed as a particle, or as a wave,
or as a field.* That is, the writer can choose to view any element of his
experience *as if it were static, or as if it were dynamic, or as if it were a
network of relationships or a part of a larger network.* Note carefully
that a unit is not *either* a particle or a wave *or* a field, but can rather
be viewed as all three.

Let's first explore a bit the implications of the *wave* perspective by talking about a particular house. A house seems to be stable and solid enough—but wait. This particular house is in the
process of decay. If we were trying to articulate this dynamic feature
of the house, we might use a phrase like "that old decaying house
about to fall down."

If we observe, "It was in its prime during the thirties," we add
to the description an element of nuclearity, of central fulfillment or
peak of usefulness over a time span.

If we add, "It was an old New England house directly joined to
the barn, so that no space or outside wall comes between them—in
fact you could not tell where house stopped and barn began," we
describe the house as a wave, with no clear-cut boundaries; instead
there is fusion, smear, or flow from the house-unit to the barn-unit.
The two units overlap inseparably.

This description of a particular house—one in which Pike
grew up—reveals three characteristics of the wave view of a unit: (1)

The wave view recognizes some dynamic feature of the unit, noting flow or movement in time, in space, or in a conceptual framework; (2) it points out the nuclear component, or peak point, of the unit; (3) it emphasizes the fusion, smear, or absence of distinct boundaries between the unit and some other unit or units.

A *particle* view of the same house, however, would highlight different features of the unit: (1) It would recognize the static nature of the unit, ignoring changes in time; (2) it would select from the dynamic whole some part, usually the nuclear bit, and "take a snapshot" of it (or select, as from a motion picture, one still frame) for presentation; (3) it would ignore the difficulties of separating one unit from another, pretending that it were possible, and would arbitrarily, if necessary, specify where the one unit left off and the next began; (4) it would isolate the unit as a "chunk," semi-insulated from its surroundings. Viewed as a particle, a unit appears well-defined, without fuzzy borders, a clean-cut member of a class; but this well-ordered look, this logical neatness, is achieved at the expense of some empirical distortion.

Consider Pike's house again. He says, "I lived in it [Note the treatment of the house as a particle, by reference through the pronoun *it*] as a boy [The boyhood time span is collapsed into a time-particle]. I would come home from school, always to find Mom there [place as particle], and would run out to the woodshed to get wood for the stove [Note that the woodshed is considered "out," apart from the barn and the house]. I wonder if it is still there [The implication is that it may have disappeared rather than decaying over time]?"

What happens when the house is viewed from a *field* perspective? (1) It is seen not as existing in its own right, isolated and independent, but as occupying a place in a system of some kind (in extreme cases, the unit shrinks to a mere point in a larger system); and (2) it is seen as a system itself, composed of interrelated subsystems. To take a field perspective on a unit means to focus on the relationships (patterns, structures, organizational principles, networks, systems, functions) that order the parts of the unit and connect it to other units within a larger system. Views of the unit as dynamic, merging and interacting with other units in a constant state of flux (wave), and as a discrete, static entity (particle) are for the moment held at the margin of our attention; ordering principles and relationships (field) are in nuclear focus.

And the house from this perspective? "It was hardly a mansion [i.e., it does not share the characteristics of the set of houses that are built in a grand manner], but it was nicely situated on the common with its lovely maples, and centrally located so Dad's patients could find him easily [Note its place as the nucleus of a physical system and the function of its location in the work of the old-time country doctor]. It was one of a cluster of buildings [that constitute a higher-level unit] around the common, a cluster that included the homes of the preacher and store keeper, a general store complete with barrels and post office, a red-brick schoolhouse with its one teacher and thirty pupils in eight grades, a white clapboard church with spire rising above the pines (before, that is, the hurricane blew it off and it got replaced with a truncated substitute), and two houses occupied by non-farming older folk. Our house was two stories high [Note that each story is a unit in a system]; my room in the upper story was unheated, with snow blowing on the bed through the window — open-a-crack during the cold winter nights."

The discussion of hierarchy and levels of magnification in Chapter 2 is relevant to understanding perspectives. Notice in the preceding paragraph how the focus shifts from the house to a larger system in which it is located, and then to smaller and smaller, clearly related subunits of the house (story, room, bed, snow on the bed). The field perspective leads obviously and inevitably to a consideration of hierarchies. Although less apparent in our description of Pike's house, particle and wave perspectives lead just as inevitably into considerations of hierarchy: Viewed as a particle a unit has appropriate or typical distributions in temporal and spatial patterns, in classes and systems of classes, each of which constitutes a higher-level unit; viewed as a wave, a unit interacts with other units in a larger context that can itself be considered a higher-level wave unit in a still larger dynamic context.

HIERARCHIES OF PERSPECTIVES

Not only is there a hierarchy within units, there is also a hierarchy of perspectives. We may choose to include reference to two or even three of the perspectives, while keeping one of them in greater prominence. In "The decaying house was sold at auction." the reference to the unit as a whole puts its particle nature in primary focus; and the modifier *decaying* adds the dynamic perspective, but in a subordinate role. To reverse the emphasis, we might say: "The house got sold even while it was in the very process of collapse" or "The house sold at auction was gradually falling down." A field perspective can be added: "The old house, with its ghostly pattern of sagging shutters, broken windows, and slanting walls, went under the gavel today."

When it is being explained, the notion of a hierarchy of perspectives may seem excessively subtle; yet it is a reasonable way of describing one important kind of emphasis in human perceptions.

But we do not need to make up examples to illustrate the notion. In a letter to his friend Anton Ridder van Rappard, Vincent van Gogh made an interesting remark: "I have been trying to express the values of crowds, and . . . I try to separate things in the dizzy whirl and chaos one can see in each little corner of Nature." His comment, as well as many of his paintings, reveals a strong emphasis on wave perspective, although he "chunks" a scene and indicates its parts and their relationships. A brief examination of your own perceptions will reveal comparable hierarchies.

PERSPECTIVES ON CONCEPTS

A solid thing, such as a particular house, can be explored by shifting perspectives, but what about the abstract concept "house"?[1] Again, differing perspectives are possible. Viewing the concept from a particle perspective we can separate it sharply from other concepts such as "mansion," even though the two are related. Abstractions of even a higher level can be viewed as particles and described: The term *homey* is a vague bundle of features labeled and treated *as if* it were a "thing"—a concept reified.

When the concept "house" is viewed as a wave, different features are highlighted. The features that constitute the concept "house" may all be present in the clearest instances or examples of "house," but there will be other instances—borderline cases—that do not fit the definitions squarely; the concept "house" may overlap with "store" (when one part of the house is a store) or with "cabin" (when the building is a small, rustic abode). The concept may change over time; what at one time in history were clear instances of houses may today be regarded as borderline cases or as instances of some other concept such as "cabin" or "mansion." A concept thus can be seen as dynamic, as an evolving thing with a unique history. One branch of history, the history of ideas, is devoted to the study of concepts from this perspective.

Similarly, the concept "house" can be viewed from a field perspective. It can be classified with other concepts of dwelling places (mansions, cabins, hotels, teepees, and so on). As this classification suggests, "house" is related to certain other concepts that (along

---

[1] By *concept* we mean a set of features shared by a class of objects; words like *chair, apple,* and *house* are labels for such sets of features. Hence when we define a word we can point to an object that clearly has these features or we can state the features themselves: *That is a house* (pointing), or *A house is a dwelling place, usually for one family,* and so on. For additional information, see "Language and experience" in Chapter 2.

with thousands of others) are parts of an individual's image and parts of his cultural heritage. The set of features that make up the concept—for example, dwelling place, limited size (usually no more than three stories), several rooms, for one or a few families—are also related to each other. The result of changing one of these features is a different but closely related concept.

The perspectives can also be used profitably to study such a question as "When is civil disobedience justified?" The term *civil disobedience* can first be studied as an abstract, static state of affairs; next as a dynamic, changing social situation; then as the conceptual framework for discussing the interplay of personal, social, moral, religious, governmental, geographic, and economic dimensions in human affairs. When the writer has done this, he can also investigate similar aspects of the term *justified*; then he can bring the two together in a larger conceptual framework.

The heuristic procedure

Thus far in this chapter we have sought to lay the foundation necessary for understanding our heuristic procedure. In doing so we have used directly only Maxims 4 (on particle, wave, and field perspectives) and 2 (on hierarchy) and indirectly Maxim 1 (which states that we segment experience into units). What happens when these maxims are supplemented with the heuristic power latent in Maxim 3 (which states that in order to understand, or define, a unit adequately, we must know its contrastive features, variant forms, and distributions)?

It should be clear that any unit viewed as a particle can be studied with reference to these three characteristics; in general it can be treated in the manner we described in Chapter 3. But a unit viewed from wave and field perspectives can also be seen as having contrastive features, variant forms, and distributions in larger contexts. A unit treated as a wave segment is an identifiable, namable entity that contrasts with comparable segments. As a continuous process a unit is a sequence of variant forms (a house when just built is quite different from what it is thirty years later, although it is the "same" house), and it interacts with other units in context. Similarly, a unit as system contrasts with other systems; its features may vary; and it has a place in larger systems.

We can construct a chart to organize these perspectives and unit characteristics into a coherent set of operations and questions. This set constitutes a fully developed heuristic procedure for explor-

	Contrast	Variation	Distribution
PARTICLE	1) View the unit as an isolated, static entity. What are its contrastive features, i.e., the features that differentiate it from similar things and serve to identify it?	4) View the unit as a specific variant form of the concept, i.e., as one among a group of instances that illustrate the concept. What is the *range* of physical variation of the concept, i.e., how can instances vary without becoming something else?	7) View the unit as part of a larger context. How is it appropriately or typically classified? What is its typical position in a temporal sequence? In space, i.e., in a scene or geographical array. In a system of classes?
WAVE	2) View the unit as a dynamic object or event. What physical features distinguish it from similar objects or events? In particular, what is its nucleus?	5) View the unit as a dynamic process. How is it changing?	8) View the unit as a part of a larger, dynamic context. How does it interact with and merge into its environment? Are its borders clear-cut or indeterminate?
FIELD	3) View the unit as an abstract, multidimensional system. How are the components organized in relation to one another? More specifically, how are they related by class, in class systems, in temporal sequence, and in space?	6) View the unit as a multidimensional physical system. How do particular instances of the system vary?	9) View the unit as an abstract system within a larger system. What is its position in the larger system? What systemic features and components make it a part of the larger system?

ing any unit (i.e., a physical object, an event, or a concept). The rows represent the perspectives of particle, wave, and field, the columns, the characteristics of a unit that must be known if it is to be understood. The result is a set of nine well-defined perspectives. Each of the chart's nine cells contains an operation ("View the unit as . . .") and one or more questions designed to elicit a certain kind of information about the unit. By following the instructions in each cell, you are led to shift perspectives systematically, focusing your attention first on one feature of the unit and then another. In doing so you fulfill the basic requirement of effective inquiry, which is to *vary your assumptions*. The purpose of the procedure is not to turn you into an intellectual machine that gathers information mechanically, but to guide and stimulate your intelligence, particularly your intuition, which is able to deal with enormous complexity in an original way.

To clarify the way the chart is used for systematic exploration of a unit, let's consider a simple and familiar object, at least an apparently simple and familiar object — a particular oak tree. Each of the nine cells in the chart leads us to examine certain features of the tree, retrieve a bit of information about it that we have stored away, and at times become aware of information that we lack. An inquirer, working down each column in turn, might answer each of the questions in this way.

1) "Old Faithful" contrasts in size and age with the surrounding trees.
2) It is shedding its leaves more slowly than the other trees. Although still stately, it has passed its lifetime peak of mature, vigorous health.
3) It is composed of roots, trunk and branches, leaves, and reproductive system (the last is not readily discernible and, for this inquirer, constitutes an unknown); each part is composed of subsystems (which again are not discernible and constitute unknowns). Since all trees have roots, trunks, branches, and so on, this oak probably differs from other kinds of trees most clearly in the peculiarities of its subsystems. The parts can be classed according to function: vegetative and reproductive. They exist in a typical spatial relationship; and each of the parts is governed by an intricate timetable — acorns appear early in the year, leaves fall late, and roots continually draw sustenance from the soil or store food for later use, and so on.
4) It is now old, nearly leafless, with one broken limb and numerous scars where others have fallen off. Ten or twenty

years ago it was the same tree, but not at its inception as a
seed. Then it was only potentially a tree. When it falls and
rots or is cut up into lumber, it will lose its identity.

5) It is clearly rotting; some of the branches are already dead
and others show signs of decay.

6) Its subsystems support, feed, and repair each other by
means of a physiological network. The state of the system
differs from hour to hour (e.g., in the regulation of moisture
loss) and from day to night (in the handling of carbon
dioxide). Some parts of the system can be lost, either tem-
porarily (leaves) or permanently (some branches) without
destroying the system.

7) It is a member of a class of trees called hardwoods, which in
turn is part of a larger class system that includes all trees.
One of the few remaining trees of the original stand of oaks
and hickories (a characteristic kind of forest in this part of
the country), it dwarfs the second-generation trees around
it.

8) As part of a scene, its branches stand out sharply against
the sky, like irregular lacework, but from a distance its
dark trunk merges almost indistinguishably with the trunks
of surrounding trees. The vines growing on it give it a special charm but probably contribute to its decay. It shelters
wildlife; it draws raw materials for growth from the earth in
which it is rooted and in turn enriches the earth with its
fallen leaves.

9) A system in itself, it fills a place in a larger system, a niche in
the ecology of the area. (Without extremely close observation
and a knowledge of ecology, these questions constitute significant unknowns.)

A number of observations must be made about this exercise.
First, the answers to the questions posed by the chart were intended only as illustrations; they do not nearly exhaust the possibilities. Each of us could easily supply additional information in response to any of the questions, particularly if the tree itself could be
examined closely. Second, each of us would answer the questions
somewhat differently. Someone with biological training, for example, might view the leaves as subsystems composed of epidermis,
mesophyll, veins, and so on. And he might locate the oak tree in
quite different classes and temporal contexts than those mentioned
here; for example, he might see the tree as a member of a class of
trees, the angiosperms, which appeared during the Cenozoic era,
very late in our evolutionary history. There are no right and wrong

answers, but some will prove more reasonable, imaginative, and useful than others. The number and kinds of answers to the questions are limited by the amount of information each of us brings to the task, by our imagination, by our energy and persistence, and, as we shall see in a moment, by the peculiarities of the problem we are trying to solve.

Third, notice that the exclusive use of any one perspective would inevitably result in an incomplete, distorted image of the tree; as Kenneth Burke points out in *Permanence and Change,* "A way of seeing is also a way of not seeing." The perspectives in the chart supplement one another; each reveals a partial truth about the unit being investigated. Approaching a unit from different perspectives gives us some assurance that we are thinking well, that we have not overlooked important data. Finally, notice that the procedure is indefinitely recursive. Any feature of the tree (one of its components, a system of which it is a part, a particular stage in its development, and so on) can itself be a new unit for investigation. Therefore, in theory at least, systematic exploration, guided by the chart, can be carried on indefinitely; the process is open-ended.

SOLVING PROBLEMS SYSTEMATICALLY

So far in our discussion of the heuristic procedure we have illustrated two of its three functions; that is, we have shown how it can be used (1) to retrieve a wide range of relevant information that the inquirer may have stored in his mind and (2) to bring to his attention information about the unit that he does not possess but can usually acquire. However, we do not often engage in exploration for the sake of exploration; normally we have a goal in mind. As we noted in Chapter 4, the activity of exploration has a role in the larger context of the process of inquiry. It prepares the mind for the discovery of hypotheses that may solve a problem.

The three functions complement one another. Adequate exploration is essential to discovery; we must know a good deal before we are prepared to discover more. "Discovery, like surprise," remarks Jerome Bruner,

> favors the well-prepared mind. In playing bridge, one is surprised by a hand with no honors in it and also by one that is all in suit. Yet all particular hands are equi-probable: to be surprised one must know something about the laws of probability. So too in discovery. The history of science is studded with examples of men "finding out" something and not knowing it. . . . Discovery, whether by a schoolboy going it on his own or by a scientist cultivating the growing edge of his field, is in its essence a matter of rearranging or transforming evidence in such a way that one is enabled to go be-

yond the evidence so reassembled to new insights. It may well be that an additional fact or shred of evidence makes this larger transformation possible. But it is often not even dependent on new information.

JEROME BRUNER, "The Art of Discovery," *On Knowing*

To illustrate all three functions, let's consider a limited body of data from an Indian language spoken in Mexico—ten utterances in Tetelcingo Aztec written in a phonetic alphabet and their probable English equivalents.[2]

1.	nıkwika	I sing.
2.	tıkwika	You sing.
3.	tıkonik	You drank.
4.	nıkonitıka	I am drinking.
5.	tıkwikas	You will sing.
6.	nıčukatıka	I am crying.
7.	tıčuka	You cry.
8.	tıčukataya	You were crying.
9.	tıkonitıka	You are drinking.
10.	nıkwikataya	I was singing.

If we assume for a moment that we need to understand this language in order to communicate with those who speak it (as might a linguist, a missionary, or a government field worker who wanted to work closely with these people), we are confronted with a genuine problem. We want to communicate, to cooperate in ways that only a knowledge of the language permits, yet we cannot. To do so we must learn the grammar of the language, its vocabulary, pronunciation, and syntax. Thus, a grammar of Tetelcingo Aztec is the unknown. To construct an adequate grammar we obviously need to study many more than ten utterances; but they are enough for a start.

Using the chart on page 127 as a guide (start with cell 1), consider each numbered utterance in Tetelcingo Aztec a particle. Treat each utterance as a "chunk" different from all the others. The mere fact that the utterances are numbered and presented in a list tells us that the person who arranged them considered them to be separable, discrete units. (Probably, also, he considered each one a word, not a sequence of words, since no spaces occur between letters. This judgment is a complex one; because the data are limited, we do not choose to discuss it, even though it is relevant to our problem of particle segmentation.)

[2] The data here are taken from William R. Merrifield and others, *Laboratory Manual for Morphology and Syntax* (Santa Ana, Calif.: Summer Institute of Linguistics, 1962), p. 3.

1) Since the utterances are represented in the phonetic alphabet, we can see immediately that they differ from each other in one
or more of their sounds. The English equivalents in the second list
indicate that they also differ in meaning. By a series of careful comparisons and contrasts we can begin to isolate lexical particles—
meaningful parts of words—inside the words. It soon becomes apparent that it is not always easy to tell where these inner particles
begin and end (i.e., how to segment the sequence) or to identify their
semantic features. The first word differs from the second, for example, by the sounds *n*- versus *t*-, and by the included meanings of "I"
versus "you." As a first guess, therefore, it is reasonable to assume
that *n*- is a particle that means "I" and that *t*- is a particle that
means "you." Building on this assumption we can similarly conclude by comparing item 3 with item 4 that -*k* probably means
"past" versus -*tıka*, which probably means "in the process of." By
comparing item 5 with item 10, we can deduce that -*s* means "future" versus -*taya*, which means "past process."

2) When we look for differences of wave form in this list of
words, we seek contrasting nuclear and peripheral elements. In our
search for word parts and their meanings, we may have found *kwika*,
("sing") in item 2 versus *čuka* ("cry") in item 7. These parts seem
more central to the meaning of the words than do the pronominal
elements preceding them. If we further guess (without proof available in the data at this point) that the elements numbered 1 through
10 are single words, then we will call *kwika* and *čuka* stems and *n*-
and *t*- prefixes; from the perspective of words as waves, stems are
nuclear.

But problems of particle segmentation already plague us. What
is the function of *ı* between *n*- and *kwika*: Is it another prefix, or is it
possibly a sound that is part of the two prefixes *nı*- and *kı*- (instead of *n*- and *k*-)? And what of -*ka* after *kwi*- and *ču*-: Is it a suffix, with an undiscovered meaning, or is it a part of the stems *kwika*
and *čuka* (as we assumed above), which just happen to be partly
alike? The problem remains unsolvable for the moment. But certainly from these data we can provisionally conclude that -*s* in item
5 is a suffix meaning "future" that has been added to *kwika*. Then
we can see that the wave structure of item 5 has a nucleus, or stem,
both preceded and followed by peripheral elements; by contrast,
item 1 has no suffix (i.e., -*ka* seems in fact to be part of *kwika*).

3) We can now begin to see something of the inner structure
of these words. They have a sequential structure composed of pronominal prefix, intransitive verb stem, and tense suffix. Also apparent are some very limited classes of lexical items that can fill the
slots in this structure: *n(ı), t(ı); kwika, čuka;* -*s.* But note the curious

fact that the *absence* of a suffix lets us know that the word is in the present tense; from a particle perspective "absence" may be treated as itself a pseudo-particle called *zero* meaning "present," just as if it were a positive, audible suffix contrasting with -*s* meaning "future".

4) The second column of the chart emphasizes variations and physical aspects of the units. Our attention is directed to the acoustic character of the sounds themselves or, in writing, to the phonetic transcriptions of the sounds. The symbol *ı*, for example, suggests a vowel made by having the lips spread apart, the tongue somewhat front and high in the mouth (as in the English word *kit*), with the vocal cords vibrating. We must be prepared to find that in Tetelcingo Aztec, as in English, the same part of one word may appear with the same meaning but a somewhat different phonetic content in other words, where the context forces a change (e.g., in English the word *knife* becomes *knives* in the plural). This kind of change proves to be a major source of difficulty in the analysis of many languages, including Aztec, but the data given here were selected so as to minimize this factor, lest the segmenting problem become too great for our present purposes. Cell 4 may also lead us to consider semantic variants, where the physical form is constant, but the meaning varies slightly. Compare the meanings of the word *crescent* in the phrases *crescent moon* and *cross and crescent*. These problems, also, have been eliminated from the data given here.

5) If we were able to examine a spectrogram of the words as they are pronounced, we would see the sounds in constant change as a result of the gradual movement of the vocal organs from one position to another. In addition, we would often be unable to specify any one precise moment at which one sound stopped and the next began; they would smear into each other. As a further result, we would be unable to determine where one meaningful part of a word ended and another began. (You can appreciate this dilemma if you pronounce *as you* rapidly until you hear between the merged words the sound that normally comes at the end of *rouge*.)

As our answers to the questions in cells 4 and 5 suggest, certain questions posed by the chart will be more useful than others in solving particular problems. These differences in usefulness are the result of unique features of the data and of the unknown. Other data and other unknowns would make other questions more productive. But we cannot always predict ahead of time which questions in the chart will yield the most useful information, so it is best to run quickly through them all. (We must always leave room for the unexpected.) But we linger with those that yield the most useful information, in this case the questions in cells 1, 2, and 3.

As for the remaining cells, we will suggest only briefly some of

the more subtle results called to attention by this heuristic procedure. By posing the question in cell 6, we attempt to elicit data
about variations of the system itself; but no data of this kind
emerge from our word list. (Compare, however, *Yesterday I went to
Boston* with *I went to Boston yesterday.*) The questions in cell 7 lead
us to consider the words as members of an intransitive class of
verbs, distributed in larger clauses or sentences. The questions in
cell 8 call our attention to the contextual sources of smearing, emphasizing the sources of those effects (already mentioned in our
response to the questions in cell 5). The questions in cell 9 suggest
the need for a larger table of forms, including, for example, a row of
intransitive versus transitive words, clauses, or sentences; plus contrasting but intersecting columns of indicative versus interrogative.

	intransitive	transitive
indicative		
interrogative		

All the data that we have fit in the upper left-hand cell.

If, now, we assume that nı- and tı- represent accurately segmented pronominal actors; *kwika, koni,* and *čuka,* verb stems; and
-*s,* -*taya,* -*tıka,* -*k,* tense suffixes, we can begin to guess at some parts
of the structure of an Aztec verb paradigm. We already have *I sing*
and *you sing* but lack *he sings;* we also lack the corresponding plurals.

nıkwika	I sing	?	we sing
tıkwika	you sing	?	you sing
?	he sings	?	they sing

The blank spaces are extremely important for they serve as a guide
to further inquiry, indicating what additional data are necessary for
subsequent analysis.

This paradigm and others we can construct from the present
data constitute hypotheses. They are, in part, based on our experience with English; that is to say, the English language contains
singular and plural pronouns and first, second, and third persons. But
since we lack evidence for these characteristics in Aztec, we cannot
be sure about their occurrence. The study of languages contains
many surprises: Some languages have no clear singular-plural contrast; others have singular versus dual (two) versus plural (more
than two); others represent various degrees of respect in first-, sec-
ond-, and third-person pronominal forms (in French both *tu* and

vous may refer to the second-person singular; in German, *du* and *Sie*).[3] In order to determine the significance of the blank spaces in the paradigm—"blank" from the point of view of an English speaker— we must get additional data from Aztec speakers.

Why can't we simply make up new words on the basis of the parts and structures we now have? We have, for example, *you sing* and *you drank* but not *you drink* or *you sang*. Can we—without risk of error—make up *you sang* by taking the stem of *I sing* and the past tense of *you drank* to form *tıkwikak*? No, not without risk of error. Nevertheless, such guesses, or hypotheses, are very helpful in guiding our search for further information. We tentatively assume that Aztec is regular at this point and make up the word according to the information we have; then we check with speakers of the language to determine whether they do in fact talk this way. If not, then the hypothesis must be rejected. Whether it is confirmed or rejected, we learn something useful that we can add to our slowly growing description of Aztec grammar.

A note on risk and failure

Like explorers in the physical world, the intellectual explorer must be willing to accept risks and the failures that so often accompany exploration. Hard work, false starts, and inadequate hypotheses seem to be preconditions for successful innovation; they are normal, perhaps necessary, features of innovative thought and should be accepted as such. As we observed in Chapter 4, effective inquiry often proceeds by a series of increasingly intelligent mistakes. No heuristic procedure can eliminate hard work and error from original inquiry; what it can do is reduce the amount of work and increase the intelligence of the mistakes. You must not be misled or disheartened by the brilliant solution to a scientific problem, the magnificent painting, or the deep-probing essay; their elegance and

---

[3] Aztec can show up to three degrees of respect, in a wide variety of circumstances, and with a fantastically elaborate set of irregularities controlling the variants. Most wives refer to their husbands with a respect form and also address them with one. Godparents and the Deity may be referred to with a doubly respectful term. On ceremonial occasions, an even higher degree of honor is shown, with simultaneous indication of three degrees. In a single word, furthermore, affixes may refer to three people or things. Each of these may at times have its separate signal of respect. In the single word (*She*) *put it on it*, meaning that the child put a dress on a doll, the word may end in *-li-li-li* or *Respectfully-she respectfully-it-the-dress respectfully-it-the-doll!* (R. S. Pittman, "Nahuatl Honorifics," *International Journal of American Linguistics*, October, 1948.)

simplicity are deceptive, for you see nothing in them of the process by which they were produced. Each accomplishment undoubtedly owes much to prior failures. Accepting error as normal helps to soften the frustrations and challenges to self-esteem that are as much a part of creative thinking as the elation of discovery.

EXERCISES

1 Construct paradigms containing the Aztec equivalents of the following English constructions. Label the rows and columns.

I cry (drink)	you cry (drink)
I am crying (drinking)	you are crying (drinking)
I cried (drank)	you cried (drank)
I was crying (drinking)	you were crying (drinking)
I will cry (drink)	you will cry (drink)

Which are hypotheses?

Examine the following data (also from Merrifield). Which of your hypotheses do the data confirm? Are you forced to reject or modify any?

11. nıkonis	I will drink.
12. nıčukak	I cried.
13. niečmačtıa malı	Mary teaches me.
14. mı¢mačtıa wan¢ı	John teaches you.
15. tıkmačtıa	You teach him.
16. tıniečmačtıa	You teach me.
17. nıkmačtıa	I teach him.
18. niečihta roberto	Robert sees me.
19. mı¢ihta malı	Mary sees you.
20. tıniečihta	You see me.
21. kıhta luisa	Louise sees him.
22. tıkılfıa	You tell him.
23. nıkılfıa	I tell him.
24. niečılfıa lito	Lito tells me.
25. tıniečılfıa	You tell me.
26. kılfıa roberto	Robert tells him.

These data introduce new units to investigate. Items 1–12 (see p. 131) are all one-word sentences with intransitive stems; items 13–26 contain another kind of verb stem and some are two-word sentences. Work through the questions in the chart again, focusing your attention first on the one-word sentences with transitive verbs and then on the two-word sentences. Note: *č* is pronounced like English *ch; ¢,* like *ts.*

What new hypotheses are generated by this exploration? In what ways does the knowledge of English grammar that you bring to the inquiry affect these hypotheses? Construct hypothetical forms for *I see him* and *John tells you;* then check your hypotheses against the Aztec forms printed at the bottom of this page. One last question: Why do you suppose Aztecs pronounce *Mary* as *malɪ* and *John* as *wan¢ɪ?* If you cannot answer the question, review the section entitled "Language and experience" in Chapter 2 and the comments on variation in this chapter and in Chapter 3.

2   Select any handy object—a book, a pen, a chair—and practice viewing it from each of the nine perspectives presented in the chart on page 127. Do this with various objects until you begin to feel comfortable with the procedure. Then try it with concepts such as democracy, civil disobedience, law, and so on. Use the procedure merely to retrieve what you know and to discover where the gaps in your knowledge are. Learning to use the procedure is somewhat like learning to drive a car; one is awkward at first and makes mistakes. But actually doing it is essential; reading about it is not enough.

3   We make the point that after one is well into the exploration certain perspectives may be more useful than others. The following passage, by the Scottish philospher Angus Sinclair, further develops this point. After reading it, try to relate each of the perspectives Sinclair takes to one or more of those in the chart on page 127.

When I look at some material object, such as a leather brief-case, I see it as a single, distinct thing, and should say, if questioned, that it *is* a single thing. I see it so because of the ways of selecting and grouping that I follow; if I followed any other ways I should not see a brief-case and could not stow my papers in it. The penalty for following ways other than the ordinary ones is confusion and unmanageability in the field in question. Of course, for special purposes I could adopt different ways, as I should if I were a production technician planning the work-room processes in the manufacture of brief-cases. I might then see the brief-case not as one thing but as three separate large pieces of leather and a number of smaller ones, namely one large folded-over main sheet and two gusset pieces, and various straps, reinforcements and the like. If I attempted to devise manufacturing processes while thinking of the brief-case as one single, distinct thing, I should fail.

I normally regard my pipe as a thing, surrounded by air, but I could regard the air which fills the bowl and the hole in the stem as a thing, surrounded by wood. I could also regard it not as one thing but as a statistical total of sub-atomic entities, and this I in fact do when I calculate that the number of possible distributions of them and of the sub-atomic entities composing the desk on which it lies which would allow of the interaction we should call 'the pipe falling through the desk' is so minute in proportion to the number of distributions which would not allow of it that we can forecast with almost absolute certainty that the pipe will lie where it is. If I want to smoke I think of it in one way; if I am working in physical theory I think of it in another. That is to say, I follow the way of selecting and grouping which is simplest and most convenient for my purpose.

ANGUS SINCLAIR, *The Conditions of Knowing*

4 Read the following essay by Marston Bates and as you read note in the margin the dominant focuses and perspectives implicit in his discussion. What focuses and perspectives does he question? Why? What does he offer as alternatives? Cite specific passages in support of your answers. What experience leads him to reject certain views and propose others?

Biotic Communities
MARSTON BATES

I have been trying to think about an organism living alone, in isolation. It is not an easy condition to imagine, but perhaps the attempt will make a good start toward understanding the interdependence of organisms in communities.

Animals are out. It is impossible to imagine any kind of animal living alone, because all animals need fairly complex carbon compounds as food, and they can only get these by eating plants, or by eating animals that in their turn have eaten plants. So we are limited to the plant kingdom in our search.

The so-called "higher plants" are out too, if only on account of nitrogen. An oak tree or a dandelion can build starches from water and atmospheric carbon dioxide, but such plants are dependent also on various chemical elements from the soil. Among these necessary elements is nitrogen. It is one of the commonest elements, making up as a gas the major bulk of the air; but neither the dandelion nor the oak can use nitrogen in its simple form; it must be combined into some soluble salt such as a nitrate.

The inert nitrogen gas of the air may be "fixed" as oxides by lightning flashes, and washed down to the soil as nitrous acids by rain; but this still is not in a form that can be used by the dandelion or oak. It must be oxidized into the nitrate form by soil bacteria. We don't know of any way these "higher" plants can get their nitrogen supply without the intervention somewhere of microorganisms. Plants of the bean family, as every farmer knows, can be used to build up the soil nitrates, but this is because the beans act in cooperation (symbiosis) with certain special bacteria: the beans, isolated from the bacteria, would be helpless.

But what about a bacterium living in isolation? Bacteria do not have chlorophyl, and thus cannot build up the carbon compounds necessary for protoplasm with solar energy, as the green plants do; most bacteria are thus dependent on green plants for their carbon compounds. A few kinds, though, have exploited completely different sources of energy, and some of these seem to be completely "autotrophic," able to live on purely inorganic materials of the sort that might be presumed to exist in the complete absence of other life. Such are the sulphur bacteria, which obtain energy from the oxidization of sulphides.

To imagine a kind of organism living all by itself, then, we are driven down to some very obscure bacterium like Thiobacillus, or perhaps to some of the simple algae that are able to utilize atmospheric nitrogen as well as atmospheric carbon dioxide. But these very bacteria and algae form, in nature, parts of complex systems of organisms which are mutually dependent in building or modifying series of compounds of these basic elements of nitrogen, carbon or sulphur. You can imagine Thiobacillus carrying on its sulphur operations in a biotic vacuum, but in fact it is thoroughly involved in the very complicated communal economy of soil organisms.

THE INTERRELATIONS OF ORGANISMS

Some kind of organism, sometime, must have crossed the bridge from the inorganic world to the world of living things all by itself. Some form of life must thus have existed alone for an eternity before, somehow, it began to diverge in function and thus become two kinds of life instead of one kind. To imagine something of this sort, on a basis of contemporary organisms, we are limited to things like the bacteria. But the bacteria today are integrated into the economy of organic nature as a whole, as dependent on the "higher plants" as the "higher plants" are on them; and the first pre-Cambrian protoplasmic ooze was probably something very different.

The point I am trying to make here is the interdependence of kinds of organisms in the world today. We have got into the habit of looking at the organic world as a mass of struggling, competing organisms, each trying to best the other for its place in the sun. But this competition, this "struggle," is a superficial thing, superimposed on an essential mutual dependence. The basic theme in nature is cooperation rather than competition — a cooperation that has become so all-pervasive, so completely integrated, that it is difficult to untwine and follow out the separate strands.

The next step, after trying to think about an organism in isolation, might be to try to think about two organisms, and to imagine the possible different relationships that might exist between them. We at once come to a major dichotomy, whether the two organisms are of the same kind or different kinds. If they are of the same kind, they may cooperate to get food, like two ants, or fight over the possible food supply, like two dogs. The two individuals may cooperate for reproduction; or being of the same sex, may struggle for the opportunity to mate with a third individual; or still being of the same sex, may peacefully share reproductive functions with the third individual. If there is a parent-offspring relationship between the two individuals, it may be protective, maternal; or it may be of the excluding, get-out-and-stand-on-your-own-feet variety.

If the two individuals are of different kinds, it is interesting to look for the direction of immediate benefit in their relationships. One may serve as food for the other. The direct benefit here flows in one direction. One may serve as protection or support for the other — the tree and the vine. In this case, "A" may derive benefit from "B" without harming "B"; or "A" may be a nuisance to "B" in varying degrees (depending on how heavily the tree becomes loaded with vines); or "A" may gain protection from "B" and give "B" a positive benefit in return. These cases of mutual benefit, of partnership, of symbiosis, are very numerous and take all sorts of forms, like the fungus and the alga uniting to make a lichen; or the protozoa in the intestine of a termite, digesting cellulose for the termite in return for protection. Or the numerous kinds of tropical trees that have developed special nectaries and cavities as home and food for stinging ants that in turn, in guarding their own nests, guard the tree.

It is probably useless even to try to catalogue the possible kinds of relationships between two different organisms, because we find that most of these relationships involve still other organisms; that the two compete to use some other kind of organism as food, or cooperate to support some other kind of organism, or utilize different parts of a third organism for food. In such an attempt to list the relationships between separate organisms, we come across the problems of the relationships within the community as a whole.

It is like trying to analyze the relationships between John, the barber, and Peter, the milkman. We soon get involved with Alfred, the grocer; with Peter's wife who works with Alfred's wife in arranging church suppers; with Elizabeth, who sells dresses imported from New York, which takes us out of the community and into ever more general and more indefinite, but none the less essential, relationships.

The logical basis for the examination of relationships among organisms is not individual organisms, or different kinds of organisms, but the biotic community. Here we encounter a problem in definition.

THE DEFINITION OF COMMUNITY

Most ecologists have worked in the temperate zone in pine forests or beech forests, and they have come to think of the biotic community as determined by a particular dominant kind of organism. The dominant is thought of as controlling the whole community either through sheer numbers of individuals, or bulk of protoplasm, or all-pervading biological effect. The whole assemblage of organisms living in a pine or beech forest is obviously dominated by the pines or beeches, so that these form a convenient guide to the limits of that particular community.

In the tropical forest, one looks in vain for any particular kind of organism that dominates in the sense that the pine or beech dominates its forest. My experience in the tropics has thus made me very dubious about the whole ecological idea of dominants. The idea works all right in the pine woods, but even in the temperate zone one must stretch the imagination to apply it in a lake or a stream or on the sea coast.

I think the essential element in the concept of the community is the interdependence of its various members to form a functioning unit. It is the next distinctive general organizational level above that of the individual and the population. Individuals of a given kind are organized, through their genetic relationships, into populations; but the behavior and history of these specific populations can only be understood in relation to the behavior and history of the other populations with which they occur. The community, it seems to me, might be defined as the smallest group of such populations that can be studied and understood as a more or less self-sufficient unit.

We thus arrive at a parallel with Toynbee's definition of an equally difficult concept, that of a "civilization." A biotic community might well be defined as "an intelligible field of study" from the point of view of the relations among different kinds of organisms. It is a unit of ecological study, just as civilization is a unit of historical study.

Toynbee has pointed out that English history is in no sense intelligible if taken as a field in itself. From its first clear chapter, the conversion of its people to Christianity, to its last, the establishment of industrial economy, the course of events in England fails to make sense except through the consideration of events in neighboring national states. But in tracing the genesis of these events, the student finds that it is not necessary to cover the whole world as a field, but that more or less definite limits in time and space are reached, limits which Toynbee in the present instance takes to define the particular field of Western Christian civilization. Within this field, the majority of relationships are directed inward, as they are in his other contemporaneous civilizations, the Orthodox Christian, the Islamic, the Hindu, and the Far-Eastern.

A concept like that of the "intelligible field of study" does not give a sharply defined series of units: but the material to be studied, at this level, is not composed of sharply defined units. Human culture is a continuum, but it is a continuum with pronounced modes both in time and in space, and the problem is to recognize these modes and to trace their development and characteristics. Even such an apparently isolated phenomenon as the Mayan civilization is related to the general nexus of culture. It must have started with people who had brought certain cultural equipment with them when they parted from the Old World along the bridge of the Aleutian Islands or across the Pacific, and this cultural equipment would be the common relationship between the civilizations developed in the Old and New Worlds. Among Old World civilizations, the relationships are, of course, numerous, in part obvious, and of a variety of sorts. The important thing is that these relationships are external, that is, their study is not essential to an understanding of the development of events within the civilization.

It is not particularly strange that civilization and biotic communities should be subject to the same type of definition process, since both are biological phenomena, involving the aggregation of individual organisms. There would be even less difficulty in making the analogy if Toynbee had been concerned with "cultures" instead of with "civilizations," which are essentially a particular kind of cultural development. Civilizations happen to be the only cultural groupings that have got much involved with the special problem of history. If one were studying human ethnology, rather than history, interest would focus on the development of cultural relationships in general, and civilization would fall into perspective as a particular type of development shown by a few scattered cultures.

THE LIMITS OF THE COMMUNITY

An oak tree may seem a world in itself. It may have hundreds of organisms of dozens of kinds that depend on it for food; it may give support to Spanish moss and other epiphytes; protection to birds that nest in its branches. The leaves that it drops decay, and the characteristics of the litter of oak leaves may determine the kind of soil organisms, and the direction of soil development.

But this complex of organisms does not form a community. It is not an intelligible unit of study. If we start to analyze the relationships of the various organisms associated with the oak tree, we find ourselves constantly led away from that association into some larger grouping. The caterpillars that feed on the oak leaves are developmental stages of a butterfly that gets food from the goldenrod in a clearing. The birds nesting in the oak tree forage through the nearby forest, and their behavior cannot be understood in terms of the

tree, but only in terms of the forest. Similarly, we find that the association of organisms in the soil depends not so much on the fact that
they are under an oak tree, as on being part of the oak forest.

Our biotic community, then, is the forest, not the association in
the tree. The complex of organisms making up the forest does form an
intelligible field of study, where the events and relationships can be
understood with only casual and occasional reference to external
phenomena. The range of the birds nesting in our particular tree depends on their relations with birds in neighboring trees, on the "territory" in the forest that is available for each family. The kind of food
that they are able to gather depends on a selection from the kinds
available in the forest. The number of caterpillars of a given kind eating the leaves of the oak tree depends on the density of population of
that particular species in the forest, which is a matter of balance of
parasites, climatic relations, and so forth. The characteristics of the
forest as a whole can be related to the regional climate, to the physical
and chemical factors of the general environment. The climate within
the forest can be understood in relation to the density and size of the
trees. The forest constitutes a biotic community.

A pool in our forest may, or may not, be inhabited by a distinct
community: the answer would soon become obvious in the course of
study of the organisms in the pool. If the pool formed an intelligible
unit without special reference to the forest, it would certainly form a
separate community. But we might find that the behavior of the inhabitants of the pool was constantly conditioned by the character of
the forest. The kind of plants growing in the pool might depend on
the shade relations with the oaks growing around the margin. A good
proportion of the animals in the pool would probably turn out to be
insect larvae, and the kind of insects in the particular pool might
depend on whether the adults were able to fit into the conditions in
the surrounding forest. The acidity of the water in the pool might
depend on the soil character of the forest and on organic matter
washed into it from the forest in rains. If, in studying our pool, we
found that we had thus constantly to refer back to the forest, we could
hardly consider it as more than a special sort of "niche" in the general forest community.

On the other hand, a small lake would probably turn out to
form an intelligible field of study in itself. The naturalist studying the
lake could likely get along very well with only occasional and casual
reference to the communities inhabiting its shores. To understand the
physical environment of the lake, he would have to study its mode of
origin, whether from glacial action, from uplift across a stream drainage system, or from some more remote sequence of geological events.
He would be concerned with the depth of the lake and with the regional climate and its relation to temperatures at various depths. The
kind of fish populations inhabiting the lake and their density would
depend on host-prey relations among these populations, on the sort
of breeding places available in marginal vegetation, and their extent.
Even the larval insects found in the vegetation at the lake margins

would probably depend more on the characteristics of the lake community than on the characteristic of the forest community adjoining the lake.

If the lake were big enough, we might find that it was inhabited by a series of communities which formed intelligible fields of study in themselves. The problem of study of great lakes thus approaches in nature the problem of studying life in the sea. The lake takes on the character of a geographical region, inhabited by many kinds of communities, tied together chiefly by factors of the regional climate, and the regional geological history.

A biotic community may form an intelligible field of study, but it is never a completely isolated field of study. The birds that nest in the oak community may spend the winter in South America. Large mammals, especially predators such as the puma and jaguar, range through all kinds of communities, although the activities of a particular individual are usually confined to a rather limited area, perhaps a single community. The fluctuations in density of a particular species of organism in a given community may depend on factors that affect the population in the whole geographical region.

SUCCESSION: THE HISTORY OF COMMUNITIES

Nor are communities stable in time. Charles Elton has described this very well in a passage in his book on *Animal Ecology:*

"If it were possible for an ecologist to go up in a balloon and stay there for several hundred years quietly observing the countryside below him, he would no doubt notice a number of curious things before he died, but above all he would notice that the zones of vegetation appeared to be moving about slowly and deliberately in different directions. The plants around the edges of a pond would be seen marching inwards toward the center until no trace was left of what had once been pieces of standing water in a field. Woods might be seen advancing over grassland or heaths, always preceded by a vanguard of shrubs and smaller trees, or in other places they might be retreating; and he might see even from that height a faint brown scar marking the warren inhabited by the rabbits which were bringing this about. Again and again fires would devastate part of the country, low-lying areas would be flooded, or pieces of water dried up, and in every case it would take a good many years for the vegetation to reach its former state. Although bare areas would constantly be formed through various agencies, only a short time would elapse before they were clothed with plants once more."

If an area of forest is cleared, a crop planted, and the land then abandoned, this land will support a succession of plant communities of different types which will form an orderly sequence until finally the stable, terminal forest community again forms. The kinds of communities in the sequence depend on the general climate of the region and the specific soil and drainage characterstics of the cleared area. We are all familiar with the obvious stages in succession called "second growth," but some rather permanent-looking types of vegetation are essentially temporary. The pine forests of Florida, for instance, are maintained by the periodic burning which the pines withstand, but which kills the oaks. If such an area is long protected from burning, it slowly changes from a pine forest to an oak forest.

Ecologists in North America have been much preoccupied with the description of this succession process, and have subjected the phenomenon to elaborate study. This is useful, because such information is necessary for the proper management of our land resources; but it seems to me that these students have put an emphasis on succession that is out of all proportion to its general role in natural history.

This emphasis is understandable in North America because it is a continent that has been devastated by man, and my own indifference to succession undoubtedly stems from the fact that I have worked in areas as remote as possible from human interference. The effect of man on the landscape is profound and far-reaching. He must form the most powerful geological force at work on the surface of the earth today. The effects of floods, of hurricanes, of earthquakes, of volcanic erruptions, of natural erosion, the effect of all of these processes fades into insignificance beside the effect of man with an axe.

The man with the axe is an integral part of nature, and the consequences of his activities make an interesting and important, though dismal, field of study. But he is, geologically, a new sort of phenomenon, and study of his activities thus has only a limited usefulness in the attempt to reach an understanding of how biological processes came to be the way they are.

The effect of man on the biota of a region is really profound. This has been brought home to me because for many years, in the Villavicencio region of Colombia, I have alternated between the neighborhood of the town, where man is firmly established, and regions where he is still only a casual intruder. The common plants, the weeds, the roadside shrubs, the second-growth trees, where man has settled, are the rare plants in the areas where he has not yet penetrated. The common roadside butterflies, whose larvae feed on these weeds, are the scarcest of insects in the untouched areas. The balance of the whole fauna and flora, from the bacteria and protozoa of the soil to the trees and rodents, the snakes and predatory cats, has been changed.

Succession is a common and natural phenomenon, but man makes it universal in the areas where he settles. In this upper Orinoco country, where man is a rare animal, the weeds and shrubs and trees so common in the settled areas are found only on new sandbars in the rivers; in spots in the forest when a giant tree, felled by lightning, has pulled its neighbors down with it, and made a little opening in the forest; on mountainsides, where a slide of rocks has laid a surface bare. Succession, in an untouched area, is limited to situations like these.

Natural succession, as distinguished from the man-made variety, may be a striking and geologically rapid phenomenon in some sorts of places, especially along beaches, in sand dune country, and in fresh-water environments. There must also have been a succession of communities everywhere, through geological time. These changes were drastic and relatively rapid in some places and times, as in the temperate zone during Pleistocene glaciation; but they have surely been exceedingly slow in other areas, such as mid-continental South America.

THE HABITAT AND THE NICHE

"Community" and "succession" are common words in the ecological vocabulary. Equally common is "habitat". The habitat of an organism is the place where it occurs. It might thus be defined as the environment of a particular kind of organism. The habitat may be co-extensive with the community, may (rarely) include several types of communities, or may represent a niche in the community. The description of the habitat would include the physical and chemical environment as well as the biological environment (communal relationships).

Generally, the habitat of an organism corresponds to a particular niche in the community. I am using "niche" here in a slightly different sense from that usual among ecologists, but since I have diverged widely from custom in defining the community, perhaps I may also use the word niche in an unorthodox way.

Niche is customarily used "to describe the status of an animal in its community, to indicate what it is *doing* and not merely what it looks like" (Elton). The trouble with that, for me, is that niche has connotations of place—the dictionary says "a place, condition, or the like, suitable for a person or thing". I would prefer to use "role" to indicate what an organism does, and "niche" to indicate its physical place in the community structure. In a forest community, the organisms living free in the tree canopy would live in a niche; those ranging over the ground (what I like to call the forest floor zone) another niche; those among the litter of dead leaves, still another; those in the soil below the forest, still another niche.

There may be endless special niches. Tracing them out in a tropical forest is an especially fascinating game, and the multiplicity of niches in such a forest makes possible the diversity of kinds of organisms that, in their sum, make up the community. Thus the epiphytic plants (orchids, ferns, many cacti, air plants, and so forth) constitute a special niche of plants that get access to the light of the upper forest zones by perching on the branches of trees. The bromeliads or air plants, the family to which the pineapple belongs, are conspicuous members of this epiphytic niche, and they in themselves form yet another niche.

The bromeliads mostly have long narrow leaves that grow from a common center, where the bases of the leaves form a watertight vessel, which the botanists aptly call the "tank". A big bromeliad may have a lot of water—sometimes several quarts, though the average would be a pint or less. This water collects debris of all sorts, and becomes a quite rich infusion which serves as a source of food for the bromeliad, but it also in itself becomes the habitat of a complex fauna. The water in these bromeliads contains, besides a host of microscopic organisms, many kinds of insect larvae such as those of mosquitoes and damsel-flies, special worms and snails, and even the tadpoles of certain kinds of tree-frogs. This complex of organisms does not form a community because the relations within the bromeliad can only be understood in terms of the forest as a whole. A major proportion of the inhabitants of the niche are larval forms of organisms whose adults live free in the forest canopy; the bromeliad itself is an organism living in the canopy zone, and the physical characteristics of the water environment in the bromeliad tank are products of the forest climate.

ROLES IN THE BIOTIC COMMUNITY

Elton's concept of niche is more directly concerned with the kind of activity of the organism in the community, with its role. Thus among the animals in a community, there is a whole series of predators, ranging from very small predators that feed on tiny organisms to big predators that feed on big animals. There is a similarly graduated series of herbivores. As Elton points out, diverse animals may play closely similar roles in different kinds of communities in different parts of the world: in many different communities there is some species of large snake that preys exclusively on other snakes; some species of bird that specializes in picking ticks off large herbivores, and so forth.

These various roles are chiefly defined in terms of food, and most studies of the interrelations of animal populations in communities have been dedicated to the description of food-chains. The classical food-chain of the fleas has perhaps been best stated by some anonymous author:

> "Great fleas have little fleas upon their back to bite 'em,
> And little fleas have lesser fleas, and so *ad infinitum*.
> The great fleas themselves in turn have greater fleas to go
>   on,
> While these again have greater still, and greater still, and
>   so on."

Working out food-chains can become a fascinating occupation —one that still has not had anything like the attention that it deserves —but the resulting diagram is apt to give too rigid an impression of the animal relationships. Such chains start with some plant, or some type of vegetation, and begin the animal chain with the smallest kinds of animals that feed on the vegetation—what Elton calls "key industry animals" because they are apt to be present in enormous numbers and furnish food for a great number of predators. A very simple chain of this sort could be: grass — grasshoppers — frogs — snakes — hawks. But one could make the shorter chain of grass — deer — puma. And one could leave the long chain at any point by going to internal parasites, or smaller fleas, instead of to bigger predators.

The game of building food-chains is only practical with the animal members of the community. Yet the community may include also hundreds of different kinds of plants, existing in some sort of population balance that obviously doesn't depend on which plant eats which. The food-chains are complicated enough, but they are still too simple a method of expressing community relationships. They stress the competitive aspects of the community and I suspect that the stability of biotic communities depends on cooperative relationships at least as much as on competitive relationships.

In a food-chain the end is some master predator, big enough and strong enough to have no enemy in turn. This seems the lord of the community, as the lion is thought of as the king of beasts. Yet these top predators occupy about the least important role. The lion isn't the king of the community. He is found in a sort of community that is rich enough or luxuriant enough to be able to afford a few master predators.

The study of communities is complicated by the fact that it is not easily attacked by the experimental method. It is difficult to remove pieces of a community one at a time to see what happens, and only the very simplest sorts of communities can be maintained under laboratory control — communities that are perhaps too simple to serve as models for the relations under complex natural conditions. We are forced, then, to depend rather largely on observation and inference in the study of communal relationships, though there is considerable room for the development of the experimental method in studying individual kinds of relationships.

5 After reading the essay by Loren Eiseley, answer the following questions: Where does he switch focus from one unit to another, and what are the units? In terms of the chart, what perspectives dominate his discussion? Cite particular passages in support of your answer. What other perspectives are clearly apparent? Cite instances.

As we have seen in the Aztec example, exploration from several perspectives may enable the writer to understand what he at first understood poorly or not at all. He is then ready to share his newly discovered knowledge with a reader. On the other hand, a particular perspective, different from the one normally taken by the reader, may be what he wants to share; he may want to communicate the fact that there is another way of looking at a familiar unit of experience and describe what it looks like from this perspective. This seems to be Eiseley's goal. How do we normally view the units he discusses? Does he describe the normal perspectives? What alternative views does he present? Describe them in terms of the chart.

Choose a commonplace event (thing, or concept) in your own life or a familiar public one, and examine it from an unconventional perspective suggested by a cell, a row, or a column of the chart. If the results seem interesting, you may have the basis for an essay that will interest others.

from

Man, Time, and Prophecy
LOREN EISELEY

Like Weigall, the desert wanderer, I have done much walking in my younger years.[1] When I climbed I almost always carried seeds with me in my pocket. Often I liked to carry sunflower seeds, acorns, or any queer "sticktight" that had a way of gripping fur or boot tops as if it had an eye on Himalayas and meant to use the intelligence of others to arrive at them. I have carried such seeds up the sheer walls of mesas and I have never had illusions that I was any different to them from a grizzly's back or a puma's paw.

They had no interest in us—bear, panther, or man—but they were endowed with a preternatural knowledge that at some point we would lie down and there they would start to grow. I have, however, aided their machinations in a way they could scarcely have intended. I have dropped sunflower seed on stony mesa tops and planted cactus in Alpine meadows amidst the sounds of water and within sight of nodding bluebells. I have sowed northern seeds south and southern seeds north and crammed acorns into the most unlikely places. You can call it a hobby if you like. In a small way I, too, am a world-changer and hopefully tampering with the planetary axis. Most of my experiments with the future will come to nothing but some may not.

Life is never fixed and stable. It is always mercurial, rolling and splitting, disappearing and re-emerging in a most unpredictable fashion. I never make a journey to a wood or a mountain without experiencing the temptation to explode a puffball in a new clearing or stopping to encourage some sleepy monster that is just cracking out of the earth mold. It is, of course, an irresponsible attitude since I cannot tell what will come of it, but if the world hangs on such matters it may be well to act boldly and realize all immanent possibilities at once. Shake

---

[1]EDITORS' NOTE: Eiseley mentioned earlier the work of the archeologist Arthur Weigall, who, in his wandering in the Egyptian desert, came upon hewn stones addressed "to the Caesars" but never dispatched. In his account of the stones, Weigall remarks that there is nothing "in this time-forsaken valley which so brings the past before one as do these blocks awaiting removal to vanished cities. . . . A door seems to open in the brain. Two thousand years have the value of the merest drop of water."

the seeds out of their pods, I say, launch the milkweed down and set the lizards scuttling. We are in a creative universe. Let us then create. After all, man himself is the unlikely consequence of such forces. In the spring when a breath of wind sets the propellers of the maple seeds to whirring, I always say to myself hopefully, "After us the dragons."

To have dragons one must have change; that is the first principle of dragon lore. Otherwise everything becomes stale, commonplace, and observed. I suspect that it is this unimaginative boredom that leads to the vulgar comment that evolution may be all very well as a theory but you can never really see anything in the process of change. There is also the even more obtuse and less defensible attitude of those who speak of the world's creative energies as being exhausted, the animals small and showing no significant signs of advance. "Everything is specialized in blind channels," some scientists contend. "Life is now locked permanently in little roadside pools, or perching dolefully on television aerials."

Such men never pause to think how *they* might have looked gasping fishily through mats of green algae in the Devonian swamps, but that is where the *homunculus* who preceded them had his abode. I have never lost a reverent and profound respect for swamps, even individually induced ones. I remember too well what, on occasion, has come out of them. Only a purblind concern with the present can lead to such attitudes, and it is my contention that a sympathetic observer, even at this moment, can witness such marvels of transitional behavior, such hoverings between the *then* and *now,* as to lay forever to rest the notion that evolution belongs somewhere in the witch world of the past.

One may learn much in those great cemeteries of which Weigall spoke, those desolate Gobis and wind-etched pinnacles that project like monuments out of the waste of time itself. One must learn, however, to balance their weight of shards and bones against a frog's leap, against a crow's voice, against a squeak in the night or something that rustles the foliage and is gone. It is here that the deception lies. The living are never seen like the dead and the living appear to be so surely what they are. We lack the penetration to see the present and the onrushing future contending for the soft feathers of a flying bird, or a beetle's armor, or shaking painfully the frail confines of the human heart.

We are in the center of the storm and we have lost our sense of direction. It is not out of sadistic malice that I have carried cockleburs out of their orbit, or blown puffball smoke into new worlds. I wanted to see to what vicissitudes they might adapt, or in what mountain meadows the old thorns might pass away. One out of all those seeds may grope forward into the future and writhe out of its current shape. It is similarly so on the windswept uplands of the human mind.

Evolution is far more a part of the unrolling future than it is of the past, for the past, being past, is determined and done. The pres-

ent, in the words of Karl Heim, "is still in the molten phase of becoming. It is still undecided. It is still being fought for." The man
who cannot perceive that battleground looks vaguely at some animal
which he expects to transform itself before his eyes. When it does not
he shrugs and says, "Evolution is all very well but you cannot see it.
Besides it does not direct you. It only teaches you that you are an
animal and had better act like one."

Yet even now the thing we are trying to see is manifesting itself. Missing links, partial adaptations, transitions from one environ-
mental world to another, animals caught in slow motion half through
some natural barrier are all about us. They literally clamor for our attention. We ourselves are changelings. Like Newton, those who possess the inclination and the vision may play on the vast shores of the
universe with the living seeds of future worlds. Who knows, through
the course of unimaginable eons, how the great living web may vi-
brate slightly and give out a note from the hand that plucked it long
ago? In the waste dumps at city edges bloom plants that have changed
and marched with man across the ages since he sat by hill barrows
and munched with the dogs. A hand there, brown with sun, threw a
seed and the world altered. Perhaps, in some far meadow, a plant of
mine will survive the onset of an age of ice. Perhaps my careless act
will root life more firmly in the dying planetary days when man is
gone and the last seeds shower gallantly against the frost.

What is true biologically is also true along the peripheries of the
mind itself. We possess our own alpine meadows, excoriating heat,
and freezing cold. There have been, according to philosophers, political man, religious man, economic man. Today there are, variously,
psychological man, technological man, scientific man. Dropped seeds,
all of them, the mind's response to its environments, its defense
against satiety. He who seeks naïvely to embrace his own time will
accept its masks and illusions. The men of one period may turn completely to religious self-examination and become dogmatically con-
tentious. Our own age, by contrast, turns outward, as if in the flight
from self of which its rockets have become the symbol. It has been
well said by Philip Rieff that every personality cure seems to expose
man to a new illness. I believe it is because man always chooses to
rest on his cure.

We have forgotten the greatest injunction of the wise traveler
from Galilee. He did not say before the Pharisees "I know where I am
staying." Instead he observed that he knew where he was going. As is
true of all great prophets, he left something unspoken hanging in the
air. Men have chosen to assume that Jesus had knowledge of his
physical fate or that he was bound to some safe haven beyond mortal
reach. It seldom occurs to us that he was definitely engaged on a journey. If, in traveling that road, it led incidentally to a high place called
Golgotha, it was because his inward journey was higher and more
dangerous still.

Five centuries ago an unknown Christian mystic wrote thus of
heaven, which his contemporaries assumed to be a definable place:

"Heaven ghostly," he said, "is as high down as up, and up as down: behind as before, before as behind, on one side as another. Insomuch, that whoso had a true desire for to be at heaven, then that same time he were in heaven ghostly. For the high and the next way thither is run by desires and not by paces of feet."

Today our glimpses of heaven have become time-projected. They are secular; they are translated into paces measured by decades and centuries. Science is the assumed instrument and progress a dynamic flow, as is the heaven we seek to create or abjure. In final analysis we deceive ourselves. Our very thought, through the experimental method, is outwardly projected upon time and space until it threatens to lose itself, unexamined, in vast distances. It does not perform the contemplative task of inward perception.

The mysterious author of *The Cloud of Unknowing* spoke rightly and his words apply equally to that future we seek to conjure up. The future is neither ahead nor behind, on one side or another. Nor is it dark or light. It is contained within ourselves; it is drawn from ourselves; its evil and its good are perpetually within us. The future that we seek from oracles, whether it be war or peace, starvation or plenty, disaster or happiness, is not forward to be come upon. Rather its gestation is now, and from the confrontation of that terrible immediacy we turn away to spatial adventures and to imagination projected forward into time as though the future were fixed, unmalleable to the human will, and only to be come upon as a seventeenth-century voyager might descry, through his spyglass, smoke rising from an unknown isle.

Not so is the human future. It is made of stuff more immediate and inescapable: ourselves. If our thought runs solely outward and away upon the clever vehicles of science, just so will there be in that future the sure intellectual impoverishment and opportunism which flight and anonymity so readily induce. It will be, and this is the difficult obstacle of our semantics, not a future come upon by accident with all its lights and shadows, guiltless, as in a foreign sea. It will be instead the product of our errors, hesitations, and escapes, returning inexorably as the future which we only wished to come upon like a geographical discoverer, but to have taken no responsibility in shaping.

If, therefore, it is my occasional task to cast auguries, I will repeat as pertinent the further words of that long-vanished seer: "Be wary that thou conceive not bodily, that which is meant ghostly, although it be spoken bodily in bodily words as be these, up or down, in or out, behind or before. This thought may be better felt than seen; for it is full blind and full dark to them that have but little while looked thereupon." If we banish this act of contemplation and contrition from our midst, then even now we are dead men and the future dead with us. For the endurable future is a product not solely of the experimental method or of outward knowledge alone. It is born of compassion. It is born of inward seeing. The unknown one called it simply *All* and he added that it was not in a bodily manner to be wrought.

6   Describe a waterfall in terms of the chart on page 127. How does your choice of priorities of perspective (of particle or of wave or of field) differ from the choice you would normally make if you thought about a house or a tree? Do you feel a permanent tension between static and dynamic perspectives that is itself pleasant? In terms of your perception of the waterfall (rather than your writing about it), do you sense transitional zones from part to part? Nuclear zones? Anticipatory elements? What about variation in the form of the falls—how is that related to the more permanent aspects of the falls? How do the words *splash, spray, foam, gorge, channel, falls, roar, power, water, H₂O, curve,* relate to perspectives of particle, wave, and field? If you were describing the falls to an electricity developer in order to try to persuade him to buy it, what terms would you emphasize? How would you describe the falls if the potential buyer were interested in a sport such as salmon fishing? If the buyer were interested in the falls as a tourist attraction?

7   Isolate a problem in your experience, or select one that occurred to you as you read Chapter 5. Using the procedure we have described, explore the problem in order first to gather as much relevant information as you can and finally to develop one or more hypotheses that could conceivably solve the problem. In preparation for the next chapter, consider how you might test the adequacy of the hypotheses.

   You may want to try your hand at the following difficult alternative task. Some people regard Isaac Babel's "Crossing into Poland" (p. 69) as a mere sketch, as incomplete and undeveloped; others consider it a whole, well-developed story. We cannot reject either position out of hand, since they are held by intelligent and knowledgeable readers; hence we are confronted with a problematic situation. Can you finish formulating the problem, and can you solve it?

   In either case, write an essay explaining your problem and your solution to the other members of the class. Notice that a good deal of the information that you accumulate during the preparatory stage of the process of inquiry (e.g., the information resulting from efforts to formulate your problem and from exploring problematic units by means of the chart) may be useful in developing your essay.

Truth is what stands the test of experience.
ALBERT EINSTEIN, "The Laws of Science and the Laws of Ethics,"
Out of My Later Years

The learner, like the discoverer, must believe
before he can know.
MICHAEL POLANYI, *Personal Knowledge*

7 Verification: evaluating hypotheses

Without free speculation one cannot innovate, but without constraints innovation is not likely to be useful. An unlimited number of hypotheses can be dreamed up that in some never-never land might solve one's problem, but what is needed is a hypothesis that will work here and now. There is a world of difference between the imaginary and the imaginative. Useful solutions are limited in number and very difficult to come by. Finding them requires a special sort of intellectual freedom, a freedom constrained by the requirements of a search procedure and by a strong sense of reality. Effective inquiry requires, then, not mere mental adventure but reasonable adventure.

Three basic tests

A hypothesis is only a tentative solution to a problem and therefore must be evaluated. It may be true or untrue, reasonable or unreasonable, acceptable or unacceptable, elegant or inelegant. But how are such evaluations formed? The remark by Albert Einstein used above as an epigraph gives a very general answer: A sound hypothesis will stand the test of experience. More specifically, a sound hypothesis is one that (1) corresponds with actual experience, (2) is consistent with that fund of reliable knowledge we accumulate over the years, and (3) is actually useful in solving problems.

CORRESPONDENCE

Perhaps the most crucial test of a hypothesis is whether it is supported by immediate experience. A hypothesis has logically predictable consequences; if these predictions are borne out by experience, then the hypothesis is likely to be sound. Although this method of testing is a powerful tool in modern science, it is not a modern innovation, nor is it restricted to scientific investigation. It is simply one way in which the mind operates in the process of verification. For example, suppose that a light suddenly goes out in a room. You may hypothesize that the bulb has burned out, predict that it will not light up again even if you put it in another socket that you know is working, and then test your prediction. If the bulb does not light, the hypothesis gains credibility; but if it does burn, the hypothesis must be rejected and inquiry must begin anew.

In the Middle Ages this kind of verification procedure was formalized in what is called the trial by ordeal. A person suspected of being a witch, for example, might be forced to undergo the ordeal by water. In this trial the accused was bound and thrown into a lake or river. If he floated, he was considered guilty; if he sank, he was considered innocent. The assumption was that pure water would not receive a sinful person, and thus only the innocent sank. It was believed that God judged men in this way, and the test was designed to precipitate a divine judgment.

The scientist uses the same basic procedure but controls it much more carefully. For example, when the Dutch physician Christiaan Eijkman suspected that a vitamin deficiency produced polyneuritis, a disease of the nerves, he fed a group of chickens only polished rice, thus eliminating vitamins (which are contained in the grain husks) from their diet. He fed another group unpolished rice. None of the second group contracted polyneuritis, but all of the first group were stricken with the disease and died. As an additional test, Eijkman fed rice husks to polyneuritic chickens; they recovered. By these tests he succeeded in establishing vitamin deficiency as the cause of the disease. The difference between Eijkman's tests and the lightbulb test or trial by water lies not in the kind of procedure used but in the rigor with which his tests were carried out. Eijkman contrived a situation in which the results of his tests could be attributed only to the presence or absence of vitamins.

Each of the three examples illustrates a process that uses prediction and direct observation as the means for testing the truth of a hypothesis. As the discussion of trial by water shows, what predictions are made and how consequences are interpreted depend in part on prior beliefs, including those that gave rise to the hypothesis in the first place. Because the procedure is somewhat circular, extensive testing with carefully controlled variables under a variety of conditions is necessary to check the soundness of a hypothesis. One reason trial by water is not an adequate test is that all the variables are not taken into account. The quality of a person's moral state may not be the only cause of his sinking or floating.

CONSISTENCY

Usually a sound hypothesis is also consistent with one's image of the world, with that very considerable fund of information, beliefs, and values that are the products of past experience. As we pointed out earlier, such a system is incredibly complex and more or less integrated. New knowledge, therefore, is not simply added to it, as we might add a book to a shelf of books; rather it is assimilated into the system. Assimilation is likely to occur only if the new is harmonious or consistent with the old. Ordinarily, if a hypothesis is to be accepted, or even considered tenable, it must not violate what we believe to be true about the world. In William Golding's powerful novel *Lord of the Flies*, a group of schoolboys try to account for the mysterious and terrifying events that take place on the island where they have been stranded after a plane crash. They consider the possibility of monsters and ghosts, but one of the boys rejects this hypothesis, arguing that if there were ghosts, "things wouldn't make sense. Houses an' streets, an'—TV—they wouldn't work." "Life," he says, "is scientific." There is no room in his image of the world for the mysterious, the inexplicable, the supernatural. Similarly, many scientists today reject the notion of mental telepathy because it is incompatible with their beliefs about the transmission of information. For instance, a telepathic communication, unlike every other type of message, appears to be completely unaffected by the distance between receiver and sender.

A person is more likely to accept a hypothesis if it is consistent with his knowledge system. If, for instance, he believes the solar system to be made up of a nucleus (the sun) and a series of satellites in regular orbits (the planets), then he is likely to consider an image of the atom as a nucleus with satellites at least tenable and quite possibly true. And if he can conceive of the solar system and the atom in this image, then he may also find convincing an image of a nation as a nucleus, surrounded by satellites within its sphere of power. Likewise, a linear conception of time—that is, the image of time as a straight line extending from the past into an infinite future with particular dates (e.g., 1776, 1812, 1929) at particular points on the line—is likely to seem reasonable to a member of our culture: To us history means movement, and almost exclusively movement in one direction, from East to West, from primeval slime to man. Americans think of nations as evolving or progressing, of some as more advanced than others; such an image seems to us reasonable and true, in large part because it is already familiar from our linear image of time. Many other people, particularly in Asia, consider time to be a cycle of recurring events analogous to the life cycle of birth, growth, decay, and death. To them, time revolves like the cycle of the seasons or the daily rotation of the sun "around the earth." (We, too, say that the sun "comes up" and "goes down.") It is apparent, then, that prior beliefs influence what a person will believe.

The consistency test is conservative, for it may lead to the rejection of possible solutions to a problem if they cannot be integrated with a present set of beliefs, even when the hypothesis is shown to have predictive power. R. Taton's account of Ignaz-Philipp Semmelweiss's discovery of the cause of puerperal infection offers an illustration.

> In the middle of the nineteenth century puerperal fever was so rampant in maternity hospitals that women in labour were truly terrified. At the time speculations on its causes were fantastic rather than scientific; we need but mention the assumed influence of some foodstuffs and even of scents. During the autopsy of a laboratory assistant, who had died of an infection that he had contracted during a dissection, Semmelweiss noticed that some anatomical and pathological symptoms were similar to those observed in women who had died of puerperal fever. From this he concluded that both diseases had similar origins, and he was confirmed in this idea by his discovery that deaths from puerperal fever were much more common in clinics where students did their obstetrics without taking any of the precautions that today are a matter of routine. He immediately communicated his observations and ideas to the Medical Council of Vienna, and stated that puerperal fever was due to blood poisoning caused by the absence of antiseptic precautions. The rapid drop in mortality which followed upon the implementation of his advice that all who came into contact with women in labour should take care to wash their hands, and that wards should be disinfected by chlorination, was a remarkable justification of Semmelweiss's point of view.

However, the leading obstetricians of Vienna fought so bitterly against this thesis that Semmelweiss had to leave the hospital where he practised. In 1855 he was appointed professor at the University of Budapest, where he continued propounding his ideas. In 1861 he published his *On the etiology, the pathology, and the prophylaxis of puerperal fever*, in which these ideas were developed further and based on new observations. Refusing to accept clearly established facts, his adversaries redoubled the violence of their attacks to such a point that Semmelweiss had to abandon his Chair. Broken by such obstinacy and by the most vicious abuse, the Hungarian doctor some years later died a sad death in a lunatic asylum.

R. TATON, Reason and Chance in Scientific Discovery

When consistency is used as the only test of truth and other tests are ignored, the knowledge system becomes inflexible. One consequence of such inflexibility is that certain problems can become unsolvable, as we suggested in Chapter 5.

USEFULNESS

A less systematic test of a hypothesis, certainly a less reliable one than either its power of prediction or its relation to present knowledge, is its practical value. It is less reliable because a tentative solution may work for reasons other than the intrinsic soundness of the hypothesis; a nation's foreign policy, for example, may appear to be working when in fact other conditions in the world have combined to bring about some desired result. Nevertheless, if a hypothesis enables one to solve problems and, perhaps equally important, to ask new and useful questions, it should be taken seriously even though it may not have been carefully tested against experience or may not fit neatly into one's knowledge system. Man's intellect is constantly exploring unknown territory and at the same time seeking to make past experience more meaningful. A hypothesis that solves problems, poses productive questions, and offers new ways of viewing old knowledge is valuable no matter what conclusions one may draw about it using other tests.

Johannes Kepler's theory of the laws governing the motion of planets in the solar system is a good illustration of this kind of hypothesis. Like all investigators, Kepler worked from what he knew, and his background knowledge included mystical conceptions based on musical harmonics and on the relationship of geometric figures to the elements that they supposedly represented. He began by assuming that the planetary system was organized according to the five regular polyhedra described by ancient mathematicians. This initial hypothesis was faulty, but it was useful for two reasons: It provided a first approximation of a simple model of the planetary system, and it led to carefully directed observations, made by means of a telescope, of the planets themselves. Ultimately, of course, the hypothesis had to be tested against experience and revised, but even in its erroneous form it served Kepler as a point of departure. Inquiry is an ongoing process; the goal at any particular stage of the process is not Truth, absolute and unchanging, but partial truth, sufficient for the moment. Viewed in these terms, a questionable but useful hypothesis, an intelligent mistake, is better than no hypothesis at all. As the nineteenth-century English logician Augustus De Morgan remarked in *A Budget of Paradoxes*, "Wrong hypotheses, rightly worked, have produced more useful results than unguided observation."

USING THE TESTS

The three tests that have been discussed — correspondence, consistency, and usefulness — are not alternative tests. None can be used to the exclusion of the others without creating difficulties. Ignoring the relevance of reliable information accumulated in the past causes one to abandon the conceptual base from which all investigation begins and to interrupt what would otherwise be a steady growth in knowledge. Ignoring the importance of experience and factual demonstration produces intellectual stagnation. Ignoring the practical uses of a hypothesis tends to slow one's thinking and make it irrelevant to human affairs. Sound hypotheses are hard to come by precisely because they must meet all the tests, not just one.

No one has invented an absolutely foolproof way of recognizing truth. What a person accepts as truth is in part based on the testing procedures he believes to be adequate, but as we have said, these tests may be fallible. It is also based partially on features of his knowledge system, but many of these are idiosyncratic and most have never been verified in any systematic way. And it is in part based on its pragmatic value, but a "truth" may be useful for reasons other than the apparent ones. Experience, then, is not an infallible guide to truth, but it is the best guide we have.

Choosing among competing hypotheses

It sometimes happens that the result of inquiry is not one but several hypotheses, all of which seem, at least at first glance, to offer solutions to a problem. In such a case the process of evaluation must include choosing what seems to be the most reasonable one. This is not always easy; even in the physical sciences, the most precise of the disciplines, incompatible hypotheses may compete for acceptance. And in the social sciences and the humanities, the conclusive testing necessary for choosing is much more difficult to perform, if not at times impossible.

But there are some guides that can make the choice less arbitrary. The principal guide, again, is the appeal to experience: Which of the hypotheses is the most helpful for making predictions? The one that can explain the greatest amount of the data of experience, and the most *kinds* of data, is the best. Moreover, the hypothesis that does least violence to what we consider reliable knowledge accumulated from past experience should be chosen. There is also a third guide for choosing among competing hypotheses: The *simplest* hypothesis that can account for all the data and solves the problem is the best.

OCCAM'S RAZOR

Hypotheses often require that certain suppositions be made for which there is no factual evidence. The hypothesis that makes the fewest of these suppositions is likely to be the most reliable. William of Occam, a fourteenth-century English logician, formulated a principle that has come to be known as *Occam's Razor:* "Entities," he said, "must not be unnecessarily multiplied." If a hypothesis can be developed that solves the problem without introducing unverifiable suppositions, there is no reason for adopting other hypotheses that do introduce them. The simplest hypothesis is best, since it has the greatest empirical content and since it is the most easily tested. The principle of simplicity does not reject more complex hypotheses out of hand; it simply places on them the burden of proof. Unsupported suppositions should be introduced only if their omission is likely to cause error, and the necessity for adding these complications must be demonstrated.

Occam's Razor can be used to cut away unnecessary suppositions and to lead one to the best of several hypotheses. In *Walden,* Henry David Thoreau explains why he left the town of Concord to live alone in the woods near Walden Pond: "I went to the woods because I wished to live deliberately, to front only the essential facts of life, and see if I could not learn what it had to teach, and not, when I came to die, discover that I had not lived." One can accept Thoreau's explanation or reject it, as did one student who cynically remarked that Thoreau really went to the woods because he wanted wealth and lacked the ability to get it, that the experiment at Walden with its attack on American materialism was actually an elaborate rationalization for Thoreau's own inadequacies. Here, then, are two hypotheses: One says that Thoreau's explanation reliably accounts for his behavior; the other says that his explanation is a rationalization concealing his real motives. Which is preferable? Without looking more closely into the details of Thoreau's life, as we would have to do in a thorough investigation, we would probably find the first hypothesis preferable, not because we may happen to like Thoreau or dislike materialism, but because it is the simpler. The second rests on suppositions from which there is no apparent evidence: that Thoreau tried his hand at business and failed, that he had a secret yearning for wealth, and so on.

Arthur M. Eastman, a professor of English literature, explains how Occam's Razor can be used in literary criticism. He reports that "after reading 'Sir Patrick Spens,' which begins,

> The king sits in Dumferling toune,
>   Drinking the blude-reid wine:
> "O whar will I get guid sailor,
>   To sail this schip of mine?"

between one-fourth and one-third of the class immediately proclaim that the king is a sot. Now the problem is not to prove these miscreants wrong but to correct them without fertilizing their delusions. The teacher may resort to the historical approach and point out that wine was the common drink in the Scotland of many centuries ago. This will do the trick, but the delusions will begin to burgeon. Since not all the students are the children of teetotalers, the teacher can ask one whether his parents have ever taken a sip of wine. If the answer is Yes, he can then ask whether the parents are sots. Usually this will do the trick without benefit to the delusions, for it appeals to the student's own experience. (If the student says his parents *are* sots, however, it is best to turn rapidly to another ballad.) A third alternative is open to the teacher, however; he can here begin to use Occam's Razor. Certainly, some students will infer, not that the king is alcoholic, but that he is simply having casual refreshment, as, in another age, he might take afternoon tea. Both interpretations include all the data; which is simpler? The second, or course, for the first has to assume data that are not essential: a blood-red nose over the blood-red wine, continued drinking, etc.

ARTHUR M. EASTMAN, "Occam's Razor and Sophomore Poetry," *College English,* November, 1949

In choosing among alternative hypotheses, one should take Alfred North Whitehead's advice: "Seek simplicity and distrust it."

Most of us in our day-to-day lives seldom evaluate solutions to problems with such care; consciously testing every hypothesis— each of us formulates many every day—would be both impractical and unnecessary. Most problems are relatively simple, familiar, and inconsequential; we manage to muddle through them without testing carefully each solution we formulate. But when a problem is important, we are obligated to examine our thinking more critically. A solution must not be accepted simply because it *seems* believable — although this is the common practice. It should be accepted only when we believe it has been adequately tested, when we have demonstrated that it *is* believable. The quality of our beliefs is at issue.

EXERCISES

1 Read the following essay by Albert Einstein. What does he mean by *scientific laws, ethical laws,* and *experience?* How are ethical laws tested?

The Laws of Science and the Laws of Ethics
ALBERT EINSTEIN

Science searches for relations which are thought to exist independently of the searching individual. This includes the case where man himself is the subject; or the subject of scientific statements may be concepts created by ourselves, as in mathematics. Such concepts are not necessarily supposed to correspond to any objects in the outside world. However, all scientific statements and laws have one characteristic in common: they are "true" or "false" (adequate or inadequate). Roughly speaking, our reaction to them is "yes" or "no."

The scientific way of thinking has a further characteristic, the concepts which it uses to build up its coherent systems do not express emotions. For the scientist, there is only "being," but no wishing, no valuing, no good, no evil—in short, no goal. As long as we remain within the realm of science proper, we can never encounter a sentence of the type: "Thou shalt not lie." There is something like a Puritan's restraint in the scientist who seeks truth: he keeps away from everything voluntaristic or emotional. Incidentally, this trait is the result of a slow development, peculiar to modern Western thought.

From this it might seem as if logical thinking were irrelevant for ethics. Scientific statements of facts and relations, indeed, cannot produce ethical directives. However, ethical directives can be made rational and coherent by logical thinking and empirical knowledge. If we can agree on some fundamental ethical propositions, then other ethical propositions can be derived from them, provided that the original premises are stated with sufficient precision. Such ethical premises play a similar role in ethics to that played by axioms in mathematics.

This is why we do not feel at all that it is meaningless to ask such questions as: "Why should we not lie?" We feel that such questions are meaningful because in all discussions of this kind some ethical premises are tacitly taken for granted. We then feel satisfied when we succeed in tracing back the ethical directive in question to these basic premises. In the case of lying, this might perhaps be done in some way such as this: Lying destroys confidence in the statements of other people. Without such confidence, social co-operation is made impossible or at least difficult. Such co-operation, however, is essential in order to make human life possible and tolerable. This means that the rule "thou shalt not lie" has been traced back to the demands: "Human life shall be preserved" and "Pain and sorrow shall be lessened as much as possible."

But what is the origin of such ethical axioms? Are they arbitrary? Are they based on mere authority? Do they stem from experiences of men and are they conditioned indirectly by such experiences?

For pure logic all axioms are arbitrary, including the axioms of ethics. But they are by no means arbitrary from a psychological and genetic point of view. They are derived from our inborn tendencies to avoid pain and annihilation, and from the accumulated emotional reaction of individuals to the behavior of their neighbors.

It is the privilege of man's moral genius, expressed by inspired individuals, to advance ethical axioms which are so comprehensive and so well founded that men will accept them as grounded in the vast mass of their individual emotional experiences. Ethical axioms are found and tested not very differently from the axioms of science. Die Wahrheit liegt in der Bewährung. Truth is what stands the test of experience.

2 Analyze the following passages. What is the problematic situation in each? What is the unknown? What hypothesis is proposed? How is it tested?

a It is well known that there are two main types of "flowers" among the higher plants. Many plants have small green blossoms without any scent, and the transfer of pollen is effected by the air. Such plants produce an abundance of pollen, which is spread by the wind and comes by chance to other blossoms of the same species. Other plants have conspicuous, brightly colored blossoms or a striking scent, or both, and it is these that we ordinarily call flowers. Only such flowers produce nectar and are therefore visited by insects, which effect the pollination by flying from one flower to the next. Biologists have long believed that flowers are colored and scented to make them more striking for their insect visitors. In this way the insects can more easily find the flowers and get their food; and the pollination is also assured.

But this view has not been accepted by all biologists. About 1910 a famous ophthalmologist, Professor C. von Hess, performed many experiments on fishes, insects, and other lower animals. He tested them while they were in a positively phototactic condition — that is, under circumstances where they moved into the brightest available light. He found that in a spectrum the animals always collected in the green and the yellow-green region, which is the brightest part of the spectrum for a color-blind human eye. Therefore, von Hess asserted, fishes and invertebrates, and in particular bees, are totally colorblind. If this were true, the colors of flowers should have no biological significance. But I could not believe it, and my skepticism was the first motive which led me to begin my studies of bees about forty years ago. I tried to find out whether bees have a color sense.

By the scent of a little honey it is possible to attract bees to an experimental table. Here we can feed them on a piece of blue cardboard, for example. They suck up the food and, after carrying it back to the hive, give it to the other bees. The bees return again and again to the rich source of food which they have discovered. We let them do so for some time, and then we take away the blue card scented with honey and put out two new, clean pieces of cardboard at the site of the former feeding place — on the left a blue card, and on the right a red one. If the bees remember that they found food on blue, and if they are able to distinguish between red and blue, they should now alight on the blue card. This is exactly what happens.

This is an old experiment. It indicates that bees can distinguish colors, but it does not prove that they have a color sense, or color perception, for these are not always the same. Thus there are totally color-blind men, although they are very rare. They see objects as we would see them in a black-and-white photograph. Yet they can distinguish between red and blue, for red appears very dark to them, and blue much lighter. Hence we cannot learn from the experiment with bees which I have just described whether the bees have distinguished red from blue by color or by shade, as a color-blind man might do. To a totally color-blind man each color appears as a gray of a certain degree of brightness. We do not know what the brightness of our various pieces of colored cardboard may be for a color-blind insect. Therefore we perform the following experiment.

On our table we place a blue card and around it we arrange gray cards of all shades from white to black. On each card we set a little watch glass, but only the glass dish on the blue card contains food (sugar-water). In this way we train the bees to come to the color blue. Since bees have a very good memory for places we frequently change the relative positions of the cards. But the sugar is always placed on the blue card so that in every case the color indicated where food is to be found. After some hours we perform the decisive experiment. The cards and the glass dishes soiled by the bees are taken away. We place on the table a new series of clean cards of different shades of gray, each with an empty glass dish, and somewhere among them we place a clean, blue card provided, like all the others, with an empty glass dish. The bees remember the blue color and alight only on the blue card, distinguishing it from all shades of gray. This means that they have a true color sense.

KARL VON FRISCH, *Bees: Their Vision, Chemical Senses, and Language*

b Aristotle, being interested both in biology and in astronomy, found himself faced with an obvious contrast. The characteristic of the world we men inhabit is incessant change by birth, growth, procreation, death, and decay. And within that world such experimental methods as had been achieved in his time could discover only an imperfect uniformity. Things happened in the same way not perfectly nor invariably but 'on the whole' or 'for the most part.' But the world studied by astronomy seemed quite different. No *Nova* had yet been observed. So far as he could find out, the celestial bodies were permanent; they neither came into existence nor passed away. And the more you studied them, the more perfectly regular their movements seemed to be. Apparently, then, the universe was divided into two regions. The lower region of change and irregularity he called Nature. . . . The upper he called Sky. . . . Thus he can speak of 'Nature and Sky' as two things. But that very changeable phenomenon, the weather, made it clear that the realm of inconstant Nature extended some way above the surface of the Earth. 'Sky' must begin higher up. It seemed reasonable to suppose that regions which differed in every observable respect were also made of different stuff. Nature was made of the four elements, earth, water, fire, and air. Air, then (and with air Nature, and with Nature inconstancy) must end before Sky began. Above the air, in true Sky, was a different substance, which he called *aether*. Thus, 'the *aether* encompasses the divine bodies, but immediately below the aethereal and divine nature comes that which is passible, mutable, perishable, and subject to death'.

C. S. LEWIS, *The Discarded Image*

C In ancient days two aviators procured to themselves wings. Daedalus flew safely through the middle air and was duly honoured on his landing. Icarus soared upwards to the sun till the wax melted which bound his wings and his flight ended in fiasco. In weighing their achievements, there is something to be said for Icarus. The classical authorities tell us that he was only "doing a stunt," but I prefer to think of him as the man who brought to light a serious constructional defect in the flying-machines of his day. So, too, in Science. Cautious Daedalus will apply his theories where he feels confident they will safely go; but by his excesses of caution their hidden weaknesses remain undiscovered. Icarus will strain his theories to the breaking-point till the weak joints gape.

SIR ARTHUR EDDINGTON, *Stars and Atoms*

d [In the following passage from *The Romance of Tristan and Iseult*, one of the world's great love stories, Iseult is being tried by her husband,

King Mark, for adultery with Tristan. Tristan is present at the trial, disguised as a pilgrim.]

On the appointed day King Mark and Iseult, and the barons of Cornwall, having ridden as far as White-Lands, arrived in fine array at the river, and massed on the other shore, the hosts of Arthur bowed their brilliant standards to them.

And just before them, sitting on the shore, was a poor pilgrim, wrapped in cloak and hood, who held his wooden platter and begged alms, in piercing, mournful tones.

Now as the Cornish boats came to the shoal of the further bank, Iseult said to the knights:

"My lords, how shall I land without befouling my clothes in the river-mud? Fetch me a ferryman."

And one of the knights hailed the pilgrim, and said:

"Friend, truss your coat, and try the water; carry you the Queen to shore, unless you fear the burden."

But as he took the Queen in his arms she whispered to him:

"Friend."

And then she whispered to him, lower still:

"Stumble you upon the sand."

And as he touched shore, he stumbled, holding the Queen in his arms; and the squires and boatmen with their oars and boat-hooks drove the poor pilgrim away.

But the Queen said:

"Let him be; some great travail and journey has weakened him."

And she threw to the pilgrim a little clasp of gold.

Before the tent of King Arthur was spread a rich Nicean cloth upon the grass, and the holy relics were set on it, taken out of their covers and their shrines.

And round the holy relics on the sward stood a guard more than a king's guard, for Lord Gawain, Girflet, and Kay the seneschal kept ward over them.

The Queen having prayed God, took off the jewels from her neck and hands, and gave them to the beggars around; she took off her purple mantle, and her overdress, and her shoes with their precious stones, and gave them also to the poor that loved her.

She kept upon her only the sleeveless tunic, and then with arms and feet quite bare she came between the two Kings, and all around the barons watched her in silence, and some wept, for near the holy relics was a brazier burning.

And trembling a little she stretched her right hand towards the bones and said: "Kings of Logres and of Cornwall; my lords Gawain, and Kay, and Girflet, and all of you that are my warrantors, by these holy things and all the holy things of earth, I swear that no man born of woman has held me in his arms saving King Mark, my lord, and that poor pilgrim who only now took a fall, as you saw. King Mark, will that oath stand?"

"Yes, Queen," he said, "and God see to it."

"Amen," said Iseult, and then she went near the brazier, pale and stumbling, and all were silent. The iron was red, but she thrust her bare arms among the coals and seized it, and bearing it took nine steps.

Then, as she cast it from her, she stretched her arms out in a cross, with the palms of her hands wide open, and all men saw them fresh and clean and cold. Seeing that great sight the Kings and the barons and the people stood for a moment silent, then they stirred together and they praised God loudly all around.

JOSEPH BÉDIER, *The Romance of Tristan and Iseult*, trans. Hilaire Belloc

e Outside the Clayborn Temple in downtown Memphis last Saturday, 20-year-old Willie Barnes, a black activist, said, "I've always been non-violent.

"I don't believe in violence as a method of getting things done. But if you try everything else and it still comes . . . then you just let it come."

DAVID WEIR AND ALISON SYMROSKI, "The Death of Non-Violence," *Michigan Daily*, April 6, 1968

3 Suppose you read the following account in a newspaper:

Early Tuesday morning Henry Smith of 120 Berkshire Road rented a boat from the Mermaid Boat Livery. Smith told the proprietor he intended to spend the day fishing on Lake Michigan. That afternoon a storm came up that authorities claim was one of the worst in the history of the area. The boat has been found, but Smith has not been located. Smith's wife told the Sheriff's Department that Smith could not swim. It is presumed he drowned.

What is the problematic situation? What is the unknown? What hypothesis is offered as a solution? Is it reasonable? Test it by the three methods we have discussed. Do tenable alternative hypotheses exist? Suggest several. Which one is preferable? Apply the tests discussed in the chapter. What additional information would serve to confirm the hypothesis that you prefer? What would lead you to change your preference?

4 Someone once said that when a person writes the first draft of an essay he must believe he is right; when he writes the second draft he must consider that he might be wrong. Certainly at some point in the process of writing, the writer must stand aside and look at his work as an outsider might. Part of his job as a writer is to be believable, to make what he presents to the

reader seem convincing. Write a brief essay in which you explain a problem and your solution of it to someone else. What must you include to make your hypothesis understandable and believable to your reader? Select as your problem one on which you worked in Chapter 5 or 6; or, if you prefer, write on the problem in Exercise 3 of this chapter.

As a guide to thinking, reread Charles Nicholle's "Mechanism of the Transmission of Typhus" (p. 78) and ask yourself why Nicholle had to test his hypothesis. Would his essay be an appropriate report on his discovery to present to a group of scientists? Why? Might it be a part of a larger report? Where in the report would it be placed? Why?

No man is an Island, entire of itself;
every man is a piece of the Continent, a part of the main.
JOHN DONNE, *Devotions upon Emergent Occasions*

Remember the first law of mating:
No love without propinquity!
HUGHES MEARNS, *Creative Power*

8 Writer and reader: prerequisites for change

Part one

No man is an island, yet, paradoxically, each of us is an island. We are all related in numerous and complex ways to other members of society, but each of us is continually reminded of the range and depth of divisions among men. Each man has a unique image of the world; each has unique desires. The uniqueness is relative, however, rather than absolute: A man is more different or less different; he is never absolutely different. Even the most sophisticated members of modern society share much with the most primitive tribes in the most remote parts of the world; the most ardent members of an ideological faction have much in common with their bitterest political enemies.

Whatever other purposes rhetoric may serve, it is, fundamentally, a means for achieving social cooperation: The writer's goal is to engage in some sort of cooperative activity with the reader. Achieving this cooperation requires change—change sometimes in the reader, sometimes in both the reader and the writer. The writer wants the reader to know what he knows, or to act in a way that benefits both of them, or to accept, or at least understand, the values that he accepts, and so on. Writing and speaking are the principal means that man has developed for promoting social cooperation and, hence, for maintaining and improving a civilized community.

Shared features as bridges

The motive for communication arises from an awareness of difference and a desire to eliminate it or at least to modify it. But there can be no interaction between writer and reader, and no changes in their thinking, unless they hold certain things in common, such as shared experiences, shared knowledge, shared beliefs, values, and attitudes, shared language. Things that are completely separated from each other cannot interact; this is as true of human minds as it is of anything else. This assumption can be stated formally as Maxim 5: *Change between units can occur only over a bridge of shared features.* Shared features, then, are prerequisites for interaction and change.

The maxim can be illustrated by the behavior of a friend of one of the authors, who works with American Indians. On entering an Indian community, she asks the Indians she works with to teach her how to be polite. (All societies have rules for good manners, although the rules vary from society to society.) Soon her knowledge of good manners becomes a fragile bridge over which more complex interaction can occur. This is, of course, an unusual situation; because we generally communicate with people who understand our language and whose images are more nearly similar to our own, bridges are usually more numerous and easier to find. But the maxim still holds true.

Shared features are, however, only prerequisites for change. *Unless the writer actively makes use of them, there will be no interaction.* The writer may acknowledge that interaction depends on sharing, but he does not always write as if he believed it. He frequently takes too much for granted, assuming that merely by speaking his mind he can change the reader's. If he fails, however, to utilize available bridges or to create new ones, his writing will not be effective. Thus it is not enough that bridges exist; they must be used — and therein lies much of the art of rhetoric.

UTILIZING THE READER'S KNOWLEDGE

Suppose someone wants to explain the distinction between nuclear and marginal focus. He begins by telling his audience that nuclear focus is centered attention and marginal focus is marginal awareness. If the audience replies that the distinction is not clear, he then explains that he has in mind the phenomenon discussed by Michael Polanyi in Chapter 4 of *Personal Knowledge*. They protest that they have not read the book; he tries again. "When we drive a nail with a hammer," he says, "we are aware of both hammer and nail, but aware of them in different ways. Our attention is centered on the effect of the hammer on the nail, but we are also aware of the hammer in our hand, of the sensations in our hand that help us guide our blows. The point of contact between hammer and nail is the center of attention, but we have a marginal awareness of the other related events that are occurring simultaneously." Finally they understand.

This exchange may be described as a quest for a bridge that will enable the speaker to convey his generalization. He first attempts to transfer it directly, but his listeners cannot assimilate it. He then tries to make it available by attaching to it information that he assumes will fall within their range of experience, but his assumption is unfounded. Finally, he manages to illustrate the generalization with an experience that does exist in their image of the world. This example is the means by which the audience is able to attach the generalization to their image.

Whenever someone asks to be given an example, which is perhaps the most common method of clarifying a generalization, he is asking us to find something in his image to which he can relate our generalization; he is asking for a familiar instance of the generalization that will provide a bridge between his image and ours. Many failures in both spoken and written communication arise from the assumption that information can be transferred without its being attached to the audience's image. The fact that a listener or a reader can parrot what he has heard or read is no indication that he has understood it. He must be able to relate the information to his own experience of the world.

UTILIZING THE READER'S VALUES

Probably the most difficult kind of writing assignment is the one that involves important attitudes and values. It is easier to convey new information to a reader than to persuade him to accept a position that conflicts with the values he regards as central to his image of the world. The situation is potentially explosive, and dealing with it requires of the writer considerable tact and sensitivity. For example, imagine a northern liberal trying to persuade a southern conservative of the desirability of the 1964 Voting Rights Act. Obviously they differ in their attitudes and values on many subjects — among them, the legitimacy and importance of states' rights and the dignity and equality of black men. They may share other attitudes and values, however, that can be bridges over which communication can occur—perhaps regard for the democratic principles of universal suffrage and the individual's right to control his own destiny; perhaps repugnance for oppression. A combination of several such bridges is likely to be more effective than a single one. In situations like this one, often the best the writer can hope for is a softening of the reader's position or an increase in his willingness to consider alternative positions.

One important question for a writer to ask in such a situation is whether an individual's values are hierarchically structured, whether some values are more important to his reader than others. Various psychologists and rhetoricians have argued that this is the case, and we can all find instances in our own experience that support their view. It seems easier to persuade someone to change the kind of car he drives than to change his political party, and easier to persuade him to change his party than his form of government. "Better dead than Chevrolet" is absurd, as is, for most people, "better dead than Democrat." But to many of the same people, "better dead than Red" makes sense. Similarly, in wartime, local animosities tend to disappear as people unite for their common defense. These examples suggest that some values take priority over others in our images of the world. Values, like so many other things, appear to be ordered hierarchically in people's minds.

If some values are more important than others to the coherence, stability, and economy of the reader's image, it follows that the writer must do more than merely make use of the values he shares with the reader. He must choose for exploitation those shared values that have priority over the unshared values. It is not clear exactly how he can determine which values in the reader's image are dominant and which subordinate; there are no rules that can guarantee right answers. Certainly the writer must make a careful assessment of his reader's habits of thinking, but even then he may not choose correctly—so little is known about the workings of the human mind.

An illustration may help to clarify the ways in which a writer can use shared values as bridges. In his first inaugural address, Abraham Lincoln made a sensitive and eloquent attempt to close the widening rift between the southern leaders and the supporters of the federal government. After discussing the nature of their differences and the undesirable consequences of secession, he concluded his speech by asking,

> Why should there not be a patient confidence in the ultimate justice of the people? Is there any better or equal hope in the world? In our

present differences is either party without faith of being in the right? If the Almighty Ruler of Nations, with His eternal truth and justice, be on your side of the North, or on yours of the South, that truth and that justice will surely prevail by the judgment of this great tribunal of the American people.

By the frame of the Government under which we live this same people have wisely given their public servants but little power for mischief, and have with equal wisdom provided for the return of that little to their own hands at very short intervals. While the people retain their virtue and vigilance no Administration by any extreme of wickedness or folly can very seriously injure the Government in the short space of four years.

My countrymen, one and all, think calmly and *well* upon this whole subject. Nothing valuable can be lost by taking time. If there be an object to *hurry* any of you in hot haste to a step which you would never take *deliberately*, that object will be frustrated by taking time; but no good object can be frustrated by it. Such of you as are now dissatisfied still have the old Constitution unimpaired, and, on the sensitive point, the laws of your own framing under it; while the new Administration will have no immediate power, if it would, to change either. If it were admitted that you who are dissatisfied hold the right side in the dispute, there still is no single good reason for precipitate action. Intelligence, patriotism, Christianity, and a firm reliance on Him who has never yet forsaken this favored land are still competent to adjust in the best way all our present difficulty.

In *your* hands, my dissatisfied fellow-countrymen, and not in *mine*, is the momentous issue of civil war. The Government will not assail *you*. You can have no conflict without being yourselves the aggressors. *You* have no oath registered in heaven to destroy the Government, while *I* shall have the most solemn one to "preserve, protect, and defend it."

I am loath to close. We are not enemies, but friends. We must not be enemies. Though passion may have strained it must not break our bonds of affection. The mystic chords of memory, stretching from every battlefield and patriot grave to every living heart and hearthstone all over this broad land, will yet swell the chorus of the Union, when again touched, as surely they will be, by the better angels of our nature.

ABRAHAM LINCOLN, "First Inaugural Address"

Notice what Lincoln does. After acknowledging that important differences on the issue of slavery exist, he argues that they are not sufficiently important to warrant secession, that the democratic process, given time, will reconcile these differences in a wise and just way. He assumes that both North and South share a faith in this process. He further assumes a shared faith in the Constitution and in Christianity, both of which, if relied on, will make war unnecessary. In closing he refers to still other common bonds—a shared love of country and a shared past. That the war came is no indication that he failed as a writer. There are limits to the power of words.

UTILIZING THE READER'S SOCIAL RELATIONSHIPS

Other kinds of sharing also characterize good writing. The society in which each of us lives is not simply a collection of similar people, like a bag of marbles. The members of a society are organized in a hierarchical system of roles that require certain kinds of behavior. "Professor," for example, is a role in a particular subsystem of society, a university. Those who fill this role are expected to behave in a certain way: teach courses, grade papers, consult with students, do research and publish the results, and so on. They occupy a certain position in the university system: above associate professors, assistant professors, and instructors; either above or below administration officials, depending on the university and the criteria it uses for ranking. One person usually belongs to several subsystems: The professor may also be a father, a member of a professional society, a citizen of a town, state, and country, and so on. In each system he has a particular role and engages in behavior appropriate to that role.

The sensitive writer is aware of both his own position in the social system and that of his readers, and he writes accordingly. To communicate effectively, writer and reader must share similar conceptions of their social roles and of the behavior appropriate to them. A student ought not to expect his professors to listen carefully if he talks down to them. Nor in most cases should a son talk to his father as an equal—not, at least, if he wishes to avoid irritating him. In our society, even a disinterested listener will often become uncomfortable when he hears a child addressing his father by his first name instead of calling him *Father* or *Dad.*

The conventions of letter-writing offer a simple illustration of the ways in which people adjust their writing to changing social relationships. A writer generally addresses older people, or strangers, or those higher in the social system with salutations indicating respect, such as *Dear Sir* or *Dear Professor Smith*; but he may address friends and those lower in the system by their first names. The different closing phrases used in letters (*Respectfully yours, Sincerely, Cordially, Love*) make similar distinctions. Social relationships are reflected not just in common conventions like these but also, implicity, throughout all well-written prose. To succeed in communicating, therefore, the writer must share with the reader an awareness of their relationship within a social system.

ESTABLISHING THE IMPORTANCE OF THE SUBJECT

We have discussed how a writer can utilize shared knowledge, attitudes, and values. Without implying that we have exhausted the subject, we will mention only one more kind of sharing that directly affects what the writer says and will leave it to you to continue the inquiry. When the reader gives his attention to a written work, he expects something in return. He may expect, for example, that the work will satisfy some need or that it will help him solve some problem. When he reads for more than mere entertainment or momentary diversion, he must believe that his reading will have one of two effects: that it will give him greater control over his environment or that it will help him to a more accurate image of the world. In addition, then, to the other sorts of sharing already discussed, writer and reader must share a sense of the importance of the subject.

The critical reader wants to know why he should read. At times he has such a strong interest in a subject that the writer need not dwell on its importance. Lincoln's audience knew why they should listen. But why would a discussion of nuclear and marginal focus be worth paying attention to? The reader should be told how he can use the information or at least how the concept of focus reveals unsuspected relationships between what seem to be isolated experiences. Failure to explain the importance of a subject can result in ineffective writing, much of which is merely skimmed and forgotten. By asking himself why a subject is significant to him, the writer can often discover the information needed to make it significant to the reader. Some subjects, however, may not be important to anyone but the writer. Discussions of these subjects belong in a journal.

We have stressed the idea that if people are to interact, they can do so only over bridges of shared language, experience, knowledge, and values. The metaphor of a bridge is worth examining more closely, for the characteristics of an actual bridge over a river can give us insight into the characteristics of a rhetorical bridge. We can travel over an actual bridge in two directions; because traffic seldom moves in one direction only, changes may occur at either end of the bridge. Consider this example: A man crosses a bridge to go to work, buys goods with the money he earns, and brings them home with him. Something is different at each end of the bridge.

We can find analogous situations by examining other sorts of bridges. A Peace Corps worker constitutes a bridge between our society and another. His work may change his hosts, but when he returns to this country he brings new knowledge and attitudes that may produce changes in our own society. In developing bridges, one cannot expect changes to occur in only one direction. If a person doesn't want to change, he had better not create the conditions that make interaction possible; the atheist who comes to a religious service to scoff may remain to pray.

When the writer builds bridges he must accept the possiblity that he, as well as his reader, may be changed. Of course he may use rhetorical techniques to manipulate others for his own ends, seeking to change them while insulating himself from ideas that might force changes in his own mind. Advertisements, political prose, legal prose, and propaganda are rich in examples of this kind of writing. But if the writer seeks to establish a true community by means of his words, he himself must be willing to change.

Discovering relevant bridges

Since effective communication requires that the writer develop his discourse in terms of what he shares with his reader, he must first know what features are shared. If he lacks this knowledge, he is confronted with a problematic situation, and the discovery of bridges becomes a special instance of the process of inquiry. When the writer knows his reader well (a parent, a close friend, a business associate), he has no problem, for they understand each other; they "talk each other's language." The bridges between them have been learned informally, often unconsciously, through long and intimate acquaintance. But when the audience is less well known to the writer, difficulties arise. Here the speaker has a great advantage over the writer, for a speaker who is alert to his listener's responses (a scowl, a wrinkled brow, a request for more information) can backtrack to introduce the needed bridges, as did, in the example above, the person explaining nuclear and marginal focus. But the writer must anticipate the reader's responses before he presents his ideas. To the extent that he fails to anticipate them accurately, he fails to communicate.

There is, of course, no infallible method for discovering relevant bridges; the writer cannot search through a reader's mind as he might through an encyclopedia. He can, however, increase his chances of discovering the necessary information by employing the heuristic procedure discussed in Chapter 6. The entire set of questions may be used, although those in the first row alone provide a simple guide for describing the reader. And this is what the writer lacks, a description of the reader or, more precisely, of those characteristics of the reader that are relevant to what the writer wants to communicate.

A reader, like an oak tree or a house, has contrastive features that separate him from other people, features that identify him. He also varies over a period of time: His knowlege of the world, his values and attitudes—including his attitude toward the writer and the writer's subject—change, just as his physical make-up changes. Furthermore, he belongs to certain classes: He is a member of various organizations (church, political party, fraternity). He is also distributed both in time—he exists at a certain point in history (personal, political, social, intellectual)—and in space—he lives somewhere (town, state, nation). Finally, he can be located in a system or in systems of categories, as we located the professor in his different social roles. All these probes can be used to describe a group of readers as well as a single reader, although the larger and more diverse the group is, the more difficult it is for the writer to describe it in any useful way.

The result of this procedure is a more complex image of the reader. The writer usually has some idea of what the reader is like, some preconception, but often it is too simple, a stereotype. The less experience he has had with his reader, the more likely the writer is to imagine him as something like what literary critics call a "flat character." By encouraging the writer to note a number of the reader's contrastive features, to observe the way he actually changes over a period of time, and to examine the various contexts within which he acts and is acted upon, the heuristic procedure tends to correct the writer's stereotypes. It is important to remember that the writer addresses his discourse not to the reader as he "really is" but to the image of the reader that he has developed in his own mind. It is not who the reader is but who the writer thinks he is that counts.

Suppose that a student interested in physics wants to describe a recent invention, a fuel cell, for example, to the members of his composition class. He might begin his quest for shared features by asking:

1) "How do my fellow students differ from other readers?"
   a) They differ from a class of physics students in that they probably have more varied backgrounds in science.
   b) They differ from newspaper readers in that on the whole they probably have more intellectual curiosity.
   c) They differ from engineering students in that they have widely different vocational and academic interests.
2) "What is the range of variation of my audience?" Although in terms of membership it is still the same class that began the semester, it has changed in certain ways.
   a) Since concrete explanation and definition of terms have been stressed in class, the students are likely to look for these features in his paper.

b) The last time the writer wrote for the class, one student said he didn't know what he was talking about and proved it. At the beginning of the semester the writer was an unknown; now he has a reputation to overcome.

3) "What is the distribution of my audience in class, sequence, space, and array?"

a) In class, they are university students, freshmen, socially and economically middle-class, and so on.

b) In sequence and space, all are freshmen in their late teens; most are urban midwesterners, and so on.

c) In systems of categories, they are, as freshmen, at the bottom of the undergraduate hierarchy; they are potential members of widely different disciplines within the university community.

The process is open-ended. For each area of inquiry, the student might ask many more related questions.

Once the writer has pushed the description as far as seems useful, he makes *inferences* about what his fellow students share that is relevant to the topic of fuel cells. He guesses about their knowledge and values on the basis of what he has learned about them so far. He may infer that they are probably familiar with basic electrical terminology (direct and alternating currents, positive and negative poles), but it would be unwise to assume much more, unwise to assume familiarity with physical laws and technical symbols. He may infer that they are probably familiar with zinc-acid batteries (the kind of battery found in automobiles, which might offer a good analogy) and that they are probably interested in recent technological advances, particularly in such glamorous ones as space and undersea exploration, in which fuel cells are used.

Although for the sake of clarity we have made the exploration rather mechanical, you should use the probes not as a rigid set of questions to be answered but as suggestions for speculation. Ultimately, it is your knowledge and imagination that are important. If you are led to insights beyond those called for by the procedure, so much the better. The procedure will have done its job.

EXERCISES

1 A principle is an eye to see with. "Looking" through Maxim 5 (change between units can occur only over a bridge of shared features), analyze the following passages. What social or personal price must one pay to use the suggested bridges?

a If you are in a region inhabited by native peoples make every effort
to get in touch with them and ask them for help. You run little danger
if you approach them in a friendly manner. Never show fear, or
threaten, or flourish a gun. As a rule it is fear on the part of natives
that makes them attack strangers and if you do nothing to cause concern you will be perfectly safe. Go up to them as you would to individuals of your own race and color, smile, offer a cigarette if you have
one, and make your wants known. You may need to use signs to
show them what you want — food, water, or directions — but natives
are accustomed to such procedure, as they often communicate in that
fashion themselves and will understand. The important thing is to
treat them with dignity. Most of them have a strong sense of self-respect and do not regard themselves as "natives" or primitive. They
will appreciate being treated as human beings just like yourself, neither as inferiors nor as superiors.

   Should the natives be inclined to be shy or unapproachable do
not rush matters by going right up to them. Stop where you are. Sit
down and light up a smoke. If you know any tricks with string, take
out a piece and proceed to do things with it. Most natives have and
are fond of an elaborate variety of string figures, such as the familiar
cat's cradle, which they make for their own amusement and on some
occasions for ceremonial purposes. They also are very curious and in
a short time some of them may not be able to hold back any longer
and will come to see what you are doing. When they do, hand them
the string and they will probably show you a few tricks. If you don't
have string take out some trinket and show interest in it. They will
want to see, too. Once the ice is broken, you can go ahead and ask for
what you need. This method of approach has been used many times
in many parts of the world by those going to study native peoples
and rarely has it failed to produce the desired results.

   U. S. OFFICE OF NAVAL INTELLIGENCE, *Survival on Land and Sea*

b If he only understands the language of a rifle, get a rifle. If he only
understands the language of a rope, get a rope. But don't waste time
talking the wrong language to a man if you really want to communicate with him.

   MALCOLM X, *Malcolm X Speaks*

c Editor, The News:

   Because I am not accustomed to agreeing with Mr. ———'s letters to the
editor, (nor, I presume, is he with mine) I should like to make special
note of the fact that a point of agreement has been glimpsed. Albeit
we both have a personal reason for interest and pride in the production, "Showtime USA" presented at ——— School, the performance
had a quality that demanded our admiration above and beyond the call
of parental (or "auntal") pride. Someone there had dreamed big and
had drawn upon and marshalled unexpected resources and unsuspected talents to make the dream into a reality.

There was so exquisite a disregard for the racial differences of the performers that each child (and there were some 300 of them) did have a chance to do and be recognized for that which he could do best and well. If there appeared at first glance to be deplorable instances of type casting the roles in another scene were so switched that one was ashamed to have even noted the previous casting at all. These folk went a giant step beyond our usual meticulous, self-conscious avoidance of any move that might be construed as either overt or subtle discrimination. Adult society could well take a lesson here and be humbled by the fact that once again it is the children who can lead us.

And further there is promise that Mr. ———— and I might find other areas of agreement. I feel better to know that he was caught, as was I, by the magic woven by a community of teachers, children and parents into the "stupendous, tremendous, star-spangled" production, "Showtime, USA."

Ann Arbor News, June 8, 1965

d [In the first of the following excerpts from Warren Miller's *The Cool World,* the narrator, a member of a black street gang in Harlem, describes the thoughts that he had after helping to kill Angel, the leader of a rival Puerto Rican gang. In the second excerpt, he speaks of his life in a reformatory after his arrest.]

They all Porto Ricans an the record store got loud speakers over the doors playin Porto Rican music. People walkin up and down talkin and laughin . . . I want to say to them. "Stop laughin I could stop you laughin if I told you. You Angel dead an layn in the bushes at the projeck."

The other guys is ok. Some of them all they think about is gettin back with the gangs again. They dont like it here. I got a friend name Ramon. Thats Raymond in Porto Rican. We in the same room an some days he help me with the flowers even though it not his job. He takin up carpentry.

WARREN MILLER, *The Cool World*

e [Helen Keller, left deaf and blind by a brain injury she suffered when she was nineteen months old, described in her autobiography the following incident from her early childhood.]

I had dolls which talked, and cried, and opened and shut their eyes; yet I never loved one of them as I loved poor Nancy. She had a cradle, and I often spent an hour or more rocking her. I guarded both doll and cradle with the most jealous care; but once I discovered my little sister sleeping peacefully in the cradle. At this presumption on the part of one to whom as yet no tie of love bound me I grew angry. I rushed upon the cradle and overturned it, and the baby might have been killed had my mother not caught her as she fell. Thus it is that when we walk in the valley of twofold solitude we know little of the tender affections that grow out of endearing words and actions and companionship. But afterward, when I was restored to my human heritage, Mildred and I grew into each other's hearts, so that we were content to go hand-in-hand wherever caprice led us . . . .

HELEN KELLER, *The Story of My Life*

f A plumber once wrote to a research bureau pointing out that he had used hydrochloric acid to clean out sewer pipes and inquired, "Was there any possible harm?" The first reply was as follows: "The efficacy of hydrocholoric acid is indisputable, but the corrosive residue is incompatible with metallic permanence." The plumber then thanked them for the information approving his procedure. The dismayed research bureau tried again, saying, "We cannot assume responsibility for the production of toxic and noxious residue with hydrochloric acid and suggest you use an alternative procedure." Once again the plumber thanked them for their approval. Finally, the bureau, worried about the New York sewers, called in a third scientist who wrote: "Don't use hydrochloric acid. It eats hell out of the pipes."

EDGAR DALE, "Clear Only If Known,"*The News Letter*, Ohio State University

2 The following passage is from Fred Hoyle's *The Nature of the Universe*. From the language he uses can you infer for whom the passage was written? Make as extensive a list as you can of the bridges that Hoyle exploits to communicate his ideas.

You might like to know something about the observational evidence that the Universe is indeed in a dynamic state of expansion. Perhaps you've noticed that a whistle from an approaching train has a higher pitch, and from a receding train a lower pitch, than a similar whistle from a stationary train. Light emitted by a moving source has the same property. The pitch of the light is lowered, or as we usually say reddened, if the source is moving away from us. Now we observe that the light from the galaxies is reddened, and the degree of reddening increases proportionately with the distance of a galaxy. The natural explanation of this is that the galaxies are rushing away from each other at enormous speeds, which for the most distant galaxies that we can see with the biggest telescopes become comparable with the speed of light itself.

My nonmathematical friends often tell me that they find it difficult to picture this expansion. Short of using a lot of mathematics I cannot do better than use the analogy of a balloon with a large number of dots marked on its surface. If the balloon is blown up the distances between the dots increase in the same way as the distances between the galaxies. Here I should give a warning that this analogy must not be taken too strictly. There are several important respects in which it is definitely misleading. For example, the dots on the surface of a balloon would themselves increase in size as the balloon was being blown up. This is not the case for the galaxies, for their internal gravitational fields are sufficiently strong to prevent any such expansion. A further weakness of our analogy is that the surface of an ordinary balloon is two-dimensional—that is to say, the points of its surface can be described by two co-ordinates; for example, by latitude and longitude. In the case of the Universe we must think of the surface as possessing a third dimension. This is not as difficult as it may sound. We are all familiar with pictures in perspective—pictures in which artists have represented three-dimensional scenes on two-dimensional canvases. So it is not really a difficult conception to imagine the three dimensions of space as being confined to the surface of a balloon. But then what does the radius of the balloon represent, and what does it mean to say that the balloon is being blown up? The answer to this is that the radius of the balloon is a measure of time, and the passage of time has the effect of blowing up the balloon. This will give you a very rough, but useful, idea of the sort of theory investigated by the mathematician.

The balloon analogy brings out a very important point. It shows we must not imagine that we are situated at the center of the Universe, just because we see all the galaxies to be moving away from us. For, whichever dot you care to choose on the surface of the balloon, you will find that the other dots all move away from it. In other words, whichever galaxy you happen to be in, the other galaxies will appear to be receding from you.

FRED HOYLE, *The Nature of the Universe*

3 Societies, as well as individuals, interact if, and only if, there are bridges between them, such as trade, travel, translation, colonization, and military occupation. Can you cite specific examples of such bridges and of the changes that result from interaction across them? For example, the rapid expansion of European trade into the Far East in the nineteenth century resulted in changes in European art, which began to employ perspectives characteristic of Chinese and Japanese art. Certain bridges have been crucial in the development of societies, civilizations, even the entire world—an ocean voyage that changed the course of history, a translation that brought together two intellectual worlds, a conquest that altered the direction of a society's growth. In terms of our assumptions about change, state your reasons for choosing the examples that you list.

4 Imagine that you are the leader of a totalitarian society and that you want to preserve your position; that is, you want to retain absolute control over the country and to maintain the

status quo. What steps could you take to prevent the occurrence of changes that might work to your disadvantage? Be specific. As a guide, examine the practices of actual dictators. Considering our comments on the prerequisites for change, can you account for their actions?

5   Think of an individual or a group with whom you have strong differences. What, specifically, are these differences? What bridges exist? What bridges might be created?

6   Using the heuristic procedure discussed on pages 178–180, analyze an audience for whom you are planning to write. What is it you want to communicate; that is, what is the unshared experience? What are the relevant features of the audience? From these features, what bridges can you infer that might be exploited? For practice, analyze your own class, substituting it for the composition class described on pages 179–180.

7   Read the following essay by E. B. White. In terms of the discussion in this chapter, explain what White is doing. What does he give as his reason for doing it?

Khrushchev and I
(A Study in Similarities)
E. B. WHITE
September 26, 1959

Until I happened to read a description of him in the paper recently, I never realized how much Chairman Khrushchev and I are alike. This fellow and myself, it turns out, are like as two peas. The patterns of our lives are almost indistinguishable, one from the other. I suppose the best way to illustrate this striking resemblance is to take up the points of similarity, one by one, as they appear in the news story, which I have here on my desk.

Khrushchev, the story says, is a "devoted family man." Well, now! Could any phrase more perfectly describe me? Since my marriage in 1929, I have spent countless hours with my family and have performed innumerable small acts of devotion, such as shaking down the clinical thermometer and accidentally striking it against the edge of our solid porcelain washbasin. My devotion is too well known to need emphasis. In fact, the phrase that pops into people's heads when they think of me is "devoted family man." Few husbands, either in America or in the Soviet Union, have hung around the house, day in and day out, and never gone anywhere, as consistently as I have and over a longer period of time, and with more devotion. Sometimes it isn't so much devotion as it is simple curiosity—the fun of seeing what's going to happen next in a household like mine. But that's all right, too, and I wouldn't be surprised if some of the Chairman's so-called devotion was simple curiosity. Any husband who loses interest in the drama of family life, as it unfolds, isn't worth his salt.

Khrushchev, the article says, "enjoys walking in the woods with his five grandchildren." Here, I have to admit, there is a difference between us, but it is slight: I have only three grandchildren, and one of them can't walk in the woods, because he was only born on June 24th last and hasn't managed to get onto his feet yet. But he has been making some good tries, and when he does walk, the woods are what he will head for if he is anything like his brother Steven and his sister Martha and, of course, me. We all love the woods. Not even Ed Wynn loves the woods better than my grandchildren and me. We walk in them at every opportunity, stumbling along happily, tripping over windfalls, sniffing valerian, and annoying the jay. We note where the deer has lain under the wild apple, and we watch the red squirrel shucking spruce buds. The hours I have spent walking in the woods with my grandchildren have been happy ones, and I hope Nikita has had such good times in his own queer Russian way, in those strange Russian woods with all the bears. One bright cold morning last winter, I took my grandchildren into the woods through deep snow, to see the place where we were cutting firewood for our kitchen stove (I probably shouldn't tell this, because I imagine Khrushchev's wife has a modern gas or electric stove in her house, and not an old woodburner, like us Americans). But anyway, Martha fell down seventeen times, and Steven disappeared into a clump of young skunk spruces, and I had all I could do to round up the children and get them safely out of the woods, once they had become separated that way. They're young, that's the main trouble. If anything, they love the woods too well.

The newspaper story says Khrushchev leads a "very busy" life. So do I. I can't quite figure out why I am so busy all the time; it seems silly and it is against my principles. But I know one thing: a man can't keep livestock and sit around all day on his tail. For example, I have just designed and built a cow trap, for taking a Hereford cow by surprise. This job alone has kept me on the go from morning till night for two weeks, as I am only fairly good at constructing things and the trap still has a few bugs in it. Before I became embroiled in building the cow trap, I was busy with two Bantam hens, one of them on ten eggs in an apple box, the other on thirteen eggs in a nail keg. This kept me occupied ("very busy") for three weeks. It was rewarding work, though, and the little hens did the lion's share of it, in the old sweet barn in the still watches of the night. And before that it was haying. And before haying it was baby-sitting—while my daughter-in-law was in the hospital having John. And right in the middle of everything I went to the hospital myself, where, of course, I became busier than ever. Never spent a more active nine days. I don't know how it is in

Russia, but the work they cut out for you in an American hospital is almost beyond belief. One night, after an exhausting day with the barium sulphate crowd, I had to sit up till three in the morning editing a brochure that my doctor handed me—something he had written to raise money for the place. Believe me, I sank down into the covers tired *that* night. Like Khrushchev, I'm just a bundle of activity, sick or well.

Khrushchev's wife, it says here, is a "teacher." My wife happens to be a teacher, too. She doesn't teach school, she teaches writers to remove the slight imperfections that mysteriously creep into American manuscripts, try though the writer will. She has been teaching this for thirty-four years. Laid end to end, the imperfections she has taught writers to remove from manuscripts would reach from Minsk to Coon Rapids. I am well aware that in Russia manuscripts do not have imperfections, but they do in this country, and we just have to make the best of it. At any rate, both Mrs. Khrushchev and my wife are teachers, and that is the main point, showing the uncanny similarity between Khrushchev and me.

Khrushchev, it turns out, has a daughter who is a "biologist." Well, for goodness' sake! *I* have a *step*daughter who is a biologist. She took her Ph.D. at Yale and heads the science department at the Moravian Seminary for Girls. Talk about your two peas! Incidentally, this same stepdaughter has three children, and although they are not technically my grandchildren, nevertheless they go walking in the woods with me, so that brings the woods total to five, roughly speaking, and increases the amazing similarity.

Khrushchev's son is an "engineer," it says. Guess what college my son graduated from! By now you'll think I'm pulling your leg, but it's a fact he graduated from the Massachusetts Institute of Technology. He hasn't launched a rocket yet, but he has launched many a boat, and when I last saw him he held the moon in his hand—or was it a spherical compass?

"The few hours Khrushchev can spare for rest and relaxation he usually spends with his family." There I am again. I hope when Khrushchev, seeking rest and relaxation, lies down on a couch in the bosom of his family, he doesn't find that a dog has got there first and that he is lying on the dog. That's my biggest trouble in relaxing—the damn dog. To him a couch is a finer invention than a satellite, and I tend to agree with him. Anyway, in the hours I can spare for rest, it's family life for me. Once in a great while I sneak down to the shore and mess around in boats, getting away from the family for a little while, but every man does that, I guess. Probably even Khrushchev, devoted family man that he is, goes off by himself once in a great while, to get people out of his hair.

Already you can see how remarkably alike the two of us are, but you haven't heard half of it. During vacations and on Sundays, it says, Khrushchev "goes hunting." That's where I go, too. It doesn't say what Khrushchev hunts, and I won't hazard a guess. As for me, I hunt the croquet ball in the perennial border. Sometimes I hunt the flea. I hunt the pullet egg in the raspberry patch. I hunt the rat. I hunt the hedgehog. I hunt my wife's reading glasses. (They are in the pocket of her housecoat, where any crafty hunter knows they would be.) Nimrods from away back, Khrush and I.

Khrushchev has been an "avid reader since childhood." There I am again. I have read avidly since childhood. Can't remember many of the titles, but I read the books. Not only do I read avidly, I read slowly and painfully, word by word, like a child reading. So my total of books is small compared to most people's total, probably smaller than the Chairman's total. Yet we're both avid readers.

And now listen to this: "Mr. Khrushchev is the friend of scientists, writers, and artists." That is exactly my situation, or predicament. Not all scientists, writers, and artists count me their friend, but I do feel very friendly toward Writer Frank Sullivan, Artist Mary Petty, Scientist Joseph T. Wearn, Pretty Writer Maeve Brennan, Artist Caroline Angell, Young Writer John Updike—the list is much too long to set down on paper. Being the friend of writers, artists, and scientists has its tense moments, but on the whole it has been a good life, and I have no regrets. I think probably it's more fun being a friend of writers and artists in America than in the Soviet Union, because you don't know in advance what they're up to. It's such fun wondering what they're going to say next.

Another point of similarity: Mr. Khrushchev, according to the news story, "devotes a great deal of his attention to American-Soviet relations." So do I. It's what I am doing right this minute. I am trying to use the extraordinary similarity between the Chairman and me to prove that an opportunity exists for improving relations. Once, years ago, I even wrote a book about the relations between nations. I was a trifle upset at the time, and the book was rather dreamy and uninformed, but it was good-spirited and it tackled such questions as whether the moon should be represented on the Security Council, and I still think that what I said was essentially sound, although I'm not sure the timing was right. Be that as it may, I'm a devoted advocate of better relations between nations—Khrush and I both. I don't think the nations are going about it the right way, but that's another story.

"No matter how busy Khrushchev is," the article says, "he always finds time to meet Americans and converse with them frankly on contemporary world problems." In this respect, he is the spit and image of me. Take yesterday. I was busy writing and an American walked boldly into the room where I was trying to finish a piece I started more than a year ago and would have finished months ago except for interruptions of one sort and another, and what did I do? I shoved everything aside and talked to this American on contemporary world problems. It turned out he knew almost nothing about them, and I've *never* known much about them, God knows, except what I see with my own eyes, but we kicked it around anyway. I have never been so busy that I wouldn't meet Americans, or they me. Hell, they drive right into my driveway, stop the car, get out, and start talking about contemporary problems even though I've never laid eyes on them before. I don't have the protection Khrushchev has. My dog welcomes any American, day or night, and who am I to let a dog outdo me in simple courtesy?

Mr. Khrushchev, the story goes on, "has a thorough knowledge of argiculture and a concern for the individual worker." Gee whizz, it's me all over again. I have learned so much about agriculture that I have devised a way to water a cow (with calf at side) in the barn cellar without ever going down the stairs. I'm too old to climb down stairs carrying a twelve-quart pail of water. I tie a halter rope to the bail of the pail (I use a clove hitch) and lower the pail through a hatch in the main floor. I do this after dark, when the cow is thirsty and other people aren't around. Only one person ever caught me at it — my granddaughter. She was enchanted. Ellsworth, my cow, knows about the routine, and she and her calf rise to their feet and walk over to the pail, and she drinks, in great long, audible sips, with the light from my flashlight making a sort of spot on cow and pail. Seen from directly above, at a distance of only four or five feet, it is a lovely sight, almost like being in church — the great head and horns, the bail relaxed, the rope slack, the inquisitive little calf attracted by the religious light, wanting to know, and sniffing the edge of the pail timidly. It is, as I say, a lovely, peaceable moment for me, as well as a tribute to my knowledge of agriculture. As for the individual worker whom Khrushchev is concerned about, he is much in my mind, too. His name is Henry.

Well, that about winds up the list of points of similarity. It is perhaps worth nothing that Khrushchev and I are not *wholly* alike — we have our points of difference, too. He weighs 195, I weigh 132. He has lost more hair than I have. I have never struck the moon, even in anger. I have never jammed the air. I have never advocated peace and friendship; my hopes are pinned on law and order, the gradual extension of representative government, the eventual federation of the free, and the end of political chaos caused by the rigidity of sovereignty. I have never said I would bury America, or received a twenty-one-gun salute for having said it. I feel, in fact, that America should not be buried. (I like the *Times* in the morning and the moon at night.) But these are minor differences, easily reconciled by revolution, war, death, or a change of climate. The big thing is that both Khrushchev and I like to walk in the woods with our grandchildren. I wonder if he has noticed how dark the woods have grown lately, the shadows deeper and deeper, the jay silent. I wish the woods were more the way they used to be. I wish they were the way they could be.

8 Read the selection from Bruno Bettelheim's *The Informed Heart*. In what ways does his discussion illustrate and clarify the points made in this chapter?

from

The Informed Heart
BRUNO BETTELHEIM

. . . In the winter of 1938 a Polish Jew murdered the German attaché in Paris, vom Rath. The Gestapo used the event to step up anti-Semitic actions, and in the camp new hardships were inflicted on Jewish prisoners. One of these was an order barring them from the medical clinic unless the need for treatment had originated in a work accident.

Nearly all prisoners suffered from frostbite which often led to gangrene and then amputation. Whether or not a Jewish prisoner was admitted to the clinic to prevent such a fate depended on the whim of an SS private. On reaching the clinic entrance, the prisoner explained the nature of his ailment to the SS man, who then decided if he should get treatment or not.

I too suffered from frostbite. At first I was discouraged from trying to get medical care by the fate of Jewish prisoners whose attempts had ended up in no treatment, only abuse. Finally things got worse and I was afraid that waiting longer would mean amputation. So I decided to make the effort.

When I got to the clinic, there were many prisoners lined up as usual, a score of them Jews suffering from severe frostbite. The main topic of discussion was one's chances of being admitted to the clinic. Most Jews had planned their procedure in detail. Some thought it best to stress their service in the German army during World War I: wounds received or decorations won. Others planned to stress the severity of their frostbite. A few decided it was best to tell some "tall story," such as that an SS officer had ordered them to report at the clinic.

Most of them seemed convinced that the SS man on duty would not see through their schemes. Eventually they asked me about my plans. Having no definite ones, I said I would go by the way the SS man dealt with other Jewish prisoners who had frostbite like me, and proceed accordingly. I doubted how wise it was to follow a preconceived plan, because it was hard to anticipate the reactions of a person you didn't know.

The prisoners reacted as they had at other times when I had voiced similar ideas on how to deal with the SS. They insisted that one SS man was like another, all equally vicious and stupid. As usual, any frustration was immediately discharged against the person who caused it, or was nearest at hand. So in abusive terms they accused me of not wanting to share my plan with them, or of intending to use one of theirs; it angered them that I was ready to meet the enemy unprepared.

No Jewish prisoner ahead of me in line was admitted to the clinic. The more a prisoner pleaded, the more annoyed and violent the SS became. Expressions of pain amused him; stories of previous services rendered to Germany outraged him. He proudly remarked that *he* could not be taken in by Jews, that fortunately the time had passed when Jews could reach their goal by lamentations.

When my turn came he asked me in a screeching voice if I knew that work accidents were the only reason for admitting Jews to the clinic, and if I came because of such an accident. I replied that I knew the rules, but that I couldn't work unless my hands were freed of the dead flesh. Since prisoners were not allowed to have knives, I asked to have the dead flesh cut away. I tried to be matter-of-fact, avoiding pleading, deference, or arrogance. He replied: "If that's all you want, I'll tear the flesh off myself." And he started to pull at the festering skin. Because it did not come off as easily as he may have expected, or for some other reason, he waved me into the clinic.

Inside, he gave me a malevolent look and pushed me into the treatment room. There he told the prisoner orderly to attend to the wound. While this was being done, the guard watched me closely for signs of pain but I was able to suppress them. As soon as the cutting was over, I started to leave. He showed surprise and asked why I didn't wait for further treatment. I said I had gotten the service I asked for, at which he told the orderly to make an exception and treat my hand. After I had left the room, he called me back and gave me a card entitling me to further treatment, and admittance to the clinic without inspection at the entrance.

THE VICTIM

This incident may serve as a starting point for discussing certain aspects of minority discrimination as a psychological defense, since it was so widespread in the camps.

There is, of course, a significant difference between aggressor and victim in the origin of this particular defense. As many have observed, the aggressor defends himself mainly against dangers that originate in himself. The victim, in his counterreaction, defends himself mainly against dangers originating in the environment; namely, the threat of persecution. But as time goes on, both defensive reactions become more a function of inner motive than outer pressure, although the individual keeps thinking they come only from without. Since both sides are now responding more to inner drives than outside reality, it becomes understandable that their reactions have significant features in common.

For example, both Jews and SS behaved as if psychological mechanisms comparable to paranoid delusions were at work in them. Both believed that members of the other group were sadistic, uninhibited, unintelligent, of an inferior race, and addicted to sexual perversions. Both groups accused each other of caring only for material goods and of having no respect for ideals, or for moral and intellectual values. In each group there may have been individual justification for some of these beliefs. But the strange similarity indicates that both groups were availing themselves of analogous mechanisms of defense. Moreover, each group thought of the other in terms of a stereotype and was thus prevented from realistically evaluating any member of the other group and thus its own situation. Unfortunately members of minority groups, in my example the Jews, were much more in need of being able to reason clearly.

During my camp experience I was impressed by the unwillingness of most prisoners to accept the fact that the enemy consisted of individuals, not just so many replicas of one and the same type. Yet they had had enough close experience with some SS to know of great individual variations. Jews realized that the SS had formed a nonsensical stereotyped picture of *the* Jew and assumed that all Jews were alike. They knew how untrue the picture was, yet they oversimplified in exactly the same way when they thought of *the* SS.

This raises the question of why prisoners could not accept the idea of individual differences among the SS. If, at the clinic entrance, they overlooked the soldier's individuality in forming their plans, some psychological mechanism prevented it. Their violent reaction to my lack of preparedness offers the necessary clue.

Prisoners seemed to derive some security and emotional relief from their preconceived, more or less elaborate, fixed plans. But these plans were based on the assumption that one SS reacted like another. Any attitude throwing their stereotyped picture of *the* SS into question aroused fears that their plans might not succeed. Without plans they would have had to face a dangerous situation without armor, with only miserable anxiety about the unknown. They were neither willing nor able to suffer such anxiety, so they assured themselves they could predict the SS man's reaction and hence plan accordingly. My insistence on approaching the SS as an individual threatened their delusional security, and their violent anger against me becomes understandable as a reaction to the threat.

Overcoming anxiety was by no means the only reason prisoners thought in stereotype of the SS. Other important functions were also fulfilled. For instance, the stereotyped picture contained, among other features, the idea that every SS man was of low intelligence, little education, low social and cultural status. These characteristics, though true for some, were ascribed to all, because otherwise their contempt for the prisoners could not be dismissed so easily. What a stupid or a depraved person thinks can be disregarded. But if those who think badly of us are intelligent and honest, then our self respect is threatened. So whatever the reality, the aggressor had to be thought stupid so that the prisoner could preserve at least a minimal self esteem.

Unfortunately, the prisoners were at the mercy of the SS. It is damaging enough to one's self respect to have to humble oneself. Even worse is having to grovel before a person of undesirable character. The prisoners therefore faced a dilemma. Either the SS were at least their equals, for instance, in intelligence, and their charges against the prisoners carried weight as the opinion of discerning men; or else the SS were stupid, and their charges could be dismissed. But in that case the prisoners had to see themselves as submissive to vastly inferior persons. For their own inner status they could not do that, particularly since many SS demands were unreasonable and amoral. The very fact that they had to obey SS orders made the SS their superiors in what they themselves lacked most, namely, actual power.

The prisoners solved this conflict by thinking of the SS as superior in some other way, though vastly inferior intellectually and morally. They thought of them as all-powerful adversaries and pretended they were not even humans. As they invested the SS with inhuman characteristics, it became possible to submit to them without being degraded. They could admit, without losing self respect, that they were unable to fight against inhuman brutality or an all-powerful conspiracy.

Inside the camps the personal contacts of prisoners with SS were frequent, but not of such a nature as to permit a real understanding of what went on in the minds of the guards. In order to understand SS behavior the prisoners had to fall back on their own experiences. The only way they could explain and understand the actions of the SS was by imputing to them motives they were familiar with. Thus they projected into the stereotype of *the* SS most, if not all, of those undesirable motives and characteristics they knew best, namely, their own. By projecting into the SS everything they considered evil, the SS became still more powerful and threatening. But the process of projection kept them from using to advantage any chance of viewing the SS man as a real person; it forced them to see him only as an *alter ego* of pure evil.

9 Read the following essay by James Baldwin. What differences separate Baldwin from the villagers? What similarities does he share with them and with white Americans?

Stranger in the Village
JAMES BALDWIN

From all available evidence no black man had ever set foot in this tiny Swiss village before I came. I was told before arriving that I would probably be a "sight" for the village; I took this to mean that people of my complexion were rarely seen in Switzerland, and also that city people are always something of a "sight" outside of the city. It did not occur to me — possibly because I am an American — that there could be people anywhere who had never seen a Negro.

It is a fact that cannot be explained on the basis of the inaccessibility of the village. The village is very high, but it is only four hours from Milan and three hours from Lausanne. It is true that it is virtually unknown. Few people making plans for a holiday would elect to come here. On the other hand, the villagers are able, presumably, to come and go as they please—which they do: to another town at the foot of the mountain, with a population of approximately five thousand, the nearest place to see a movie or go to the bank. In the village there is no movie house, no bank, no library, no theater, very few radios, one jeep, one station wagon; and, at the moment, one typewriter, mine, an invention which the woman next door to me here had never seen. There are about six hundred people living here, all Catholic—I conclude this from the fact that the Catholic church is open all year round, whereas the Protestant chapel, set off on a hill a little removed from the village, is open only in the summertime when the tourists arrive. There are four or five hotels, all closed now, and four or five *bistros*, of which, however, only two do any business during the winter. These two do not do a great deal, for life in the village seems to end around nine or ten o'clock. There are a few stores, butcher, baker, *épicerie*, a hardware store, and a money-changer—who cannot change travelers' checks, but must send them down to the bank, an operation which takes two or three days. There is something called the *Ballet Haus*, closed in the winter and used for God knows what, certainly not ballet, during the summer. There seems to be only one schoolhouse in the village, and this for the quite young children; I suppose this to mean that their older brothers and sisters at some point descend from these mountains in order to complete their education—possibly, again, to the town just below. The landscape is absolutely forbidding, mountains towering on all four sides, ice and snow as far as the eye can reach. In this white wilderness, men and women and children move all day, carrying washing, wood, buckets of milk or water, sometimes skiing on Sunday afternoons. All week long boys and young men are to be seen shoveling snow off the rooftops, or dragging wood down from the forest in sleds.

The village's only real attraction, which explains the tourist season, is the hot spring water. A disquietingly high proportion of these tourists are cripples, or semi-cripples, who come year after year—from other parts of Switzerland, usually—to take the waters. This lends the village, at the height of the season, a rather terrifying air of sanctity, as though it were a lesser Lourdes. There is often something beautiful, there is always something awful, in the spectacle of a person who has lost one of his faculties, a faculty he never questioned until it was gone, and who struggles to recover it. Yet people remain people, on crutches or indeed on deathbeds; and wherever I passed, the first summer I was here, among the native villagers or among the lame, a wind passed with me—of astonishment, curiosity, amusement, and outrage. That first summer I stayed two weeks and never intended to return. But I did return in the winter, to work; the village offers, obviously, no distractions whatever and has the further advantage of being extremely cheap. Now it is winter again, a year later, and I am here again. Everyone in the village knows my name, though they scarcely ever use it, knows that I come from America—though, this, apparently, they will never really believe: black men come from Africa — and everyone knows that I am the friend of the son of a woman who was born here, and that I am staying in their chalet. But I remain as much a stranger today as I was the first day I arrived, and the children shout *Neger! Neger!* as I walk along the streets.

It must be admitted that in the beginning I was far too shocked to have any real reaction. In so far as I reacted at all, I reacted by trying to be pleasant — it being a great part of the American Negro's education (long before he goes to school) that he must make people "like" him. This smile-and-the-world-smiles-with-you routine worked about as well in this situation as it had in the situation for which it was designed, which is to say that it did not work at all. No one, after all, can be liked whose human weight and complexity cannot be, or had not been, admitted. My smile was simply another unheard-of phenomenon which allowed them to see my teeth — they did not, really, see my smile and I began to think that, should I take to snarling, no one would notice any difference. All of the physical characteristics of the Negro which had caused me, in America, a very different and almost forgotten pain were nothing less than miraculous — or infernal — in the eyes of the village people. Some thought my hair was the color of tar, that it had the texture of wire, or the texture of cotton. It was jocularly suggested that I might let it all grow long and make myself a winter coat. If I sat in the sun for more than five minutes some daring creature was certain to come along and gingerly put his fingers on my hair, as though he were afraid of an electric shock, or put his hand on my hand, astonished that the color did not rub off. In all of this, in which it must be conceded there was the charm of genuine wonder and in which there was certainly no element of intentional unkindness, there was yet no suggestion that I was human: I was simply a living wonder.

I knew that they did not mean to be unkind, and I know it now; it is necessary, nevertheless, for me to repeat this to myself each time that I walk out of the chalet. The children who shout *Neger!* have no way of knowing the echoes this sound raises in me. They are brimming with good humor and the more daring swell with pride when I stop to speak with them. Just the same, there are days when I cannot pause and smile, when I have no heart to play with them; when, indeed, I mutter sourly to myself, exactly as I muttered on the streets of a city these children have never seen, when I was no bigger than these children are now: *Your* mother *was a nigger.* Joyce is right about history being a nightmare — but it may be the nightmare from which no one *can* awaken. People are trapped in history and history is trapped in them.

There is a custom in the village — I am told it is repeated in many villages — of "buying" African natives for the purpose of converting them to Christianity. There stands in the church all year round a small box with a slot for money, decorated with a black figurine, and into this box the villagers drop their francs. During the *car-*

naval which precedes Lent, two village children have their faces blackened—out of which bloodless darkness their blue eyes shine like ice—and fantastic horsehair wigs are placed on their blond heads; thus disguised, they solicit among the villagers for money for the missionaries in Africa. Between the box in the church and the blackened children, the village "bought" last year six or eight African natives. This was reported to me with pride by the wife of one of the *bistro* owners and I was careful to express astonishment and pleasure at the solicitude shown by the village for the souls of black folk. The *bistro* owner's wife beamed with a pleasure far more genuine than my own and seemed to feel that I might now breathe more easily concerning the souls of at least six of my kinsmen.

I tried not to think of these so lately baptized kinsmen, of the price paid for them, or the peculiar price they themselves would pay, and said nothing about my father, who having taken his own conversion too literally never, at bottom, forgave the white world (which he described as heathen) for having saddled him with a Christ in whom, to judge at least from their treatment of him, they themselves no longer believed. I thought of white men arriving for the first time in an African village, strangers there, as I am a stranger here, and tried to imagine the astounded populace touching their hair and marveling at the color of their skin. But there is a great difference between being the first white man to be seen by Africans and being the first black man to be seen by whites. The white man takes the astonishment as tribute, for he arrives to conquer and to convert the natives, whose inferiority in relation to himself is not even to be questioned; whereas I, without a thought of conquest, find myself among a people whose culture controls me, has even, in a sense, created me, people who have cost me more in anguish and rage than they will ever know, who yet do not even know of my existence. The astonishment with which I might have greeted them, should they have stumbled into my African village a few hundred years ago, might have rejoiced their hearts. But the astonishment with which they greet me today can only poison mine.

And this is so despite everything I may do to feel differently, despite my friendly conversations with the *bistro* owner's wife, despite their three-year-old son who has at last become my friend, despite the *saluts* and *bonsoirs* which I exchange with people as I walk, despite the fact that I know that no individual can be taken to task for what history is doing, or has done. I say that the culture of these people controls me—but they can scarcely be held responsible for European culture. America comes out of Europe, but these people have never seen America, nor have most of them seen more of Europe than the hamlet at the foot of their mountain. Yet they move with an authority which I shall never have; and they regard me, quite rightly, not only as a stranger in their village but as a suspect latecomer, bearing no credentials, to everything they have—however unconsciously —inherited.

For this village, even were it incomparably more remote and incredibly more primitive, is the West, the West onto which I have been so strangely grafted. These people cannot be, from the point of view of power, strangers anywhere in the world; they have made the modern world, in effect, even if they do not know it. The most illiterate among them is related, in a way that I am not, to Dante, Shakespeare, Michelangelo, Aeschylus, Da Vinci, Rembrandt, and Racine; the cathedral at Chartres says something to them which it cannot say to me, as indeed would New York's Empire State Building, should anyone here ever see it. Out of their hymns and dances come Beethoven and Bach. Go back a few centuries and they are in their full glory—but I am in Africa, watching the conquerors arrive.

The rage of the disesteemed is personally fruitless, but it is also absolutely inevitable; this rage, so generally discounted, so little understood even among the people whose daily bread it is, is one of the things that makes history. Rage can only with difficulty, and never entirely, be brought under the domination of the intelligence and is therefore not susceptible to any arguments whatever. This is a fact which ordinary representatives of the *Herrenvolk*, having never felt this rage and being unable to imagine it, quite fail to understand. Also, rage cannot be hidden, it can only be dissembled. This dissembling deludes the thoughtless, and strengthens rage and adds, to rage, contempt. There are, no doubt, as many ways of coping with the resulting complex of tensions as there are black men in the world, but no black man can hope ever to be entirely liberated from this internal warfare—rage, dissembling, and contempt having inevitably accompanied his first realization of the power of white men. What is crucial here is that, since white men represent in the black man's world so heavy a weight, white men have for black men a reality which is far from being reciprocal; and hence all black men have toward all white men an attitude which is designed, really, either to rob the white man of the jewel of his naïveté, or else to make it cost him dear.

The black man insists, by whatever means he finds at his disposal, that the white man cease to regard him as an exotic rarity and recognize him as a human being. This is a very charged and difficult moment, for there is a great deal of will power involved in the white man's naïveté. Most people are not naturally reflective any more than they are naturally malicious, and the white man prefers to keep the black man at a certain human remove because it is easier for him thus to preserve his simplicity and avoid being called to account for crimes committed by his forefathers, or his neighbors. He is inescapably aware, nevertheless, that he is in a better position in the world than black men are, nor can he quite put to death the suspicion that he is hated by black men therefore. He does not wish to be hated, neither does he wish to change places, and at this point in his uneasiness he can scarcely avoid having recourse to those legends which white men have created about black men, the most usual effect of which is that the white man finds himself enmeshed, so to speak, in his own language which describes hell, as well as the attributes which lead one to hell, as being as black as night.

Every legend, moreover, contains its residuum of truth, and the root function of language is to control the universe by describing it. It is of quite considerable significance that black men remain, in the imagination, and in overwhelming numbers in fact, beyond the disciplines of salvation; and this despite the fact that the West has been "buying" African natives for centuries. There is, I should hazard, an instantaneous necessity to be divorced from this so visibly unsaved stranger, in whose heart, moreover, one cannot guess what dreams of vengeance are being nourished; and, at the same time, there are few things on earth more attractive than the idea of the unspeakable liberty which is allowed the unredeemed. When, beneath the black mask, a human being begins to make himself felt one cannot escape a certain awful wonder as to what kind of human being it is. What one's imagination makes of other people is dictated, of course, by the laws of one's own personality and it is one of the ironies of black-white relations that, by means of what the white man imagines the black man to be, the black man is enabled to know who the white man is.

I have said, for example, that I am as much a stranger in this village today as I was the first summer I arrived, but this is not quite true. The villagers wonder less about the texture of my hair than they did then, and wonder rather more about me. And the fact that their wonder now exists on another level is reflected in their attitudes and in their eyes. There are the children who make those delightful, hilarious, sometimes astonishingly grave overtures of friendship in the unpredictable fashion of children; other children, having been taught that the devil is a black man, scream in genuine anguish as I approach. Some of the older women never pass without a friendly greeting, never pass, indeed, if it seems that they will be able to engage me in conversation; other women look down or look away or rather contemptuously smirk. Some of the men drink with me and suggest that I learn how to ski—partly, I gather, because they cannot imagine what I would look like on skis—and want to know if I am married, and ask questions about my *métier*. But some of the men have accused *le sale nègre*—behind my back—of stealing wood and there is already in the eyes of some of them that peculiar, intent, paranoiac malevolence which one sometimes surprises in the eyes of American white men when, out walking with their Sunday girl, they see a Negro male approach.

There is a dreadful abyss between the streets of this village and the streets of the city in which I was born, between the children who shout *Neger!* today and those who shouted *Nigger!* yesterday—the abyss is experience, the American experience. The syllable hurled behind me today expresses, above all, wonder: I am a stranger here. But I am not a stranger in America and the same syllable riding on the American air expresses the war my presence has occasioned in the American soul.

For this village brings home to me this fact: that there was a day, and not really a very distant day, when Americans were scarcely Americans at all but discontented Europeans, facing a great unconquered continent and strolling, say, into a marketplace and seeing black men for the first time. The shock this spectacle afforded is suggested, surely, by the promptness with which they decided that these black men were not really men but cattle. It is true that the necessity on the part of the settlers of the New World of reconciling their moral assumptions with the fact—and the necessity—of slavery enhanced immensely the charm of this idea, and it is also true that this idea expresses, with a truly American bluntness, the attitude which to varying extents all masters have had toward all slaves.

But between all former slaves and slave-owners and the drama which begins for Americans over three hundred years ago at Jamestown, there are at least two differences to be observed. The American Negro slave could not suppose, for one thing, as slaves in past epochs had supposed and often done, that he would ever be able to wrest the power from his master's hands. This was a supposition which the modern era, which was to bring about such vast changes in the aims and dimensions of power, put to death; it only begins, in unprecedented fashion, and with dreadful implications, to be resurrected today. But even had this supposition persisted with undiminished force, the American Negro slave could not have used it to lend his condition dignity, for the reason that this supposition rests on another: that the slave in exile yet remains related to his past, has some means—if only in memory—of revering and sustaining the forms of his former life, is able, in short, to maintain his identity.

This was not the case with the American Negro slave. He is unique among the black men of the world in that his past was taken from him, almost literally, at one blow. One wonders what on earth the first slave found to say to the first dark child he bore. I am told that there are Haitians able to trace their ancestry back to African kings, but any American Negro wishing to go back so far will find his journey through time abruptly arrested by the signature on the bill of sale which served as the entrance paper for his ancestor. At the time —to say nothing of the circumstances—of the enslavement of the captive black man who was to become the American Negro, there was not the remotest possibility that he would ever take power from his master's hands. There was no reason to suppose that his situation would ever change, nor was there, shortly, anything to indicate that his situation had ever been different. It was his necessity, in the words of E. Franklin Frazier, to find a "motive for living under American culture or die." The identity of the American Negro comes out of this extreme situation, and the evolution of this identity was a source of the most intolerable anxiety in the minds and the lives of his masters.

For the history of the American Negro is unique also in this: that the question of his humanity, and of his rights therefore as a human being, became a burning one for several generations of Americans, so burning a question that it ultimately became one of those used to divide the nation. It is out of this argument that the venom of the epithet *Nigger!* is derived. It is an argument which Europe has never had, and hence Europe quite sincerely fails to understand how or why the argument arose in the first place, why its effects are so frequently disastrous and always so unpredictable, why it refuses until today to be entirely settled. Europe's black possessions remained — and do remain — in Europe's colonies, at which remove they represented no threat whatever to European identity. If they posed any problem at all for the European conscience, it was a problem which remained comfortingly abstract: in effect, the black man, *as a man,* did not exist for Europe. But in America, even as a slave, he was an inescapable part of the general social fabric and no American could escape having an attitude toward him. Americans attempt until today to make an abstraction of the Negro, but the very nature of these abstractions reveals the tremendous effects the presence of the Negro has had on the American character.

When one considers the history of the Negro in America it is of the greatest importance to recognize that the moral beliefs of a person, or a people, are never really as tenuous as life — which is not moral — very often causes them to appear; these create for them a frame of reference and necessary hope, the hope being that when life has done its worst they will be enabled to rise above themselves and to triumph over life. Life would scarcely be bearable if this hope did not exist. Again, even when the worst has been said, to betray a belief is not by any means to have put oneself beyond its power; the betrayal of a belief is not the same thing as ceasing to believe. If this were not so there would be no moral standards in the world at all. Yet one must also recognize that morality is based on ideas and that all ideas are dangerous — dangerous because ideas can only lead to action and where the action leads no man can say. And dangerous in this respect: that confronted with the impossibility of remaining faithful to one's beliefs, and the equal impossibility of becoming free of them, one can be driven to the most inhuman excesses. The ideas on which American beliefs are based are not, though Americans often seem to think so, ideas which originated in America. They came out of Europe. And the establishment of democracy on the American continent was scarcely as radical a break with the past as was the necessity, which Americans faced, of broadening this concept to include black men.

This was, literally, a hard necessity. It was impossible, for one thing, for Americans to abandon their beliefs, not only because these beliefs alone seemed able to justify the sacrifices they had endured and the blood that they had spilled, but also because these beliefs afforded them their only bulwark against a moral chaos as absolute as the physical chaos of the continent it was their destiny to conquer. But in the situation in which Americans found themselves, these beliefs threatened an idea which, whether or not one likes to think so, is the very warp and woof of the heritage of the West, the idea of white supremacy.

Americans have made themselves notorious by the shrillness and the brutality with which they have insisted on this idea, but they did not invent it; and it has escaped the world's notice that those very excesses of which Americans have been guilty imply a certain, unprecedented uneasiness over the idea's life and power, if not, indeed, the idea's validity. The idea of white supremacy rests simply on the fact that white men are the creators of civilization (the present civilization, which is the only one that matters; all previous civilizations are simply "contributions" to our own) and are therefore civilization's guardians and defenders. Thus it was impossible for Americans to accept the black man as one of themselves, for to do so was to jeopardize their status as white men. But not so to accept him was to deny his human reality, his human weight and complexity, and the strain of denying the overwhelmingly undeniable forced Americans into rationalizations so fantastic that they approached the pathological.

At the root of the American Negro problem is the necessity of the American white man to find a way of living with the Negro in order to be able to live with himself. And the history of this problem can be reduced to the means used by Americans — lynch law and law, segregation and legal acceptance, terrorization and concession — either to come to terms with this necessity, or to find a way around it, or (most usually) to find a way of doing both these things at once. The resulting spectacle, at once foolish and dreadful, led someone to make the quite accurate observation that "the Negro-in-America is a form of insanity which overtakes white men."

In this long battle, a battle by no means finished, the unforeseeable effects of which will be felt by many future generations, the white man's motive was the protection of his identity; the black man was motivated by the need to establish an identity. And despite the terrorization which the Negro in America endured and endures sporadically until today, despite the cruel and totally inescapable ambivalence of his status in his country, the battle for his identity has long ago been won. He is not a visitor to the West, but a citizen there, an American; as American as the Americans who despise him, the Americans who fear him, the Americans who love him — the Americans who became less than themselves, or rose to be greater than themselves by virtue of the fact that the challenge he represented was inescapable. He is perhaps the only black man in the world whose relationship to white men is more terrible, more subtle, and more meaningful than the relationship of bitter possessed to uncertain possessor. His survival depended, and his development depends, on his ability to turn his peculiar status in the Western world to his own advantage and, it may be, to the very great advantage of that world. It remains for him to fashion out of his experience that which will give him sustenance, and a voice.

The cathedral at Chartres, I have said, says something to the people of this village which it cannot say to me; but it is important to understand that this cathedral says something to me which it cannot say to them. Perhaps they are struck by the power of the spires, the glory of the windows; but they have known God, after all, longer than I have known him, and in a different way, and I am terrified by the slippery bottomless well to be found in the crypt down which heretics were hurled to death, and by the obscene, inescapable gargoyles jutting out of the stone and seeming to say that God and the devil can never be divorced. I doubt that the villagers think of the devil when they face a cathedral because they have never been identified with the devil. But I must accept the status which myth, if nothing else, gives me in the West before I can hope to change the myth.

Yet, if the American Negro has arrived at his identity by virtue of the absoluteness of his estrangement from his past, American white men still nourish the illusion that there is some means of recovering the European innocence, of returning to a state in which black men do not exist. This is one of the greatest errors Americans can make. The identity they fought so hard to protect has, by virtue of that battle, undergone a change: Americans are as unlike any other white people in the world as it is possible to be. I do not think, for example, that it is too much to suggest that the American vision of the world—which allows so little reality, generally speaking, for any of the darker forces in human life, which tends until today to paint moral issues in glaring black and white—owes a great deal to the battle waged by Americans to maintain between themselves and black men a human separation which could not be bridged. It is only now beginning to be borne in on us—very faintly, it must be admitted, very slowly, and very much against our will—that this vision of the world is dangerously inaccurate, and perfectly useless. For it protects our moral high-mindedness at the terrible expense of weakening our grasp of reality. People who shut their eyes to reality simply invite their own destruction, and anyone who insists on remaining in a state of innocence long after that innocence is dead turns himself into a monster.

The time has come to realize that the interracial drama acted out on the American continent has not only created a new black man, it has created a new white man, too. No road whatever will lead Americans back to the simplicity of this European village where white men still have the luxury of looking on me as a stranger. I am not, really, a stranger any longer for any American alive. One of the things that distinguishes Americans from other people is that no other people has ever been so deeply involved in the lives of black men, and vice versa. This fact faced, with all its implications, it can be seen that the history of the American Negro problem is not merely shameful, it is also something of an achievement. For even when the worst has been said, it must also be added that the perpetual challenge posed by this problem was always, somehow, perpetually met. It is precisely this black-white experience which may prove of indispensable value to us in the world we face today. This world is white no longer, and it will never be white again.

It is the man determines what is said, not the words.
If a mean person uses a wise maxim,
I bethink me how it can be interpreted
so as to commend itself to his meanness;
but if a wise man makes a commonplace remark,
I consider what wider construction it will admit.
HENRY DAVID THOREAU, *The Journal of Henry D. Thoreau*

9 Writer and reader: prerequisites for change

Part two

FREQUENTLY the impact of what a person says or writes has very little to do with the literal meaning of his message. The intended effect of a sarcastic remark, for instance, is always the opposite of its content: The speaker's tone of voice, the length of his pauses, the movements of his eyes, his facial expressions, his posture all combine to betray the hostile intent behind such innocent statements as "That was a brilliant remark!" and "An excellent suggestion!" Often one learns more about the speaker's feelings from these extraverbal forms of communication than from the verbal content of the message. One psychologist has even worked out a formula to indicate the contribution that each component makes to the total impact: Total Impact = 0.7 verbal + .38 vocal + .55 facial. . . . Isn't science grand.[1]

[1] Both the formula and the sarcastic remark are from Albert Mehrabian, "Communication Without Words," *Psychology Today*, September, 1968.

Attitudinal meaning is somewhat more difficult to express in writing than in speech. It requires skill for a writer to translate a facial expression or a hand gesture into words. However, purely verbal ways to express attitudes do exist; for example, many adverbs express attitudes — *sadly, happily, unfortunately, surely, probably, obviously*. In written form, the sentence

1) The Tigers won the game.

does not convey the writer's attitude toward the event. But notice how one can alter the sentence to reveal attitudes by using adverbs, metaphors, punctuation, and other, subtler means:

2) Unfortunately, the Tigers won the game.
3) The Tigers stole the game.
4) Our Tigers won the game.
5) Those Tigers won the game.
6) The Tigers have won the game!

Most readers will agree that sentence 5 suggests a more detached attitude than does 4 and that sentence 6 suggests more surprise or shock than does 1.

Communication and the sense of threat

When the writer's attitudes toward his subject and his reader clash with the attitudes of the reader, the reader is inclined to reject rather than investigate the writer's message. This tendency creates an important problem in communication: All but the most saintly or self-assured of us tend to feel threatened when someone challenges a feature of our image that is important to us, be it a theory, a baseball team, a religion, a school, a governmental system, a friend. Yet because differences — unshared experiences and new images — are the most worthwhile subjects to write about, most significant and interesting writing is in some degree challenging, and hence threatening, to the reader.

When the reader feels threatened, he seeks to defend himself rather than to weigh the merits of the writer's message. He may begin to elaborate his own position in opposition to the writer's, or to search for defects in the message or in the writer himself; he may distort the message so that it can easily be rejected, or even shove the writer's work aside in a fit of irritation. Thus it is possible for writer and reader to interact without entering into the cooperative enterprise that characterizes true communication. Defensiveness does not preclude interaction, but it does preclude cooperation.

Since the writer cannot force changes in the reader's mind, he must create conditions that encourage the reader to make these changes himself.

EVALUATIVE AND DESCRIPTIVE WRITING

Often the writer unintentionally works against himself by stating his ideas in a way that causes the reader to become defensive. One way of doing this is to evaluate an experience instead of describing it. An evaluation makes a judgment about an experience according to some scale of values; the experience is seen as good or bad, desirable or undesirable, profitable or unprofitable, and so on. A description, on the other hand, does not make judgments; instead, it presents a series of statements about the characteristics or content of the experience. When the third edition of Webster's unabridged dictionary was published, many people felt threatened by it and reacted defensively; their response produced in turn a sense of threat in the defenders of the dictionary. The controversy became polarized, and for some time people with conflicting beliefs about the functions of dictionaries found it nearly impossible to talk reasonably to each other: There was much interaction, little communication. The two passages that follow illustrate quite different overall attitudes.

1) The 1934 dictionary had been, heaven knows, no citadel of conservatism, no last bastion of puristical bigotry. But it had made shrewd reports on the status of individual words; it had taken its clear, beautifully written definitions from fit uses of an enormous vocabulary by judicious users; it had provided accurate, impartial accounts of the endless guerrilla war between grammarian and anti-grammarian and so given every consultant the means to work out his own decisions. Who could wish the forthcoming revision any better fortune than a comparable success in applying the same standards to whatever new matter the new age imposed?

Instead, we have seen a century and a third of illustrious history largely jettisoned; we have seen a novel dictionary formula improvised, in great part out of snap judgments and the sort of theoretical improvement that in practice impairs; and we have seen the gates propped wide open in enthusiastic hospitality to miscellaneous confusions and corruptions. In fine, the anxiously awaited work that was to have crowned cisatlantic linguistic scholarship with a particular glory turns out to be a scandal and a disaster. Worse yet, it plumes itself on its faults and parades assiduously cultivated sins as virtues without precedent.

WILSON FOLLETT, "Sabotage in Springfield,"
Atlantic Monthly, January, 1962

2) We are in a different language climate from that in which the Second Edition was prepared. Since then, linguistics has been recognized as a science. This dictionary is the result of a scientific or "test-tube" approach, an impersonal photographing of English speech. Philip Gove, editor in chief, lists five basic concepts that motivated the dictionary staff: 1. Language changes constantly; 2. Change is normal; 3. Spoken language is the language; 4. Correctness rests upon usage; 5. All usage is relative.

MILLICENT TAYLOR, "The New Dictionary,"
Christian Science Monitor, November 29, 1961

Passage 1, which is highly evaluative, forces the reader to take sides. If the reader agrees with the writer's judgments — that is, if they share the same beliefs about the proper nature and function of a dictionary — he has found a champion and urges the writer on. If he disagrees, he bristles and may even stop reading. In this situation a meeting of minds is impossible; incompatible positions merely become more rigid. Passage 2, on the other hand, presents verifiable information. The reader need not take sides; he is therefore more likely to consider the writer's position and perhaps be influenced by it.

The writer should avoid evaluative statements whenever description alone is sufficient for his purpose. But when, as often happens, he must make judgments, he can make them in a way that minimizes the reader's sense of threat. First, he can avoid the use of loaded and abusive language, such as that used in passage 1 — "snap judgments," "miscellaneous confusions and corruptions," "scandal," "disaster." Second, he can acknowledge the personal element in his judgment, taking care not to present it as if it possessed the same unqualified reliability as the answer to a carefully worked arithmetic problem. There is a subtle but important difference between saying "I don't like it" and "It's bad." The first statement suggests that other judgments are possible; the second implies that there is only one proper response and that to disagree is somehow to separate oneself from the community of right-thinking men. Third, before making his judgment the writer can describe the experience in order to clarify what is being judged. People often disagree on evaluations because they are not evaluating the same thing. When he moves on to the judgment itself, he leads the reader from something readily shared to something less readily shared. Finally, the writer can specify the basis for his judgment. For example, in the evaluation of a dictionary one basis for judgment is whether the dictionary fulfills its proper function. If, as in the controversy above, there is disagreement about the proper function of a dictionary — one side arguing that a dictionary should establish proper usage and the other that it should describe current usage—the writer must argue the reasonableness of his position. He *must not* assume that his beliefs are shared by all men.

DOGMATIC AND PROVISIONAL WRITING

A second, related way of arousing in the reader a sense of threat is to write dogmatically, to write as if one knew the Truth. The dogmatic writer often seems less interested in communication than in indoctrination, to which few men react happily. He conveys the impression that to differ with him is heresy. His mind is closed, impervious to change. Cooperation in a search for truth is possible (1) only if each of us in the discussion is ready to lay his basic position open to careful scrutiny and test and is ready to accept modification of that position if facts brought to our attention warrant it, and (2) only if others can see that this is in fact our attitude.

> "It's no use arguing with Ruskin when he says wild things," said a friend of the British writer. "I tried once and had to give it up. I had begun by saying, 'Now, Ruskin, you surely do not believe that?' 'Believe it! Sir, I know it.' "
>
> In WALTER E. HOUGHTON, *The Victorian Frame of Mind*

Of course all men do—they must—believe in some things strongly; our concern here is the way they state their beliefs to others. The problem with dogmatism is that, like evaluation, it forces the reader to take sides. Conflicting positions tend to become rigid, and the possibility of cooperation diminishes.

Provisional writing, on the other hand, focuses on the process of inquiry itself and acknowledges the tentative nature of conclusions. This focus enables the reader to see clearly the basis of the writer's generalizations; it gives him an opportunity to differ with them and to develop alternatives. Provisional writing implies that more than one reasonable conclusion is possible. In the following passage, the writer poses a problem, explores it, and offers a reasoned, *provisional* solution.

> [Many social scientists argue that they are not interested in predicting human behavior, only in understanding it.] When asked what the proponents of "understanding" mean by it, they are in difficulties. It is as difficult to convey the meaning of "understanding" (in its subjective sense, as it is used here) as it is to convey the meaning of "appreciation" or of "perception." Yet these words are full of "meaning," of sorts. All of us "know" what they mean in the same sense that we "know" what vinegar smells like or how velvet feels. Pressing the issue of the "meaning" of understanding is not fair in

this situation. But is it fair to raise the question whether it is proper to give the name "science" to an activity which aims only at subjective understanding of this sort.

This is not a rhetorical question. I am not at all sure that the answer is categorically "no," although I suspect that I prefer "no" to "yes." Yet there is no denying that this intuitive organization of perception (akin to appreciation) is an important component in the psychology of science. Without it I doubt whether any but utilitarian motivation would exist for scientific activity, and I doubt whether science could get very far on utilitarian motives alone.

ANATOL RAPOPORT, "Various Meanings of 'Theory,'"
American Political Science Review, December, 1958

The English critic and poet Matthew Arnold seems to have had this kind of prose in mind when he expressed a preference for the prose style of the "explorer" over that of the "doctor." By "doctor" he meant a writer who presents to his reader *the* single correct doctrine. What he sought to develop in his own writing was an attitude that was free, curious, elastic, accepting of risk — an attitude, and a style, that was in Montaigne's words *ondoyant et divers* ("undulating and diverse"). When the writer indicates a willingness to examine and even to experiment with his own ideas and beliefs, he reduces the reader's defensiveness. He is more likely to find a sympathetic ear if instead of presenting his generalizations as absolute truths, he makes clear that he has sought to construct a provisional system to organize data and solve problems, a system that can be altered or replaced when its deficiencies are perceived.

THE ASSUMPTION OF SIMILARITY

The reader's response is affected as much by the writer's attitude toward him as by the writer's attitude toward the subject. Prose that encourages careful, open-minded reading implies that the writer regards the reader as essentially similar to him in intellectual capacity and moral qualities, even though they may differ significantly in other ways. The writer makes what might be called an *assumption of similarity*. The reader is addressed as if he were intelligent, curious, honest, sincere — in short, as if he possessed the same qualities that the writer attributes to himself. A writer who indicates that he feels superior, that he wishes to preserve his distance, or that he regards others as commodities, things to be counted or manipulated, is likely to arouse the reader's defenses. The reader responds with accusations of "arrogance," "high-and-mighty attitude," "snobbery" and so on.

Here and in earlier chapters we have insisted on the importance of shared features as bridges over which change can occur.

We have not, however, directly discussed why sharing is necessary to persuasion. Perhaps the preceding paragraph suggests one of the reasons: An element of trust must be present in every persuasive situation. The reader believes in the writer's scientific integrity (including his moral integrity as a scientist), or he accepts as true the writer's report of personal experience, or he assumes that the arguments advanced are genuine efforts to present a truth and not selfish attempts to gain an advantage. When trust is not present, rational persuasion becomes impossible, and the likelihood of coercion increases. Yet where does this trust come from? Often it arises at the precise points where sharing has occurred. Shared features offer a basis on which the reader can judge the writer's integrity, professional competence, and personal characteristics.

There is a second reason why persuasion occurs at points of sharing: If writer and reader begin by holding in common some feature relevant to the subject, the writer can attempt to broaden this area of agreement. On the one hand, if they agree on crucial matters (matters nuclear to the argument), the writer can try to extend the area of agreement by showing that the peripheral matters about which they disagree should be included within the broad area of agreement. On the other hand, if they agree on less important matters (matters peripheral to the crucial point), the writer can try to use these aspects, trivial though they may seem, to establish the trust that must be present before the crucial point can be argued successfully.

A few years ago many people became disturbed by a report that assessed the probable consequences to this country of an atomic war. In it, various possibilities were analyzed with mathematical precision; effects on population were estimated in "megadeaths." Much of the agitation and indignation felt by those who read the report derived not so much from their being forced to confront a problem they would rather not think about, as from the way the report treated human tragedy exclusively in statistical terms. Because the report failed to establish a satisfactory basis of shared human concern, the readers were unready to accept the abstract data. All men want to be regarded as individuals with special worth; clinical attitudes disturb them. Behind the clinician they want to see a man, a man like themselves.

Furthermore, men do not like to feel that they are being manipulated by arguments in which the users themselves do not believe. For example, there is in this country a general cynicism toward advertisements and political speeches. We look askance at advertisements that seem overly concerned about our welfare and at politicians who claim to seek only an opportunity to serve us. Such

politicians no doubt do exist, but the public response to their promises is often an indiscriminate "What's in it for him?" Through bitter experience men have learned to defend themselves against the
daily assault made on their minds by those who try to use others for
their own ends. As one of Dostoyevsky's characters remarks, men
will go to any lengths to prove that "men are still men and not the
keys of a piano."

The writer may trigger defensive responses in a number of
ways: Among them, by feigning emotion (such as the "friendliness"
or dazzling high spirits of magazine advertisements), by obviously
suppressing information or skirting issues that could prejudice his
position, by including heavily loaded language in a supposedly
objective account, by seeming to use logical fallacies deliberately.
In general, any behavior that leads the reader to suspect a difference
between what is said and what is intended will cause him to doubt
the writer's sincerity and to be insulted by the estimation made of
his intelligence. The writer must assume that the reader knows the
difference between something that is done *for* him and something
that is done *to* him.

The effort to manipulate is not always subtle; at times it is
both explicit and extreme. But the more blatantly coercive the effort
to control, the greater the reader's sense of threat and defiance.
What, for example, is your response to the following letter, which
was published in the *Michigan Daily*, a student newspaper?

From: Ku Klux Klan and White Citizen Council
       and White Citizens of Alabama
To: Students & Faculty,
       University of Michigan

DEAR STUDENTS & FACULTY:

I write for the Ku Klux Klan of Alabama as to a reply and a warning
to you about the recent letter Governor John received from you recently; We, the people of our great State think that we can run our own
affairs and are capable of it without interference of out siders; We, the
people of the State of Alabama are proud of our superb advance in
education.

The Coons in our great State of Alabama, have, at present,
School facilities above the whites, and also Employment above whites
such as At Goodyear, US. Steel, and Allis Chalmers.

I and the rest of my buddies do not like the present Criticisiz-
ing of Governor John he was capable of being one of the Justices and
Attorneys for the Nurenburg war Crime Trials.

We are all strong in Alabama there will not be another Little
Rock here; We will turn all of our Congressional Medals of Honor and
Distinguished Service Crosses in and turn to arms again; In the First

Choice I have a 358 Magnum Snipperscope bullet with the head of the N.A.A.C.P.s Name on it. I am a Sharpshooter with all weapons including the Thompson Sub machine Gun, Grease Gun, 30 & 50 Caliber Machine Guns and the others are Qualified with anything from hand Grenades, and Poison Gas; We say Clean up Detroit, and Michigan, and then tell another State how to run its Affairs; Thank You.

(P.S.) N.A.A.C.P. is the Contributors to Communism, Naziism, and such as to cause Caos within the Constitution of the United States; RED BIRDS DO NOT BUILD THEIR NESTS WITH BLUE BIRDS.

Sincerely,
K.K.K. of Alabama

In this discussion of attitudes, the ethical dimension of the art of rhetoric is evident. The attempt to reduce another's sense of threat in the effort to reach the goal of cooperation and mutual benefit is as much a moral act as it is a strategy for effective communication. From a simple remark to a complete essay, the writer's attitudes toward his subject and his reader, attitudes often conveyed in subtle ways, are a major part of the meaning of his work — or, as the psychologist expressed it (with some clinical detachment), .93 of Total Impact.

EXERCISES

1 Classify the following statements as either descriptive or evaluative. Descriptive statements usually can be verified empirically; evaluations usually cannot. As a guide, ask yourself whether it would make sense to vote on each statement. An evaluation, being a matter of opinion, can be voted on; to vote on a descriptive statement, however, would be absurd, since it can be verified empirically.

1) John lives at 25 Avon Street.
2) The food was poor.
3) I am a freshman.
4) I am only a freshman.
5) He's a beatnik.

Make comparable lists of observations and judgments, explaining the basis for your classification of each statement. Are any of your statements difficult to classify? If so, why?

2   Identify as best you can the reader to whom each of the following passages is addressed. Then analyze each passage in terms
of the writer's attitudes toward subject and reader. Which passages are likely to be threat-producing? Which seem threat-
reducing? Point out specific features to support your judgments.
What does the writer imply that he shares with the reader? Do
you as a reader share these features?

a   [The following letter from Elizabeth I of England to the Bishop of Ely
was a response to the Bishop's refusal to part with Ely Place, which
the Queen wished to give to a favorite.]

PROUD PRELATE,

You know what you were before I made you what you are now. If you
do not immediately comply with my request, I will unfrock you, by
God.

ELIZABETH

The Letters of Queen Elizabeth, ed. G. B. Harrison

b   Is there a way of setting up a construct which will provide us with a
frame of reference within which we can discuss the relationship between change of systems in general, and the status of the languages of
the bilingual or the dialects or styles of the monolingual?
        As a basis of discussion we suggest four propositions. We at-
tempt to put them in a form which is rigid, so that it will be easier to
refute them by counter examples and force complete abandonment, or
— more profitably — modify them to make them more useful.
        KENNETH L. PIKE, "Toward a Theory of Change and Bilingualism,"
Studies in Linguistics, 1960

C   The views expressed by the friend whom I so much honour [Romain
Rolland, who argued that the "oceanic feeling," a sense of mystical
union with the whole external world, was the source of religion], . . .
caused me no small difficulty. I cannot discover this "oceanic" feeling
in myself. It is not easy to deal scientifically with feelings. One can
attempt to describe their physiological signs. Where this is not possible — and I am afraid that the oceanic feeling too will defy this kind of
characterization — nothing remains but to fall back on the ideational
content which is most readily associated with the feeling. If I have
understood my friend rightly, he means the same thing by it as the
consolation offered by an original and somewhat eccentric dramatist
to his hero who is facing a self-inflicted death. "We cannot fall out of
this world." That is to say, it is a feeling of an indissoluble bond, of
being one with the external world as a whole. I may remark that to
me this seems something rather in the nature of an intellectual perception, which is not, it is true, without an accompanying feeling-

tone, but only such as would be present with any other act of thought of equal range. From my own experience I could not convince myself of the primary nature of such a feeling. But this gives me no right to deny that it does in fact occur in other people. The only question is whether it is being correctly interpreted and whether it ought to be regarded as the *fons et origo* of the whole need for religion.

SIGMUND FREUD, *Civilization and Its Discontents*, trans. James Strachey

d A passel of double-domes at the G. and C. Merriam Company joint in Springfield, Mass., have been confabbing and yakking for twenty-seven years—which is not intended to infer that they have not been doing plenty work—and now they have finalized Webster's Third New International Dictionary, Unabridged, a new-edition of that swell and esteemed word book.

"Webster's New Word Book," *New York Times,* October 12, 1961

e In a previous Forum article (Nov., 1952), "without any attempt to insure statistical accuracy" I indicated that, in published writing, after the "there is" formula a compound subject with a singular first member frequently occurs with a singular verb, probably more frequently than with a plural verb. To gather some statistics about the construction, I read four recent issues of both the *Atlantic Monthly* and *Harper's Magazine* (Dec., 1952, Jan., Feb., Mar., 1953). To discover whether usage had changed in recent years, I also read the eight issues published just thirty years earlier. Approximately 1900 pages provide the following statistics:

				There is	There are
Harper's	Dec.	'52–Mar.	'53	18	2
Atlantic	Dec.	'52–Mar.	'53	29	2
Harper's	Dec.	'22–Mar.	'23	36	1
Atlantic	Dec.	'22–Mar.	'23	28	1

ROBERT J. GEIST, " 'There Is' Again," *College English,* December, 1954

f The number of souls in this kingdom being usually reckoned one million and a half, of these I calculate there may be about two hundred thousand couple whose wives are breeders; from which number I subtract thirty thousand couples, who are able to maintain their own children, although I apprehend there cannot be so many under the present distresses of the kingdom, but this being granted, there will remain an hundred and seventy thousand breeders. I again subtract fifty thousand for those women who miscarry, or whose children die by accident, or disease within the year. There only remain an hundred and twenty thousand children of poor parents annually born: The question therefore is, how this number shall be reared, and provided for . . . .

JONATHAN SWIFT, "A Modest Proposal"

g When the American Ambassador tells us—in some degree at least seriously—that better English is spoken in America than in England, it is really a little too much. . . . [The Americans] are rich. They are—or seem to be—confident of themselves. They excel at the business of games. They make things "hum." But it is absurd to pretend they speak good English.

Their English and their spelling of English . . . are most unpleasant. Their twang is sometimes so.

Saturday Review (London), December 13, 1913

h Imagine that we stand on any ordinary seaside pier, and watch the waves rolling in and striking against the iron columns of the pier. Large waves pay very little attention to the columns—they divide right and left and re-unite after passing each column, much as a regiment of soldiers would if a tree stood in their road; it is almost as though the columns had not been there. But the short waves and ripples find the columns of the pier a much more formidable obstacle. When the short waves impinge on the columns, they are reflected back and spread as new ripples in all directions. To use the technical term, they are "scattered." The obstacle provided by the iron columns hardly affects the long waves at all, but scatters the short ripples.

We have been watching a sort of working model of the way in which sunlight struggles through the earth's atmosphere . . . .

SIR JAMES JEANS, *The Stars in Their Courses*

3 Guided by the discussions in Chapters 8 and 9, analyze the following description of an event. Do not overlook the sentence that begins, "He is really a wonderful guy."

Big battle with Sam today. Through some relatively little misunderstandings about plans and leadership for the mental hospital visitation this fall we both got upset. He called me a son-of-a-bitch and I threw some beer at him. Fortunately Peter and Jamie from up the hall happened to be in the room and shouted us into sanity and it didn't go any farther than that. Then we both sat there, each stunned at ourselves and the other guy. He is really a wonderful guy, though, and proved it by suggesting that we talk about what had happened. Apparently the whole shebang had started back the middle of last year, when I had taken a slightly superior attitude toward him, being, I thought, more intellectually astute than he! It had gradually built up from there. Talking it through brought us closer together I think—a kind of I-Thou growing out of hand-to-hand warfare!

JOSEPH HAVENS, *The Journal of a College Student*

4 The editorial page of a newspaper can be instructive reading for students of rhetoric. Study the editorials and the letters to the editor, particularly some series of exchanges on a single

social problem; then try to account for the behavior of the writers in terms of the discussions in Chapters 8 and 9. Such exchanges are clear revelations of the state of Babel after the Fall.

5 We have not by any means described all the things that one can do to arouse or allay threat in an audience. Repeated interruptions in a conversation, for example, make people angry, as does flat contradiction, although the latter may be only a species of dogmatism. Write a brief manual entitled "How to Make a Man Mad," giving instructions and illustrations drawn from your own experience. Also, speculate on defense-reducing alternatives for each example. Since your manual is a set of hypotheses about psychological behavior, test one, some, or all of the techniques in a way that seems to you reliable; then report the results.

The meaning of a message
is the change which it produces in the image.
KENNETH E. BOULDING, *The Image*

10   Writer and reader: intention

THE task of the writer is to set in motion a process that will result in a particular change in the reader's image. This change may be one of three kinds: (1) a change that results in reconstruction of the image or some part of it, (2) a change that expands the image, that adds to it, or (3) a change that alters the clarity or the certainty with which some part of the image is held. We might add a fourth possible result of the writer's efforts: no change at all.[1] Although it is difficult, perhaps impossible, to determine precisely what effect a message has had or will have on a particular reader's image, these categories are useful because they help us grasp more tightly the meaning of *intention*. They also help explain the different strategies that writers use when they are trying to induce changes in the reader, a subject to which we will turn in the following chapter.

[1] In this discussion the authors are greatly indebted to Kenneth E. Boulding, *The Image* (Ann Arbor: University of Michigan Press, 1961).

Changes in the reader's image

RECONSTRUCTION

Suppose you are told that someone whom you have always considered a good friend has made a cruel remark about you. You may at first deny that your friend could have said it. "He's not that sort of person," you protest. But if the evidence is irrefutable, you may be forced in the end to alter your image of him, concluding that he is not the person you thought him to be. Your image, or at least one feature of it, has been radically changed. Consider another example. Kenneth E. Boulding reports that after reading Vasiliev's *History of the Byzantine Empire* he experienced this effect:

> I have considerably revised my image of at least a thousand years of history. I had not given the matter a great deal of thought before, but I suppose if I had been questioned on my view of the period, I would have said that Rome fell in the fifth century and that it was succeeded by a little-known empire centering in Constantinople and a confused medley of tribes, invasions, and successor states. I now see that Rome did not fall, that in a sense it merely faded away, that the history of the Roman Empire and of Byzantium is continuous, and that from the time of its greatest extent the Roman Empire lost one piece after another until only Constantinople was left; and then in 1453 that went.
>
> KENNETH E. BOULDING, *The Image*

Often, then, what a person reads (or does or hears or sees) triggers a process that results in a reconstruction of his image.

The fact that one frequently resists such changes suggests that more is taking place than a simple addition to his image. As we pointed out earlier, in our discussion of problems in Chapter 5, there are conservative forces at work in the reader's mind, constantly seeking to maintain harmony or consistency among the numerous features of his image. Resistance to change indicates that the reader finds an inconsistency between the image and the new message—a problematic situation. A change in the image eliminates both inconsistency and resistance.

Reconstruction of the image may be relatively marginal or it may be nuclear. Some changes involve values and beliefs that are not particularly important to the stability of the image; the change in Boulding's historical beliefs seems to have been of this sort, since he mentions no resistance to the change. A politician may change his vote on a bill after hearing a speech; a housewife may change brands of soap after being persuaded that a new brand will put a bigger giant in her washing machine. All of us have experienced similar changes; they occur often and are accompanied by minimal resistance.

Other changes, however, may be strongly resisted, for they affect values that we regard as essential to our identity, even to our survival. Values are hierarchically structured; some are more significant, more eminent, than others. This may explain why psychoanalysis is such a long and painful process: The patient is being forced to relinquish nuclear beliefs and attitudes; giving them up sets in motion an extensive reorganization of his entire image. Other illustrations of strong resistance to change are common enough; for instance, the letter from the Ku Klux Klan discussed in Chapter 9 or the reaction of the Viennese obstetricians to Semmelweiss's theory of the cause of puerperal fever discussed in Chapter 7. The following letter, written in response to a student's argument in favor of legalizing the use of marijuana, offers still another example.

Mr. ————:

Any fool can go to college these days. The campus is filled with idiots, the dormitory with prostitutes. That's why you are there, so, in spending your time and energy on as vile a thing as smoking marijuana and demanding it be legalized, is no worse than promiscuous sex. You can't make a whistle out of a pig's tail.

It's too bad young people won't listen to older people. . . .

I have always heard that a cigarette is a fire on one end and a fool on the other. What will you call a marijuana cigarette?

You probably are just another Zionist Jew, trying to degrade the Gentile race, and bring it down to the Jew level.

One who knows

Michigan Daily, February 14, 1967

The reader's image may influence his evaluation of alternatives in such a way that the alternatives seem immoral or anarchistic, not "reasonable" at all. There is a rule of thumb for estimating the strength of the reader's resistance to changes in features of his image: Resistance varies directly with the importance of the feature to the economy of the image. The more important the feature, the stronger the resistance, and the more carefully and consciously the writer must proceed if he is to induce a change.

EXPANSION

By contrast, expansion of the reader's image involves, not inconsistency, but an extension or elaboration of features already established. Such elaboration is readily accepted, as you know if you have, for example, taken a mathematics course: The new information seldom conflicts with prior knowledge and attitudes. Likewise, when you look up a new word in a dictionary or consult an atlas to discover how far Accra is from Johannesburg, you accept the information readily since it contradicts nothing in your image. Changes like these are additive; the image becomes richer, more complex, but its integrity is not affected. Most writing is designed to induce this kind of change.

The ease with which we accept new information does not imply, however, that additions to the image are inconsequential or that they cannot strike us as immensely significant. When ignorance is replaced by knowledge, the effect is often exciting. This excerpt from a letter written by a medical student to a man who had earlier been his religious counselor is particularly interesting. In addition to illustrating additive change, it suggests the way in which new information is assimilated into one's image, taking its place in an incredibly complex and dynamic system of relationships.

> Very early this school year I happened to be doing some reading for a talk I had been asked to give at a suburban club, and I ran across some information that fascinated me. I won't bore you with the details, but it's work being done at Yale and it has to do with the biomagnetic fields which each living organism produces. The remarkable thing is that these fields are apparently very sensitive to changes in the much larger electrical fields of the earth and sun which surround us. There is scientific evidence that our mood swings, our physical state, our available energies are to some extent dependent on the cyclical changes—day-night, fortnightly and monthly, seasonal and annual—of these electrical tides. This so intrigued me that I found time to do additional reading about the implications of all this, and ran across some ideas which seemed to stimulate my religious imagination again, if you know what I mean.
>
> JOSEPH HAVENS, *The Journal of a College Student*

John Keats's response to his first reading of Chapman's translation of Homer captures the excitement that can accompany additive change.

> Much have I travell'd in the realms of gold,
>   And many goodly states and kingdoms seen;
>   Round many western islands have I been
> Which bards in fealty to Apollo hold.
> Oft of one wide expanse had I been told
>   That deep-brow'd Homer ruled as his demesne;
>   Yet did I never breathe its pure serene
> Till I heard Chapman speak out loud and bold:

> Then felt I like some watcher of the skies
>   When a new planet swims into his ken;
> Or like stout Cortez when with eagle eyes
>   He star'd at the Pacific—and all his men
> Look'd at each other with a wild surmise—
>   Silent, upon a peak in Darien.
>
> JOHN KEATS, "On First Looking into Chapman's Homer"

Experiences like these account for much of the pull of good education.

CLARIFICATION AND REINFORCEMENT

"The image," says Boulding,

> has a certain dimension, or quality, of certainty or uncertainty, probability or improbability, clarity or vagueness. Our image of the world is not uniformly certain, uniformly probable, or uniformly clear. Messages, therefore, may have the effect not only of adding to or of [reconstructing] the image, they may also have the effect of clarifying it, that is, of making something which previously was regarded as less certain more certain, or something which was previously seen in a vague way, clearer.
>
> KENNETH E. BOULDING, *The Image*

The image of the future that most Americans hold today is more uncertain than, say, the comparable image held by those Christians who believe that the Day of Judgment is not far off. The Marxist, who believes that history is moving inevitably toward a communist society, also has a clearer and more certain image of the future. As time passes, events tend either to reinforce an image or to cloud and weaken it.

Our earlier discussion of hypotheses is relevant to a consideration of the quality, the relative clarity and certainty, of beliefs. When someone formulates a hypothesis, he develops a new way of interpreting problematic data; that is, he constructs a new image of certain features of the world. This image may be rather vague, and it is always tentative. Subsequent analysis and attempts at verification can increase both the clarity and the certainty of the hypothesis; Charles Nicholle's account in Chapter 4 of his discovery of the carrier of typhus offers an excellent illustration of this process. But analysis and testing can also force one to modify a hypothesis or to abandon it altogether.

Clearly, messages can decrease as well as increase the certainty with which any feature of an image is held; that is, they can create a sense of doubt about the beliefs and values to which one is committed. Understanding this kind of change is important for at least two reasons. First, when the positions of writer and reader clash strongly, reconstructing the reader's image may be out of the question; but inducing him to reexamine and doubt his position is often possible. If the conflict cannot be eliminated, it can at least be mitigated. Second, a state of doubt can be seen as a transitional stage in the process of moving from old beliefs to new. In creating a sense of doubt, the writer also creates the opportunity to induce further changes in the reader's image, since uncertainty is an unstable state in which one cannot live comfortably for long. St. Augustine's conversion from Manicheism to Christianity offers an instructive example. As a teacher of rhetoric, Augustine spent considerable time in analyzing the speeches of Bishop Ambrose, an eloquent spokesman of the infant church. About this analysis Augustine remarks:

> Although I took no trouble to learn what he spake, but only to hear how he spake . . . yet, together with the words which I prized, there came into my mind also the things about which I was careless; for I could not separate them. And whilst I opened my heart to admit "how skillfully he spake," there also entered with it, but gradually, "how truly he spake!"
>
> The Works of Aurelius Augustine, ed. Marcus Dods and trans. J. G. Pilkington

But his conversion came slowly, for although he was led to question Manichean philosophy, he could not yet commit himself to Christianity.

> So, then . . . doubting of everything and fluctuating between all, I decided that the Manichaeans were to be abandoned; judging that, even while in that period of doubt, I could not remain in a sect to which I preferred some of the philosophers; to which philosophers, however, because they were without the saving name of Christ, I utterly refused to commit the cure of my fainting soul.

NO CHANGE

A message may also have a fourth effect: no change at all. Several errors may account for this failure. A message may be stated in language that the reader doesn't understand; most of us have read essays so full of highly technical terms that they almost seemed to be written in a foreign language. A message may also be stated so haphazardly that it is unclear. But even when the message is intelligible, it may fail to hold the reader's attention: He may merely skim it or put it aside without finishing it. As we pointed out in Chapter 8, one reason for this inattention is the writer's failure to explain the importance of the subject. If a message is to be attended to for long, it must seem significant. Furthermore, if a message is to produce a change in the image, it must not only be intelligible and significant, but must also be to some extent new. If the reader already knows and believes the message, the most it can do is to clarify or reinforce some feature of his image.

MULTIPLE INTENTIONS AND MULTIPLE CHANGES

For the sake of clarity we have discussed various kinds of changes as if they were simple and sharply separable in the mind. But if a message is complex (more complex than, say, a single sentence or the number given in an almanac to represent the population of Tokyo), it may produce several closely related changes in one's knowledge system. The messages with which we are concerned in this book — essays, scientific reports, letters — are extremely complex. Although the dominant effect of an essay, for example, may be a reconstruction of the reader's image, the work may also contain parts that add information or change the quality of certain of the image's features — parts such as a definition, a brief history of the problem to be solved, a piece of information about the writer himself, a discussion of alternative solutions, and so on. Thus we can speak of primary and secondary changes produced by a single, complex message, although even this explanation no doubt oversimplifies what actually occurs.

The notion of intention

Our discussion of the kinds of change that messages can induce in men's minds suggests a way of defining *intention. The intention of the writer is the primary change that he seeks to induce in the reader's mind.* His intention may be to replace some feature of the reader's image, or to add to it, or to clarify a particular feature, or to strengthen or weaken it. Since these changes occur within a mind, they cannot be observed; but the consequences are often overt and indicate whether the writer has been successful. If he has succeeded, the reader may be able to assemble a machine or to write a better essay; he may support a cause or vote for a candidate. Our discussion of change and intention leads us back to — in Sir Philip Sidney's phrase — the "ending end" of communication. For the goal of the writer, and of rhetoric, is to induce changes that will result in greater cooperation among men.

The writer may state his intention in his discourse, or he may leave it to be inferred by the reader. In some cases he may even tell the reader explicitly that he wants to explain how to do something (i.e., wants to add knowledge of a process to the reader's image), or that he wants to clarify an idea, or the like. He will probably not employ the abstract terminology that we have used to discuss intention, but will instead make equivalent statements that are directly related to his topic. Notice the way Ladis Kovach begins his essay that defines *nonlinear*:

> It was inevitable that the question would be asked. I've been working with nonlinear problems for a number of years and various books have found their way into our home. Books like *Nonlinear Problems in Random Theory* by Norbert Wiener and *Nonlinear Analysis* by Cunningham. One day my nine-year-old son asked, "What does non-lie-near (sic) mean?" Remembering that a parent should always answer questions about the facts of life, I pretended to ponder for a few minutes until my mind could get into high gear.
>
> LADIS KOVACH, "Life Can Be *So* Nonlinear"

Clearly, his intention is to add to his son's, and his reader's, image. The opening passage of Martin Luther King's "Letter from Birmingham Jail" indicates that his purpose in writing is to reconstruct the images of those readers who believe his activities to be "unwise and untimely."

> While confined here in the Birmingham city jail, I came across your recent statement calling our present activities "unwise and untimely." Seldom do I pause to answer criticism of my work and ideas. If I sought to answer all the criticisms that cross my desk, my secretaries would have little time for anything other than such correspondence in the course of the day and I would have no time for constructive work. But since I feel that you are men of genuine good will and your criticisms are sincerely set forth, I want to try to answer your statement in what I hope will be patient and reasonable terms.
>
> MARTIN LUTHER KING, JR., "Letter from Birmingham Jail"

By contrast, Aldo Leopold's "Thinking like a Mountain" in Chapter 5 contains no statement of intention. Fictional literature, too, generally omits such statements. In cases like these, the reader is left to infer the writer's intention if he so chooses. There is no reason to assume that one method is always superior to the other, although statements of intention do help the reader understand better what the writer is trying to do.

The writer cannot state his intention until he has determined both his message and the audience to whom it is directed. Intention emerges from the *relation* of the message to the reader's knowledge, attitudes, and values. Unlike the speaker, who confronts his audience, the writer cannot always know who will read his message. But he does know whom he wants to read it, and he designs his discourse for these readers. Writing is not quite like putting a letter in a bottle and throwing it into the sea.

Recapitulation: the writer-reader relationship

From the discussion thus far of units of experience, of alternative perspectives, of the process of inquiry, and of change, a complex conception of the writer-reader relationship emerges.

1) On the one hand, partial sharing by writer and reader of knowledge, values, beliefs, and so on is prerequisite for communicating things unshared. On the other hand, it is the presence of differences between writer and reader that makes discussion worthwhile — otherwise, as between old friends, a nod of the head, a touch of the hand, a glance of the eye would be sufficient.

2) In preparation for his attempt to share what is unshared, the writer must work at understanding the reader and the knowledge and perspectives that the reader is likely to bring to the encounter. If he fails to understand, he may miss the target. But it is equally important that he understand himself and articulate to himself the set of perspectives from which he views the situation. Both kinds of understanding are necessary if he is to evaluate the whole accurately and thereby increase the chances of changing his reader.

3) The ultimate goal of the writer is the construction of an enlarged system of human relationships, a system in which he and the reader are in some sense one, sharing knowledge, values, and perspectives in a single community; this community in turn is a unit that can be isolated and studied. The rhetorical effort to tell and to listen is the bridge over which partially isolated human particles can interact in a process that results in an integrated human system.

Such changes of separate human particles into a single human system are well known and need little comment; we all share an understanding of, and need only exchange a smile of appreciation over, at least one example. A single particle-man and a single particle-woman meet as isolated units and establish communion over bridges of shared interests. Their marriage creates a new family with shared psychological, social, physical, and spiritual properties — a new basic unit to be studied (and lived) in its own right. In terms of the chart presented in Chapter 6, the perspective has shifted from cell 1 (contrasting particles) to cell 9 (a system within a hierarchy of systems: a family within a structured society).

EXERCISES

1 From your own experience cite instances of each kind of change discussed in this chapter.

2 Read the entire editorial page of a newspaper, maintaining a nuclear focus on the content of the articles and a marginal focus on the effect that each has on your mind. Describe these effects in terms of the kinds of change discussed in this chapter. Do any of the articles induce more than one kind of change? If so, can you relate each change to a specific part of the article?

3 Read several letters to the editor in your local newspaper. Who is the intended audience of each? What is the main idea, or thesis? What is the intention? Is the intention stated, or must you infer it?

4 Review several of the essays you have already studied (e.g., Bruno Bettelheim, p. 190; Richard B. Gregg, p. 101; James Baldwin, p. 193). Who is the intended audience of each? What is the thesis of the writer's message? What is his intention? Does he allude to it, or must you infer it? Does the writer have what might be called secondary intentions? (For example, if his primary intention is to reconstruct the image, does he at times seek also to add to or to clarify some feature?) Can you associate these secondary intentions with specific sections of the essay?

5 Invent several hypothetical writing situations that would involve different kinds of intention. For instance, if a letter arguing for federal control of medical services were addressed to a journal read by members of the American Medical Association, it would probably be intended to reconstruct the reader's image.

6 Examine an essay that you have written. For whom was it written? What was your thesis? What was your intention? Did you allude to it or leave it to be inferred? Did you fulfill your intention? How do you know?

7 What is the probable effect on the relationship between speaker and listener of each of the following?

1) A Fourth of July oration.

    2) A sermon in a church service.
    3) An over-long introduction of a guest speaker.
    4) A class lecture on theoretical physics.

8 How does each of the following larger systems of relationships differ from the relationship of lecturer to audience or of writer to reader?

    1) A student bull session.
    2) A formal debate.
    3) An argument between a labor leader and a business executive, mediated by a government arbitrator.
    4) A discussion between a doctor and a patient with terminal cancer.

9 In terms of the underlying relationships found in larger groups, analyze the following statement, made by Professor Leon Lipson of Yale University in a private conversation with one of the authors:

It's foolish to suppose that we can liberate ourselves from conventional wisdom at no other cost than that of deriding conventional wisdom. History is full of examples of lonely thinkers who were belittled by the established figures of the time and who, it now turns out, were deservedly neglected!

10 Assume that the writer-reader relationship is paralleled by that between a political cartoonist and his reading audience. Now imagine that you have before you a news photograph of former President Johnson or of President Nixon and a cartoonist's caricature of the same man in approximately the same pose. If we consider the interrelation of the man's facial features as a system, what does the cartoonist tell us about his version of that system? How does his version differ from that of the news photographer? How would it differ from the version presented in a portrait that hung in the National Gallery? What total view of the system can you derive from the sum of the perspectives? What degree of sharing exists among them? How does the total, the community perspective, change after a particular political event, and how is the change reflected in cartoons? What can you learn from this exercise in comparisons about the manner in which a writer might search for a perspective when he is favorably disposed toward the person he is to write about? When he disapproves of his subject? When he is trying to be objective?

All acts have in common the character of being intended
or willed. But one act is distinguishable from another
by the content of it, the expected result of it,
which is here spoken of as its intent.
CLARENCE IRVING LEWIS, *An Analysis of Knowledge and Valuation*

11 Writer and reader: strategies for change

Part one

IN several of the preceding chapters we described heuristic procedures for solving some of the problems inherent in the process of communication: procedures for defining, for stating problems, for discovering ordering generalizations, for testing the adequacy of generalizations, for isolating relevant characteristics of the audience, and so on. In this chapter we shall discuss procedures that can aid in developing a discourse designed to change the reader's image: to reconstruct some feature of it, to add to it, or to alter its quality. The procedures are general guides for selecting and ordering information—plans for developing promising first drafts.

By placing this chapter at this juncture of the book, we do not mean to imply that the process of writing is strictly linear, that the writer first senses a difficulty, articulates it, explores it, discovers a possible solution, verifies it, then decides to communicate the results of his inquiry, considers his potential readers and intention, and

229

finally puts his thoughts on paper. At times he may write this way, but often he does not. Sometimes the writer is committed to writing something before he knows what he will say; this is frequently the case with both students and professional writers. Many times the writer maintains a marginal focus on his intended readers in the earliest stages of inquiry. Also, he is often led to modify his thinking by the act of writing itself, on occasion even to abandon his ideas once he sees them fully developed on paper. For the activity of writing has heuristic value; it encourages further, detailed exploration of one's ideas. Nevertheless, at some time in the rhetorical process the writer must begin to develop and organize a discourse. This chapter is devoted to that beginning.

Reconstructing the reader's image: traditional argument

"Show me in the clearest and most unambiguous manner," wrote William Godwin, an eighteenth-century political thinker, "that a certain mode of proceeding is most reasonable in itself, or most conducive to my interest, and I shall infallibly pursue that mode, so long as the views you suggest to me continue present in my mind." Behind Godwin's remark is a theory of persuasion that has been studied and used in the Western world for most of recorded history. Basic to this theory is the assumption that men are rational beings, that they can be persuaded by reason.

Reason is usually defined as logical thought: An argument is reasonable when it conforms to the rules of logic. Although logic is primarily a tool for inquiry, an aid in developing and evaluating hypotheses, it is relevant to communication. For a persuasive discourse is concerned with evaluation, with judging truth and falsity, goodness and badness, desirability and undesirability. It is designed not only to present the evaluation made by the writer but also to induce a comparable evaluation in the mind of the reader. Logic provides the writer with guides for making reasonable evaluations and for presenting them to the reader "in the clearest and most unambiguous manner." It is not our purpose here to describe the rules of logic and their use in the process of inquiry. Logic is an elaborate and difficult discipline; to develop even an elementary competence in it requires extensive explanation and drill. We can, nevertheless, discuss how the writer can use logic to present his message to the reader in a clear and convincing way. We hope an awareness of the nature and importance of the role of logic in persuasive discourse will lead you to develop your logical skills further.[1]

There are two basic kinds of argument: inductive and deductive. *Inductive, or empirical, argument is a kind of reasoning that proceeds from observations about particular things to a generalization about the things.* *Deductive* argument proceeds from generalizations, or premises, to valid inferences about particulars. We can illustrate the use of logical argument in discourse by focusing on one type of deductive argument, the categorical argument, discussing its nature, its use in organizing and stating evaluations, and its place in the discourse as a whole.

CATEGORICAL ARGUMENT

In a categorical argument one reasons about categories, or classes, of things and about the members of these categories. This characteristic can be seen more clearly when the categorical argument is reduced to its simplest form, which is called a *syllogism*. For example, there is a category of living organisms called bacteria, all the members of which — that is, all actual bacteria — share certain features; among them, that of asexual reproduction. Since cholera is a kind of bacteria, it must reproduce asexually. This illustration is stated in syllogistic form as:

MAJOR PREMISE: All bacteria are organisms that reproduce asexually.

MINOR PREMISE: All cholera organisms are bacteria.

CONCLUSION: All cholera organisms are organisms that reproduce asexually.

Consider a second example, the syllogism underlying one argument in Martin Luther King's "Letter from Birmingham Jail":

MAJOR PREMISE: All unjust laws are laws that one has no moral responsibility to obey.

MINOR PREMISE: All segregation laws are unjust laws.

CONCLUSION: All segregation laws are laws that one has no moral responsibility to obey.

[1] Three books that provide good introductions to logic are Manuel Bilsky, *Patterns of Argument* (New York: Holt, Rinehart and Winston, 1963); John C. Sherwood, *Discourse of Reason: A Brief Handbook of Semantics and Logic* (New York: Harper & Row, 1964); and Morris Cohen and Ernest Nagel, *Introduction to Logic and Scientific Method* (New York: Harcourt, Brace & World, 1934). The last book is more detailed and demanding than the first two, which are introductions designed specifically for students of rhetoric.

Notice that although the statements in the two syllogisms discuss quite different subjects, the underlying form is the same in both:

MAJOR PREMISE: All A's are B's.
MINOR PREMISE: All C's are A's.
CONCLUSION: All C's are B's.

It is apparent, then, that people often argue from general "truths" to particular cases, that the truths are about classes of things, and that the particular cases are seen as members of the classes and therefore share the characteristics of the classes. If the premises are indeed true and if the rules of logical inference are followed, the conclusion is assumed to be necessary and true. Since we have no desire to introduce here the principles of logical reasoning, we have said nothing about these rules of inference or about the different forms of categorical argument. What you should learn from this discussion is that logic can provide you with patterns for ordering the statements in your message clearly and persuasively.[2]

If you study actual examples of persuasive discourse (newspaper editorials, political and legal debates, popular and scientific arguments in journals), you will seldom find the arguments presented as formally as those that we have been discussing. Frequently the writer omits one of the premises or the conclusion. These "informal" syllogisms are called *enthymemes*.

For example, a person might argue that since cholera is a kind of bacteria, it reproduces asexually (here the major premise is omitted). In his "Letter from Birmingham Jail" King might have argued that since we have no obligation to obey unjust laws, we

---

[2] As we have suggested, categorical argument is only one kind of deductive argument. Logicians also distinguish hypothetical, alternative, and disjunctive arguments, each of which provides a basic pattern for organizing statements. Typical forms of each are:

HYPOTHETICAL:
If A is B, then C is D.   If war is declared, the draft call will soar.
A is B.   War is declared.
C is D.   The draft call will soar.

ALTERNATIVE:
Either A or B.   Either we hang together or we will all hang separately.
Not A.   We do not hang together.
B.   We will all hang separately.

DISJUNCTIVE:
Not both A and B.   It is not possible that a man can both love his country
                             and betray it.
A.   Jones loves his country.
Not B.   Jones did not betray it.

have no obligation to obey segregation laws (here the minor premise is omitted). Omissions are possible because the reader is usually able to supply the missing information. They are permissible, however, only when both writer and reader are convinced that the missing premise is indisputably true; that is, when the premise is a belief that writer and reader share. To conceal questionable assumptions by omitting them is to compromise oneself morally as well as to run the risk of arousing the defenses of a perceptive reader. King's inclusion of both premises suggests not only a desire to make his argument as clear as possible but also an assumption that one or both premises express beliefs not shared by his readers.

Writers frequently employ other kinds of arguments that are less logically compelling but nevertheless persuasive: authoritative statements, for example, and analogies. King relies heavily on passages from the Bible and on statements of theologians and philosophers, authorities that are likely to be persuasive *to his readers,* a group of clergymen. And he cites several instances of civil disobedience that are analogous to his own efforts:

> Of course, there is nothing new about this kind of civil disobedience. It was evidenced sublimely in the refusal of Shadrach, Meshach, and Abednego to obey the laws of Nebuchadnezzar, on the ground that a higher moral law was at stake. It was practiced superbly by the early Christians, who were willing to face hungry lions and the excruciating pain of chopping blocks rather than submit to certain unjust laws of the Roman Empire. To a degree, academic freedom is a reality today because Socrates practiced civil disobedience. In our own nation, the Boston Tea Party represented a massive act of civil disobedience.
>
> We should never forget that everything Hitler did in Germany was "legal" and everything the Hungarian freedom fighters did in Hungary was "illegal." It was "illegal" to aid and comfort a Jew in Hitler's Germany. Even so, I am sure that, had I lived in Germany at the time, I would have aided and comforted my Jewish brothers. If today I lived in a Communist country where certain principles dear to the Christian faith are suppressed, I would openly advocate disobeying that country's antireligious laws.
>
> MARTIN LUTHER KING, JR., "Letter from Birmingham Jail"

If King's readers consider these acts moral and desirable, then they must approve his acts in Birmingham.

DEVELOPING THE MESSAGE

In actual discourse, a logical argument seldom constitutes the entire message; rather, it generally forms the nucleus of a larger structure. For the sake of clarity, explanatory statements are usually added to each premise, and when the reader is likely to doubt the truth of the premises, each is substantiated by additional arguments. (Notice the care with which King explains and argues his major and minor premises. He does not assume that his readers will accept either one as indisputably true.) Furthermore, statements are usually added to introduce and conclude the argument: to introduce the subject and the writer, to explain the importance of the problem that the writer seeks to solve, to point out the implications of the writer's position, and so on. In short, the argument is placed in a larger context that serves to make it clearer and more persuasive.

The following outline is a set of instructions, a heuristic procedure for reconstructing the reader's image; it can help you develop both your argument and its context. By using this procedure you increase your chances of producing a well-developed first draft.

1) Introduction
   a) Direct the reader's attention to the subject or problem.
   b) Explain your experience with the subject, the reasons why you can write with authority.
   c) Establish bridges with the reader by pointing out shared beliefs, attitudes, and experiences.
2) Background
   a) Explain the nature of the problem — its history and causes.
   b) Explain its relevance to the reader's problems, desires, and interests — the reasons why the problem is important to him.
3) Argument
   a) State the major premise. Include any information that is necessary for making it clear and acceptable.
   b) State the minor premise. Include any information that is necessary for making it clear and acceptable. (It is usually the minor premise that needs the most substantial support. Cite authoritative statements, facts, statistics, personal experiences and experiences of others, and so on.)
   c) State your conclusion.
   d) Demonstrate the superiority of your position by pointing out defects in the premises or inferences of alternative positions. Explain why the alternatives cannot solve the problem; or if they can, why your solution solves it better.
4) Conclusion
   a) Explain the implications of the argument, such as the benefits to the reader of accepting it and the undesirable consequences of rejecting it.

     b) Summarize your argument: the problem (2a), your con-
     clusion (3c), and the reasons for accepting it (3a and 3b).

When this procedure is used thoughtfully, it can increase both the efficiency of the writing process and the effectiveness of the discourse. Since it can serve as a checklist of kinds of information that might be included, it can help you discover what you need in order to develop a discourse. In addition, since it separates and describes the stages of the discourse, it enables you to focus attention on one stage at a time and thus avoid being overwhelmed by the complexity of the task. It helps you state your assumptions, inferences, and evidence in a clear and orderly way that makes your argument corrigible (i.e., capable of being analyzed, verified, and corrected). Finally, because each stage is addressed to the reader's assumed needs, psychological as well as logical, it increases the chances that your discourse will in fact satisfy his needs. Mastery of this method enables you to develop appropriate and lucid arguments quickly.

VARIANT FORMS

While actual persuasive essays have many of the features of the pattern just described, they may vary widely one from another. These variations result in part from the nature of your argument, the extent of your knowledge, and the conventions of the kind of discourse that you are writing (e.g., the structure and language of a political argument differ from those of a scientific argument). But these variations depend most significantly on your conception of your reader—the extent of his relevant knowledge and the nature and strength of his values and attitudes. If, for example, the reader already regards you as an authority, your experience with the problem (1b) may be omitted or mentioned only briefly. If the reader is familiar with the problem and the way it concerns him, 2a and 2b may likewise be omitted or merely mentioned. If he is hostile to your position, 3a and 3b must be developed extensively. On the other hand, if one of the premises is a widely shared belief, the argument may be reduced to an enthymeme. If the implications are obvious to the reader or if the discourse is short (e.g., a letter to the editor of a newspaper), 4a may be appropriately modified or omitted. The heuristic procedure is not a set of pigeonholes into which information is put, but a flexible plan for producing a discourse adjusted to the unique features of a specific situation: to a particular writer and a particular reader, to a particular subject, and to the conventions that govern the particular occasion and type of discourse.

Expanding the reader's image

The procedure for expanding the reader's image does not differ greatly from the one for reconstructing it, except in the way the writer states the nucleus of his discourse. Discourses designed to add to the reader's image are difficult to characterize, for there are no elaborate, well-defined conventions that govern them, no forms analogous to the conventions of deductive and inductive argument. We can, however, point out some features that, though obvious perhaps, are nevertheless true and, we hope, useful.

STATING AND EXPLAINING THE THESIS

The writer always, or nearly always, states his *thesis*, his interpretation of an experience; and the thesis statement strongly influences the organization of his discourse and the kind of information that he includes. One thesis may require narration of an event or description of a scene; another, division into parts and discussion of each in turn; a third, a sustained comparison and contrast; and so on. The thesis statement creates expectations in the reader's mind, and its explanation satisfies them. The beginning of E. B. White's "Khrushchev and I" clearly illustrates the nature and function of the thesis. In the first paragraph the thesis is stated and then immediately restated twice.

> Until I happened to read a description of him in the paper recently, I never realized how much Chairman Khrushchev and I are alike. This fellow and myself, it turns out, are like as two peas. The patterns of our lives are almost indistinguishable, one from the other.
>
> E. B. WHITE, "Khrushchev and I"

Although White specifically tells us what will follow (a list of similarities), we could have inferred this from the thesis, which lets us know what to expect.

> I suppose the best way to illustrate this striking resemblance is to take up the points of similarity, one by one . . . .

Furthermore, there is always an oscillation between generalizations and more concrete statements, just as there is in argumentative discourse, the dominant one being the shift from the thesis to its explanation. (The discussion of paragraphs in Chapter 14 will further develop this relationship of general to particular statement.) Our minds seem to be so constituted that we have difficulty in grasping abstractions divorced from experience. How many times have you heard people ask for an example when they are confronted with an abstract statement? Adequate explanation of abstractions requires rooting them in the physical world around us. The "fusion of a large generality with an insistent particularity," as Alfred North Whitehead puts it in *Modes of Thought*, seems to be necessary to any conscious understanding of experience. The concrete statements chosen to connect an abstraction with the world of experience should exploit already shared knowledge; the abstraction presents the larger conceptual system that the writer hopes to share with the reader.

One of the most common errors of beginning writers is the failure to root their generalizations in the world of experience. If the writer cannot readily cite specific examples, he had better question the truth of the general statement. By oscillating between generalities and particulars, he not only increases the chances that he will be understood but also tests, informally, the adequacy of his generalizations.

The need for rigorously logical interrelationships among statements is less insistent in expository than in argumentative discourse. Logically compelling demonstration softens to explanation. The conclusion of a deductive argument, along with the premises and the supporting evidence from which it derives, has its counterpart in expository discourse in the thesis, with its accompanying explanation and illustration. Since the expository writer seeks only to add to the reader's image, not to root out and replace some feature of it, there is no need for the power of logical demonstration. Instead, the emphasis is on clarity of focus (a precisely stated thesis), on clarity of structure (a well-defined, well-signaled organizational pattern), and on clarity and appropriateness of explanation (definition of unshared terms; use of shared knowledge, experience, and values). This writer's chief task is to connect new information with old, stating and ordering his generalizations and explanations as clearly as possible.

DEVELOPING THE MESSAGE

The thesis and its explanation, like a logical argument, seldom stand alone; they are usually embedded in a larger structure that is designed to increase their effectiveness. The following is a heuristic procedure for producing a rough draft of a discourse that adds information to the reader's image.

1) Introduction
   a) Direct the reader's attention to the subject or problem.
   b) Explain your experience with it.

2) Background
   a) Explain the nature of the problem — its history and causes.
   b) Explain why the problem is important to the reader.
3) Thesis and explanation
   a) State the thesis.
   b) Develop it.
4) Conclusion
   a) Explain the implications (social, philosophical, psychological, and so on) of the information.
   b) Summarize your discussion: the problem (2a), your thesis (3a), and your explanation (3b).

As we noted earlier, how you use this procedure depends on a number of variables: the nature of the message, its length and complexity, the extent of the reader's relevant knowledge, his knowledge of you, and his attitude toward you. If the reader regards you as an authority, 1b may be passed over briefly or omitted. If he is familiar with the background of the problem and its significance for him, 2a and 2b may be similarly reduced or omitted. If the discourse is short, omit 4b. And so on.

Changing the quality of the reader's image

We are tempted to say that the two procedures described so far are adequate guides not only for reconstructing or expanding the reader's image but for changing its quality as well; that is, for changing the strength of the reader's commitment to a value or belief or for clarifying notions that he only partially understands. Traditional argument often has the effect of either strengthening or weakening belief rather than revolutionizing it, and writing apparently designed to give new information often serves instead to clarify what is obscurely known. Nevertheless, at times the writer does clearly intend to alter the quality of some feature of the reader's image. Close scrutiny of how writers handle these situations reveals techniques that seem designed specifically to fulfill this intention.

INCREASING THE READER'S COMMITMENT

The reader who has only a weak commitment to a belief often holds other beliefs that are incompatible with it; he is hence unable to commit himself to any of them. He sits on a psychological fence and doubts. Changing the quality of his belief, that is, changing from doubt to conviction, depends heavily on the writer's ability to diagnose the source of conflict in the reader's mind. Once he has done this, his principal task is to remove the obstacles that prevent commitment.

We have already cited a clear instance of this method in Chapter 1 — Anatol Rapoport's description of his efforts to overcome doubt in the minds of his students:

> Once when teaching elementary physics, I was impressed with the resistance of mature intelligent students to some fundamental facts and concepts. For example, when a man falling in a parachute has reached constant velocity, the forces acting on him add up to zero. Beginners almost invariably resist this conclusion. "If there is no resultant force acting on a falling body," they ask, "why does it fall?" Proof by appeal to the fundamental equation of motion is of little avail. They "believe" the equation, but they *believe* their preconceptions.
>
> Getting to the core of the matter usually helps. One must point out *where the preconceptions come from.* They come from an inner conviction (based on direct experience!) that it takes a force to move a body. The force in the muscles is felt directly, but the opposing force, say of friction or air resistance (which must be equal and opposite if the body is moved with constant velocity) is not directly felt and therefore ignored. Hence the false notion that an unbalanced force is acting on a body moving with constant velocity.
>
> Another idea difficult to put across was that underlying the operation of a Venturi tube. As the stream of air passes through the constriction in this device, the velocity of the flow increases, and the pressure decreases. The prevailing image resists these facts. Most students believe that pressure is greater in the narrower portions and the velocity of flow is smaller. When the probable origin of this notion is pointed out ("You are thinking of squeezing tooth paste and of traffic jams") the mental resistance usually collapses.
>
> ANATOL RAPOPORT, *Fights, Games, and Debates*

Consider another example. Responding to those people who believe that passive resistance, attractive though it may be as a means of resolving conflicts, is inconsistent with Western values and experience, Richard B. Gregg argues that it *is* sufficiently consistent to provide an effective substitute for war:

> But the similarities between war and nonviolent resistance are not merely an interesting set of analogies. This entire chapter up to this point answers two doubts: namely, whether this method of struggle is not utterly foreign and new and suited only to Oriental people, and therefore whether it could be adopted by people with the modern Western attitude of mind. The facts that the military virtues are used and needed in this new form of struggle, and that the principles of military strategy apply here too, show that if we adopt this new mode of settling conflicts we will not be entirely reversing our previous

experience, nor abandoning whatever true principles and values the human race may have garnered from its age-long experience of war. It may be that, for its first great mass success, nonviolent resistance had to be used among a people who have much social awareness and who had been thoroughly inculcated and disciplined for many centuries with ideas of nonviolence, as the Indians with their Buddhist, Jain, and Hindu traditions have been. But after its first success, a desire to try it has risen in other countries, and its rationale is coming to be understood. For obvious reasons, their desire and understanding will increase. Given desire and understanding, the courage, organizing ability, and disciplinary capacity of other peoples, whether Asian, African or Western, is not less than that of Indians. Hence the use of the method may be expected to spread. The new method is an advance, an improvement in the art of deciding public disputes, but not so utterly foreign as to be unworkable by other peoples. By fully understanding these relationships between war and nonviolent resistance we may provide ourselves an assurance with which we may advance to this new procedure.

RICHARD B. GREGG, "An Effective Substitute for War,"
The Power of Nonviolence

The strength of a person's commitment to a particular belief seems to depend on the consistency of the belief with other features of his image. If this is true, then your task in trying to strengthen your reader's commitment is to show him (1) that the inconsistencies, or conflicts, are only apparent and can be explained away, or (2) that the idea is consistent with beliefs that he holds strongly, or (3) that although there are inconsistencies, alternative positions are even more inconsistent and therefore even more open to objection. Such arguments make up the nucleus of your message; your analysis of the conflict or inconsistency constitutes the explanation of the problem, which precedes your arguments (see 2a and 3, p. 234).

CLARIFYING THE READER'S IMAGE

In an attempt to clarify the reader's image the writer's ability to diagnose the source of the reader's confusion is again extremely important. Unless he has a fairly precise notion of the difficulty, the writer's only recourse is to review the whole subject, in the hope that by doing so he will at some point in the discussion eliminate the difficulty.

Discourse designed to clarify something that is obscure or confused often begins with a statement about the origin and nature of the reader's difficulty. (See 2a, p. 238.) There are two common kinds of difficulty, one arising from obscure generalizations and the other from inadequate development. The first difficulty can usually be eliminated by definition of unshared terms or by restatement of the entire generalization. For example, people who read Francis Bacon's discussion of the art of communication are often puzzled by his statement that the art is composed of three disciplines called the "organ of tradition," the "method of tradition," and the "illustration of tradition." Although his subsequent discussion helps clarify the concept of tradition, many readers remain somewhat puzzled. The difficulty can be removed, however, by the explanation that to Bacon *tradition* does not mean a custom or an established practice, as it does to us, but rather the act of delivery or transfer (from the Latin *tradere,* which means to hand over). Thus Bacon is saying that the art of communication is concerned with how we transfer knowledge—an entirely familiar notion.

At other times the source of the difficulty lies in the development of the generalization. Unless the generalization is linked to features of the reader's image, the reader will not feel that he understands it completely. As we pointed out earlier, understanding seems to require that abstractions be linked with the known and the particular. When trying to clarify an abstraction, make sure the reader can assimilate it by citing several instances that are familiar *to him.* It does not seem to be an excessively broad generalization to say that the most significant technique for clarifying an idea is redundancy—saying the same thing in a number of different ways. Restating generalizations, defining terms, and piling up specific instances are all forms of redundancy.

Conventionally, redundant statements in a discourse are regarded as undesirable. But we can grant that nonfunctional redundancy is undesirable (since it is both inefficient and tedious) and still maintain that at times redundancy has considerable value as a technique of communication, particularly in the situation that we have been describing. One way redundant statements function in clarifying features of the reader's image is by increasing the chances of introducing shared features into the discourse—a scatter-gun approach. For example, if you present a number of illustrations of a single abstraction, it is likely that at least one of them will be familiar to the reader. Redundant statements also serve to create bridges where necessary links are missing. Information new to the reader on first statement appears a bit more familiar after it is restated, often in a new guise or in more detail. Once it is presented for a third time, parts of the information may be understood; these newly shared parts act as bridges to fuller understanding. By means of redundant statements, then, the reader cycles toward understanding.

EXERCISES

1 Read the following essay by James Madison, identifying the kinds of arguments he employs. Analyze the essay for other features characteristic of traditional argumentative discourse (i.e., those features described in 1, 2, and 4 of the procedure on pp. 234–35). Do the same for the essay by Martin Luther King, Jr. (p. 10). Both essays are instances of traditional argumentative discourse. Can you account for the differences between the two?

The Federalist, Number X
JAMES MADISON

Among the numerous advantages promised by a well constructed union, none deserves to be more accurately developed than its tendency to break and control the violence of faction. The friend of popular governments, never finds himself so much alarmed for their character and fate, as when he contemplates their propensity to this dangerous vice. He will not fail, therefore, to set a due value on any plan which, without violating the principles to which he is attached, provides a proper cure for it. The instability, injustice, and confusion, introduced into the public councils, have, in truth, been the mortal diseases under which popular governments have everywhere perished; as they continue to be the favourite and fruitful topics from which the adversaries to liberty derive their most specious declamations. The valuable improvements made by the American constitutions on the popular models, both ancient and modern, cannot certainly be too much admired; but it would be an unwarrantable partiality, to contend that they have as effectually obviated the danger on this side, as was wished and expected. Complaints are every where heard from our most considerate and virtuous citizens, equally the friends of public and private faith, and of public and personal liberty, that our governments are too unstable; that the public good is disregarded in the conflicts of rival parties; and that measures are too often decided, not according to the rules of justice, and the rights of the minor party, but by the superior force of an interested and overbearing majority. However anxiously we may wish that these complaints had no foundation, the evidence of known facts will not permit us to deny that they are in some degree true. It will be found, indeed, on a candid review of our situation, that some of the distresses under which we labour, have been erroneously charged on the operation of our governments; but it will be found, at the same time, that other causes will not alone account for many of our heaviest misfortunes; and, particularly, for that prevailing and increasing distrust of public engagements, and alarm for private rights, which are echoed from one end of the continent to the other. These must be chiefly, if not wholly, effects of the unsteadiness and injustice, with which a factious spirit has tainted our public administrations.

By a faction, I understand a number of citizens, whether amounting to a majority or minority of the whole, who are united and actuated by some common impulse of passion, or of interest, adverse to the rights of other citizens, or to the permanent and aggregate interests of the community.

There are two methods of curing the mischiefs of faction: The one, by removing its causes; the other, by controlling its effects.

There are again two methods of removing the causes of faction: The one, by destroying the liberty which is essential to its existence; the other, by giving to every citizen the same opinions, the same passions, and the same interests.

It could never be more truly said, than of the first remedy, that it was worse than the disease. Liberty is to faction what air is to fire, an aliment, without which it instantly expires. But it could not be a less folly to abolish liberty, which is essential to political life because it nourishes faction, than it would be to wish the annihilation of air, which is essential to animal life, because it imparts to fire its destructive agency.

The second expedient is as impracticable, as the first would be unwise. As long as the reason of man continues fallible, and he is at liberty to exercise it, different opinions will be formed. As long as the connection subsists between his reason and his self-love, his opinions and his passions will have a reciprocal influence on each other; and the former will be objects to which the latter will attach themselves. The diversity in the faculties of men, from which the rights of property originate, is not less an insuperable obstacle to an uniformity of interests. The protection of these faculties is the first object of government. From the protection of different and unequal faculties of acquiring property, the possession of different degrees and kinds of property immediately results; and from the influence of these on the sentiments and views of the respective proprietors, ensues a division of the society into different interests and parties.

The latent causes of faction are thus sown in the nature of man; and we see them every where brought into different degrees of activity, according to the different circumstances of civil society. A zeal for different opinions concerning religion, concerning government, and many other points, as well of speculation as of practice; an attachment to different leaders, ambitiously contending for pre-eminence and power; or to persons of other descriptions, whose fortunes have been interesting to the human passions, have, in turn, divided mankind into parties, inflamed them with mutual animosity, and rendered them much more disposed to vex and oppress each other, than to co-operate for their common good. So strong is this propensity of mankind, to fall into mutual animosities, that where no substantial occasion presents itself, the most frivolous and fanciful distinctions have been sufficient to kindle their unfriendly passions, and excite their most violent conflicts. But the most common and durable source of factions, has been the various and unequal distribution of property. Those who hold, and those who are without property, have ever formed distinct interests in society. Those who are creditors, and those who are debtors, fall under a like discrimination. A landed interest, a manufacturing interest, a mercantile interest, a moneyed interest, with many lesser interests, grow up of necessity in civilized nations, and divide them into different classes, actuated by different sentiments and views. The regulation of these various and interfering interests forms the principal task of modern legislation, and involves the spirit of party and faction in the necessary and ordinary operations of government.

No man is allowed to be a judge in his own cause because his interest will certainly bias his judgment, and, not improbably, corrupt his integrity. With equal, nay, with greater reason, a body of men are unfit to be both judges and parties at the same time; yet what are many of the most important acts of legislation, but so many judicial determinations, not indeed concerning the rights of single persons, but concerning the rights of large bodies of citizens? and what are the different classes of legislators, but advocates and parties to the causes which they determine? Is a law proposed concerning private debts? It is a question to which the creditors are parties on one side, and the debtors on the other. Justice ought to hold the balance between them. Yet the parties are, and must be, themselves the judges: and the most numerous party, or, in other words, the most powerful faction, must be expected to prevail. Shall domestic manufactures be encouraged, and in what degree, by restrictions on foreign manufactures? are questions which would be differently decided by the landed and the manufacturing classes; and probably by neither with a sole regard to justice and the public good. The apportionment of taxes, on the various descriptions of property, is an act which seems to require the most exact impartiality; yet there is, perhaps, no legislative act, in which greater opportunity and temptation are given to a predominant party, to trample on the rules of justice. Every shilling, with which they overburden the inferiour number, is a shilling saved to their own pockets.

It is in vain to say, that enlightened statesmen will be able to adjust these clashing interests, and render them all subservient to the public good. Enlightened statesmen will not always be at the helm: nor, in many cases, can such an adjustment be made at all, without taking into view indirect and remote considerations, which will rarely prevail over the immediate interest which one party may find in disregarding the rights of another, or the good of the whole.

The inference to which we are brought is, that the *causes* of faction cannot be removed; and that relief is only to be sought in the means of controlling its *effects*.

If a faction consists of less than a majority, relief is supplied by the republican principle, which enables the majority to defeat its sinister views, by regular vote. It may clog the administration, it may convulse the society; but it will be unable to execute and mask its violence under the forms of the constitution. When a majority is included in a faction, the form of popular government, on the other hand, enables it to sacrifice to its ruling passion or interest, both the public good and the rights of other citizens. To secure the public good, and private rights, against the danger of such a faction, and at the same time to preserve the spirit and the form of popular government, is then the great object to which our inquiries are directed. Let me add, that it is the great desideratum by which alone this form of government can be rescued from the opprobrium under which it has so long laboured, and be recommended to the esteem and adoption of mankind.

By what means is this object attainable? Evidently by one of two only. Either the existence of the same passion or interest in a majority, at the same time must be prevented; or the majority, having such coexistent passion or interest, must be rendered, by their number and local situation, unable to concert and carry into effect schemes of oppression. If the impulse and the opportunity be suffered to coincide, we well know, that neither moral nor religious motives can be relied on as an adequate control. They are not found to be such on the injustice and violence of individuals, and lose their efficacy in proportion to the number combined together; that is, in proportion as their efficacy becomes needful.

From this view of the subject, it may be concluded, that a pure democracy, by which I mean a society consisting of a small number of citizens, who assemble and administer the government in person, can admit of no cure from the mischiefs of faction. A common passion or interest will, in almost every case, be felt by a majority of the whole; a communication and concert, results from the form of government itself; and there is nothing to check the inducements to sacrifice the weaker party, or an obnoxious individual. Hence it is, that such democracies have ever been spectacles of turbulence and contention; have ever been found incompatible with personal security, or the rights of property; and have, in general, been as short in their lives, as they have been violent in their deaths. Theoretic politicians, who have patronized this species of government, have erroneously supposed, that by reducing mankind to a perfect equality in their political rights, they would, at the same time, be perfectly equalized and assimilated in their possessions, their opinions, and their passions.

A republic, by which I mean a government in which the scheme of representation takes place, opens a different prospect, and promises the cure for which we are seeking. Let us examine the points in which it varies from pure democracy, and we shall comprehend both the nature of the cure and the efficacy which it must derive from the union.

The two great points of difference, between a democracy and a republic, are, first, the delegation of the government, in the latter, to a small number of citizens elected by the rest; secondly, the greater number of citizens, and greater sphere of country, over which the latter may be extended.

The effect of the first difference is, on the one hand, to refine and enlarge the public views, by passing them through the medium of a chosen body of citizens, whose wisdom may best discern the true interest of their country, and whose patriotism and love of justice, will be least likely to sacrifice it to temporary or partial considerations. Under such a regulation, it may well happen, that the public voice, pronounced by the representatives of the people, will be more consonant to the public good, than if pronounced by the people themselves, convened for the purpose. On the other hand, the effect may be inverted. Men of factious tempers, of local prejudices, or of sinister designs, may by intrigue, by corruption, or by other means, first obtain the suffrages, and then betray the interests of the people. The question resulting is, whether small or extensive republics are most favourable to the election of proper guardians of the public weal; and it is clearly decided in favour of the latter by two obvious considerations.

In the first place, it is to be remarked, that however small the republic may be, the representatives must be raised to a certain number, in order to guard against the cabals of a few; and that however large it may be, they must be limited to a certain number, in order to guard against the confusion of a multitude. Hence, the number of representatives in the two cases not being in proportion to that of the constituents, and being proportionally greatest in the small republic, it follows, that if the proportion of fit characters be not less in the large than in the small republic, the former will present a greater option, and consequently a greater probability of a fit choice.

In the next place, as each representative will be chosen by a greater number of citizens in the large than in the small republic, it will be more difficult for unworthy candidates to practice with success the vicious arts, by which elections are too often carried; and the suffrages of the people being more free, will be more likely to centre in men who possess the most attractive merit, and the most diffusive and established characters.

It must be confessed, that in this, as in most other cases, there is a mean, on both sides of which inconveniences will be found to lie. By enlarging too much the number of electors, you render the representative too little acquainted with all their local circumstances and lesser interests; as by reducing it too much, you render him unduly attached to these, and too little fit to comprehend and pursue great and national objects. The federal constitution forms a happy combination in this respect; the great and aggregate interests being referred to the national, the local and particular to the state legislatures.

The other point of difference is, the greater number of citizens, and extent of territory, which may be brought within the compass of republican, than of democratic government; and it is this circumstance principally which renders factious combinations less to be dreaded in the former, than in the latter. The smaller the society, the fewer probably will be the distinct parties and interests composing it; the fewer the distinct parties and interests, the more frequently will a majority be found of the same party; and the smaller the number of individuals composing a majority, and the smaller the compass within which they are placed, the more easily will they concert and execute their plans of oppression. Extend the sphere, and you take in a greater variety of parties and interests; you make it less probable that a majority of the whole will have a common motive to invade the rights of other citizens; or if such a common motive exists, it will be more difficult for all who feel it to discover their own strength, and to act in unison with each other. Besides other impediments, it may be remarked, that where there is a consciousness of unjust or dishonourable purposes, communication is always checked by distrust, in proportion to the number whose concurrence is necessary.

Hence, it clearly appears, that the same advantage, which a republic has over a democracy, in controlling the effects of faction, is enjoyed by a large over a small republic—is enjoyed by the union over the states composing it. Does this advantage consist in the substitution of representatives, whose enlightened views and virtuous sentiments render them superior to local prejudices, and to schemes of injustice? It will not be denied, that the representation of the union will be most likely to possess these requisite endowments. Does it consist in the greater security afforded by a greater variety of parties, against the event of any one party being able to outnumber and oppress the rest? In an equal degree does the increased variety of parties, comprised within the union, increase this security. Does it, in fine, consist in the greater obstacles opposed to the concert and accomplishment of the secret wishes of an unjust and interested majority? Here, again, the extent of the union gives it the most palpable advantage.

The influence of factious leaders may kindle a flame within their particular states, but will be unable to spread a general conflagration through the other states; a religious sect may degenerate into a political faction in a part of the confederacy; but the variety of sects dispersed over the entire face of it, must secure the national councils against any danger from that source: a rage for paper money, for an abolition of debts, for an equal division of property, or for any other improper or wicked project, will be less apt to pervade the whole body of the union, than a particular member of it; in the same proportion as such a malady is more likely to taint a particular county or district, than an entire state.

In the extent and proper structure of the union, therefore, we behold a republican remedy for the diseases most incident to republican government. And according to the degree of pleasure and pride we feel in being republicans, ought to be our zeal in cherishing the spirit, and supporting the character of federalists.

2   We have said nothing about the rules that govern logical argument. One way of developing an understanding of the difference between good argument and bad is to study typical examples of bad argument. Read Irving M. Copi's essay, which offers an introduction to logical fallacies. To test your understanding, find instances of the fallacies he discusses. Letters to the editor of your local newspaper offer a rich source of examples.

Informal Fallacies
IRVING M. COPI

There is no universally accepted classification of fallacies. This situation is not surprising: as the early modern logician De Morgan aptly said, "There *is* no such thing as a classification of the ways in which men may arrive at an error: it is much to be doubted whether there ever *can be*."

The word "fallacy" is used in various ways. One perfectly proper use of the word is to designate any mistaken idea or false belief, like the "fallacy" of believing that all men are honest. But logicians use the term in the narrower sense of an error in reasoning or in argument. A fallacy, as we shall use the term, is a type of incorrect argument. Since it is a *type* of incorrect argument, we can say of two different arguments that they contain or commit the *same* fallacy. Many arguments, of course, are so obviously incorrect as to deceive no one. It is customary in the study of logic to reserve the term "fallacy" for arguments which, although incorrect, are psychologically persuasive. We therefore define a fallacy as a form of argument that *seems* to be correct but which proves, upon examination, not to be so. It is profitable to study such arguments, for familiarity and understanding will help keep us from being misled by them. To be forewarned is to be forearmed.

Traditionally, fallacies are divided into two broad groups, formal and informal. Formal fallacies are most conveniently discussed in connection with certain patterns of valid inference to which they bear a superficial resemblance. . . . For the present, we shall be concerned with informal fallacies, errors in reasoning into which we may fall either because of carelessness and inattention to our subject matter or through being misled by some ambiguity in the language used to formulate our argument. We may divide informal fallacies into fallacies of *relevance* and fallacies of *ambiguity*. No attempt will be made at completeness; only eighteen informal fallacies will be considered, the most common and deceptive ones.

I. FALLACIES OF RELEVANCE

Common to all arguments which commit fallacies of relevance is the circumstance that their premises are *logically irrelevant* to, and therefore incapable of establishing the truth of, their conclusions. The irrelevance here is logical rather than psychological, of course, for unless there were some psychological connection, there would be no persuasiveness or *seeming* correctness. How psychological relevance can be confused with logical relevance is most satisfactorily explained by reference to the fact that language can be used directively and expressively as well as informatively.

A number of particular types of irrelevant argument have traditionally been given Latin names. Some of these Latin names have become part of the English language, "ad hominem," for example. Others are less familiar. We shall consider only a few of them here, making no pretense to an exhaustive treatment. How they succeed in being persuasive despite their logical incorrectness is in many cases to be explained by their expressive function of evoking such attitudes as fear, pity, reverence, disapproval, or enthusiasm.

1. Argumentum ad Baculum (appeal to force). The *argumentum ad baculum* is the fallacy committed when one appeals to force or the threat of force to cause acceptance of a conclusion. It is usually resorted to only when evidence or rational arguments fail. The *ad baculum* is epitomized in the saying "might makes right." The use and threat of "strong-arm" methods to coerce political opponents provide contemporary examples of this fallacy. Appeal to nonrational methods of intimidation may of course be more subtle than the open use or threat of concentration camps or "goon squads." The lobbyist uses the *ad baculum* when he reminds a representative that he (the lobbyist) represents so many thousands of voters in the representative's constituency, or so many potential contributors to campaign funds. Logically these considerations have nothing to do with the merits of the legislation the lobbyist is attempting to influence. But they may be, unfortunately, very persuasive. On the international scale, the *argumentum ad baculum* means war or the threat of war. An amusing though at the same time frightening example of *ad baculum* reasoning at the international level is told in Harry Hopkins' account of the "Big Three" meeting at Yalta toward the end of World War II. Churchill is reported to have told the others that the Pope had suggested that such-and-such a course of action should be followed. And Stalin is supposed to have indicated his disagreement by asking, "And how many divisions did you say the Pope had available for combat duty?"

2. Argumentum ad Hominem (abusive). The phrase *"argumentum ad hominem"* translates literally into "argument directed to the man." It is susceptible of two interpretations, whose interrelationship will be explained after the two are discussed separately. We may designate this fallacy on the first interpretation as the "abusive" variety. It is committed when, instead of trying to *disprove the truth* of what is asserted, one attacks the man who made the assertion. Thus it may be argued that Bacon's philosophy is untrustworthy because he was removed from his chancellorship for dishonesty. This argument is fallacious, because the personal character of a man is logically irrelevant to the truth or falsehood of what he says or the correctness or incorrectness of his argument. To argue that proposals are bad or assertions false because they are proposed or asserted by Communists (or by "economic royalists," or by Catholics, or by anti-Catholics, or by wife beaters) is to argue fallaciously and to be guilty of committing an *argumentum ad hominem* (abusive). The way in which this irrelevant argument may sometimes persuade is through the psychological process of transference. Where an attitude of disapproval toward a person can be evoked, it may possibly tend to overflow the strictly emotional field and become disagreement with what that person says. But this connection is only psychological, not logical. Even the most wicked of men may sometimes tell the truth or argue correctly.

The classic example of this fallacy has to do with British law procedure. There the practice of law is divided between *solicitors*, who prepare the cases for trial, and *barristers*, who argue or "plead" the cases in court. Ordinarily their cooperation is admirable but sometimes it leaves much to be desired. On one such latter occasion, the barrister ignored the case completely until the day it was to be presented at court, depending upon the solicitor to investigate the defendant's case and prepare the brief. He arrived at court just a moment before the trial was to begin and was handed his brief by a solicitor. Surprised at its thinness, he glanced inside to find written: "No case; abuse the plaintiff's attorney!"

3. Argumentum ad Hominem (circumstantial). The other interpretation of the fallacy of *argumentum ad hominem*, the "circumstantial" variety, pertains to the relationship between a person's beliefs and his circumstances. Where two men are disputing, one may ignore the question of whether his own contention is *true* or *false* and seek instead to prove that his opponent ought to accept it because of his opponent's special circumstances. Thus if one's adversary is a clergyman, one may argue that a certain contention *must* be accepted because its denial is incompatible with the Scriptures. This is not to prove it *true* but to urge its acceptance by that particular individual because of his special circumstances, in this case his religious affiliation. Or if one's opponent is, say, a Republican, one may argue, not that a certain proposition is *true*, but that he ought to assent to it because it is implied by the tenets of his party. The classical example of this fallacy is the reply of the hunter when accused of barbarism in sacrificing unoffending animals to his own amusement. His reply is to ask his critic, "Why do *you* feed on the flesh of harmless cattle?" The sportsman here is guilty of an *argumentum ad hominem* because he does not try to prove that it is right to sacrifice animal life for human pleasure, but merely that it cannot consistently be decried by his critic because of the critic's own special circumstances, in this case his not being a vegetarian. Arguments such as these are not *cor-*

rect; they do not present good evidence for the *truth* of their conclusions but are intended only to win assent to the conclusion from one's opponent because of his special circumstances. This they frequently do; they are often very persuasive.

In the preceding paragraph we described the use of the circumstantial *ad hominem* to get one's adversary to *accept* a conclusion. It is also used as the basis for *rejecting* a conclusion defended by one's adversary, as when it is argued that the conclusions arrived at by one's opponent are dictated by his special circumstances rather than based upon reason or evidence. Thus if a manufacturer's arguments in favor of tariff protection are rejected on the grounds that a manufacturer would naturally be expected to favor a protective tariff, his critic would be committing the fallacy of *argumentum ad hominem* (circumstantial). This type of argument, though often persuasive, is clearly fallacious.

The connection between the abusive and the circumstantial varieties of *argumentum ad hominem* is not difficult to see. The circumstantial variety may even be regarded as a special case of the abusive. The first use of the circumstantial *ad hominem* charges the man who disputes your conclusion with inconsistency, either among his beliefs or between his preaching and his practice, which *may* be regarded as a kind of reproach or abuse. The second use of the circumstantial *ad hominem* charges the adversary with being so prejudiced that his alleged reasons are mere rationalizations of conclusions dictated by self-interest. And that is certainly to abuse him.

4. Argumentum ad Ignorantiam (argument from ignorance).
The fallacy of *argumentum ad ignorantiam* is illustrated by the argument that there must be ghosts because no one has ever been able to prove that there aren't any. The *argumentum ad ignorantiam* is committed whenever it is argued that a proposition is true simply on the basis that it has not been proved false, or that it is false because it has not been proved true. But our ignorance of how to prove or disprove a proposition clearly does not establish either the truth or the falsehood of that proposition. This fallacy often arises in connection with such matters as psychic phenomena, telepathy, and the like, where there is no clear-cut evidence either for or against. It is curious how many of the most enlightened people are prone to this fallacy, as witness the many students of science who affirm the falseness of spiritualist and telepathic claims simply on the grounds that their truth has not been established.

This mode of argument is not fallacious in a court of law, because there the guiding principle is that a person is presumed innocent until proven guilty. The defense can legitimately claim that if the prosecution has not proved guilt, this warrants a verdict of *not guilty.* But since this claim is based upon the special legal principle mentioned, it is consistent with the fact that the *argumentum ad ignorantiam* constitutes a fallacy in other contexts.

It is sometimes maintained that the *argumentum ad hominem* (abusive) is not fallacious when used in a court of law in an attempt to impeach the testimony of a witness. True enough, doubt can be cast upon a witness' testimony if it can be shown that he is a chronic liar and perjurer. Where that can be shown, it certainly reduces the credibility of the testimony offered. But if one goes on to infer that the witness' testimony establishes the falsehood of that to which he testifies, instead of concluding merely that his testimony does not establish its truth, then the reasoning is fallacious, being an *argumentum ad ignorantiam*. Such errors are more common than one would think.

A qualification should be made at this point. In some circumstances it can safely be assumed that *if* a certain event had occurred, evidence of it could be discovered by qualified investigators. In such circumstances it is perfectly reasonable to take the absence of proof of its occurrence as positive proof of its non-occurrence. Of course, the proof here is not based on ignorance but on our *knowledge* that if it had occurred it would be known. For example, if a serious F.B.I. investigation fails to unearth any evidence that Mr. X is a communist, it would be wrong to conclude that their research had left them ignorant. It has rather established that Mr. X is *not* one. Failure to draw such conclusions is the other side of the bad coin of innuendo, as when one says of a man that there is "no proof" that he is a scoundrel. In some cases not to draw a conclusion is as much a breach of correct reasoning as it would be to draw a mistaken conclusion.

5. Argumentum ad Misericordiam (appeal to pity). The *argumentum ad misericordiam* is the fallacy committed when pity is appealed to for the sake of getting a conclusion accepted. This argument is frequently encountered in courts of law, when a defense attorney may disregard the facts of the case and seek to win his client's acquittal by arousing pity in the jurymen. Clarence Darrow, the celebrated trial lawyer, was a master at using this device. In defending Thomas I. Kidd, an officer of the Amalgamated Woodworkers Union, who was indicted on a charge of criminal conspiracy, Darrow spoke these words to the jury:

I appeal to you not for Thomas Kidd, but I appeal to you for the long line — the long, long line reaching back through the ages and forward to the years to come — the long line of despoiled and downtrodden people of the earth. I appeal to you for those men who rise in the morning before daylight comes and who go home at night when the light has faded from the sky and give their life, their strength, their toil to make others rich and great. I appeal to you in the name of those women who are offering up their lives to this modern god of gold, and I appeal to you in the name of those little children, the living and the unborn.*

* As quoted in *Clarence Darrow for the Defense* by Irving Stone. Copyright, 1941, by Irving Stone. Published by Garden City Publishing Company, Inc., Garden City, N. Y.

Is Thomas Kidd guilty as charged? Darrow's appeal was sufficiently moving to make the average juror want to throw questions of evidence and of law out the window. Yet, however persuasive such a plea might be, from the point of view of logic that argument is fallacious which draws from "premises" such as these the conclusion that the accused is innocent.

An older and considerably more subtle example of the *argumentum ad misericordiam* is reported by Plato in the *Apology*, which purports to be a record of Socrates' defense of himself during his trial.

Perhaps there may be some one who is offended at me, when he calls to mind how he himself on a similar, or even a less serious occasion, prayed and entreated the judges with many tears, and how he produced his children in court, which was a moving spectacle, together with a host of relations and friends; whereas I, who am probably in danger of my life, will do none of these things. The contrast may occur to his mind, and he may be set against me, and vote in anger because he is displeased at me on this account. Now if there be such a person among you,—mind, I do not say that there is,—to him I may fairly reply: My friend, I am a man, and like other men, a creature of flesh and blood, and not "of wood or stone," as Homer says; and I have a family, yes, and sons, O Athenians, three in number, one almost a man, and two others who are still young; and yet I will not bring any of them hither in order to petition you for acquittal.

The *argumentum ad misericordiam* is sometimes used with ludicrous effect, as in the case of the youth who was tried for a particularly brutal crime, the murder of his mother and father with an axe. Confronted with overwhelming evidence, he pleaded for leniency on the grounds that he was an orphan.

6. Argumentum ad Populum. The *argumentum ad populum* is sometimes defined as the fallacy committed in directing an emotional appeal "to the people" or "to the gallery" to win their assent to a conclusion unsupported by valid argument. But this definition is so broad as to include the *ad misericordiam*, the *ad hominem* (abusive), and most of the other fallacies of relevance. We may define the *argumentum ad populum* fallacy a little more narrowly as the attempt to win popular assent to a conclusion by arousing the feelings and enthusiasms of the multitude. This is a favorite device with the propagandist, the demagogue, and—the advertiser. Faced with the task of mobilizing public sentiment for or against a particular measure, the propagandist will avoid the laborious process of collecting and presenting evidence and rational argument by using the short-cut methods of the *argumentum ad populum*. Where the proposal is for a change and he is against it, he will express suspicion of "newfangled innovations" and praise the wisdom of "the existing order." If he is for it, he will be for "progress" and opposed to "antiquated prejudice." Here we have the use of invidious terms with no rational attempt made to argue for them or to justify their application. This technique will be supplemented by displaying the flag, brass bands, and what-

ever else may serve to stimulate and excite the public. The demagogue's use of the *argumentum ad populum* is beautifully illustrated by
Shakespeare's version of Marc Antony's funeral oration over the body
of Julius Caesar.

It is to the huckster, the ballyhoo artist, the twentieth-century
advertiser that we may look to see the *argumentum ad populum* elevated
almost to the status of a fine art. Here every attempt is made to set
up associations between the product being advertised and objects
of which we can be expected to approve strongly. To eat a certain
brand of processed cereal is proclaimed a patriotic duty. To bathe
with a certain brand of soap is described as a thrilling experience.
Strains of symphonic music precede and follow the mention of a certain dentifrice on the radio and television programs sponsored by its
manufacturer. In pictorial advertisements, the people portrayed as
using the products advertised are always pictured as wearing the
kind of clothing and living in the kind of houses calculated to arouse
the approval and admiration of the average consumer. The young
men pictured as delightedly using the products are clear-eyed and
broad-shouldered, the older men are invariably "of distinction." The
women are all slim and lovely, either very well dressed or hardly
dressed at all. Whether you are interested in economical transportation or in high-speed driving, you will be assured by each automobile manufacturer that his product is "best," and he will "prove" his
assertion by displaying his car surrounded by pretty girls in bathing
suits. Advertisers "glamorize" their products and sell us daydreams
and delusions of grandeur with every package of pink pills or garbage disposal unit.

Here, *if* they are trying to prove that their products adequately
serve their ostensible functions, their procedures are glorified examples of the *argumentum ad populum*. Besides the "snob appeal" already referred to, we may include under this heading the familiar
"band-wagon argument." The campaigning politician "argues" that
he should receive our votes because "everybody" is voting that way.
We are told that such and such a breakfast food, or cigarette, or motor
car is "best" because it is America's largest seller. A certain belief
"must be true" because "everyone knows it." But popular acceptance
of a policy does not prove it to be wise; widespread use of certain
products does not prove them to be satisfactory; general assent to a
claim does not prove it to be true. To argue in this way is to commit
the *ad populum* fallacy.

7. Argumentum ad Verecundiam (appeal to authority). The
argumentum ad verecundiam is the appeal to authority, that is, to the
feeling of respect people have for the famous, to win assent to a conclusion. This method of argument is not always strictly fallacious, for
the reference to an admitted authority in the special field of his
competence may carry great weight and constitute relevant evidence.
If laymen are disputing over some question of physical science and
one appeals to the testimony of Einstein on the matter, that testimony

is very relevant. Although it does not prove the point, it certainly tends to confirm it. This is a relative matter, however, for if experts rather than laymen are disputing over a question in the field in which they themselves are experts, their appeal would be only to the facts and to reason, and any appeal to the authority of another expert would be completely without value as evidence.

But when an authority is appealed to for testimony in matters outside the province of his special field, the appeal commits the fallacy of *argumentum ad verecundiam*. If in an argument over religion one of the disputants appeals to the opinions of Darwin, a great authority in biology, the appeal is fallacious. Similarly, an appeal to the opinions of a great physicist like Einstein to settle a political or economic argument would be fallacious. The claim might be made that a person brilliant enough to achieve the status of an authority in an advanced and difficult field like biology or physics must have correct opinions in fields other than his specialty. But the weakness of this claim is obvious when we realize that in this day of extreme specialization, to obtain thorough knowledge of one field requires such concentration as to restrict the possibility of achieving authoritative knowledge in others.

Advertising "testimonials" are frequent instances of this fallacy. We are urged to smoke this or that brand of cigarettes because a champion swimmer or midget auto racer affirms their superiority. And we are assured that such-and-such a cosmetic is better because it is preferred by opera singers or movie stars. Of course, such an advertisement may equally well be construed as snob appeal and listed as an example of an *argumentum ad populum*. But where a proposition is claimed to be literally *true* on the basis of its assertion by an "authority" whose competence lies in a different field, we have a fallacy of *argumentum ad verecundiam*.

8. Accident. The fallacy of *accident* consists in applying a general rule to a particular case whose "accidental" circumstances render the rule inapplicable. In Plato's *Republic,* for example, an exception is found to the general rule that one should pay one's debts: "Suppose that a friend when in his right mind has deposited arms with me and he ask for them when he is not in his right mind, ought I to give them back to him? No one would say that I ought or that I should be right in doing so. . . ." What is true "in general" may not be true universally and without qualification, because circumstances alter cases. Many generalizations known or suspected to have exceptions are stated without qualification, either because the exact conditions restricting their applicability are not known, or because the accidental circumstances that render them inapplicable occur so seldom as to be practically negligible. When such a generalization is appealed to in arguing about a particular case whose accidental circumstances prevent the general proposition from applying, the argument is said to commit the fallacy of *accident.*

Some examples of the fallacy of *accident* are no better than jokes, as: "What you bought yesterday, you eat today; you bought raw meat yesterday; therefore, you eat raw meat today." In this argument the premiss "What you bought yesterday, you eat today" applies only in general, to the substance of what is bought, rather than to its condition. It is not intended to cover every accidental circumstance, such as the raw condition of the meat. Of this example De Morgan wrote: "This piece of meat has remained uncooked, as fresh as ever, a prodigious time. It was raw when Reisch mentioned it in the *Margarita Philosophica* in 1496: and Dr. Whately found it in just the same state in 1826."*

In its more serious forms, however, the fallacy of *accident* is often fallen into by moralists and legalists who try to decide specific and complicated issues by appealing mechanically to general rules. As H. W. B. Joseph remarked, ". . . there is no fallacy more insidious than that of treating a statement which in many connections is not misleading as if it were true always and without qualification."**

9. Converse Accident (hasty generalization). If one considers only exceptional cases and hastily generalizes to a rule that fits them alone, the fallacy committed is that of *converse accident*. For example, observing the value of opiates when administered by a physician to alleviate the pains of those who are seriously ill, one may be led to propose that narcotics be made available to everyone. Or considering the effect of alcoholic beverages only on those who indulge in them to excess, one may conclude that all liquor is harmful and urge that its sale and use should be forbidden by law. Such reasoning is erroneous, illustrating the fallacy of *converse accident* or *hasty generalization*.

10. False Cause. The fallacy of *false cause* has been variously analyzed in the past and given alternative Latin names, such as *non causa pro causa* and *post hoc ergo propter hoc*. The first of these is more general, and means to mistake what is not the cause of a given effect for its real cause. The second is the inference that one event is the cause of another from the bare fact that the first occurs earlier than the second. We shall regard any argument that incorrectly attempts to establish a causal connection as an instance of the fallacy of *false cause*.

What actually constitutes a good argument for the presence of causal connections is perhaps the central problem of inductive logic or scientific method . . . . It is easy to see, however, that the mere fact of coincidence or temporal succession does not establish any causal connection. Certainly we should reject the savage's claim that beating his drums is the cause of the sun's reappearance after an eclipse, even though he can offer as evidence the fact that every time drums have been beaten during an eclipse, the sun has reappeared! No one would

* *Formal Logic* by Augustus De Morgan, The Open Court Company, 1926.
** *An Introduction to Logic* by H. W. B. Joseph, Oxford University Press, 1906.

be misled by this argument, but countless people are "suckers" for patent-medicine testimonials which report that Mrs. X suffered from a head cold, drank three bottles of a "secret" herb decoction and in two weeks lost her cold!

11. Petitio Principii (begging the question). In attempting to establish the truth of a proposition, one often casts about for acceptable premisses from which the proposition in question can be deduced as conclusion. If one assumes as a premiss for his argument the very conclusion he intends to prove, the fallacy committed is that of *petitio principii*, or begging the question. If the proposition to be established is formulated in exactly the same words both as premiss and as conclusion, the mistake would be so glaring as to deceive no one. Often, however, two formulations can be so different as to obscure the fact that one and the same proposition occurs both as premiss and conclusion. This situation is illustrated by the following argument given by Whately: "To allow every man unbounded freedom of speech must always be, on the whole, advantageous to the state; for it is highly conducive to the interests of the community that each individual should enjoy a liberty, perfectly unlimited, of expressing his sentiments."*

It should be noted that the premiss is not logically irrelevant to the *truth* of the conclusion, for if the premiss is true the conclusion must be true also — since it is the same proposition. But the premiss is logically irrelevant to the purpose of *proving* the conclusion. If the proposition is acceptable without argument, no argument is needed to establish it; and if the proposition is not acceptable without argument, then no argument which requires its acceptance as a premiss could possibly lead any one to accept its conclusion. In any such argument the conclusion asserts exactly what was explicitly asserted by the premisses, and hence the argument, though perfectly valid, is utterly incapable of establishing the truth of its conclusion.

Sometimes a chain of several arguments is used in attempting to establish a conclusion. Thus one may argue that Shakespeare is a greater writer than Spillane because people with good taste in literature prefer Shakespeare. And if asked how one tells who has good taste in literature, one might reply that such persons are to be identified by their preferring Shakespeare to Spillane. Such a *circular argument* clearly begs the question and commits the fallacy of *petitio principii*.

12. Complex Question. The next fallacy of relevance to be considered is that of the *complex question*. We all know that there is something "funny" about questions like "Have you given up your evil ways?" or "Have you stopped beating your wife?" These are not simple questions to which a straightforward "yes" or "no" answer is possible. Such questions as these presuppose that a definite answer

* *Elements of Logic* by Richard Whately, London, 1826.

has already been given to a prior question that was not even asked. Thus the first assumes that the answer "yes" has been given to the unasked question "Have you in the past followed evil ways?" and the second assumes an affirmative answer to the unasked question "Have you ever beaten your wife?" In either case, if a simple "yes" or "no" answer to the "trick" question is given, it has the effect of ratifying or affirming the implied answer to the unasked question. A question of this sort does not admit of a simple "yes" or "no" answer because it is not a simple or single question but a complex question which consists of several questions rolled into one.

The fallacy of the *complex question* is committed when the plurality of questions is undetected and a single answer is demanded or returned to a complex question as if it were a simple one. This fallacy is not confined to obvious jokes like our first two examples. In cross-examination a lawyer may ask complex questions of a witness to confuse or even to incriminate him. He may ask: "Where did you hide the evidence?" "What did you do with the money you stole?" or the like. In propaganda, where a flat statement might be extremely difficult to prove or get accepted, the idea may be "put across" very persuasively by means of the *complex question*. A spokesman for utilities interests may propound the question: "Why is private development of resources so much more efficient than any public control?" A jingo may demand of his audience: "How long are we going to tolerate foreign interference with our national interests?"

In all such cases, the intelligent procedure is to treat the complex question not as a simple one, but to analyze it into its component parts. It may well be the case that when the implicit or implied prior question is correctly answered, the second or explicit one simply dissolves. If I did not hide any evidence, the question of where I hid it does not make sense.

There are other varieties of the *complex question*. A mother may ask her youngster if he wants to be a good boy and go to bed? Here the matter is less deceptive. There are clearly two questions involved; one does not presuppose a particular answer to the other. The fallacy here lies in the implication that one and the same answer must be given to *both* of the questions. Are you "for" the Republicans and prosperity, or not? Answer "yes" or "no"! But here is a complex question, and it is at least conceivable that the two questions have different answers.

In parliamentary procedure, the motion "to divide the question" is a *privileged* motion. This rule acknowledges that questions may be complex and can therefore be considered more intelligently when separated. Our practice with respect to the President's veto power is less enlightened. The President can veto a measure as a whole, but he cannot veto the part he disapproves and sign the remainder. The President cannot divide the question but must veto or approve, answer "yes" or "no," to any question no matter how complex. This restriction has led, as is well known, to the congressional practice of attaching, as "riders" to measures that the President is generally known to approve, certain additional—often completely irrelevant—clauses to which he is known to be opposed. When presented with such a bill, the President must either approve something of which he disapproves or veto something he approves.

Another version of this fallacy lies in the use of question-begging epithets, as when one asks "Is so-and-so a screwball radical?" or "an unthinking conservative?" or "Is this policy going to lead to ruinous deflation?" Here, as elsewhere, one must *divide* the complex question. The answers might be, "a radical, yes, but not a screwball," "a conservative, yes, but not unthinking," or "It will lead to deflation, yes; however, that will not be ruinous but a healthy readjustment."

13. Ignoratio Elenchi (irrelevant conclusion). The fallacy of *ignoratio elenchi* is committed when an argument supposedly intended to establish a particular conclusion is directed to proving a different conclusion. For example, when a particular proposal for housing legislation is under consideration, a legislator may rise to speak in favor of the bill and argue only that decent housing for all the people is desirable. His remarks are then logically irrelevant to the point at issue, for the question concerns the particular measure at hand. Presumably everyone agrees that decent housing for all the people is desirable (even those will pretend to agree who do not really think so). The question is: will this particular measure provide it, and if so, will it provide it better than any practical alternative? The speaker's argument is fallacious, committing the fallacy of *ignoratio elenchi* or *irrelevant conclusion*.

In a law court, in attempting to prove that the accused is guilty of murder, the prosecution may argue at length that murder is a horrible crime. He may even succeed in *proving* that conclusion. But when he infers from his remarks about the horribleness of murder that the defendant is guilty of it, he is committing the fallacy of *ignoratio elenchi*.

The question naturally arises, how do such arguments ever fool anybody? Once it is seen that the conclusion is logically irrelevant, why should the argument mislead anyone? In the first place, it is not always obvious that a given argument *is* an instance of *ignoratio elenchi*. During the course of an extended discussion, fatigue may lead to inattention and errors and irrelevancies may tend to pass unnoticed. That is only part of the answer, of course. The other part has to do with the fact that language may serve to evoke emotion as well as to communicate information.

Consider the first example of *ignoratio elenchi*. By urging that decent housing for all the people is desirable the speaker may succeed in evoking an attitude of approval for himself and for what he says, and this attitude may tend to get transferred to his final conclusion, by psychological association rather than by logical implication. The speaker may have succeeded in evoking such a positive sentiment for housing improvement that his hearers will vote more enthusiastically for the bill he supports than if he had really proved its passage to be in the public interest.

Again, in the second example, if the prosecution has given a sufficiently moving picture of the horribleness of murder, the jury may be so aroused, such horror and disapproval may be evoked in them, that they will bring in a verdict of "guilty" more swiftly than if the prosecutor had "merely" proved that the defendant had *committed* the crime.

Although every emotional appeal is logically irrelevant to the truth or falsehood of one's conclusion, not every case of *ignoratio elenchi* need involve an emotional appeal. An argument may be stated in cold, aseptic, neutral language and still commit the fallacy of irrelevant conclusion. It does so if its premises are directed toward a conclusion different from the one that is supposed to be established by them.

EXERCISES

Identify the fallacies of relevance in the following passages and explain how each specific passage involves that fallacy or fallacies.

1. You can't believe what Professor Threadbare says about the importance of higher salaries for teachers. As a teacher himself he would naturally be in favor of increasing teachers' pay.

2. I am sure that their ambassador will be reasonable about the matter. After all, man is a rational animal.

3. The wives of successful men wear expensive clothing, so the best way for a woman to help her husband become a success is to buy expensive clothing.

4. Anytus: "Socrates, I think that you are too ready to speak evil of men: and, if you will take my advice, I would recommend you to be careful. Perhaps there is no city in which it is not easier to do men harm than to do them good, and this is certainly the case at Athens, as I believe that you know."   (Plato, *Meno*)

5. Our team is the outstanding team in the conference, because it has the best players and the best coach. We know it has the best players and the best coach because it will win the conference title. And it will win the conference title because it *deserves* to win the conference title. Of course it deserves to win the conference title, for it is the outstanding team in the conference.

6. Mr. Scrooge, my husband certainly deserves a raise in pay. I can hardly manage to feed the children on what you have been paying him. And our youngest child, Tim, needs an operation if he is ever to walk without crutches.

7. Our tests have shown that the product will not adequately do the work for which it was designed. We also found that it is ex-

tremely breakable, and cannot stand up under normal usage. We conclude, therefore, that the product can not be sold successfully, but will be a commercial failure.

8. During the war enemy espionage rings were exposed by tapping the telephone wires of suspects. Therefore the authorities should have the telephone wires of all suspicious persons tapped.

9. However, it matters very little now what the king of England either says or does; he hath wickedly broken through every moral and human obligation, trampled nature and conscience beneath his feet, and by a steady and constitutional spirit of insolence and cruelty procured for himself an universal hatred.

(Thomas Paine, *Common Sense*)

10. No breath of scandal has ever touched the Senator. Therefore he must be incorruptibly honest.

11. In that melancholy book, *The Future of an Illusion*, Dr. Freud, himself one of the last great theorists of the European capitalist class, has stated with simple clarity the impossibility of religious belief for the educated man of today.

(John Strachey, *The Coming Struggle for Power*)

12. The Inquisition must have been justified and beneficial, if whole peoples invoked and defended it, if men of the loftiest souls founded and created it severally and impartially, and its very adversaries applied it on their own account, pyre answering to pyre.

(Croce, *Philosophy of the Practical*)

13. It is too my turn to pitch today! After all, it's my ball!

14. Why do I know more than other people? Why, in general, am I so clever? I have never pondered over questions that are not really questions. I have never wasted my strength.

(Nietzsche, *Ecce Homo*)

15. Of course socialism is desirable. Look at the facts. At one time all utilities were privately owned, now more and more of them are owned by the government. The social-security laws embody many of the principles that socialists have always maintained. We are well on our way to socialism, and its complete triumph is inevitable!

16. If we want to know whether a state is brave we must look at its army, not because the soldiers are the only brave people in the community, but because it is only through their conduct that the courage or cowardice of the community can be manifested.

(R. L. Nettleship, *Lectures on the Republic of Plato*)

17. "But I observe," says Cleanthes, "with regard to you, Philo, and all speculative sceptics, that your doctrine and practice are as much at variance in the most abstruse points of theory as in the conduct of common life." (Hume, *Dialogues Concerning Natural Religion*)

18. The Golden Rule is basic to every system of ethics ever devised, and everyone accepts it in some form or other. It is, therefore, an undeniably sound moral principle.

19. No mathematician has ever been able to demonstrate the truth of the famous "last theorem" of Fermat, so it must be false.

20. But can you doubt that air has weight when you have the clear testimony of Aristotle affirming that all the elements have weight including air, and excepting only fire?

(Galileo Galilei, *Dialogues Concerning Two New Sciences*)

21. What the farmer sows in the spring he reaps in the fall. In the spring he sows two-dollar-a-bushel corn. Therefore in the fall the farmer reaps two-dollar-a-bushel corn.

22. Of course there is a Santa Claus. But he doesn't bring any presents to children who don't believe in him.

23. The alarmists have not succeeded in proving that radio-active fall-out is dangerously harmful to human life. Therefore it is perfectly safe to continue our program of testing thermonuclear weapons.

24. I'm absolutely certain about how fast I was driving, Officer, and it was well below the speed limit. I've had tickets before, and if you give me one now it will cost me over fifty dollars. And if I have to pay a fifty-dollar fine I won't be able to afford to have my wife operated on—and she's been sick a long time and needs that operation desperately!

25. There's no point in hiring a skilled worker to do the job, because many who are regarded as skilled workers are no more skilled than anybody else.

26. Nietzsche was personally more philosophical than his philosophy. His talk about power, harshness, and superb immorality was the hobby of a harmless young scholar and constitutional invalid. (Santayana, *Egotism in German Philosophy*)

27. Are you in favor of increased governmental service and taxes? If you are, those whose taxes are already too high will vote against you. If you are not, those who need more services from the government will vote against you. In no case can you hope to win general support.

28. In his work an attorney is always free to consult law books. And a physician often looks up cases in his medical texts. Everyone should be allowed a similar freedom of reference. So students should be permitted to use their textbooks during examinations.

29. While General Grant was winning battles in the West, President Lincoln received many complaints about Grant's being a drunk-

ard. When a delegation told him one day that Grant was hopelessly addicted to whiskey, the President is said to have replied: "I wish General Grant would send a barrel of his whiskey to each of my other Generals!"

30. The story is told about Wendell Phillips, the abolitionist, who one day found himself on the same train with a group of Southern clergymen on their way to a conference. When the Southerners learned of Phillips' presence, they decided to have some fun at his expense. One of them approached and said, "Are you Wendell Phillips?"

"Yes, sir," came the reply.

"Are you the great abolitionist?"

"I am not great, but I am an abolitionist."

"Are you not the one who makes speeches in Boston and New York against slavery?"

"Yes, I am."

"Why don't you go to Kentucky and make speeches there?"

Phillips looked at his questioner for a moment and then said, "Are you a clergyman?"

"Yes, I am," replied the other.

"Are you trying to save souls from hell?"

"Yes."

"Well—why don't you go there?"

II. FALLACIES OF AMBIGUITY

The informal fallacies to be considered next have traditionally been called "fallacies of ambiguity" or "fallacies of clearness." These occur in arguments whose formulations contain ambiguous words or phrases, whose meanings shift and change more or less subtly in the course of the argument and thus render it fallacious. The following are all fallacies of ambiguity, but it is helpful to divide and classify them according to the different ways in which their ambiguities arise.

1. Equivocation. The first fallacy of ambiguity we shall consider is that which arises through simple *equivocation*. Most words have more than one literal meaning, as the word "hide" may denote either the process of concealing something or the skin of an animal. When we keep these different meanings apart, no difficulty arises. But when we confuse the different meanings a single word or phrase may have, using it in different senses in the same context, we are using it *equivocally*. If the context happens to be an argument, we commit the fallacy of *equivocation*.

A traditional example of this fallacy is the following: "The end of a thing is its perfection; death is the end of life; hence, death is the perfection of life." This argument is fallacious because two different senses of the word "end" are confused in it. The word "end" may mean either "goal" or "last event." Both these meanings are, of course, legitimate. But what is illegitimate is to confuse the two, as in this argument. The premises are plausible only when the word "end" is interpreted differently in each of them, as: "The *goal* of a thing is its perfection," and "Death is the *last event* of life." But the conclusion that "death is the perfection of life" does not even apparently follow from *these* premises. Of course the *same* sense of "end" could be used in both premises, but then the argument would lose all its plausibility, for it would have either the unplausible premiss "The *last event* of a thing is its perfection" or the patently false premiss "Death is the *goal* of life." Some examples of the fallacy of *equivocation*, so absurd as to fool no one, are a kind of joke. Such, for example, would be:

> Some dogs have fuzzy ears.
> My dog has fuzzy ears.
> Therefore my dog is some dog!

There is a special kind of equivocation that deserves special mention. This has to do with "relative" terms, which have different meanings in different contexts. For example, the word "tall" is a relative word; a *tall man* and a *tall building* are in quite different categories. A tall man is one who is taller than most men, a tall building is one which is taller than most buildings. Certain forms of argument which are valid for nonrelative terms break down when relative terms are substituted for them. The argument "an elephant is an animal; therefore a gray elephant is a gray animal," is perfectly valid. The word "gray" is a nonrelative term. But the argument "an elephant is an animal; therefore a small elephant is a small animal," is ridiculous. The point here is that "small" is a relative term: a small elephant is a very large animal. The fallacy is one of *equivocation* on the relative term "small." Not all equivocation on relative terms is so obvious, however. The word "good" is a relative term and is frequently equivocated on when it is argued, for example, that so and so would be a good President because he is a good general, or must be a good man because he is a good mathematician, or is a good teacher because he is a good scholar.

2. Amphiboly. The fallacy of *amphiboly* occurs in arguing from premises whose formulations are ambiguous because of their grammatical construction. A statement is *amphibolous* when its meaning is unclear because of the loose or awkward way in which its words are combined. An amphibolous statement may be true on one interpretation and false on another. When it is stated as premiss with the interpretation which makes it true, and a conclusion is drawn from it on the interpretation which makes it false, then the fallacy of *amphiboly* has been committed.

The classic example of *amphiboly* has to do with Croesus and the Oracle of Delphi. *Amphibolous* utterances were, of course, the chief stock in trade of the ancient oracles. Croesus, the king of Lydia, was contemplating war with the kingdom of Persia. Being a prudent man, he did not wish to war unless he were sure to win. He consulted Delphi on the matter and received the oracular reply that "If Croesus went to war with Cyrus, he would destroy a mighty kingdom." Delighted with this prediction, Croesus went to war and was speedily defeated by Cyrus, king of the Persian host. Afterwards, his life having been spared, Croesus wrote a bitterly complaining letter to the Oracle, presumably signing it "irate subscriber." His letter was answered by the priests of Delphi who claimed that the Oracle had been right. In going to war Croesus *had* destroyed a mighty kingdom —his own! Amphibolous statements make dangerous premisses. They are, however, seldom encountered in serious discussion.

Some amphibolous sentences are not without their humorous aspects, as in posters urging us to "Save Soap and Waste Paper," or when anthropology is defined as "The science of man embracing woman." We should be mistaken if we inferred immodest dress on the woman described in a story: ". . . loosely wrapped in a newspaper, she carried three dresses." Amphiboly is often exhibited by newspaper headings and brief items, as in "The farmer blew out his brains after taking affectionate farewell of his family with a shotgun."

3. Accent. Like all fallacies of ambiguity, the fallacy of *accent* is committed in an argument whose deceptive but invalid nature depends upon a change or shift in meaning. The way in which the meaning shifts in the fallacy of *accent* depends upon what parts of it may be emphasized or accented. That some statements have quite different meanings when different words are stressed is clear. Consider the different meanings that are given according to which of the italicized words is stressed in the injunction:

We should not speak ill of our friends.

When read without any undue stresses, the injunction is perfectly sound. If the conclusion is drawn from it, however, that we should feel free to speak ill of someone who is *not* our friend, then this conclusion follows *only* if the premiss has the meaning it acquires when its last word is accented. But when its last word is accented, it is no longer acceptable as a moral law, it has a different meaning, and is in fact a different premiss. The argument is a case of the fallacy of *accent*. So too would be the argument which drew from the same premiss the conclusion that we are free to *work* ill upon our friends if only we do it silently. And similarly with the other fallacious inferences which suggest themselves. In the same light vein, depending upon how it is accented, the statement:

Woman without her man would be lost.

would be perfectly acceptable to either sex. But to infer the statement with one accent from the statement accented differently would be an instance of the fallacy of *accent*.

A more serious commission of this fallacy, in a slightly wider sense of the term, can occur in making a quotation, where inserting or deleting italics may change the meaning. Another kind of fallacious accenting may occur without any variation in the use of italics, when the passage quoted is torn from its context. For often a passage can be correctly understood only in the light of its context, which may make clear the *sense* in which the passage is intended, or may contain explicit qualifications without which the passage has a quite different meaning. Therefore a responsible writer who makes a direct quotation will indicate whether or not any words italicized in his quotation were italicized in the original, and will indicate any omission of words or phrases by the use of dots.

A statement which is literally true but quite uninteresting when read or written "normally" may be made quite exciting when accented in certain ways. But this accenting may change its meaning, and with its different meaning it may no longer be true. Thus truth is sacrificed to sensationalism by means of the fallacious inference produced by accenting (typographically) one part of a sentence more than another. This technique is a deliberate policy of certain tabloid newspapers to make their headlines arresting. Such a paper may run as a headline in large boldface type the words,

REVOLUTION IN FRANCE

and then below, in considerably less prominent and smaller type, may be found the words "feared by authorities." The complete statement that "Revolution in France (is) feared by authorities" may be perfectly true. But as accented in the tabloid the assertion is given an exciting but utterly false significance. The same kind of misleading accenting is found in many advertisements. Where a presumably net price is quoted for a particular commodity, closer inspection of the announcement may reveal the words, invariably in much smaller print, "plus tax" or perhaps the phrase "and up." In advertisements directed toward a presumably less literate section of the public, this kind of accenting is often quite flagrant.

How even the literal truth can be a vehicle for falsehood when *accented* by being put in a misleading context is illustrated by the following sea story. At almost the very outset of a certain ship's voyage, there had been a falling-out between the captain and his first mate. The dissension was aggravated by the mate's tendency to drink, for the captain was a fanatic on temperance and seldom let an occasion go by without lecturing the mate on his failings. Needless to say, this nagging only made the mate drink more heavily. After repeated warnings, one day when the mate had imbibed even more than usual, the captain entered the fact in the ship's log book, writing, "The mate was drunk today." When next it was the mate's turn to keep the log he was horrified to find this official record of his misbehavior. The log would be read by the ship's owner, whose reaction would probably mean the mate's discharge, with a bad reference to boot. He pleaded with the captain to remove the entry, but the captain refused. The mate was unhappy until he finally hit upon a method of revenge. At the end of the regular entries he made in the log book that day he added, "The captain was sober today."

4. Composition. The term "fallacy of composition" is applied to both of two closely related types of invalid argument. The first may be described as reasoning fallaciously from the properties of the parts of a whole to the properties of the whole itself. A particularly flagrant example would be to argue that since every part of a certain machine is light in weight, the machine "as a whole" is light in weight. The error here is manifest when we consider that a very heavy machine may consist of a very large number of lightweight parts. Not all examples of this kind of fallacious *composition* are so obvious, however. Some are misleading. I have heard it seriously argued that since each scene of a certain play was a model of artistic perfection, the play as a whole was artistically perfect. But this is as much a fallacy of *composition* as it would be to argue that since every player on a team is an outstanding athlete the team must be an outstanding team.

The other type of *composition* fallacy is strictly parallel to that just described. Here the fallacious reasoning is from properties possessed by individual elements or members of a collection to properties possessed by the class or collection as such. This *may* be regarded as an equivocation on the verb "to be," for in connection with this fallacy we may distinguish between two senses of that verb. The statement "Men are mortal," means that each and every member of the class of men is mortal. Here we have the *distributive* sense of the verb, where a property is predicated of men taken *severally* as members of the class of men. The verb "to be" may also be used in the *collective* sense, as in the equally true statement "Men are numerous,." Here we are clearly not predicating of each and every man the property of being numerous, for that would simply not make sense. What is intended is to predicate numerousness of men *collectively*, of the class or collection as a whole. Similarly, in the statement "Rodents have four feet," we mean to predicate the property four-footedness of rodents *distributively*; that is, we assert that each and every rodent has four feet. But in the statement "Rodents are widely distributed over the earth," we are speaking of rodents *collectively*; it is certainly not intended to assert of each and every rodent that *it* is widely distributed over the earth – whatever that might mean. This second kind of *composition* fallacy may be defined as the invalid inference that what may truly be predicated of a class *distributively* may also be truly predicated of the class *collectively*. Thus the atomic bombs dropped during World War II did more damage than the ordinary bombs dropped – but only distributively. The matter is exactly reversed when the two kinds of bombs are considered *collectively*, because there were so many more bombs of the conventional type dropped than atomic ones. Ignoring this distinction in an argument would permit the fallacy of *composition*.

These two varieties of *composition*, although parallel, are really distinct, because of the difference between a mere collection of elements and a whole constructed out of those elements. Thus a mere collection or class of parts is no machine; a mere collection or class of bricks is neither a house nor a wall. A whole like a machine, a house, or a wall has its parts organized or arranged in certain definite ways. And since organized wholes and mere classes or collections are distinct, so are the two versions of the *composition* fallacy, one proceeding invalidly to wholes from their parts, the other proceeding invalidly to classes from their members or elements.

5. Division. The fallacy of *division* is simply the reverse of the fallacy of *composition*. In it the same confusion is present but the inference proceeds in the opposite direction. As in the case of *composition*, two varieties of the fallacy of *division* may be distinguished. The first kind of *division* consists in arguing fallaciously that what is true of a whole must also be true of each of its parts. To argue that since a certain corporation is very important, and Mr. Doe is an official of that corporation, therefore Mr. Doe is very important, is to commit the fallacy of *division*. This first variety of the *division* fallacy would be committed in any such argument, as in going from the premiss that a certain machine is heavy, or complicated, or valuable, to the conclusion that this or any other *part* of the machine must be heavy, or complicated, or valuable. To argue that so-and-so must be an outstanding athlete because he plays on an outstanding team would be still another instance of this first kind of *division*.

The second type of *division* fallacy is committed when one argues from the properties of a collection of elements to the properties of the elements themselves. To argue that since all the trees in the park make a thick shade, therefore every tree in the park makes a thick shade would be to commit the second kind of *division* fallacy. Clearly *each* tree might be skimpy and throw a meagre shadow, yet there might be so many that together they give a solid thick shade. Here it would be true that all trees in the park, *collectively*, make a thick shade but false that all trees in the park, *distributively*, do so. Instances of this variety of the fallacy of *division* often look like valid arguments, for what is true of a class *distributively* is certainly true of each and every member. Thus the argument:

> Dogs are carnivorous.
> Japanese Spaniels are dogs.
> _____
> Therefore Japanese Spaniels are carnivorous.

is perfectly valid. But although it closely resembles the foregoing, the argument:

> Dogs are common.
> Japanese Spaniels are dogs.
> _____
> Therefore Japanese Spaniels are common.

is invalid, committing the fallacy of division. Some instances of *division* are obviously jokes, as when the classical example of valid argumentation:

> Men are mortal.
> Socrates is a man.
> _____
> Therefore Socrates is mortal.

is parodied by the fallacious:

> American Indians are disappearing.
> That man is an American Indian.
> _____
> Therefore that man is disappearing.

The old riddle "Why do white sheep eat more than black ones?" turns on the confusion involved in the fallacy of *division.* For the answer, "Because there are more of them," treats *collectively* what seemed to be referred to *distributively* in the question.

EXERCISES

Identify the fallacies of ambiguity in the following passages and explain how each specific passage involves that fallacy or fallacies.

1. To press forward with a properly ordered wage structure in each industry is the first condition for curbing competitive bargaining; but there is no reason why the process should stop there. What is good for each industry can hardly be bad for the economy as a whole.
(*Twentieth Century Socialism*, p. 74. Penguin Books, 1956)

2. Russian threats are no news. Therefore Russian threats are good news, since no news is good news.

3. Traffic accidents are increasing. Collisions between Model T Fords are traffic accidents. Therefore collisions between Model T Fords are increasing.

4. The Bible tells us to return good for evil. But Jones has never done me any evil. Hence it will be all right to play him a dirty trick or two.

5. . . . each person's happiness is a good to that person, and the general happiness, therefore, a good to the aggregate of all persons.
(Mill, *Utilitarianism*)

6. Leaking badly, manned by a skeleton crew, one infirmity after another overtakes the little ship. — *The Herald Tribune Books Section.*
Those game little infirmities!
(*The New Yorker*, Nov. 8, 1958)

7. Since every third child born in New York is a Catholic, Protestant families living there should have no more than two children.

8. Her father has a very distinguished appearance, so he must be a very distinguished man.

9. Each manufacturer is perfectly free to set his own price on the product he produces, so there can be nothing wrong with all manufacturers getting together to fix the prices of the articles made by all of them.

10. Psychological testing established that Mr. Jones' concern with money was above average and that Mrs. Jones' concern with money was below average. It follows that Jones likes money more than his wife. Their marriage is not likely to last, for how can a man stand a woman to whom he prefers money?

11. American buffalo are practically extinct. This animal is an American buffalo, so it must be practically extinct.

12. White: I do not see any good reasons for making the trip. So I have given up my intention of going.

    Black: Aha! You admit there are good reasons for making the trip—those are your very words! I am glad to hear of your "intention of going."

13. Improbable events happen almost every day, but what happens almost every day is a very probable event. Therefore improbable events are very probable events.

14. Good steaks are rare these days, so don't order yours well-done.

15. And to judge still better of the minute perceptions which we cannot distinguish in the crowd, I am wont to make use of the example of the roar of noise of the sea which strikes one when on its shore. To understand this noise as it is made, it would be necessary to hear the parts which compose this whole, i.e. the noise of each wave, although each of these little noises . . . would not be noticed if the wave which makes it were alone. For it must be that we are affected a little by the motion of this wave, and that we have some perception of each one of these noises, small as they are; otherwise we would not have that of a hundred thousand waves, since a hundred thousand nothings cannot make something.

    (Leibnitz, *New Essays Concerning Human Understanding*)

III. THE AVOIDANCE OF FALLACIES

Fallacies are pitfalls into which any of us may tumble in our reasoning. Just as danger signals are erected to warn travelers away from dangerous places, so the labels for fallacies . . . may be regarded as so many danger signals posted to keep us away from the bogland of incorrect argument. Familiarity with these errors and the ability to name and analyze them may well keep us from being deceived by them.

    There is no "royal road" for the avoidance of fallacies. To avoid the fallacies of relevance requires constant vigilance and awareness of the many ways in which irrelevance can intrude. . . . A realization of the flexibility of language and the multiplicity of its uses will keep us from mistaking an *exhortation* to *accept* and *approve* a conclusion for an *argument* designed to *prove* that conclusion *true*.

The fallacies of ambiguity are subtle things. Words are slippery, and most of them have a variety of different senses or meanings. Where these different meanings are confused in the formulation of an argument, the reasoning is fallacious. To avoid the various fallacies of ambiguity, we must have and keep the meanings of our terms clearly in mind. One way to accomplish this is by defining the key terms that are used. Since shifts in the meanings of terms can make arguments fallacious, and since ambiguity can be avoided by careful definition of the terms involved, definition is an important matter for the student of logic.

3   Letters of application for jobs tend to have the following underlying pattern: (1) the lead, in which the writer states that he is an applicant for a particular position and describes the position, often mentioning the source of his information about it; (2) a description of his education and experience; (3) a list of his references; and (4) a request for an interview or for further information. Translate this pattern into one of those we have discussed: the pattern for reconstructing the reader's image, the pattern for adding to his image, or the pattern for changing the quality of his image. Which pattern you translate the letter form into depends on what you believe to be the usual intention of a job applicant. Would you say that a letter of application generally seeks to reconstruct the reader's image, to add to it, or to change its quality? Why? What could cause the intention to change? What does the possibility of translation suggest about the usefulness of the procedures and patterns discussed in this chapter?

4   Francis Bacon, speculating on appropriate patterns for presenting the results of scientific investigation, suggested that "knowledge . . . ought to be delivered . . . *in the same method wherein it was invented*. . . . Man may revisit and descend unto the foundations of his knowledge and consent; and so transplant it into another as it grew in his own mind." Compare the essays by Albert H. Hastorf and Hadley Cantril (p. 31), Aldo Leopold (p. 109), and Charles Nicholle (p. 78). In what ways do they exemplify Bacon's suggestion? How would you characterize the intention of each essay? What evidence can you cite in support of your answer?

5 Hastorf and Cantril employ the pattern suggested by the American Psychological Association for organizing scientific reports: (1) a statement of the problem (either the questions asked and the reasons for asking them or the hypothesis to be tested, along with relevant arguments and background information); (2) a description of the experimental method that is detailed enough for the reader to duplicate the procedure; (3) a statement of the results of the experiment; (4) a discussion of the results that points out the limitations of the conclusions and their theoretical or practical implications; (5) a summary. What are the similarities and differences between this pattern and that of traditional argument? Which do you think is better suited for empirical and scientific argument? Why?

Nicholle tells us that he verified his hypothesis experimentally. What would you guess to have been the structure of his report? Where, if anywhere, would he have included the information in the essay you have read?

6 The heuristic procedures discussed in this chapter imply that the writer responds to two kinds of problems: (1) conceptual problems to which his thesis is an answer and (2) communication problems that arise from a difference between his image and the reader's—a difference that the discourse is designed to eliminate. Analyze the essays by Ladis Kovach (p. 111) and Aldo Leopold (p. 109) for both kinds of problems.

7 Write a dialogue in which you and another person, real or imaginary, are the actors. Select a problem that you regard as significant and for which you have developed an answer. Attempt to communicate the problem and your solution to the other actor. The task is likely to be interesting only if you set for yourself obstacles as formidable as those in the real world; for example, an audience that is apathetic or hostile to you or to your solution or convinced of an alternative solution, an audience that lacks the knowledge necessary for understanding your message, and so on. Give the other actor a specific character: His behavior should clearly reflect what he is and what he wants. Be sure to keep the basic conceptual and communication problems in focus; never lose sight of the relevant differences between you and the other actor. Specify the setting (when and where) and consider whether it would affect what is said. Set up the dialogue as a play; give it a title; list the characters.

But reason is only reason,
and it only satisfies man's rational requirements.

FEODOR DOSTOYEVSKY, *Notes from Underground*

If I face a human being as my Thou,
and say the primary word I-Thou *to him,*
he is not a thing among things, and does not consist of things.

MARTIN BUBER, *I and Thou*

12 Writer and reader: strategies for change

Part two

THE effectiveness of traditional argument depends heavily on the nature of the argumentative situation and on the strength of the audience's commitment to the values and beliefs that the writer wants to change. In one type of argumentative situation, probably the most common, the writer (or the speaker) addresses his message directly to the audience he seeks to change. Such a two-sided situation is described as *dyadic*. There are also three-sided, or *triadic*, situations comprised of the writer (or the speaker), his opponent, who is his ostensible audience, and a third party, who is his true audience. In these situations the writer seeks to change the third party by attacking the opponent's position. Political and legal debates are obvious illustrations. In such debates the arguer usually has no desire to change—and little chance of changing—his opponent. For example, it would be highly unusual, to say the least, if a defense attorney were persuaded by the prosecution's arguments and acknowledged in court that his client was guilty. The jury, not the opposing attorney, is the true audience. Many debates in the letters-to-the editor column in newspapers are best seen as triadic, as are attacks and rebuttals in scholarly journals. Although the opponents address each other, the newspaper or journal readers are the true audience; winning the argument requires changing them.

Limitations of traditional argument

Although traditional argument is used in both dyadic and triadic situations, often very effectively, it tends to be ineffective in those dyadic situations that involve strong values and beliefs. In confrontations between young and old, East and West, white and black—in short, whenever commitments to values are powerful and emotions run high—logical demonstration may seem irrelevant and conventional argumentative strategies suspect. In situations like these even minimal changes often seem unattainable. Over the last few years, however, an argumentative strategy appropriate to these dyadic situations has been developed, principally by the psychotherapist Carl R. Rogers. Although it is not totally new (various aspects of the strategy are often apparent when men seek to resolve conflicts), the strategy has only recently been developed to the point that it can be considered an effective alternative to traditional argument.

Rogerian argument

Rogerian argument rests on the assumption that out of a need to preserve the stability of his image, a person will refuse to consider alternatives that he feels are threatening, and hence, that *changing a person's image depends on eliminating this sense of threat.*[1] Much of men's resistance to logical argument seems explainable by this assumption. A strong sense of threat may render the reader immune to even the most carefully reasoned and well-supported argument. The Rogerian strategy seeks to reduce the reader's sense of threat so that he will be able to consider alternatives that may contribute to the creation of a more accurate image of the world and to the elimi-

---

[1] For an extended discussion and illustration of this idea, see Anatol Rapoport, *Fights, Games, and Debates* (Ann Arbor: University of Michigan Press, 1960), to which we are heavily indebted. At this point you may also wish to review the discussions of change in Chapters 8 and 9, since they anticipate much of what we will say about Rogerian argument.

nation of conflict between writer and reader. As Rogers suggests, a willingness to consider alternatives is evidence of the establishment of real communication, which greatly increases the chances that a reasonable solution can be reached.

The writer who uses the Rogerian strategy attempts to do three things: (1) to convey to the reader that he is understood, (2) to delineate the area within which he believes the reader's position to be valid, and (3) to induce him to believe that he and the writer share similar moral qualities (honesty, integrity, and good will) and aspirations (the desire to discover a mutually acceptable solution). We stress here that these are only tasks, not stages of the argument. Rogerian argument has no conventional structure; in fact, users of the strategy deliberately avoid conventional persuasive structures and techniques because these devices tend to produce a sense of threat, precisely what the writer seeks to overcome. We do not mean, of course, that the argument has no structure, but only that the structure is more directly the product of a particular writer, a particular topic, and a particular audience. The Rogerian strategy places a premium on empathy between writer and reader and on the peculiarities of the topic.

CONVEYING TO THE READER THAT HE IS UNDERSTOOD

Understanding here means something more than merely a grasp of the basic ideas of the opponent's position. It goes considerably beyond categorizing the opponent's position and noting its contrastive features. In "Communication: Its Blocking and Its Facilitation" Rogers explains that *understanding* means "*to see the expressed idea and attitude from the other person's point of view, to sense how it feels to him, to achieve his frame of reference in regard to the thing he is talking about.*" It requires empathy, requires getting inside the other person's skin and seeing the world through his eyes, or, to speak less metaphorically, it requires considering the beliefs and perspectives of the reader in the context of his attitudes, values, and past experience.

The task of the writer is to induce the reader to consider his position and to understand it. The writer tries to make the reader understand this position as it is interrelated with the larger system of values and beliefs that comprise the writer's image; he wants the reader to understand as an insider rather than an outsider. Curiously enough, one method of eliciting this response is to demonstrate that the *reader's* position has been understood. To do this, the writer states the reader's position as accurately, completely, and sensitively as he can, taking care not to judge it. Many conventional arguments fail either because the reader refuses to listen or because he distorts the argument, making it conform to his preconceptions of the writer and the writer's position. In either case, the reader is not trying to understand; he is trying to defend himself. He *will,* however, pay careful attention to a statement of his own position. The writer's first task, then, is to state the reader's position so carefully that the reader will agree that it has been well stated. If the writer "wins" this part of the argument, the reader is likely to continue listening. Furthermore, he is now motivated to understand the writer's position, for the reader too wants to score a victory. Demonstrating to the reader that a problem has been understood from *his* point of view is a powerful method of threat-reduction; not only can it induce the reader to listen to another position and try to understand it, but it can also create in him a willingness to pursue the argument, to reconsider his own position, and perhaps, finally, to change it.

DELINEATING THE AREA OF VALIDITY

When a person argues, he usually seeks to refute an opponent's position by evaluating it, pointing out what he considers to be its defective, or invalid, aspects. But as we pointed out in Chapter 9, such a procedure is often threat-producing. The writer can mitigate this sense of threat by focusing on the aspects of the reader's position that clearly *are valid.* Just as isolating the invalid aspects of a position implies the existence of valid aspects, so isolating valid aspects implies that there are invalid ones. Logically, the two acts amount to much the same thing; their effects, however, are different psychologically. Focusing on the valid rather than the invalid reduces the reader's sense of threat and offers him further evidence that he is understood. It also encourages him to discover the valid aspects of the writer's position. When writer and reader discover validity in each other's positions, they discover important shared features that can form the basis of further interaction.

Generally speaking, a statement is neither entirely valid nor entirely invalid; its validity is relative to a context. (See column 3, row 1, of the chart in Chapter 6 for the perspective implied by this assumption.) An awareness of this relativity makes it somewhat easier for the writer to understand opposing positions and to accept disagreement with his own position. Consider a trivial and obvious example: "Slate is hard." This statement is true if slate is being compared with talc, not true if it is being compared with diamond. Out of context, the statement seems an undeniable truth with which no reasonable person could disagree. In different contexts, however (i.e., if slate is compared with talc, with diamond, and so on), the statement is subject to rational discussion. Many people engaged in arguments ignore the effect that different contexts can have on a statement; they often say flatly, "It's true, and I can't imagine how any reasonable man could disagree with it." They might get further in an argument if they said, "If we consider it in such-and-such a context, or if we assume certain conditions, then it is true." Consider another example. Suppose someone says that underdeveloped countries should import Western technology. To most Americans, this proposal would seem entirely reasonable, for we would contemplate how technology can free people from hunger and disease. Thus we would place the statement in a context in which it is reasonable and true. But someone else, someone with a strong anthropological or historical bias, might disagree, arguing that artificially imposed technological development would destroy the cultural values of the society, those values that give it order and stability, or that the introduction of technology would lead to the kind of suffering that was experienced in sweatshops during the Industrial Revolution. Here is still another example: "Literature is important to national survival." This statement is not true if you consider it in a military context, for literature lacks the immediate force of arms. It may be true if you put it in a political or a sociological context, for literature can be a powerful propaganda instrument (e.g., much of modern Russian literature, or for that matter some of our own, particularly that written during times of national stress). The statement is also true in a psychological context: Literature can help people become more perceptive about human problems and human conflict, and as a result more willing and able to deal with them intelligently.

Opponents in an argument often, perhaps usually, disagree not because of fallacious reasoning or ignorance of the facts but because of the different contexts in which they see the problem. They may think that they are talking about the same subject when actually they aren't. Our discussion of the image and its effect on perception helps to clarify this point. People "edit" experience in different ways; hence the same problem may well seem quite different to men on opposite sides of an argument. Facts will have different degrees of importance; attitudes and values, different weights. Perceptions and their meanings are to a great extent determined by the image of the observer.

Ignoring the contexts of statements leads opponents to make categorical denials or affirmations; positions in the argument then become polarized, and the chances for reaching an agreement are reduced. A statement of the conditions under which a position is valid, however, encourages discussion; the argument tends to become provisional, and a problem-solving orientation is developed. "The opposing views," says Anatol Rapoport,

> stem largely from different criteria for *selecting what to see, what to be aware of*. Therefore, the object in a debate is to induce the opponent to admit stimuli which he had not admitted before, in short to enlarge his vision. To do this, some feel, it is best to show him not the limits outside of which he is wrong, but, on the contrary, the limits inside of which he is right. They are, of course, the same limits! But putting it one way is likely to emphasize the threat to the image, while putting it the other way is likely to dilute the threat.
>
> ANATOL RAPOPORT, *Fights, Games, and Debates*

Definitions can be another source of disagreement. But the writer can often benefit from exploiting the fact that any definition is to some extent arbitrary. He usually loses little by agreeing to use his opponent's definitions (at least his denotative definitions) of key terms in the debate. And he may gain much, for he gives further evidence of his good will and understanding. Note, however, that before he can agree to use the reader's definitions, he must be aware of all the dimensions of their meaning. *Communist, worker,* and *capitalist* may have roughly similar denotations for a communist and a capitalist, but their connotations may differ radically. Ultimately, the meaning of a term is not its dictionary definition, nor even the meaning that people agree to assign to the word in a particular situation. The meaning arises from the living contexts within which the word occurs in connected speech or writing. A word is ultimately defined by its distribution in relation to the other words with which it is used. (In terms of the chart in Chapter 6, the perspectives described in column 3, rows 1 and 2, are necessary for an understanding of the meaning of a word.) The word *sincere*, for example, ordinarily refers to a correspondence between a person's inner and outer attitudes. Yet consider its meaning in the following context: "Always be sincere—whether you mean it or not."

Denotative definitions (e.g., the kind used in the scientific description of objects) are often easy to accept, and by doing so, the writer can clarify some of the issues of the debate. Connotative definitions, however, often encompass areas of genuine disagreement, for they carry with them evaluations of a situation—evaluations that may reflect profound differences in values, beliefs, and experience. For example, the writer may be able to grant to the communist his denotative definition of *capitalist*—that is, one or more of its economic meanings—but its connotation for the communist of ruthless exploiter or enemy of the worker may be precisely what the writer is trying to change by means of his argument. The most that the writer can do in this situation is recognize the definition's area of validity, accepting the truth that is there and hoping that the reader will come to see in what way the term is limited.

Rapoport explains that defining terms and delineating their area of validity is a necessary step in argument.

> If by changing definitions or properly delineating the area of validity, we can accept some of the opponent's assertions as true (whereas they had seemed false to us otherwise), let us do so. By doing so, we make it easier for him to do the same for us. If the issue of the debate evaporates on that account, then the debate was not really worth the effort.
>
> Most serious debates are *not* simply about words; so we cannot, as a rule, expect the issues to disappear as a result of semantic analysis and improved comunication. But this preliminary job of understanding must first be done to make sure that it is not only words we are concerned with, and if it is not, to get down to the real business.
>
> ANATOL RAPOPORT, *Fights, Games, and Debates*

The techniques that we have been discussing in this section can help minimize irrelevant opposition and emotional explosion. They can also help the writer to distinguish the areas of real disagreement from the areas of agreement, which may provide bridges over which changes can take place.

INDUCING THE ASSUMPTION OF SIMILARITY

The immediate goal of the Rogerian strategy is to get the opponent to reciprocate—to induce him to understand the writer's position as the writer has understood his position. To some extent, demonstrating that the reader's position is understood and establishing where its area of validity lies are both techniques that encourage the reader to reciprocate. Inducing the reader to acknowledge that his position has been stated well constitutes a kind of victory; the reader realizes that he too can "win" if he studies the writer's position and states it equally well. He is also likely to become interested in pointing out the region of validity and invalidity in the writer's position, since it is to his advantage to demonstrate that this position too has its limitations. There are other reasons for a willingness to reciprocate. If he has been relieved of his sense of threat, it is to his advantage to reciprocate in order to prevent the writer's sense of threat from destroying the potential for cooperation that has begun to develop. Finally, a reader whose sense of threat has been reduced is more willing to consider alternative positions, including the writer's.

Attempts at persuading the reader to treat the writer as he himself has been treated are likely to fail if the reader thinks that the writer is different from himself in significant ways. He may not even try to understand the writer's position if he sees the writer as unreasonable, for example, refusing to grant what seem to the reader to be obvious, verifiable facts; or if he sees him as Machiavellian, deliberately using words as traps or employing arguments whose stated purposes mask different and unscrupulous ones. The Rogerian strategy requires that opponents confront each other as equals in an atmosphere of mutual trust. But how can the reader be brought to trust the writer, to regard him as worthy of being believed, and finally to understand his position?

The threat-reducing acts we have already discussed can help to create trust; a more explicit and direct method, however, is to show that writer and reader are similar in relevant ways. The writer can either build or discover bridges (e.g., shared attitudes, experiences, and values; see Chapters 8 and 9) that will encourage trust and lead to further interaction. Consider the following imaginary debate between a Russian communist and an American liberal. In this excerpt, the liberal is pointing out historical, cultural, and ideological features that are shared by the two societies.

> Science is the common heritage in both our societies, and both societies are unquestionably adapted to utilizing the power which science confers on man over his environment—but only to a limited extent. The limitations on both sides stem from commitments to dogma, the antithesis of the scientific attitude. Dogma is that portion of one's outlook which is immune to modification.
>
> It will be futile for me to maintain that you as Communists are bound more rigidly by dogma than we, although it appears that way to us. Rather than try to measure the unmeasurable, I maintain from the start that both our societies are impeded by dogmatic attitudes from developing their full potentials. The difference is that you recognize dogma explicitly and call it Marxism (or dialectical materialism in the natural science sphere), while we deny that our fetishes (like "liberty") are symptoms of dogma. The effects are similar. In the name of liberty we dare not undertake measures to safeguard minimum standards of economic security and health, which we can well afford. In the name of the "only correct philosophy" you have failed to extend the realm of scientific investigation to the nature of man and society, which you have unequaled opportunity to do.
>
> I believe that taking refuge in dogma is a fear reaction. The irrational fear of planning, so conspicuous in the United States, stems from a dread of *overt* restraints on the activities of the individual. As so often happens, an overpowering fear incapacitates one in dealing with real dangers. In our pathological avoidance of overt restraints, we have succumbed to innumerable covert ones and have drifted into a drabness of conformity.

Your irrational fear stems from the dread of "idealism." You see "idealism" in any intellectual position which, however remotely, admits the perceptual or the cognitive structure of an individual in the start of a theoretical investigation. You keep fighting the intellectual battle of the nineteenth century, the battle against the hegemony of religious dogma, an issue which has since lost all significance in the intellectual sphere.

. . .

The witch hunts in the years of our McCarthy eclipse are well matched by the outbursts of intellectual lynching of the type the Russians call *razgrom* . . . .

ANATOL RAPOPORT, *Fights, Games, and Debates*

Trust is encouraged by showing the opponent that he is trusted. There is considerable wisdom in one of the techniques used for bringing about a military truce: The initiator of the truce deliberately exposes himself to attack by laying aside his weapons and going to meet his opponent. His act implies that although the opponent distrusts him, he considers the opponent worthy of trust. It also suggests that they share certain values and interests that could form the basis for some sort of accommodation. In his argument with the Russian, the American liberal deliberately exposes the shortcomings of his own side: He acknowledges the existence of dogma in American political thought, our resulting inability to solve pressing social problems, the conformity pervading our social life, the political "witch hunts" of the early 1950's, and so on. He also makes explicit a definition of *dogma,* which, if left unstated, might inhibit understanding. And he lists the important features that both societies share: their common scientific heritage, the ability to utilize this heritage for human betterment, the burdens of dogmas. What could be better evidence of good faith and willingness to cooperate than letting down one's guard?

In situations involving great stress, where powerful values and beliefs clash, we tend to see our opponent as an extremist, as rigid, unreasonable, even dangerous; and no doubt we see ourselves as honest, reasonable, and responsible. But it is important to remember that our opponent is likely to hold the opposite view, to think that *he* is the one who is reasonable and that we are the unreasonable and rigid ones. We may increase our chances of being listened to and understood by imagining that our opponent shares the qualities we attribute to ourselves and by behaving as if he did. As Rapoport points out, "Maybe he does not, but maybe this 'delusion' of ours will induce a similar delusion in him about us."

Rogerian argument and traditional argument

Rogerian argument may at first seem somewhat puzzling and difficult to grasp. The cause of confusion may well be that traditional argument has been taught in schools so long and has been applied so extensively that it has shaped your image of what constitutes effective argument. The Rogerian strategy requires you to modify your image of effective argument; you may resist this change to some extent, since the characteristics of Rogerian argument may at times seem to contradict the techniques you are used to. In Rogerian argument, instead of stating your own case and refuting your opponent's, you state the opponent's case with as much care as your own, and you analyze the sound points of his argument. Instead of building up your own character and qualifications and attacking those of your opponent, you seek to gain your opponent's trust, even at the cost of acknowledging your own inadequacies. Logic, too, is used differently: In traditional argument it acts as a tool for presenting your case and refuting your opponent's; in Rogerian argument it serves an exploratory function, helping you to analyze the conditions under which the position of either side is valid. And language is used in different ways: Traditional argument often exploits language's capacity for arousing emotion in order to strengthen a position; Rogerian argument emphasizes the descriptive, dispassionate use of language. The goals of the two strategies also differ. The goal of traditional argument is to make your position prevail, to replace some feature of the opponent's image with one that you consider correct. The goal of Rogerian argument is to create a situation conducive to cooperation; this may well involve changes in *both* your opponent's image and your own. As we pointed out in Chapter 8, bridges encourage two-way traffic.

One last difference is worth noting. Traditional argument is highly conventional and draws on an armory of persuasive techniques, only a few of which were examined in Chapter 11. Rogerian argument avoids conventional techniques and structures because they tend to be threat-producing. This absence of conventional structures, however, is more characteristic of oral argument than of written. Written argument excludes the possibility of continual readjustment of the discourse as the result of observing the opponent's reactions. Your opponent cannot show you where you have failed to state his position adequately and give you an opportunity to modify your statement before continuing the discussion. In written argument, then, especially great care must be taken to state his position well the first time. Furthermore, since the opponent is not present, he cannot state your position for you; you must state it yourself, pointing out its regions of validity and invalidity just as you did with his. Written argument thus lacks the flexibility of oral argument. And if the writer does not use a conventional, sharply defined structure, there are at least phases to his argument. These phases can be ordered as follows:

1) An introduction to the problem and a demonstration that the opponent's position is understood.
2) A statement of the contexts in which the opponent's position may be valid.
3) A statement of the writer's position, including the contexts in which it is valid.
4) A statement of how the opponent's position would benefit if he were to adopt elements of the writer's position. If the writer can show that the positions complement each other, that each supplies what the other lacks, so much the better.

We should here note that the assumption of similarity is best seen not as a phase of the argument but as an attitude revealed throughout the discourse.

If some people are puzzled by Rogerian argument, others react to it with skepticism. They grant its ethical attractiveness but object that it is impractical and self-deluding. Although reasonable, generous, and honest behavior under great stress is not to be dismissed lightly, Rogerian argument need not be defended exclusively on moral grounds. Its goal is an eminently practical one: to induce changes in an opponent's mind in order to make mutually advantageous cooperation possible. And its means, strange as they may seem at first, have been proven effective in a wide variety of social situations. Essentially, the writer induces his opponent to listen to his position, to understand it, and to see the truth in it, by demonstrating that he has done the same with the opponent's position. If we pause for a moment to consider how we would respond to someone who behaved in this way toward us, the strategy is not likely to seem so impractical after all. Reasonable, moral behavior can be a means to an end as well as an end in itself.

EXERCISES

1 Read the following essay by Carl R. Rogers and answer these questions. What does Rogers mean by *communication?* What does he believe to be the principal obstacle to communication?

How can it be avoided? Why isn't Rogers' method used more often?

Rogers suggests a laboratory experiment to test the quality of your understanding of an opponent's position. Try it out in an argument; then write a brief essay describing the argument, your application of his procedure, and the results of the experiment. If your results differed from the ones that Rogers predicted, try to explain why.

Communication: Its Blocking and Its Facilitation*
CARL R. ROGERS

It may seem curious that a person whose whole professional effort is devoted to psychotherapy should be interested in problems of communication. What relationship is there between providing therapeutic help to individuals with emotional maladjustments and the concern of this conference with obstacles to communication? Actually the relationship is very close indeed. The whole task of psychotherapy is the task of dealing with a failure in communication. The emotionally maladjusted person, the "neurotic," is in difficulty first because communication within himself has broken down, and second because as a result of this his communication with others has been damaged. If this sounds somewhat strange, then let me put it in other terms. In the "neurotic" individual, parts of himself which have been termed unconscious, or repressed, or denied to awareness, become blocked off so that they no longer communicate themselves to the conscious or managing part of himself. As long as this is true, there are distortions in the way he communicates himself to others, and so he suffers both within himself, and in his interpersonal relations. The task of psychotherapy is to help the person achieve, through a special relationship with a therapist, good communication within himself. Once this is achieved he can communicate more freely and more effectively with others. We may say then that psychotherapy is good communication, within and between men. We may also turn that statement around and it will still be true. Good communication, free communication, within or between men, is always therapeutic.

It is, then, from a background of experience with communication in counseling and psychotherapy that I want to present here two ideas. I wish to state what I believe is one of the major factors in blocking or impeding communication, and then I wish to present what in our experience has proven to be a very important way of improving or facilitating communication.

I would like to propose, as an hypothesis for consideration, that the major barrier to mutual interpersonal communication is our very natural tendency to judge, to evaluate, to approve or disapprove, the

*This paper was originally presented on October 11, 1951, at Northwestern University's Centennial Conference on Communications.

statement of the other person, or the other group. Let me illustrate my meaning with some very simple examples. As you leave the meeting tonight, one of the statements you are likely to hear is, "I didn't like that man's talk." Now what do you respond? Almost invariably your reply will be either approval or disapproval of the attitude expressed. Either you respond, "I didn't either. I thought it was terrible," or else you tend to reply, "Oh, I thought it was really good." In other words, your primary reaction is to evaluate what has just been said to you, to evaluate it from *your* point of view, your own frame of reference.

Or take another example. Suppose I say with some feeling, "I think the Republicans are behaving in ways that show a lot of good sound sense these days," what is the response that arises in your mind as you listen? The overwhelming likelihood is that it will be evaluative. You will find yourself agreeing, or disagreeing, or making some judgment about me such as "He must be a conservative," or "He seems solid in his thinking." Or let us take an illustration from the international scene. Russia says vehemently, "The treaty with Japan is a war plot on the part of the United States." We rise as one person to say "That's a lie!"

This last illustration brings in another element connected with my hypothesis. Although the tendency to make evaluations is common in almost all interchange of language, it is very much heightened in those situations where feelings and emotions are deeply involved. So the stronger our feelings, the more likely it is that there will be no mutual element in the communication. There will be just two ideas, two feelings, two judgments, missing each other in psychological space. I'm sure you recognize this from your own experience. When you have not been emotionally involved yourself, and have listened to a heated discussion, you often go away thinking, "Well, they actually weren't talking about the same thing." And they were not. Each was making a judgment, an evaluation, from his own frame of reference. There was really nothing which could be called communication in any genuine sense. This tendency to react to any emotionally meaningful statement by forming an evaluation of it from our own point of view, is, I repeat, the major barrier to interpersonal communication.

But is there any way of solving this problem, of avoiding this barrier? I feel that we are making exciting progress toward this goal and I would like to present it as simply as I can. Real communication occurs, and this evaluative tendency is avoided, when we listen with understanding. What does that mean? It means *to see the expressed idea and attitude from the other person's point of view, to sense how it feels to him, to achieve his frame of reference in regard to the thing he is talking about.*

Stated so briefly, this may sound absurdly simple, but it is not. It is an approach which we have found extremely potent in the field of psychotherapy. It is the most effective agent we know for altering the basic personality structure of an individual, and improving his relationships and his communications with others. If I can listen to what he can tell me, if I can understand how it seems to him, if I can see its personal meaning for him, if I can sense the emotional flavor which it has for him, then I will be releasing potent forces of change in him. If I can really understand how he hates his father, or hates the university, or hates communists—if I can catch the flavor of his fear of insanity, or his fear of atom bombs, or of Russia—it will be of the greatest help to him in altering those very hatreds and fears, and in establishing realistic and harmonious relationships with the very people and situations toward which he has felt hatred and fear. We know from our research that such empathic understanding—understanding *with* a person, not *about* him—is such an effective approach that it can bring about major changes in personality.

Some of you may be feeling that you listen well to people, and that you have never seen such results. The chances are very great indeed that your listening has not been of the type I have described. Fortunately I can suggest a little laboratory experiment which you can try to test the quality of your understanding. The next time you get into an argument with your wife, or your friend, or with a small group of friends, just stop the discussion for a moment and for an experiment, institute this rule. "Each person can speak up for himself only *after* he has first restated the ideas and feelings of the previous speaker accurately, and to that speaker's satisfaction." You see what this would mean. It would simply mean that before presenting your own point of view, it would be necessary for you to really achieve the other speaker's frame of reference—to understand his thoughts and feelings so well that you could summarize them for him. Sounds simple doesn't it? But if you try it you will discover it one of the most difficult things you have ever tried to do. However, once you have been able to see the other's point of view, your own comments will have to be drastically revised. You will also find the emotion going out of the discussion, the differences being reduced, and those differences which remain being of a rational and understandable sort.

Can you imagine what this kind of an approach would mean if it were projected into larger areas? What would happen to a labor-management dispute if it was conducted in such a way that labor, without necessarily agreeing, could accurately state management's point of view in a way that management could accept; and management, without approving labor's stand, could state labor's case in a way that labor agreed was accurate? It would mean that real communication was established, and one could practically guarantee that some reasonable solution would be reached.

If then this way of approach is an effective avenue to good communication and good relationships, as I am quite sure you will agree if you try the experiment I have mentioned, why is it not more widely tried and used? I will try to list the difficulties which keep it from being utilized.

In the first place it takes courage, a quality which is not too widespread. I am indebted to Dr. S. I. Hayakawa, the semanticist, for pointing out that to carry on psychotherapy in this fashion is to take a very real risk, and that courage is required. If you really understand another person in this way, if you are willing to enter his private world and see the way life appears to him, without any attempt to make evaluative judgments, you run the risk of being changed yourself. You might see it his way, you might find yourself influenced in your attitudes or your personality. This risk of being changed is one of the most frightening prospects most of us can face. If I enter, as fully as I am able, into the private world of a neurotic or psychotic individual, isn't there a risk that I might become lost in that world? Most of us are afraid to take that risk. Or if we had a Russian communist speaker here tonight, or Senator Joe McCarthy, how many of us would dare to try to see the world from each of these points of view? The great majority of us could not *listen;* we would find ourselves compelled to *evaluate,* because listening would seem too dangerous. So the first requirement is courage, and we do not always have it.

But there is a second obstacle. It is just when emotions are strongest that it is most difficult to achieve the frame of reference of the other person or group. Yet it is the time the attitude is most needed, if communication is to be established. We have not found this to be an insuperable obstacle in our experience in psychotherapy. A third party, who is able to lay aside his own feelings and evaluations, can assist greatly by listening with understanding to each person or group and clarifying the views and attitudes each holds. We have found this very effective in small groups in which contradictory or antagonistic attitudes exist. When the parties to a dispute realize that they are being understood, that someone sees how the situation seems to them, the statements grow less exaggerated and less defensive, and it is no longer necessary to maintain the attitude, "I am 100% right and you are 100% wrong." The influence of such an understanding catalyst in the group permits the members to come closer and closer to the objective truth involved in the relationship. In this way mutual communication is established and some type of agreement becomes much more possible. So we may say that though heightened emotions make it much more difficult to understand *with* an opponent, our experience makes it clear that a neutral, understanding, catalyst type of leader or therapist can overcome this obstacle in a small group.

This last phrase, however, suggests another obstacle to utilizing the approach I have described. Thus far all our experience has been with small face-to-face groups—groups exhibiting industrial tensions, religious tensions, racial tensions, and therapy groups in which many personal tensions are present. In these small groups our experience, confirmed by a limited amount of research, shows that this basic approach leads to improved communication, to greater acceptance of others and by others, and to attitudes which are more positive and more problem-solving in nature. There is a decrease in defensiveness, in exaggerated statements, in evaluative and critical behavior. But these findings are from small groups. What about trying to achieve understanding between larger groups that are geographically remote? Or between face-to-face groups who are not speaking for themselves, but simply as representatives of others, like the delegates at Kaesong? Frankly we do not know the answers to these questions. I believe the situation might be put this way. As social scientists we have a tentative test-tube solution of the problem of breakdown in communication. But to confirm the validity of this test-tube solution, and to adapt it to the enormous problems of communication-breakdown between classes, groups, and nations, would involve additional funds, much more research, and creative thinking of a high order.

Even with our present limited knowledge we can see some steps which might be taken, even in large groups, to increase the amount of listening *with,* and to decrease the amount of evaluation *about.* To be imaginative for a moment, let us suppose that a therapeutically oriented international group went to the Russian leaders and said, "We want to achieve a genuine understanding of your views and even more important, of your attitudes and feelings, toward the United States. We will summarize and resummarize these views and feelings if necessary, until you agree that our description represents the situation as it seems to you." Then suppose they did the same thing with the leaders in our own country. If they then gave the widest possible distribution to these two views, with the feelings clearly described but not expressed in name-calling, might not the effect be very great? It would not guarantee the type of understanding I have been describing, but it would make it much more possible. We can understand the feelings of a person who hates us much more readily when his attitudes are accurately described to us by a neutral third party, than we can when he is shaking his fist at us.

But even to describe such a first step is to suggest another obstacle to this approach of understanding. Our civilization does not yet have enough faith in the social sciences to utilize their findings. The opposite is true of the physical sciences. During the war when a test-tube solution was found to the problem of synthetic rubber, millions of dollars and an army of talent was turned loose on the problem of using that finding. If synthetic rubber could be made in milligrams, it could and would be made in the thousands of tons. And it was. But in the social science realm, if a way is found of facilitating communication and mutual understanding in small groups, there is no guarantee that the finding will be utilized. It may be a generation or more before the money and the brains will be turned loose to exploit that finding.

In closing, I would like to summarize this small-scale solution to the problem of barriers in communication, and to point out certain of its characteristics.

I have said that our research and experience to date would make it appear that breakdowns in communication, and the evaluative tendency which is the major barrier to communication, can be avoided. The solution is provided by creating a situation in which each of the different parties come to understand the other from the *other's* point of view. This has been achieved, in practice, even when feelings run high, by the influence of a person who is willing to understand each point of view empathically, and who thus acts as a catalyst to precipitate further understanding.

This procedure has important characteristics. It can be initiated by one party, without waiting for the other to be ready. It can even be initiated by a neutral third person, providing he can gain a minimum of cooperation from one of the parties.

This procedure can deal with the insincerities, the defensive exaggerations, the lies, the "false fronts" which characterize almost every failure in communication. These defensive distortions drop away with astonishing speed as people find that the only intent is to understand, not judge.

This approach leads steadily and rapidly toward the discovery of the truth, toward a realistic appraisal of the objective barriers to communication. The dropping of some defensiveness by one party leads to further dropping of defensiveness by the other party, and truth is thus approached.

This procedure gradually achieves mutual communication. Mutual communication tends to be pointed toward solving a problem rather than toward attacking a person or group. It leads to a situation in which I see how the problem appears to you, as well as to me, and you see how it appears to me, as well as to you. Thus accurately and realistically defined, the problem is almost certain to yield to intelligent attack, or if it is in part insoluble, it will be comfortably accepted as such.

This then appears to be a test-tube solution to the breakdown of communication as it occurs in small groups. Can we take this small scale answer, investigate it further, refine it, develop it and apply it to the tragic and well-nigh fatal failures of communication which threaten the very existence of our modern world? It seems to me that this is a possibility and a challenge which we should explore.

2 In Chapter 8 we discussed a simple heuristic procedure for describing a particular audience. Using this procedure results in what Rogers would call understanding "about" the audience. It may also aid empathic understanding, understanding "with" a person, but this kind of understanding requires more imagination — and courage. Empathy is the process of imaginatively entering into the personality of another in order to understand the way he interprets experience, to understand his beliefs, desires, fears, joys, sorrows — something that we can all do even though psychologists do not fully understand how the process works. One way of explaining the process is to say that we come to understand the internal states of other people by first observing their behavior and then making inferences based on our memory of similar behavior of our own and of the internal states that produced our behavior. Another explanation is that we imaginatively put ourselves

into the shoes of another; in our minds we play the part of another, trying to see the world as the other person sees it and to respond to it as he responds. Both explanations offer further guides for achieving the more intimate understanding that seems essential to the kind of communication we have been discussing.

As an exercise in empathic understanding, select from a newspaper or magazine a letter to the editor that presents an argument with which you strongly disagree, and try to empathize with its writer. Do you notice a change in your own attitudes toward the argument and the writer?

3 Isolate from your reading or your conversations with others two or three statements with which you sharply disagree. From what perspectives or in what contexts might they be considered valid? Write a paragraph that delineates each statement's area of validity.

4 Write a letter to the editor of your local newspaper, replying to a letter that has irritated you or aroused your sense of threat. Use the strategy described in this chapter. If replies to your letter are published, try to account for their characteristics. (An absence of replies may also be interesting. Why?)

5 Reread the excerpt from the argument between the American liberal and the Russian communist (p. 280). How would an American conservative be likely to react to this excerpt? Why? How do you react? Why? What do these reactions suggest about the nature of communication in general and of Rogerian argument in particular?

6 We have noted some of the limitations of traditional argument. Does Rogerian argument have comparable limitations? The following questions may aid speculation. Are there dyadic situations in which Rogerian argument might prove ineffectual or unnecessary? When, or for what purposes, might it be useful in triadic situations? When wouldn't it be useful? What qualities does it demand of the user?

What underlying beliefs about the future are implied by Rogers' optimism when he says that adequate restatement of each other's views would "practically guarantee that some reasonable solution would be reached"? Do you share these beliefs? To what extent does willingness to use the strategy depend on one's belief about the nature of man?

BRYAN COLLEGE

DAYTON, TENNESSEE 37321

CLASS GRADE REPORT

280

STUDENT'S NAME — John S Lacey

SEMESTER — Fall   YEAR — 77-78

PRINT NAME —

ADDRESS — and Mrs Jack E Lacey

ADDRESS OF PARENTS — 2039 Saratoga Dr.

CITY — Waterloo   STATE — Iowa   ZIP — 50702

A - SUPERIOR
B - GOOD
C - AVERAGE
D - BELOW AVERAGE

F - FAILED
I - INCOMPLETE
WP - WITHDREW PASSING
WF - WITHDREW FAILING

S - SATISFACTORY
U - UNSATISFACTORY
NR - NOT REPORTED
NC - NO CREDIT

COURSE NO.	TITLE	MID-TERM GRADE	FINAL GRADE	SEMESTER HOURS	QUALITY POINTS
EH 101A	FRESHMAN ENG	C+			

INSTRUCTOR'S SIGNATURE - MID TERM

COMMENTS - MID TERM — Louise Bentley

INSTRUCTOR'S SIGNATURE - FINAL

COMMENTS - FINAL

304-10-18 (10/71)

*The major reason that language skills appear to be
more complex than perceptual-motor skills
is the overwhelming richness of alternative situations
where language is employed.*
PAUL M. FITTS AND MICHAEL I. POSNER, *Human Performance*

*The great writer seldom regards himself as a personality
with something to say: his mind to him is simply a place
where something happens to words.*
NORTHROP FRYE, Lecture at the University of Toronto

13 Dimensions of linguistic choice

NORTHROP Frye's statement suggests another conception of the process of writing: that writing is more than accurate *description,* more than the writer's *expression* of his personal image of the world, and more than effective *communication* with a reader. It is all of these, but it is also *verbal creation*—an extremely complex sequence of linguistic choices resulting in a structure of words, which in its wholeness is a new thing. Implicit in each chapter of this book is one or another of these conceptions. In the early chapters we discussed the characteristics of adequate description; later we suggested how you can systematically explore and enrich your image of the world. Then we concentrated on your relationship with your reader—how you can come to know him and change him in various ways. Our focus in this chapter and in the following two chapters is on linguistic choice; we will be concerned not so much with what is said as with how it is said. We will examine several properties of language that, if understood, can help you avoid or correct some of the problems most common to all writers — in particular, problems of structure, coherence, focus, and loading. Bear in mind as you read, however, that verbal creation, development of personal knowledge, and interaction with the reader are not completely separable activities, although for the sake of clarity we speak of them as if they were. They overlap and interpenetrate to such an extent that they must finally be regarded as aspects of a single, extraordinarily complex process.

Language as meaning and form

Language can be thought of as very complex coding behavior for interpreting and recording experience. One of its most significant features is that the same basic "meaning" can be represented in several different forms; hence, one of the choices a writer must make is the choice of a form to encode his meaning.[1] For example, the following sentences all have the same, or nearly the same, meaning.

1) The police arrested my roommate for picketing against the tuition increase that the president announced yesterday.
2) My roommate was arrested by the police for picketing against the tuition increase that the president announced yesterday.
3) Yesterday the president announced that there would be an increase in tuition. My roommate picketed against the increase and the police arrested him.
4) I have a roommate and he picketed against the tuition increase. It was announced by the president yesterday. My roommate was arrested by the police for this.

What is the same in all these versions? Underlying them all is a proposition (P) that might be expressed as:

P_1 = Agent (*the police*), Act (*arrest*), Affected or Goal (*my roommate*), Reason (*for picketing against the tuition increase that the president announced yesterday*).

Embedded in this proposition, under the category labeled Reason,

---

[1] One current linguistic theory, known as tagmemics, treats language (1) as one kind of human behavior and (2) as relevant only in relation to its setting (a) in nonverbal behavior and (b) in contexts of nonverbal things or events. From this point of view, meaning is, in part, the relation of verbal to nonverbal behavior.

In some sense, however, meaning *is* choice: unless choice is possible, no meaning occurs.

are two other propositions (or possibly more[2]). We can designate the underlying proposition P_1. The two embedded propositions are:

P_2 = Agent (*my roommate*), Act (*picket against*), Goal (*tuition increase*).

P_3 = Agent (*the president*), Act (*announce*), Goal (*the tuition increase*), Time (*yesterday*).

P_1 (including embedded P_2 and P_3) can, grammatically, take any of the forms listed above. Out of all possible grammatical forms, the writer chooses the one that is the most strategic with reference to his reader and to the larger verbal contexts of which the proposition is a part. (Criteria for choosing one form over another are discussed in Chapter 15.)

In order for a proposition to take form as one or more sentences, the various categories in the proposition must be assigned grammatical roles in the sentence. That is, a category such as Agent is assigned a particular grammatical role — subject, or predicate, or adjunct, and so on.

Agent as subject: *The police* arrested my roommate.

Agent as predicate: The streets were well *policed.*

Agent as adjunct: My roommate was arrested *by the police.*

Because the different categories of a proposition can take various grammatical roles, and propositions can be combined in different ways, we can have a variety of sentences that have nearly the same meaning. In examples 1 through 4 above, P_1, P_2, and P_3 are combined in various ways.

Just how many categories there are remains an open question — guesses by linguists range from five or six to nearly fifty, and the process by which one assigns underlying categories to grammatical roles has not been described completely. Yet the assumption that sentences do have underlying propositions or something like them seems necessary in order to explain how a writer changes the form of what he writes while in some sense leaving the basic meaning unchanged.[3]

---

[2] This analysis is illustrative and not complete. Constituents like *my roommate* can be broken down further: Agent (*I*), Process (*have*), Affected or Goal (*a roommate*). Features such as tense, aspect, and mood are considered by some scholars features of sentences, not of propositions.

[3] Tagmemic theory insists, however, on studying language as a *form-meaning composite*. No language forms can be profitably studied without reference to *some* degree of meaning, and no meanings can be studied without either direct or indirect reference to forms that manifest them. If it were not for the fact that this book automatically meets the problem — since it is stressing writing, the creation of meaningful forms — the assumption that language is a form-meaning composite would have been set up as a maxim.

Language as a hierarchical system

Another related structural characteristic of language that makes choice possible is the hierarchical arrangement of its parts. As Herbert A. Simon suggests in "The Architecture of Complexity" (p. 43), a language system is a hierarchical structure composed of complete but interrelated subsystems: Paragraphs, for example, normally include complete sentences; sentences, complete clauses; clauses, complete phrases; and phrases, complete words. This hierarchy is more complex than it first appears, for it is made up of three separate yet interlocking hierarchical systems: a lexical hierarchy, a phonological hierarchy, and a grammatical (or syntactic) hierarchy. Thus every sentence contains words, sounds (or, in writing, letters and punctuation), and grammatical units, such as subject and object.

The lexical hierarchy includes, potentially, all the words in the English dictionary. Lexical units, however, can be smaller or much larger than words. The parts of Aztec words we studied in Chapter 6 are examples of the smaller lexical units. Similarly, in the English word *un-gentle-man-li-ness*, each part set off by a hyphen is a lexical unit. A larger lexical unit may be a group of words, such as an idiom, which must be considered a unit, since its meaning as a whole is not the sum of the meanings of the parts: for example, *out on a limb, off the cuff, step on the gas.* There are lexical units of a still higher level, such as particular clauses and sentences. As we shall see in the next chapter, this hierarchy extends beyond the sentence to syllogisms, paragraphs, poems, even whole books.

The phonological hierarchy is composed of units of sound: individual sounds represented (roughly) by the letters in our spelling system, syllables, rhythmic feet, stress groups, and those still larger units that are identifiable by the way the voice is used—a prayer, for instance, or an oration, or a newscast. In writing, phonological features are symbolized, imperfectly, by various graphic devices: English spelling more or less indicates the sequence of sounds in a word; italics sometimes show the nucleus, or accented syllable, of a stress group; punctuation reflects something of the intonational patterns of the voice—its rising and falling pitch, its stresses, its breaks and pauses.[4] Listen to what your voice does as you read the following sentences aloud:

[4] The range of phonological choices that are open to us when we speak is extraordinary, and scarcely known to us though we use language constantly. In this sense English is practically an unwritten language. (Even some of what we do "know" about it is probably false. As a simple example, a question often, but by no means always, ends with a rising pitch.) Writing eliminates some of the normal tools of communication. But the paucity of tools and their artificiality make it all the more important that the writer learn to use the dull saw to shape his intricate cabinet.

> The men went away.
> The men went away?
> The men went away!
> The men who were here went away.
> The men, who were here, went away.

The grammatical hierarchy includes grammatical units, or *tag-memes*. A tagmeme is a composite (1) of a functional slot in a grammatical pattern (e.g., object slot), (2) with accompanying generalized plot element (a propositional category, such as Affected), (3) plus a class of appropriate fillers (such as noun phrase), (4) manifested by one chosen member of the class (such as *my roommate*):

$$\text{subject} + \text{predicate} + \begin{bmatrix} \text{object:} & \text{noun phrase} \\ \text{Affected:} & my \ roommate \end{bmatrix}$$

As in *The police arrested my roommate.*

Slots and their fillers are combined in hierarchical patterns. Small units are parts of larger ones; for example, the phrase *my roommate* includes a head (*roommate*) and modifier (*my*). And larger units are parts of still larger ones. As we suggested earlier, the hierarchy extends beyond the sentence, since the sentence as a whole may be part of a larger construction:

> The police arrested my roommate yesterday for singing his favorite song, "Green with Envy, Purple with Passion, White with Anger, Scarlet with Fever, What Were You Doing in Her Arms Last Night Blues." It's a good song, but he ought not to have been singing it on the street corner at three in the morning.

Choice occurs at slots in a *pattern*—which we define as a conventional sequence of slots with a set of possible alternatives, or choices, that can fill the slots. Patterns, like tagmemes, are grammatical units, with slots filled by particular lexical items.

Other lexical items of a category may be substituted; for example, *they* or *the cops* may be substituted for *the police*; *him* or *my friend* for *my roommate*. Higher-level substitutions are also possible; for instance, one clause for another clause; one sentence for another sentence; one paragraph for another paragraph. It is usually possible to substitute parts without significantly changing the whole; indeed, much of the activity of writing, particularly editing, involves making such substitutions.

The hierarchical structure of language also permits choice in the *scope* of a proposition. A proposition can be stretched over two or three sentences (or even a larger span) as in example 4 (p. 292).

> I have a roommate and he picketed against the tuition increase. It was announced by the president yesterday. My roommate was arrested by the police for this.

Or can it can be compressed into a single slot of a sentence. P_1 (p. 292), for instance, can become a noun phrase:

> *My roommate's arrest by the police* . . . was a blow to his parents.

Or:

> *It* was a blow to his parents.

Language systems, then, utilize the principle of hierarchy to achieve tremendous complexity of the whole with fairly simple, manipulable parts.[5]

Constraints on linguistic choice

GRAMMATICAL CONSTRAINTS

Choices within any of the hierarchies of language, lexical, phonological, or grammatical, and at any of the levels of these hierarchies can be grammatically correct or incorrect. The English language is a public code; as such, it has rules. Our knowledge of these lexical, phonological, and grammatical rules enables us to produce an indefinite number of original, comprehensible statements, to understand the statements produced by others, and to identify statements formulated in some other language or in incorrect English. These rules are constraints on the user, just as the rules of tennis are constraints on the tennis player. Without rules there can be no game.

For example,

Loves John Mary.

is obviously not a correct English sentence; contrary to normal practice, the subject is placed after the verb. But which is the subject, Mary or John? Notice that there is no way of capturing the proposition underlying this sentence; as a result, there is no easy way of

---

[5] We have chosen to limit discussion in this chapter to *language* structure. Tagmemic theory insists, however, that language structure and language behavior are but one subsystem of the structure of behavior as a whole. All the principles used here can be used in the study of football games, house construction, or lollipop eating. See the first footnote in this chapter about language and behavior; see also Exercise 2 and the related discussion in Chapter 3.

correcting it. We recognize a general type of error (incorrect word order), but in trying to correct it we produce several grammatically acceptable possibilities:

> John loves Mary.
> Mary loves John.
> Does John love Mary?
> Does Mary love John?

The problem here is that we cannot identify the propositional categories of the participants (e.g., Is *John* Agent or Affected?), nor can we be sure of their grammatical roles (e.g., Is *John* subject or object?).[6] With an intransitive verb there is no dilemma:

> Away ran John.

agreement

Although *John* is out of its normal position, it is clearly the subject of the sentence. (Similar deviations from normal word order are common in storytelling, particularly in children's stories—a strange convention, since children presumably require simpler constructions than adults do in order to understand.) The rules of English do not specify what you discuss, but they do specify the forms available to you—forms that you must use if you wish to be able to talk and write and be understood.

As speakers and writers of English, we seldom—if ever—produce statements as completely incomprehensible as *Loves John Mary.* But we do at times make incorrect linguistic choices that may produce other undesirable consequences, even though they do not block understanding. For example, we have all written sentences containing errors in agreement between subject and verb; such errors are fairly common in complex constructions.

> The student who is sitting in the last row behind the two
> girls working on their compositions (*write* or *writes?*) well.

spelling

And we all have misspelled words; misspelling is a common error in English even among good writers. Mistakes in agreement, spelling, and so on have social as well as linguistic implications. Ordinarily,

---

[6] The following sentences are incorrect in a more subtle way. We can recognize the underlying propositions and the grammatical roles; the rules violated involve restrictions on the co-occurrence of certain underlying categories or grammatical roles.

> The old man and the wind died.
> I have a pipe but some tobacco.
> I don't have some money.

A discussion of this kind of constraint can be found in Alton L. Becker, *A Generative Description of the English Subject Tagmemes,* unpublished doctoral dissertation, University of Michigan, 1967.

incorrect spelling does not seriously impair recognition of the linguistic code; we usually know what the writer meant. Often, however, a misspelling produces a highly undesirable reaction in the
reader, a reaction far out of proportion to the seriousness of the error. For many readers, an error in spelling carries implications
about the writer's social background and moral character. Such responses may be unreasonably harsh, but they are a fact of life.

RHETORICAL CONSTRAINTS

There are other less clearly defined constraints on the choices
we make when we write and speak, constraints that we will label
rhetorical, since they derive less from the rules of the linguistic code
itself than from the usual responses of people to the way the code is
used. Grammatical correctness is not in itself sufficient to ensure
effective communication. For instance, it is possible to write a
grammatically "correct" English sentence that will baffle most readers:

The rat the cat the dog chased caught died.[7]

Two sentences (*The dog chased the cat* and *The cat caught the rat*) are
embedded into a third sentence (*The rat died*) as relative clauses,
and the relative pronouns are deleted. The embedded clauses overload the resulting sentence, making it almost totally obscure to the
general reader. It is poor strategy if the writer's goal is communication.

Likewise, a sentence (or any other syntactic pattern, including
a paragraph) may be grammatically correct but strategically poor
because it is ambiguous. The sentence *John gave Bill his driver* obviously has at least two possible readings. The ambiguity of the
sentence *John and Bill came to Ann Arbor* is more subtle: The reader
may take the sentence to mean that John and Bill came together to
Ann Arbor (i.e., John came with Bill) or that each came separately.
Although ambiguous sentences seldom seem ambiguous to the writer (who knows what he means), it is safe to predict that most of
them will be read the wrong way by a large percentage of readers.

This fact is hard for the writer to accept. Since his meaning
seems clear enough to him, he may resent being told by a fellow
student, his wife, his editor, or his teacher that his writing is un-

---

[7] That is to say, this sentence would be "correct" within any theory of grammar that
does not set a limit on the frequency of embedding or the extent of overloading in
its specifications of appropriate patterns or acceptable rules. Tagmemic theory holds
that such probabalistic constraints must eventually be included formally in adequate
grammatical descriptions and in discussions of correctness; current tagmemic descriptions, however, do this only informally.

clear. He often concludes that his readers must be stupid to miss his meaning. But he should remember that the reader was not following along with him as he made his choices; if the reader had participated, the meaning would probably be clear. The reader does not know which alternatives were considered and rejected; he knows only the results of the choices made. The effective writer learns to predict his reader's reactions to his words and to act accordingly.

Other constraints on linguistic choices are matters of social convention. These conventions determine not only the appropriate thing to say in a particular social situation but also the appropriate way to say it. For instance, we write in one way to intimates, in another to friends, in another to business acquaintances, and in still another to professional colleagues. We may say the "same things" in each case, but the way we say them differs. The linguistic choices that we make vary in response to variations in the social situation. In highly informal discourse, our punctuation is likely to be unstudied (we tend to substitute a dash for more discriminating punctuation); our spelling is frequently simplified; our syntax is often elliptical and fragmented; and the words we choose may include a high proportion of casual terms and slang. More formal discourse is more studied and discriminating and more carefully edited. The variations in the way we address different readers are called *functional varieties* of English. (Much of the current antagonism felt by adults toward student writing, particularly the writing in underground newspapers, is attributable to the writers' refusal to recognize the social norms that govern linguistic choice.)

Language choice also varies with the topic under discussion. Normally, topics considered to be serious are discussed in one of the more formal functional varieties; less serious topics, in one of the more informal varieties. Incongruities between the weight of the topic and the functional variety that is used to discuss it may produce shocking or humorous effects. The following passage from "Buck Fanshaw's Funeral" by Mark Twain illustrates a failure to adapt language to both a particular audience and topic. Shorty is merely trying to arrange a funeral for a friend, but his efforts to communicate with the minister are hopeless as well as hilarious.

> "Are you the duck that runs the gospel-mill next door?"
> "Am I the—pardon me, I believe I do not understand?"
> With another sigh and a half-sob, Scotty rejoined:
> "Why you see we are in a bit of trouble, and the boys thought maybe you would give us a lift, if we'd tackle you—that is, if I've got the rights of it and you are the head clerk of the doxology-works next door."
> "I am the shepherd in charge of the flock whose fold is next door."

"The which?"

"The spiritual adviser of the little company of believers whose sanctuary adjoins these premises."

Scotty scratched his head, reflected a moment, and then said:

"You ruther hold over me, pard. I reckon I can't call that hand. Ante and pass the buck."

"How? I beg pardon. What did I understand you to say?"

"Well, you've ruther got the bulge on me. Or maybe we've both got the bulge, somehow. You don't smoke me and I don't smoke you. You see, one of the boys has passed in his checks, and we want to give him a good send-off, and so the thing I'm on now is to roust out somebody to jerk a little chin-music for us and waltz him through handsome."

"My friend, I seem to grow more and more bewildered. Your observations are wholly incomprehensible to me. Cannot you simplify them in some way? At first I thought perhaps I understood you, but I grope now. Would it not expedite matters if you restricted yourself to categorical statements of fact unencumbered with obstructing accumulations of metaphor and allegory?"

MARK TWAIN, "Buck Fanshaw's Funeral," *Roughing It*

Much of the humor comes from the fact that neither of the speakers has control over more than one functional variety of English. Although both men are constructing grammatically correct sentences, neither is making rhetorically appropriate choices, lexical choices in particular. If they are to communicate, they must, at the very least, make their lexical choices from a subset of items that they share.

There are also aesthetic constraints on the use of language. For example, obvious or unintentional puns are aesthetically unappealing to many English-speaking people (we commonly apologize for them), although in some other languages and cultures they are considered a sign of inspiration and linguistic sensitivity. We also object to the use in contemporary prose of alliteration, rhymes, homophones, and meter — at least when they call attention to themselves. Consider these sentences by John Lyly, a sixteenth-century writer who was regarded by his contemporaries as an elegant prose stylist.

Descend into your own consciences; consider with your selves the great difference between staring and stark blind, wit and wisdom, love and lust; be merry but with modesty; be sober but not too sullen; be valiant but not too venturous; let your attire be comely but not too costly; your diet wholesome but not excessive; use pastime as the word importeth, to pass the time in honest recreation. Mistrust no man without cause, neither be you credulous without proof; be not light to follow every man's opinion, neither obstinate to stand in your own conceits; serve God, fear God, love God, and God will bless you, as either your hearts can wish, or your friends desire.

Realizing that different ages have different aesthetic norms, the modern reader has no trouble in accepting such prose, although it may sound strange. But if it had been written today, it would strike most of us as pretentious and inappropriate, for the stylistic norm of modern prose is educated conversation. Radical departures from this norm seem to us either inept or mannered.

Although we have by no means exhausted the subject, it should be apparent that the task of writing involves making a multitude of linguistic choices and that these choices are affected by both the linguistic and the extralinguistic context in which they are made—by what might be called the writer's *universe of discourse.* This observation is fundamental enough to warrant being stated as the sixth in our list of maxims: *Linguistic choices are made in relation to a universe of discourse.* Many, perhaps most, of the choices that we make are the result of intuition rather than conscious analysis. Nevertheless, we must have either a conscious or a subconscious awareness of the particular universe of discourse that constrains our choices if we are to choose intelligently.

Intelligent choices are *simultaneously* appropriate to all the dimensions of a universe of discourse: to other linguistic features of the verbal system that is being created, to the peculiarites of writer and reader, to the topic, to the kind of discourse being written—in short, to all the aspects of the writing situation that we have discussed both in this chapter and in the preceding ones. If such complexity seems overwhelming when it is first analyzed, it is nevertheless something that human beings can learn to handle—and, with sufficient study and practice, can learn to handle with relative ease. One of the astonishing characteristics of the human mind is its ability to process extraordinary complexity readily and with great rapidity. Another word of comfort: The possibility of choice creates the possibility of correcting choices that we have already made. Every choice need not be right the first time; we can edit what we have written.

Innovation in linguistic choice

We have said that effective choices are those that are grammatically correct and rhetorically appropriate, but let us qualify this generalization. It is possible to make "incorrect" and "inappropriate" choices that are nevertheless effective. For example, even though *smilt* and *grube* do not happen to have any meaning in English, they are possible English words because they follow the rules of English phonology; *lgnet* and *shbih*, on the other hand, are non-English, for they violate rules of English phonology. With two exceptions (words beginning with *shr* and a few foreign words—the names of people, places, and so on), no English word beginning with *sh* has another consonant before the first vowel. But when cartoonist Al Capp introduced and popularized the word *shmo*, he established a precedent for forming other words on the same model. Such words are now appropriate in humorous contexts; acceptance in more formal contexts, however, will take longer.

Suppose a writer included a poem in a technical essay on quantum mechanics. His readers would no doubt be surprised, for its presence in such a context is extremely unusual. If, however, he was able to use the poem skillfully to clarify or emphasize a point, his "elegant inappropriateness" would be rewarded by close attention, improved communication, and better retention. Appropriateness implies the existence of some kind of norm; at times departures from this norm can produce a higher appropriateness. The accomplished poet is well aware of this and often uses words in unusual (abnormal) contexts or "breaks the rules of grammar" for special effects. But one need not be a poet in order to exercise such license. The writer of nonfiction prose may also regard current grammatical and rhetorical norms as creative opportunities. Our best writers do.

Without constraints—rules, conventional patterns, norms of various sorts—nothing could be said at all; no communication could occur without conventional forms. We usually make use of the extensive areas of choice that are available within the conventions; occasionally, however, we exploit a "higher" area of choice by flouting convention. Yet such deviations can go only so far before we are speaking a different language, living a different culture, and stopping communication dead. Ultimately, innovation that destroys all conventions destroys the possibility of innovation itself. But whether the writer chooses to experiment with conventions for unusual effects or to stay well within the norms, what he does cannot be reduced to a mechanical process, a set of rules that might be programmed into a computer. Writing is an art, with choices abounding.

EXERCISES

1 Using the categories Agent, Act, Affected or Goal, Instrument, Beneficiary, Time, Place, Cause, Purpose, Accompaniment, and Manner, describe the propositions underlying the follow-

ing sentences. Note that a sentence may include more than one proposition.

> EXAMPLE: I'll get the book for you if you'll wait here a moment.
> P_1 = Agent (*I*), Act (*get*), Goal (*book*), Beneficiary (*you*).
> P_2 = Agent (*you*), Act (*wait*), Place (*here*), Time (*moment*).

a The little fellow who is labeled for posterity as Lawrence of Arabia detested the title.

> E. M. FORSTER, "T. E. Lawrence," *Abinger Harvest*

b A man who is working as a skilled laborer and has never held any other type of job may struggle to rise from the ranks of labor into a white-collar position.

> C. WRIGHT MILLS, "The Trade Union Leader," *Power, Politics and People*

c The protagonist of Doctor Faustus, Adrien Leverkuhn, makes a pact with the devil, willfully contracts syphilis with a prostitute, and finally goes utterly mad.

> MICHAEL HARRINGTON, "Images of Disorder," *The Accidental Century*

d The silent substance is also the place where a man is re-created.

> MAX PICARD, *The World of Silence*

e I went to the woods because I wished to live deliberately. . . .

> HENRY DAVID THOREAU, *Walden*

Adding and subtracting as little meaning as possible, express the proposition(s) underlying each sentence in two other ways. Discuss reasons why one version might be preferable to another. (Chapter 15 will supply you with additional reasons.)

2 Bearing in mind the hierarchical structure of linguistic units, discuss the functions of each of these conventions of writing: a table of contents; chapter numbers; an epigraph to a book and to a chapter of a book; an introductory paragraph to a book, to a chapter of a book, and to an essay; headings within chapters and essays; paragraph indentions; summary paragraphs.

Why do you suppose a good reader studies the table of contents of a book before he begins to read the book? Why do you suppose he skims each chapter before reading it? What parts is he likely to pay more attention to as he skims?

3   After reading Lewis Carroll's "Jabberwocky," describe as precisely as you can the linguistic peculiarities of the poem. Does Carroll violate any rules of English grammar and phonology? What features of language make it possible for you to get some meaning from the poem? Or, to ask the same question in another way, why does Alice remark after hearing the poem that "somehow it seems to fill my head with ideas—only I don't know exactly what they are!"

Jabberwocky
LEWIS CARROLL

'Twas brillig, and the slithy toves
    Did gyre and gimble in the wabe;
All mimsy were the borogoves,
    And the mome raths outgrabe.

"Beware the Jabberwock, my son!
    The jaws that bite, the claws that catch!
Beware the Jubjub bird, and shun
    The frumious Bandersnatch!"

He took his vorpal sword in hand:
    Long time the manxome foe he sought—
So rested he by the Tumtum tree,
    And stood awhile in thought.

And as in uffish thought he stood,
    The Jabberwock, with eyes of flame,
Came whiffling through the tulgey wood,
    And burbled as it came!

One, two! One, two! And through and through
    The vorpal blade went snicker-snack!
He left it dead, and with its head
    He went galumphing back.

"And hast thou slain the Jabberwock?
    Come to my arms, my beamish boy!
O frabjous day! Callooh! Callay!"
    He chortled in his joy.

'Twas brillig, and the slithy toves
    Did gyre and gimble in the wabe;
All mimsy were the borogoves,
    And the mome raths outgrabe.

4 Consult a dictionary's appendix on punctuation. Which punctuation marks can be substituted for one another; that is, which marks can be interchanged with little or no effect on meaning? Which cannot be interchanged? Illustrate your answers by writing the same sentence several times using different punctuation each time.

5 We have reprinted the following passage without punctuation. Try to read it aloud slowly. What happened? What is missing? Add your own punctuation. If your curiosity lives long enough to haunt you, compare your version with the original (p. 163).

science searches for relations which are thought to exist independently of the searching individual this includes the case where man himself is the subject or the subject of scientific statements may be concepts created by ourselves as in mathematics such concepts are not necessarily supposed to correspond to any objects in the outside world however all scientific statements and laws have one characteristic in common they are true or false adequate or inadequate roughly speaking our reaction to them is yes or no

6 How would you characterize the functional varieties of English that are used in James Madison's "Federalist," Number X (p. 242), and in E. B. White's "Khrushchev and I" (p. 185)? Rewrite the first paragraph of Madison's essay in the functional variety that would be appropriate to a letter addressed to close friends. Rewrite the first paragraph of White's essay in the functional variety that would be appropriate to a treatise on politics and communication addressed to political scientists. What kinds of changes did you institute? Make appropriate and inappropriate lexical substitutions in each opening paragraph and explain why they are appropriate or inappropriate. (For a detailed discussion of such variant forms of discourse, see Martin Joos, *The Five Clocks,* New York: Harcourt, Brace & World, 1967.)

7 Read the following passages and answer the questions after each one.

a What's worse than raining cats and dogs?
ANSWER: Hailing taxis.

What substitutions can be made in both statements without destroying the joke? What substitutions destroy the joke? What peculiarity of the word *hail* makes the joke possible?

b During the reign of Queen Mary of England (1553–58) a country gentleman chosen to be speaker of Parliament was ridiculed because he "made no difference between an Oration or publike speach to be delivered to th'ear of a Princes Maiestie and state of a Realme, than he would have done of an ordinary tale to be told at his table in the countrey, wherein all men know the oddes is very great."

In w. s. howell, *Logic and Rhetoric in England, 1500–1700*

As we suggested in this chapter we all share social and aesthetic norms that affect our sense of what is acceptable prose. Find specific instances of modern discourse comparable to those described in the quotation. Do the linguistic differences between the modern examples strike you as being "very great"?

c During one period of his political career, Machiavelli was exiled from his native city of Florence to a country estate. There he wrote his famous treatise on statecraft, *The Prince*. His days were spent talking and gambling with the local people. "We quarrel over farthings," he wrote. "When evening comes I return to the house and go to my study. Before I enter I take off my rough mud-stained country dress. I put on my royal and curial robes and thus fittingly attired I enter into the assembly of men of old times."

NICCOLO MACHIAVELLI, *Letters*

Changing clothes obviously has symbolic meaning for Machiavelli. In terms of our discussion in this chapter can you explain his behavior?

d *You, Noam Chomsky*
SISTER MARY JONATHAN, O.P.

*Sentences (1) and (2) are equally nonsensical,
but any speaker of English will recognize
that only the former is grammatical.
(1) Colorless green ideas sleep furiously.
(2) Furiously sleep ideas green colorless.*
NOAM CHOMSKY, *Syntactic Structures*

Colorless green ideas sleep furiously
in the fan-shaped eyes, that welcomed
only the color of the relevant world,
wearing a face of man,

their green (in violent sleep, the nightmare
day) draining to white or vagueness
in a stretch of fear.

Address yourself, Ideas, to sleep.
Furiously sleep, Ideas, green, colorless,
involved in green, careless of responsibility.

Let all fury, entangled with your grammar,
be a colorless green.

What is the area of validity of Chomsky's statement? What is
Sister Mary Jonathan trying to demonstrate? What changes
does she make in the original sentences? Why? What is the
source of the title and why did the author use it? What does
understanding the allusion in the title add to your understanding and appreciation of the poem?

e "I don't know what you mean by 'glory,' " Alice said.
       Humpty Dumpty smiled contemptuously. "Of course you don't
—till I tell you. I mean 'there's a nice knock-down argument for you!' "
       "But 'glory' doesn't mean 'a nice knock-down argument,' " Alice
objected.
       "When *I* use a word," Humpty Dumpty said in rather a scornful
tone, "it means just what I choose it to mean—neither more nor less."
       "The question is," said Alice, "whether you *can* make words
mean so many different things."
       "The question is," said Humpty Dumpty, "which is to be mas-
ter—that's all."
       LEWIS CARROLL, *Through the Looking-Glass, and What Alice Found There*

What are the areas of validity and invalidity in the arguments
of Alice and Humpty Dumpty?

8   After reading the following essay by Charles V. Hartung, answer these questions. On what assumptions about language
does each of the doctrines rest? What is the area of validity of
each doctrine? What are the limits of each doctrine? Which of
the doctrines were you taught in grade school and high
school? What are its advantages and disadvantages? Is one of
the doctrines correct? Are certain doctrines more reasonable
than others?

from
Doctrines of English Usage
CHARLES V. HARTUNG

. . . Generally speaking, the four main doctrines current among those
concerned with judging the propriety of language usage are: (1) the
doctrine of rules; (2) the doctrine of general usage; (3) the doctrine of
appropriate usage; (4) the doctrine of the linguistic norm. Rarely do

those interested in language adhere consistently to any one of these doctrines, instead there is the usual divergence between theory and practice; some linguists profess one doctrine and practice another. Also there is the usual eclectic compromise. Nevertheless, it is possible to make roughly approximate groupings of schools of opinion according to the degrees of emphasis given to these various doctrines.

THE DOCTRINE OF RULES

From the point of view of the modern school of linguistics the doctrine of rules is, or at least should be, moribund. But even a cursory glance at handbooks and grammars of recent date reveals what a tenacious hold it has on life. And even when the doctrine is disclaimed in theory, we find grammarians following it in spirit and practice. For example, in the preface to R. W. Pence's *A Grammar of Present-Day English*, we find the following statement: "Grammar is not a set of rules thought up by and imposed by some invisible godlike creature."[4] Yet the text itself consists of a set of prescriptions in the spirit of the eighteenth century grammarians and having the effect if not the form of the old rules. Here is an example:

. . . inasmuch as an interrogative pronoun normally introduces a clause and so may not have the position that a noun of like function would have, the function of an interrogative pronoun may be easily mistaken. Care needs to be exercised to meet the demands of subjective complements of finite verbs and of infinitives. But especial care needs to be taken that the proper objective form is used when an interrogative pronoun coming first functions as the object of a preposition that is delayed.
1. Subjective complement
   Whom do you mean? [*Whom* is the object of *do mean.*]
2. Object of a preposition
   Whom were you with last night?
   [*Whom* is the object of the preposition *with. Not:* Who were you with last night?][5]

In a note some concession is made to the demands of spoken discourse: "Who are you looking for? [Accepted by some in spoken discourse.]" But in the same note we find this comment: "This use of the nominative in informal spoken discourse is regarded by a few as acceptable, although the fastidious person will probably look upon it as sloppy speech." It is noteworthy that the text in which this judgment is to be found reached its seventh printing in 1953. Yet the sentence *Who are you looking for* is listed as *Accepted* in the Leonard survey printed in 1932.

It would be possible, of course, to multiply examples of the continuing hold that the doctrine of rules still has on a large proportion

[4] New York: The Macmillan Co., 1947, p. v.
[5] *Ibid.*, pp. 204–05.

of present day students of language, but it is more to the point to examine the reasons for this hold. Probably the most important reason is that the doctrine has behind it the weight of over a century and a half of almost undisputed dominance. This is the result of two main sources of authority: the assumed correspondence of the rules of grammar with basic principles of reason and the supposed correspondence of the rules with the usage of the best writers. Some grammarians have assumed that reason has the prior claim and determines usage; others have placed usage first and have claimed that rules are inductively derived from the best usage. The eighteenth century grammarian William Ward gives typical expression to the view of the first group:

Use and Custom are considered as the only Rules by which to judge of what is right or wrong in Process. But is the Custom which is observed in the Application of any Language the Effect of Chance? Is not such a Custom a consistent Plan of communicating the Conceptions and rational discursive Operations of one Man to another? And who will maintain, that this is, or can be, the Effect of unmeaning Accident? If then it be not so, it must be the Effect of the Reason of Man, adjusting certain means to a certain End: And it is the Business of Speculative or Rational Grammar to explain the Nature of the Means, and to show how they are applied to accomplish the End proposed. If this can be done with sufficient Evidence, the most simple of the Elements of Logic will become familiar to those who engage in a Course of Grammar, and Reason will go Hand in Hand with Practice. [6]

Ward's linking of grammar and logic was a common eighteenth century practice and carried over into the nineteenth century, receiving the approval of even such a great philosopher as John Stuart Mill. Mill says that "the principles and rules of grammar are the means by which forms of language are made to correspond with the universal forms of thought."[7] The weakness of this thesis was, of course, evident to the language experts of Mill's own time. Henry Sweet and A. H. Sayce brought to bear their great knowledge of comparative philology to show how little actual correspondence there is between logic and grammar, and modern linguists and semanticists have agreed with them. Probably the most judicious summation of the problem is that of Otto Jespersen:

Most linguists are against any attempt to apply a logical standard to language. Language, they say, is psychology, not logic; or "language is neither logical nor illogical, but a-logical." That is to say, language has nothing to do with logic. To many philologists the very word, logic, is like a red rag to a bull. . . . It would be surprising however if language which serves to express thoughts should be quite independent of the laws of correct thinking.[8]

[6] William Ward, *English Grammar* (1765). Quoted by C. C. Fries, *The Teaching of English* (Ann Arbor: The George Wahr Publishing Co., 1949), p. 13.

[7] See I. A. Richards, *Interpretation in Teaching* (London: Routledge & Kegan Paul, 1938), p. 280.

[8] *Mankind, Nation and the Individual* (London: Geo. Allen, 1946), p. 114.

As Jespersen demonstrates, however, what often has pretended to be logic is no more than Latin grammar disguised, and arguments declaring the correspondence of grammar with logic have often been little more than the forcing of English into Latin syntactical patterns. For example, the rule that the predicative must stand in the same case as the subject is not, as has been claimed, an incontrovertible law of thought but merely a rule of Latin grammar. Many languages of different types violate this so-called incontrovertible law.

The authority that the rules have derived from deductive logic has never been equal to the support given them by the belief that rules are inductively derived from examination of the best usage. George Campbell's dictum that reputable, national, and present usage determines correctness has been cited with approval from the days of Lindley Murray, probably the most popular of eighteenth century grammarians, to the present day. Many writers on language have, in fact, cited Campbell's doctrine as liberalizing in effect, but it is difficult to see how such a belief can be accepted. Campbell so restricted the field of acceptable usage that the doctrine of rules lost little of the force it had held in the writings of such prescriptive grammarians as Bishop Lowth and William Ward. Lowth had, of course, declared the independence of grammar from the usage of even the best writers, whereas Campbell paid lip service to the doctrine of usage. But in practice Campbell, as S. A. Leonard has shown, repudiated the very theory he had set up as a guide. We can see what the doctrine of usage actually became when we examine the following statement from a latter day follower of Campbell:

By good usage is meant the usage generally observed in the writers of the best English authors and in the speech of well-educated people. Dictionaries, grammars, and books on rhetoric and composition record this usage, on the basis of wide observation and study.[9]

This definition follows a pattern dating from the eighteenth century and repeated in scores of nineteenth century handbooks and grammars. The doctrine of usage in the hands of the grammarians has been practically identical with the doctrine of rules.

THE DOCTRINE OF GENERAL USAGE

Joseph Priestley, the eighteenth century scientist and grammarian, was probably the first writer in English to show a consistent regard for the doctrine of general usage. But his views were neglected, and it was not until the rise of scientific linguistics in the late nineteenth century that the doctrine began to make headway against the doctrine of rules. Among the pioneers were W. D. Whitney, Fitzedward Hall, and Alexander Bain. The first full-fledged popular exposition and exemplification of the doctrine, J. Lesslie Hall's *English Usage* (1917),

---

[9] Edwin C. Woolley, *Handbook of Composition,* Revised Edition (Boston: D. C. Heath, 1920), p. 1.

was not published until well into the twentieth century. In contrast with most of his predecessors, who only paid lip service to the doctrine of usage, Hall is consistent and documents his opinion with particular examples. In his article, "Who for Whom," for instance, Hall cites the opinions of contemporary liberal grammarians in favor of *who* as the objective form in questions, and he gives a number of examples from usage, citing Shakespeare, Marlowe, Defoe, Kingsley, and Froude, as well as less well-known writers.

Comprehensive as it is, Hall's work is limited primarily to an examination of written documents, and it was not until Leonard's *Current English Usage* that there was a systematic survey of spoken usage to support Hall's findings. Strictly speaking, the Leonard report is not a survey of the facts of English usage but of opinion about the relative standing of various debatable items. The guiding principle of the survey is indicated succinctly in the statement that "allowable usage is based on the actual practice of cultivated people rather than on rules of syntax or logic."[10] In keeping with this principle, Leonard submitted a number of items of debatable usage to a jury consisting of linguistic specialists, editors, authors, business men, and teachers of English and speech. These judges were to decide the standing of the items according to what they thought the actual usage to be. Four levels of acceptability were indicated: "literary English," "standard, cultivated, colloquial English," "trade or technical English," and "naïf, popular, or uncultivated English." The findings of the report provided evidence to demonstrate the discrepancy between actual usage and the rules of the common school grammar. Among the items indicated as *established,* or acceptable on the cultivated colloquial level by more than seventy-five percent of the judges, were *it is me, who are you looking for, I feel badly,* and many other locutions that had long been proscribed by the handbooks and grammars.

The Leonard report was not a survey of "general" usage but of "cultivated" usage. It is not until the research studies of C. C. Fries that we find a truly inclusive and adequately documented study of general usage. Eschewing the guidance of the grammars and even of polls of "educated" usage, Fries stated that "it is probably much more sound to decide that the spontaneous usage of that large group who are carrying on the affairs of English speaking people is the usage to be observed and to set the standard."[11] To provide evidence of actual usage, Fries has used letters and transcripts of telephone conversations. Like other modern advocates of the doctrine of usage, Fries has not held to the theory that the standard of general usage should apply in all language situations. In concession to the demands of effective communication and to the practical problems of the teacher in the classroom he has given assent to the doctrine of appropriateness. The

---

[10] Sterling Andrus Leonard, *Current English Usage* (Chicago: The National Council of Teachers of English, 1932), p. 95.
[11] *The Teaching of English,* p. 35.

problem of the teacher, according to Fries, is to develop in the student the habits that will enable him to use freely the language appropriate to his ideas, the occasion of their expression, and the needs of his hearers. To bring about this end, the teacher needs to become sensitive to the different levels and functional varieties of usage and to develop a program of study designed to meet the particular needs of each class. Although the teacher must take into account the prevailing demand that he equip his pupils with the language habits that have attained the most social acceptability, he needs to develop also an intelligently liberal attitude toward the particular language habits of any group of students.

THE DOCTRINE OF APPROPRIATENESS

In its essentials the doctrine of appropriateness has not changed since the full exposition by George Philip Krapp in his *Modern English* (1909). Krapp introduces his exposition by making a distinction between "good" English and "conventional" or "standard" English. Good English, according to Krapp, is any language which "hits the mark." Since the purpose of language is the satisfactory communication of thought and feeling, any language which satisfactorily performs this function is good English. Standard English is that usage which is recognized and accepted as customary in any particular community. Such locutions as *he don't* or *these kind of people* or *I will* may be standard in one community and not standard in another. Custom is the only relevant determinant of the standard. Krapp's relativism is evident in the following statement:

What is defended as customary use by a community, or even by a single speaker, to carry the matter to its final analysis, is standard, or conventional, or "right," or "correct," in that community or for that speaker.[12]

In analyzing the concept of "good" English, Krapp arrives at the doctrine of appropriateness. He describes three tendencies in English speech—"popular English," "colloquial English," and "formal or literary English"—and declares that each of these has its appropriate uses. They are three kinds of arrows by which the speaker attempts to hit the mark of good English. Whether the speaker hits the mark or not depends upon his skill and upon his acumen in sizing up the particular speech situation:

. . . the degree of colloquialism which one permits, in one's self or in others depends on the subject of conversation, on the intimacy of the acquaintanceship of the persons speaking, and in general on all the attendant circumstances . . . language which may be adequately expressive, and therefore good, under one set of circumstances, under a different set of circumstances becomes inadequately expressive, because it says more or less than the speaker intended, and so becomes bad English. One learns thus the lesson of complete relativity of the value of language, that there is no such thing as an absolute English

[12] New York: Charles Scribners' Sons, 1909, p. 332.

but that language is valuable only as it effects the purpose one wishes to attain, that what is good at one time may be bad at another, and what is bad at one time may be good at another.[13]

This doctrine has been somewhat qualified by some of its recent exponents, particularly by Pooley and Perrin, but it has not been changed in its essentials. And it is still subject to the same sort of objection that J. Lesslie Hall made to Krapp's statement of it. Hall pointed out that Krapp's conception of "good" English was unprecedented and varied from the commonly accepted meaning of the term. He also deprecated Krapp's advocacy of "a sort of isolated, neighborhood English" and declared that the consistent carrying out of Krapp's ideas would mean the decline of a *general* and reputable usage for which students of language had been struggling. Consistent application of the doctrine of appropriateness would mean that every newcomer to a community would need to learn a new set of speech habits and that every traveler would need to be sensitive to innumerable local dialects and to cater to the personal language habits of his listeners. This would finally result in the decline of a general standard of cultivated speech understood everywhere and acceptable everywhere. In answer to Hall's objections Krapp might very well have repeated what he had said in *Modern English:* that the completely consistent adherence to the idea of general usage would mean finally a fixed language inadmissive of improvement and that the interplay of standard English and good English makes for a language constantly improving in expressiveness and effectiveness of communication.

THE DOCTRINE OF THE LINGUISTIC NORM

Under the heading of the linguistic norm may be grouped those concepts which emphasize that language is above all responsible to an expressive ideal. Some advocates of the normative approach hold that language should not be subservient to usage and should be judged by consciously derived criteria. I. A. Richards, for instance, has characterized the doctrine of usage as "the most pernicious influence in current English teaching."[14] In attacking the doctrine of usage, Richards does not recommend a return to the doctrine of rules and of what he calls the illegitimate application of logic and philosophy to language. Instead he recommends a self-critical reflection about the conduct of thought in language. Richards' evaluation of modern linguistic theories and his own program are explicitly stated in his latest book:

There are vast areas of so-called "purely descriptive" linguistics which are a grim danger at present to the conduct of language, to education, to standards of intelligence, to the reserves in theory and in sensibility of the mental tester. . . . The appeal to mere *usage:* "If it's widely in use, it's O.K.," is a case in point.

[13] *Ibid.,* pp. 327, 329–30.
[14] *Op. cit.,* p. 174.

Every useful feature of language was *not in use* once upon a time. Every degradation of language too starts somewhere. Behind usage is the question of efficiency. Inefficient language features are not O.K., however widespread their use. Of course, to the linguistic botanist it is important to preserve all varieties until they have been collected and described. But that is not the point of view of the over-all study of language, its services and its powers. That over-all view is, I am insisting, inescapably NORMATIVE. It is concerned (as every speaker and ever listener is always concerned) with the maintenance and improvement of the use of language.[15]

As instances of degradation in language Richards cites the current practice of using *uninterested* and *disinterested* and *imply* and *infer* as synonyms. In each instance the confusion has brought about a loss in precision without a corresponding gain.

Not all adherents to the concept of a linguistic norm have held as strongly as Richards to the principle of consciously critical evaluation of language. Instead such linguistic scholars as Otto Jespersen and Edward Sapir have held that linguistic efficiency is often the result of the spontaneous and intuitive expression of the folk. Probably the best known statement of the belief that language tends constantly toward a norm of maximum expressiveness with least effort is Otto Jespersen's theory of energetics, most recently restated in his *Efficiency in Linguistic Change* (1941).[16] According to Jespersen's theory, linguistic changes involve a constant interplay of opposing demands, one by the individual seeking ease of expression and the other of a social character calling for distinctness of communication. The first tendency is subversive of traditional forms of expression; the second is conservative and tends to keep alive the traditional norm. The interaction between these two demands brings about language changes designed to conserve the energy of the speaker and at the same time to retain the power of exact communication.

Edward Sapir's *Language* contains a discussion of the expression *Who did you see* that may serve to illustrate Jespersen's theory.[17] Sapir declares that the syntax of "whom" in *whom did you see* is logically and historically sound but psychologically shaky. The construction is kept alive by social snobbery but will eventually succumb to the pressure put on it by the uncontrolled speech of the folk. Meanwhile, users of *whom* are torn between an unconscious desire to say *who* and a fear of social penalty. The correctness of *whom* is fundamentally false and within a couple of hundred years the "whom" will probably be as delightfully archaic as the Elizabethan "his" for "its." In his analysis, Sapir cites four reasons for the linguistic shakiness of *whom*. First, *who* is becoming invariable because of its linguistic similarity to such invariable forms as the interrogative and relative pronouns, *which, what,*

---

[15] *Speculative Instruments* (Chicago: University of Chicago Press, 1955), pp. 123–24.

[16] Copenhaven: Ejnar Munksgaard, 1941, pp. 15–16.

[17] New York: Harcourt, Brace, 1921, pp. 156–62.

and *that* and the interrogative adverbs *where, when,* and *how*. Second, interrogative pronouns normally play an emphatic part in the sentence, and emphatic elements are typically invariable. The third powerful reason for the interrogative use of *who* rather than *whom* is its position in the sentence. Normal word order in English places the subject at the beginning of the sentence, before the verb. And the word in the subject position normally takes the subjective form. A fourth difficulty in *whom did you see* is that the *m* sound slows down the movement of the sentence and calls for a deliberate mental and physical effort at odds with the spontaneous speech situations in which the expression is normally used. For these reasons then *whom* is on psychologically shaky grounds and will eventually be replaced by the more natural and expressive *who*. As another instance of the prevalence of psychology over logic in language usage we may cite the rule about the placement of adverbial modifiers. The latest version of Woolley's handbook still carries the following precept and example: "Place such adverbs as *only, merely, just, almost, ever, hardly, scarcely, quite, nearly* next to the words they modify. COLLOQUIAL: *I only want three.* BETTER: *I want only three;* [or] *I want three only.*"[18] It may be that the constructions labeled BETTER are more logically sound, but rhetorically and psychologically they may not be as effective as the COLLOQUIAL version. The intention of the speaker may be to emphasize the reasonableness of his request, not the request itself or the exact amount being requested. If such is his intention, the sooner he introduces the idea of reasonableness into his expression the truer he is to his actual meaning and the more likely he is to get a favorable response. The placement of a modifier depends therefore not on an invariable rule of logic or grammar but on the speaker's full meaning. It is this insistence on precision and fullness of meaning which gives force to the doctrine of the linguistic norm. In its expressive aims it is similar to the doctrine of appropriateness, but whereas the doctrine of appropriateness emphasizes the social situation, particularly the effect on an audience, the doctrine of the linguistic norm holds in balance the intention of the speaker, the nature of the language itself, and the probable effect on the audience.

Because of its over-all point of view the doctrine of the linguistic norm is probably the best vantage ground for the teacher. It provides criteria by which to evaluate both the conservative and the liberalizing forces in language. It does not, to be sure, provide the sense of psychological security and social approval so long associated with the doctrine of rules. But submission to dogmatic authority merely out of a desire to gain security hardly seems a constructive attitude. Nor does it seem desirable to compromise personal conviction in the way so often demanded by consistent adherence to either the doctrine of general usage or the doctrine of appropriateness. The most suitable philosophy of language for the teacher would seem to be

---

[18] *College Handbook of Composition* (Boston: D. C. Heath, 1951), p. 89.

one calling for a disinterested and yet constantly critical evaluation of language as a means to maximum expression. And this is the point of view of the doctrine of the linguistic norm.

9 In which of the following statements do the choices change the meaning? In which statements do they produce the same meaning? In the latter group, do the choices that you make depend on an unspecified universe of discourse? If so, what is it? Can you vary elements in the universe of discourse (e.g., different readers, different occasions, different linguistic contexts) to make the alternative choices appropriate? Do any of the alternatives violate the rules of English grammar?

1) He (don't, doesn't) do it.
2) A bored and (disinterested, uninterested) judge.
3) I (will, shall) go tomorrow.
4) (Who, Whom) do you want to see?
5) Knowing as much as you do, you can explain the situation easily. Knowing as much as you do, the situation is easily explained.
6) He wanted secretly to investigate the matter.
   He wanted to secretly investigate the matter.
   He wanted to investigate the matter secretly.
7) (Can, May) I have a ride downtown?
8) Only I want $10.
   I only want $10.
   I want only $10.
9) Let's you and (I, me) stay here.

Which of Hartung's doctrines of usage underlies the choices that you have just made? Consult Margaret Nicholson, *Dictionary of American-English Usage* (New York: Oxford University Press, 1957), and Bergen and Cornelia Evans, *Dictionary of Contemporary American Usage* (New York: Random House, 1957), on each of these choices. Do they differ? Can you infer which doctrines underlie their comments?

An essay is an attenuated play.
KENNETH BURKE, *Perspectives by Incongruity*

14 Editing: plots in discourse

Language, we have said, is a kind of public bridge linking men with one another. But language can be used in a completely private way. The language of schizophrenics, for example, like that of small children, is often completely private. Unable or unwilling to share the beliefs and perspectives of others, schizophrenics cannot imagine the difficulties that others find in understanding them. They do not seem aware that their own images of the world are not shared by all. The following passage is an example of the private, disorganized conversation of a schizophrenic:

> You go out and stand pat—pat, you hear! Who was Pat ? What does he wear when he's in Ireland? This hair won't stay out of my eyes [brushes it aside and touches pillow]. See this pillow [raising it behind head]? Now is it even, even or odd? Even or odd, by God: I take it even, by God. By God we live, by God we die, and that's my allegiance to these United States. See my little eagle [bedsheet wrapped

around feet and stretched taut]? These are my wings. No, I have wings of a girl. [Patient sings Prisoner's Song, making flying movements with her arms to accompany the lines, "Over these prison walls I would fly." Then sings,] "One little Indian, two little Indians," [and suddenly shouts,] Heap big Indian chief! I'm not afraid. I got a heart right here, I've got a key to my heart. I don't want instant death. No, not one little teensy, eensy, weensy, not one little teensy, eensy, wittsy, wonsy bit. Right is right, wrong is wrong, two rights don't make a wrong. So they are, all over the world, God made the world, but this isn't Adam speaking, it's me. Mr. Adam, you just can't walk out of here. It's O.K. by me, I've said my say. Out you go! Take me if you want to or leave me. Shoot if you want to. I have just one heart, a right heart. I'm so tired. So shoot, shoot, but only once. Point the gun at the right breast. I'll know him wherever I see him, dead or alive. Shoo-oot. Oh, Columbia, the gem of the ocean [sung]. Shoot, I'm ready. One-two-three, shoot [hand over heart, eyes closed]. My husband, my sweetheart. Oh, how my heart aches, oh, it aches, I'm tired, I'm tired, I'm tired.

In NORMAN CAMERON, *The Psychology of Behavior*

Language of this sort is sad but, for our purposes, very interesting: It challenges us to puzzle out the relationships between the sentences and to try to imagine what is going on in the mind of the speaker. The sentences are connected illogically, by rhymes and puns and outside distractions, as the speaker jumps from topic to topic. Furthermore, nearly every sentence relates only to the sentences immediately preceding and following it; there is no overall pattern connecting the entire series of sentences. For instance, the first sentence has nothing to do with any other sentence in the passage except the one directly after it, to which it is connected only by a pun.

It is true, of course, that each language act is unique, the creation of a unique person in a unique situation. This might be called the personal aspect of language. But language has a social aspect, too — an aspect with which the schizophrenic cannot cope. As we pointed out in Chapter 2, all of us conceive of the world in terms of repeatable units of experience; people, objects, and events recur, as do relationships among them. Social coherence depends on this recurrence, since contracts, marriages, and other social institutions are all based on laws and customs that must have some degree of continuity. Our use of language reflects this way of seeing the world: We apply a single label (e.g., *chair*, *boat*, and so on) to a variety of different objects that are in some way similar, and we use commonly understood words and phrases (i.e., the plot cues that are discussed below) to indicate repeatable patterns or relationships.

Although the schizophrenic also uses labels that we understand and applies them in conventional sentences, she does not, as we have seen, relate the sequence of sentences in any discernible pattern. To say that her language is disorganized and incomprehensible is to say that it is asocial—almost entirely personal. The effective writer takes into consideration the social demands of writing—the potential problems that his readers will face in trying to comprehend his message—and takes care that his discourse does not become incomprehensibly personal.

Discovering the pattern in discourse

One way of discovering the overall pattern of a piece of writing is to summarize it in your own words. The act of summarizing is much like stating the plot of a play. For instance, if you were asked to summarize the story of Shakespeare's *Hamlet,* you might say:

> It's the story of a young prince of Denmark who discovers that his uncle and his mother have killed his father, the former king. He plots to get revenge, but in his obsession with revenge he drives his sweetheart to madness and suicide, kills her innocent father, and in the final scene poisons and is poisoned by her brother in a duel, causes his mother's death, and kills the guilty king, his uncle.

This summary contains a number of dramatic elements: a cast of characters (the prince; his uncle, mother, and father; his sweetheart; her father, and so on.), a scene (Elsinore Castle in Denmark), instruments (poison, swords), and actions (discovery, dueling, killing). It also has an overall pattern—a pattern that might well be followed for different characters, a different scene, different instruments, and different actions:

> A boy in Alaska finds out that a wolf has killed his dog. He plans to hunt the wolf down and kill him. He sets traps for the wolf but catches many innocent animals instead. Finally he meets the wolf in the forest and shoots him, but gets caught in one of his own traps and dies.

The summary of *Hamlet,* with its particular cast, setting, and actions, we will call its *specific plot.* The semantic pattern that is shared by *Hamlet* and our story about the boy in Alaska we will call the *generalized plot.* A generalized plot is made up of a sequence of semantic slots which may be filled with a variety of specific semantic elements provided that the choice of an element to fill one slot is appropriate to the choices made for the other slots. The generalized plot shared by the two specific plots above might be stated in this way: (1) a wish for revenge, (2) formulation of a plan, and (3) revenge and death. With variations and added subplots, this same plot underlies many plays, stories, novels, and epics. It is a widely shared image of experience, a significant pattern of events. Shakespeare's greatness lies not in his invention of this generalized plot — as a matter of fact he borrowed most of the story — but in the way he used it as a framework around which to build his play, a skeleton to support and organize the flesh of words and actions. The generalized plot is but one part of a play; it is a necessary part, however, if one is to have a play.

Other modes of writing besides drama and narrative have recurring generalized plots. There are argumentive plots (e.g., the formal patterns underlying syllogisms), plots for jokes, plots for news stories, and many others. Some of these have been mentioned in preceding chapters. For example, the propositions underlying sentences were described earlier as miniature generalized plots with agents, acts, instruments, locations, times, and other plot elements. The sentence "The police arrested my roommate for picketing against the tuition increase that the president announced yesterday" is a story in miniature; it contains an underlying proposition or plot into which particular dramatic characters have been inserted. And the strategies that we discussed in Chapter 11 may be seen as generalized plots, although they were presented as sets of operations for producing discourse rather than as rigid and conventional systems of slots.

Paragraphs also have plots, patterns that organize sentences into a whole unit. For instance, if you were asked to summarize the specific plot of the preceding paragraph, you might say that "they said that other kinds of discourse besides stories have plots and then they mentioned some examples." The generalized plot of that paragraph, which is implicit in the specific plot, could be summarized and labeled in any of several ways (since there is no conventional set of labels for generalized plots, we must devise our own): as Statement and Examples, or Assertion and Instances, or "B, C, and so on are instances of A." It provides the framework that structures the specific elements of the paragraph. This particular generalized plot, the most common of paragraph plots, occurs in all kinds of discourse.

Every piece of writing is composed of a hierarchy of patterns: Related sentences form paragraphs, related paragraphs form units of a still higher level — sections of essays, complete essays, chapters of books. The writer usually builds this hierarchy intuitively; he does not ordinarily think about these patterns as he writes. The overall pattern is the result of his mental image of the whole structure of his work — an image that may be clear in his mind when he begins to write or that may evolve gradually through repeated trials made during the act of writing. As he writes, the writer shifts his attention back and forth from the whole to some part of the whole. Like an artist composing a picture, he senses intuitively that a sentence, a paragraph, a word, or a phrase either fits or does not fit at a particular stage of his work. He selects, arranges, and rearranges the units of his work in accordance with this mental image of the whole.

During this activity, however, the writer does not always make the right choices, for the number of choices that he must make as he writes is vast; hence rewriting and careful editing are necessary. In the following pages we will suggest some useful editing procedures for correcting problems of structure, particularly problems of plot at the paragraph level.

Editing paragraph structures

One job of the writer as he edits what he has written is to make the structure as clear as possible to the reader, to bring to the surface the patterns that relate the parts. The following paragraph, written by an engineering student, illustrates what happens when the writer fails to reveal the patterns that relate his ideas:

> Live and dead moments are reported separately. Live load moment curves are valid for bridges accomodating two lanes of H-20 truck traffic, with curves 25.5 feet apart. For bridges of any width-span ratio, curves denoting dead load moments are valid.

The writer has given very few clues to the plot underlying these sentences. The plot is probably clear to him; he may well perceive an "obvious" pattern in what he has written. He has failed, however, to reveal it to his audience. Nevertheless, we can guess at it. After some study, we hypothesize that there are two generalized plots relating the sentences. Sentences 2 and 3 seem to offer reasons why "live and dead moments" (whatever they are) should be "reported separately." The generalized plot, then, is Effect and Cause, or "A because B." Sentences 2 and 3 also seem to be related by contrast: Each gives the *contrastive features* of one kind of "moment." In this case, the generalized plot is "B_1 is different from B_2 because B_1 has features X and Y and B_2 does not." Perceiving these relationships, we can combine the two plots into a complex plot for the whole paragraph: "A [Distinguish ('report separately') B_1 and B_2 ('live and dead moments')] because B [B_1 ('live moments') has features X and Y (cases in which B_1 is 'valid') and B_2 ('dead moments') does not]."

EDITING THE PLOT FOR CLARITY

This analysis reconstructs the plot underlying the engineering student's paragraph. The paragraph can now be rewritten to make this underlying structure clear. We have indicated the relationships among the parts of the paragraph by means of brackets and parentheses; but writers have at their disposal devices that are more conventional and much more capable of conveying subtle relationships. Among these devices is a specific set of words and phrases whose function is to mark relationships of units within plots.

These words and phrases, labeled in various ways, may be called *plot cues,* for their major function is to indicate the relationship of one linguistic unit to another within a specific, or surface, plot—of one sentence to another within a paragraph, of one paragraph to another within an essay. There are too many such words and phrases for us to list them all here, but some examples follow.

GENERALIZED PLOTS	PLOT CUES
B is an instance of A.	for example, for instance, e.g.
B is a cause of A or a reason for A.	because, since, therefore, consequently
B is a restatement or a clarification of A.	that is, in other words, i.e.
B is different from A.	on the other hand, however, but
B is similar to A.	likewise, in the same manner, also
A and B exist in temporal sequence.	then, next, before, subsequently
A and B exist in spatial array.	next to, beside, under, alongside

This list is merely illustrative, not exhaustive. No one has yet given a complete list of the various kinds of generalized plots and the cues related to each.

Plot cues are usually absent in obscure writing, chiefly because the writer is either unaware of the reader's difficulties in understanding him or indifferent to them. Notice how the addition of plot cues (*because, while, on the other hand*) brings to the surface the obscured plot underlying the engineering student's paragraph:

> Live and dead moments on bridges are reported separately because curves denoting live load moments are valid only for bridges that (1) accomodate two lanes of H-20 truck traffic and (2) have curves 25.5 feet apart, while curves denoting dead load moments, on the other hand, are valid for bridges of any width-span ratio.

One of the simplest ways to make a plot clear to a reader is to formulate it as a question and answer, or as a series of questions and answers, as in the following paragraph:

> Of what use is a college training? We who have had it seldom hear the question raised; we might be a little nonplussed to answer it offhand. A certain amount of meditation has brought me to this as the pithiest reply which I myself can give: The best claim that a college education can possibly make on your respect, the best thing it can aspire to accomplish for you, is this: that it should *help you to know a good man when you see him*. This is as true of women's as of men's colleges; but that it is neither a joke nor a one-sided abstraction I shall now endeavor to show.
>
> WILLIAM JAMES, "The Social Value of the College-Bred," *Memories and Studies*

All plots can be translated directly into question-and-answer patterns. Considered from this perspective, the development of a plot seems to parallel the process of inquiry; the writer begins with a problem, formulates the problem as a question, and concludes when the question has been answered to the satisfaction of the reader.

EDITING THE PLOT FOR COMPLETENESS

Seen as a question and answer, a plot, like the process of inquiry, conveys a sense of *closure* and *completeness*. A question specifies within itself the dimensions of its answer — not the specific content of the answer but the form that the answer must take. For example, if the question is

Where is John?

we know that the answer must substitute for the word *where;* that is, it must locate the subject *John* at the present time (*is*). Thus none of the following are adequate answers to this question:

John is hungry.
John was in San Francisco.
John is my brother.

An acceptable answer must satisfy the demands of the question by specifying a location. Only when the location is given is the pattern completed; only then is there a sense of closure:

John is sitting *at the top of the apple tree.*

In other words, a question arouses in the reader anticipations that, when satisfied, give him a sense of form. In *Counter-statement* Kenneth Burke puts it this way, "A work has form in so far as one part of it leads a reader to anticipate another part, to be gratified by the sequence." Like music, a written work carries the reader through a sequence of psychological tensions and releases.

Even though a passage may not begin with a question (most do not), the writer creates a similar sense of anticipation and closure by other means. When we read the statement "Live and dead moments on bridges are reported separately," we expect to be told *why* or, if we know why, *how* or *when* this reporting is done. The initial sentence of a paragraph usually serves to arouse the reader's anticipation of what will follow. This initial sentence, which poses a question either explicitly or implicitly, is usually called the *topic sentence* of a paragraph. (In description and narrative prose, topic sentences are often only implied.) Consider what anticipations are aroused by the following statement, which begins a biblical proverb: "There be three things which are too wonderful for me, yea, four which I know not . . . ." Surely in the statements that follow, these four things will be identified. The initial statement does not predict for us what they will be, but, like a question, it specifies the dimensions of what is to come:

> There be three things which are too wonderful for me, yea, four which I know not: The way of an eagle in the air; the way of a serpent on a rock; the way of a ship in the midst of the sea; and the way of a man with a maid.
>
> Proverbs 30: 18–19

This view of paragraphs as structures that arouse and fulfill anticipations helps to clarify an important editing problem. A common, and fundamental, defect in many paragraphs is that they arouse anticipations that are never fulfilled. There are two causes for this: (1) a sentence that appears to serve as the topic sentence may actually perform some other function in the plot, thus arousing false anticipations in the reader's mind, or (2) the sentences that follow a topic sentence may not develop all the dimensions of the topic, thus failing to gratify the anticipations raised.

What does the initial sentence of this passage lead you to expect?

> Some observers are much quicker than others and will therefore yield more accurate results when dealing with quantities in a state of flux. Some consistently read a given instrument low and others consistently read it high. Some can estimate readings between scale divisions more accurately than others.

The strong parallelism in the sentence structure suggests that although the initial sentence at first appears to be the topic sentence, it is actually part of the development of the writer's idea. The paragraph lacks a topic sentence, that is, a statement that establishes, explicitly or implicitly, a question to be answered. Phrased as a question, this sentence might read:

> How do observers differ in their ways of reading precision instruments?

With the question stated indirectly, the initial sentence might read:

> Observers reading precision instruments differ in several ways.

Or, more specifically:

> Observers reading precision instruments differ in speed, consistency, and accuracy.

Notice that the last statement, by specifying the three differences that will be considered, constrains the reader's anticipations much more than do the other statements.

The following paragraph, on the other hand, does begin with a topic sentence, one that clearly establishes the dimensions of what should follow. (Notice that its generalized plot is the same as that of the biblical passage.)

> There are five different types of input that may be used with the digital computer: (1) keyboard, (2) electric typewriter, (3) Hollerith card, (4) perforated tape, and (5) magnetic tape. The Hollerith is well known and will be recognized if the IBM punched card is cited as the most popular example of the Hollerith card. The perforated tape contains holes mechanically punched in a roll of paper according to a fixed code. The machine reads the input through a photoelectric cell and light arrangement. The magnetic tape is the fastest to date. Numbers are introduced as a positive tape saturation. This is done by incorporating a binary system of numbers.

Here again, anticipations are aroused but not fulfilled: We are led to expect an explanation of all five different types of input used with digital computers; however, only three of them are discussed.

A final note on editing plots

All of the examples explored in this chapter have been paragraphs. Although problems of plot are also found in longer passages, paragraphs are the most convenient unit for studying plots and particularly the editing problems that result from a failure to present plots clearly and completely. As J. G. R. McElroy, a nineteenth-century rhetorician, remarked, "A paragraph is in fact a whole composition in miniature." The exercises and discussion questions for this chapter, which ask you to recognize plots and to edit obscure prose, therefore focus almost exclusively on paragraphs. If you learn how to edit paragraphs well, your editing of larger units should also improve.

In editing prose that seems obscure, you must find the generalized plot of the passage under consideration and rewrite it to make this plot recognizable to the reader. You can discover underlying plots by attempting to summarize the passage or by figuring out what question the passage answers, thereby recovering the topic sentence. Plots should be checked for closure and completeness, and plot cues should be added whenever possible to help the reader follow the plot.

EXERCISES

1   Try to summarize the schizophrenic's conversation given at the beginning of this chapter. How do you explain the results?

2   All of us use numerous plots for ordering discourse; we are subtly aware of the existence of many more. As a way of clarifying your understanding of the notion of generalized plot in discourse, list as many plots as you can (e.g., the limerick plot — there was an A from B, who . . . ; the categorical syllogism — all A's are B's, all C's are A's, therefore . . . .) We suggested in Chapter 11 that letters of application and scientific reports of experiments had conventional structures, which we might now regard as generalized plots. Is there a generalized plot underlying many advertisements? Can you isolate one and cite a number of its specific manifestations? Try making a comparable analysis of folk and fairy tales.

One can carry this line of inquiry over into nonverbal behavior as well. Games such as baseball, hide-and-seek, and tennis can be seen to have generalized plots as well as specific ones. What is the plot of a church service? Of courtship? (If you are still curious, read Eric Berne, *Games People Play*, New York: Grove Press, 1964.)

3   Reread the essay by Aldo Leopold (p. 109). Why does Leopold

put paragraph indentions where he does? Point out the plot cues and several generalized plots in his paragraphs.

4 Rewrite the following paragraphs to bring the underlying plots to the surface. Follow this procedure as an aid to rewriting:

> 1) Attempt to summarize the paragraph.
> 2) Formulate the question that the paragraph poses and answers.
> 3) Check the paragraph for closure and completeness.
> 4) Add plot cues when possible.

a Radar can be used in any type of weather. It is not affected by darkness. It has what is called a "high data rate," meaning that it develops information very rapidly and hence can make a rapid search of large enemy areas. Finally, it can indicate areas of enemy activity by developing what is called MTI (moving target information).

b The period of interest in shutdown situations is the first few seconds following the occurrence of the difficulty. Some time must elapse before the reactor is shut down. The case of loss of power to the main coolant pumps is a good illustration. The inertia of the coolant systems must be examined in each design and in some cases additional inertia added to insure that the transient heat energy is safely removed.

c The lines of mercury vapor occur principally in the ultra-violet region, with a very strong line appearing at 2537 A.U. (Angstrom Units). A few lines, however, do appear in the visible spectrum (about 4000 to 8000 A.U.), giving the lamp a bluish-purple appearance. The mercury-vapor lamp radiates light energy only at certain resonant wavelengths called lines, as mentioned above. It does this when a voltage of several hundred volts is impressed across the electrodes of the lamp. When this happens, a glow discharge occurs through the mercury vapor, causing it to become incandescent. The phenomenon occurs within a glass tube containing mercury vapor under a pressure of about one-tenth of an atmosphere, the electrodes being at each end of the tube.

d Our experience in municipal engineering has covered virtually all of the facilities necessary to operate and maintain a modern city. We have prepared preliminary reports as well as contract plans and specifications. Many of the reports have been the basis of revenue bond financing. Financing the construction of public projects through the sale of revenue bonds has come more and more into favor during recent years. Revenue bonds are sold mainly on the basis of preliminary engineering estimates of revenue, operating and maintenance expenses, and construction costs. Such surveys and reports have become an increasingly important phase of our activities. We have supervised construction of various types of water works and sewerage improvements, street paving and lighting, traffic control systems, municipal garbage and refuse incinerators, and a variety of municipal buildings. Since 1935, we have continously served Cicero, Illinois (population 68,000) on nearly all of its engineering and architectural problems.

5   Find two obscure paragraphs in your own writing and rewrite them following the procedure outlined in Exercise 4. If you can't find any, have someone else find them for you; it is often revealing to discover that what is obvious to you is obscure to someone else.

6   The clarity with which relationships between sentences are marked seems to depend in part on the writer's way of speaking. If he is in the habit of speaking very slowly, pausing to think between many of his sentences, his plot cues, transitions, topic sentences, and so on, may never be outwardly expressed. These speaking habits are likely to affect his writing habits; for example, he may not give the reader the necessary plot cues.

The following analysis provides the basis for a near-mechanical test to determine whether plot cues are present. It is based on work by Robert Longacre on twenty-five languages of the Philippines. In the following passage, Longacre describes what mght be called *chain linking* in narrative paragraphs.

Just as the *sine qua non* of NARRATIVE genre is chronological sequence, so such sequence is likewise central to the NARRATIVE PARAGRAPH. While, however, a variety of devices secure chronological sequence on the discourse level, on the paragraph level the linking mechanisms are simpler. In describing this linking mechanism it is necessary to take account of variation both in the grammatical form of the linkage and also in its lexical form as well.

Regardless, however, of the varying grammatical or lexical forms of narrative linkage, the device basically consists in repeating, paraphrasing, or referring in some manner at the onset of a succeeding sentence to the whole or part of the preceding sentence. The repeated material in each succeeding sentence serves as a *Ground* for the novel material which is the *Figure* for that sentence. In proceeding through a series of BUILD-UP tagmemes overtly linked by this device the *Figure* of each sentence becomes the *Ground* of the succeeding sentence.

This is exemplified in the following Itneg paragraphs:

EXAMPLE 1

Ground	Figure	
	They went to the place where they were going to do the singeing.	BU_1
It was bad, when they arrived	they were going to singe a boar.	BU_2
When they had singed it	the old man took half of it, he almost didn't leave any, he consumed the viand they had made.	BU_3
After they had eaten like that	they went home.	BU_n

EXAMPLE 2

Ground	Figure	
	He went.	BU_1
When he arrived in the forest	he chopped the trees.	BU_2
When he had chopped them	he shaped them.	BU_3
When he had shaped them	he went home again.	BU_n

ROBERT LONGACRE, *Discourse, Paragraph, and Sentence Structure in Selected Philippine Languages*

Choose from your writing a paragraph that you were unable to make clear to a reader. Arrange the sentences one by one in chart fashion, marking with an arrow the link from statement to following recapitulation. If no such link is present, add one. For the writer whose readers tend to find his paragraphs indecipherable, use of a series of "chain linkup" sentences can make obscure relationships become obvious. (Of course, this procedure is chiefly therapeutic: A mechanical application of the device doesn't produce good prose!) For all of us, this device can be a useful editing procedure for bringing a plot to the surface and for learning to see sequence relationships among parts of paragraphs and between paragraphs. Try it on one of your own problem paragraphs or on any paragraph in this book.

7 Read the following essay by Joseph Weizenbaum. How is ELIZA like a human reader? Different from a human reader? In Weizenbaum's view, is a plot (i.e., a belief structure) always ordered in the writer's mind? If it is not, what is one task of the writer-editor?

Many people feel threatened by attempts such as Weizenbaum's to program human cognitive functions. Can you explain why?

Relate concepts discussed by Weizenbaum to sections of this book. For example, consider the relationship between his statement about the nature of "recognition" and our discussion of Maxim 1. Or consider the similarities and differences between his concept of understanding and the concepts discussed in Chapters 3 and 12. To which of Weizenbaum's concepts would you relate our discussion of the image? Universe of discourse?

Compare and contrast the chart by Longacre in the preceding exercise, the passage by the schizophrenic, and the conversation from the ELIZA and DOCTOR programs. Can you draw any conclusions about characteristics of meaningful discourse?

Contextual Understanding by Computers
JOSEPH WEIZENBAUM

We are here concerned with the recognition of semantic patterns in text.

I compose my sentences and paragraphs in the belief that I shall be understood — perhaps even that what I write here will prove persuasive. For this faith to be at all meaningful, I must hypothesize at least one reader other than myself. I speak of *understanding*. What I must suppose is clearly that my reader will recognize patterns in these sentences and, on the basis of this recognition, be able to recreate my present thought for himself. Notice the very structure of the word "recognize," that is, know again! I also use the word "recreate." This suggests that the reader is an active participant in the two-person communication. He brings something of himself to it. His understanding is a function of that something as well as of what is written here. I will return to this point later.

Much of the motivation for the work discussed here derives from attempts to program a computer to understand what a human might say to it. Lest it be misunderstood, let me state right away that the input to the computer is in the form of typewritten messages — certainly not human speech. This restriction has the effect of establishing a narrower channel of communication than that available to humans in face-to-face conversations. In the latter, many ideas that potentially aid understanding are communicated by gestures, intonations, pauses, and so on. All of these are unavailable to readers of telegrams — be they computers or humans.

Further, what I wish to report here should not be confused with what is generally called content analysis. In the present situation we are concerned with the fragments of natural language that occur in conversations, not with complete texts. Consequently, we cannot rely on the texts we are analyzing to be grammatically complete or correct. Hence, no theory that depends on parsing of presumably well-formed sentences can be of much help. We must depend on heuristics and other such impure devices instead.

The first program to which I wish to call attention is a particular member of a family of programs which has come to be known as DOCTOR. The family name of these programs is ELIZA. This name was chosen because these programs like the Eliza of Pygmalion fame, can be taught to speak increasingly well. DOCTOR causes ELIZA to respond roughly as would certain psychotherapists (Rogerians). ELIZA performs best when its human correspondent is initially instructed to "talk" to it, via the typewriter, of course, just as one would to a psychiatrist.

I chose this mode of conversation because the psychiatric interview is one of the few examples of categorized dyadic natural language communication in which one of the participating pair is free to assume the pose of knowing almost nothing of the real world. If, for example, one were to tell a psychiatrist "I went for a boat ride" and he responded "Tell me about boats," one would not assume that he knew nothing about boats, but that he had some purpose in so directing the subsequent conversation. It is important to note that this assumption is one made by the speaker. Whether it is realistic or not is an altogether separate question. In any case, it has a crucial psychological utility in that it serves the speaker to maintain his sense of being heard and understood. The speaker further defends his impression (which even in real life may be illusory) by attributing to his conversational partner all sorts of background knowledge, insights and reasoning ability. But again, these are the speaker's contribution to the conversation. They manifest themselves inferentially in the interpretations he makes of the offered responses. From the purely technical programming point of view, the psychiatric interview has the advantage that it eliminates the need for storing explicit information about the real world.

The human speaker will contribute much to clothe ELIZA's responses in vestments of plausibility. However, he will not defend his illusion (that he is being understood) against all odds. In human conversation a speaker will make certain (perhaps generous) assumptions about his conversational partner. As long as it remains possible to interpret the latter's responses to be consistent with those assumptions, the speaker's image of his partner remains undamaged. Responses which are difficult to so interpret may well result in an enhancement of the image of the partner, by additional rationalizations which then make more complicated interpretations of his responses reasonable. When, however, such rationalizations become too massive and even self-contradictory, the entire image may crumble and be replaced by another ("He is not, after all, as smart as I thought he was"). When the conversational partner is a machine (the distinction between machine and program is not useful here), the idea of credibility may well be substituted for that of plausibility in the above.

"When in conversation with ELIZA, the user types in some statement or set of statements in natural language using normal punctuation and sentence structures. The user's statement is terminated by a double carriage return which serves to turn control over to ELIZA. ELIZA then analyzes the user's statement and generates some response which it types out. Control is then again with the user.

"A typical conversation is the following:

Men are all alike.
IN WHAT WAY
They're always bugging us about something or other.
CAN YOU THINK OF A SPECIFIC EXAMPLE
Well, my boyfriend made me come here.
YOUR BOYFRIEND MADE YOU COME HERE
He says I'm depressed much of the time.
I AM SORRY TO HEAR YOU ARE DEPRESSED
It's true. I am unhappy.
DO YOU THINK COMING HERE WILL HELP YOU NOT TO BE UNHAPPY
I need some help, that much seems certain.
WHAT WOULD IT MEAN TO YOU IF YOU GOT SOME HELP
Perhaps I could learn to get along with my mother.
TELL ME MORE ABOUT YOUR FAMILY
My mother takes care of me.
WHO ELSE IN YOUR FAMILY TAKES CARE OF YOU
My father.
YOUR FATHER
WHAT RESEMBLANCE DO YOU SEE
You are not very aggressive but I think you don't want me to notice that.
WHAT MAKES YOU THINK I AM NOT VERY AGGRESSIVE
You don't argue with me.
WHY DO YOU THINK I DON'T ARGUE WITH YOU
You are afraid of me.
DOES IT PLEASE YOU TO BELIEVE I AM AFRAID OF YOU
My father is afraid of everybody.
WHAT ELSE COMES TO MIND WHEN YOU THINK OF YOUR FATHER
Bullies.
DOES THAT HAVE ANYTHING TO DO WITH THE FACT THAT YOUR BOYFRIEND MADE YOU COME HERE

The capitalized lines are the machine responses.

"I described the original ELIZA program in some detail in [6]. For the present it is sufficient to recall that ELIZA's conversational powers are governed by a *script*. A script consists of a set of key words and key phrases each of which is associated with a set of so-called decomposition and reassembly rules. A decomposition rule is a data structure which searches a text for specified patterns, and, if such patterns are found, decomposes the text into disjoint constituents. A reassembly rule is a specification for the construction of a new text by means of recombinations of old and possible addition of new constituents. From one point of view, an ELIZA script is a program and ELIZA itself an interpreter. From another perspective, ELIZA appears as an actor who must depend on a script for his lines. The script determines the contextual framework within which ELIZA may be expected to converse plausibly.

"The gross procedure of the program is quite simple; the text is read and inspected for the presence of a key word. If such a word is found, the sentence is transformed according to a rule associated with the key word; if not, a content-free remark or, under certain conditions, an earlier transformation is retrieved. A rule-cycling mechanism delays repetition of responses to identical keys as long as possible. The text so computed or retrieved is then printed out."[1]

One of the principle aims of the DOCTOR program is to keep the conversation going — even at the price of having to conceal any misunderstandings on its own part. We shall see how more ambitious objectives are realized subsequently. In the meanwhile, the above discussion already provides a framework within which a number of useful points may be illuminated.

By far the most important of these relates to the crucial role *context* plays in all conversations. The subject who is about to engage in his first conversation with the DOCTOR is told to put himself in a role-playing frame of mind. He is to imagine that he has some problem of the kind one might normally discuss with a psychiatrist, to pretend he is actually conversing with a psychiatrist, and under no circumstances to deviate from that role. While some of the responses produced by the program are not very spectacular even when the subject follows his instructions, it is remarkable how quickly they deteriorate when he leaves his role. In this respect, the program mirrors life. Real two-person conversations also degenerate when the contextual assumptions one participant is making with respect to his partner's statements cease to be valid. This phenomenon is, for example, the basis on which many comedies of error are built.

These remarks are about the *global* context in which the conversation takes place. No understanding is possible in the absence of an established global context. To be sure, strangers do meet, converse, and immediately understand one another (or at least believe they do). But they operate in a shared culture — provided partially by the very language they speak — and, under any but the most trivial circumstances, engage in a kind of hunting behavior which has as its object the creation of a contextual framework. Conversation flows smoothly only after these preliminaries are completed. The situation is no different with respect to visual pattern recognition — a visual pattern

[1] The cooperation of the editors of the *Communications of the ACM* in permitting the extensive quotations from the paper "ELIZA," Vol. 9, No. 1, January, 1966, by the author is hereby gratefully acknowledged.

may appear utterly senseless until a context within which it may be recognized (known again, i.e., understood) is provided. Very often, of course, a solitary observer arrives at an appropriate context by forming and testing a number of hypotheses. He may later discover that the pattern he "recognized" was not the one he was intended to "see," i.e., that he hypothesized the "wrong" context. He may see the "correct" pattern when given the "correct" context. It doesn't mean much to say that the pattern "is" such and such. We might, for example, find a string of Chinese characters beautiful as long as we don't know what they spell. This, an apparent impoverishment, i.e., really a broadening, of context will enhance the esthetic appeal of a pattern. Similarly, many people think anything said in French is charming and romantic precisely *because* they don't understand the language.

In real conversations, global context assigns meaning to what is being said in only the most general way. The conversation proceeds by establishing subcontexts, sub-subcontexts within these, and so on. It generates and, so to speak, traverses a contextual tree. Beginning with the topmost or initial node, a new node representing a subcontext is generated, and from this one a new node still, and so on to many levels. Occasionally the currently regnant node is abandoned — i.e., the conversation ascends to a previously established node, perhaps skipping many intermediate ones in the process. New branches are established and old ones abandoned. It is my conjecture that an analysis of the pattern traced by a given conversation through such a directed graph may yield a measure of what one might call the consequential richness of the conversation. Cocktail party chatter, for example, has a rather straight line character. Context is constantly being changed — there is considerable chaining of nodes — but there is hardly any reversal of direction along already established structure. The conversation is inconsequential in that nothing being said has any effect on any questions raised on a higher level. Contrast this with a discussion between, say, two physicists trying to come to understand the results of some experiment. Their conversation tree would be not only deep but broad as well, i.e., they would ascend to an earlier contextual level in order to generate new nodes from there. The signal that their conversation terminated successfully might well be that they ascended (back to) the original node, i.e., that they are again talking about what they started to discuss.

For an individual the analog of a conversation tree is what the social psychologist Abelson calls a *belief structure*. In some areas of the individual's intellectual life, this structure may be highly logically organized — at least up to a point; for example, in the area of his own profession. In more emotionally loaded areas, the structure may be very loosely organized and even contain many contradictions. When a person enters a conversation he brings his belief structures with him as a kind of agenda.

A person's belief structure is a product of his entire life experience. All people have some common formative experiences, e.g., they

were all born of mothers. There is consequently some basis of understanding between any two humans simply because they are human.
But, even humans living in the same culture will have difficulty in
understanding one another where their respective lives differed radically. Since, in the last analysis, each of our lives is unique, there is a
limit to what we can bring another person to understand. There is an
ultimate privacy about each of us that absolutely precludes full communication of any of our ideas to the universe outside ourselves and
which thus isolates each one of us from every other noetic object in
the world.

There can be no total understanding and no absolutely reliable
test of understanding.

To know with certainty that a person understood what has been
said to him is to perceive his entire belief structure and *that* is equivalent to sharing his entire life experience. It is precisely barriers of
this kind that artists, especially poets, struggle against.

This issue must be confronted if there is to be any agreement as
to what machine "understanding" might mean. What the above argument is intended to make clear is that it is too much to insist that a
machine understands a sentence (or a symphony or a poem) only if
that sentence invokes the same imagery in the machine as was present in the speaker of the sentence at the time he uttered it. For by
that criterion no human understands any other human. Yet, we agree
that humans do understand one another to *within acceptable toler-
ances*. The operative word is "acceptable" for it implies *purpose*.
When, therefore, we speak of a machine understanding, we must
mean understanding as limited by some objective. He who asserts
that there are certain ideas no machines will ever understand can
mean at most that the machine will not understand these ideas tolera-
bly well because they relate to objectives that are, in his judgement,
inappropriate with respect to machines. Of course, the machine can
still deal with such ideas symbolically, i.e., in ways which are reflec-
tions—however pale—of the ways organisms for which such objectives are appropriate deal with them. In such cases the machine is no
more handicapped than I am, being a man, in trying to understand,
say, female jealousy.

A two-person conversation may be said to click along as long as
both participants keep discovering (in the sense of uncovering) identical nodes in their respective belief structures. Under such circumstances the conversation tree is merely a set of linearly connected
nodes corresponding to the commonly held parts of the participants'
belief structures. If such a conversation is interesting to either participant, it is probably because the part of the belief structure being
made explicit has not been consciously verbalized before, or has
never before been attached to the higher level node to which it is
then coupled in that conversation, i.e., seen in that context, or because
of the implicit support it is getting by being found to coexist in someone else.

Backtracking over the conversation tree takes place when a new context is introduced and an attempt is made to integrate it into the ongoing conversation, or when a new connection between the present and a previous context is suggested. In either case, there is a need to reorganize the conversation tree. Clearly the kind of psychotherapist initiated by the DOCTOR program restricts himself to pointing out new connectivity opportunities to his patients. I suppose his hope is that any reorganization of the conversation tree generated in the therapy session will ultimately reflect itself in corresponding modifications of his patients' belief structures.

I now turn back to the program reproduced earlier. I hope the reader found the conversation quoted there to be smooth and natural. If he did, he has gone a long way toward verifying what I said earlier about the investment a human will make in a conversation. Any continuity the reader may have perceived in that dialogue—excepting only the last machine response—is entirely illusionary. A careful analysis will reveal that each machine response is a response to the just previous subject input. Again with the exception of the last sentence, the above quoted conversation has no subcontextual structure at all. Nor does the description of the program given in [6] give any clues as to how subcontexts might be recognized or established or maintained by the machine.

To get at the subcontext issue, I want to restate the overall strategy in terms somewhat different from those used above. We may think of the ELIZA script as establishing the global context in which subsequent conversations will be played out. The DOCTOR script establishes the Rogerian psychiatric context. The key word listings are guesses about what significant words might appear in the subject's utterances. The appearance of any of these words in an actual input tentatively directs the system's attention to decomposition rules associated with the identified word. These rules are hypotheses about what an input containing such words might mean. An important property of the system is that just as the entire set of key words need not be searched in the analysis of every input sentence, neither does the whole list of hypotheses about what *any* input might mean have to be tested in order to generate a response to a specific sentence. Should the set of hypotheses associated with the currently regnant key word be exhausted without success, there is a way (although not here described) to go to decomposition rules associated with lower ranking key words that may have appeared in the input string.

Much is known about an input sentence once it matches a decomposition rule. If, for example, the rule

(O MY (/FAMILY) DRINKS O)

matches a sentence, then we know that the subject matter is a family member, and that this person drinks. (The notation "(/A B C)" means that in that position a word "tagged" with any of the symbols A or B or C is looked for. Words are tagged as part of the script. This mechanism is not further discussed here.) A reassembly rule can subsequently identify the family member in question, e.g., father. The successful matching of a decomposition rule — hence, the verification of a hypothesis — is therefore an opportunity not only to generate a plausible response but also to establish a subcontextual node. The laying down of such a node does not mean merely remembering what is now being talked about, but what is more important, making hypotheses about what is likely to be said next within the new contextual framework.

The realization of such a mechanism in an ELIZA script involves attaching a substructure to decomposition rules which says, in effect, that if a so modified decomposition rule matches an input sentence and a suitable subcontext exists, then control is transferred to a set of decomposition and reassembly rules appropriate to that subcontext. The details of mechanization are not important here. I will, however, show its effect by exhibiting the following conversational fragment from the DOCTOR program:

Because you are so stubborn.
IS THAT THE REAL REASON
Maybe
WHAT IS A BETTER REASON THEN
My stomach hurts.
TELL ME ABOUT YOUR PAINS IN GENERAL
My head bothers me, too.
YOU SEE SOME PSYCHOLOGICAL REASON WHY YOUR HEAD SHOULD
PAIN YOU
Maybe.
YOU THINK COMING HERE MIGHT HELP ALLEVIATE YOUR HEAD PAIN
Certainly.
LET'S TALK ABOUT YOUR FEELINGS WHEN YOU THINK OF YOUR HEAD
AND ITS PAINS

We are here in the middle of a dialog. The first sentence is an input to the program, the next a machine response, and so on in alternation.

The word "because" was the key that triggered the first machine response. At the same time the *reason* subcontext, so to speak, was established. Notice that the next subject input, i.e., the word "maybe", was interpreted as meaning "no," as is appropriate in that particular context, and that a contextually correct machine response was produced. The next input serves to establish a "hurt" subcontext. I believe the conversation is self-explanatory from that point on. Notice, however, that in the new subcontext the word "maybe" which was earlier interpreted to mean "no" is now seen as meaning "yes." Under still other circumstances it would be understood as indicating uncertainty.

My secretary watched me work on this program over a long period of time. One day she asked to be permitted to talk with the system. Of course, she knew she was talking to a machine. Yet, after I watched her type in a few sentences she turned to me and said "Would you mind leaving the room, please?" I believe this anecdote testifies to the success with which the program maintains the illusion of understanding. However, it does so, as I've already said, at the price of concealing its own misunderstandings. We all do this now and then, perhaps in the service of politeness or for other reasons. But we cannot afford to elevate this occasional tactic to a universal strategy. Thus, while the DOCTOR program may be useful as an instrument for the analysis of two-person conversations, and while it is certainly fun, its aim must be changed from that of concealment of misunderstanding to its explication.

Another difficulty with the system currently under discussion is that it can do very little other than generate plausible responses. To be sure, there are facilities for keeping and testing various tallies as well as other such relatively primitive devices, but the system can do no generalized computation in either the logical or numerical sense. In order to meet this and other deficiencies of the original ELIZA system, I wrote a new program, also called ELIZA, which has now replaced its ancestor.

The ELIZA differs from the old one in two main respects. First, it contains an *evaluator* capable of accepting expressions (programs) of unlimited complexity and evaluating (executing) them. It is, of course, also capable of storing the results of such evaluations for subsequent retrieval and use. Secondly, the idea of the script has been generalized so that now it is possible for the program to contain three different scripts simultaneously and to fetch new scripts from among an unlimited supply stored on a disk storage unit, intercommunication among coexisting scripts is also possible.

The major reason for wishing to have several scripts available in the core (i.e., high speed) memory of the computer derives from the arguments about contexts I made above. The script defines, so to speak, a global context within which all of the subsegment conversation is to be understood. We have seen that it is possible for a single script to establish and maintain subcontexts. But what is a subcontext from one point of view is a major (not to say global) one as seen from another perspective. For example, a conversation may have as its overall framework the health of one of the participants but spend much time under the heading of stomach disorders and headache remedies.

In principle one large, monolithic ELIZA script could deal with this. However, such a script would be very long and extremely difficult to modify and maintain. Besides, long exposure to computer programming should at least instill a healthy respect for subroutines, their power and utility. In the new ELIZA system scripts are in fact very much like subroutines. One script plays the role of the so-called "main program," i.e., it is the one for calling in and replacing subscripts. This is the one which, in an important sense, governs the computer's role in the conversation. Such a script may, for example, play the role of an initial interviewer in a hospital, i.e., a person who knows just enough about the field of medicine and the organization of the hospital to be able to determine, by means of appropriate questions, to whom the incoming patient is to be directed. A more highly specialized script then plays the role of that person. It may call on still further levels of scripts—and each script, except for the "main" one, can return the issue up one or more levels with information "explaining" that action.

We saw earlier how the word "maybe" was differentially interpreted in what might be called different micro contexts. The hierarchy of scripts now under discussion makes much more nearly global contextual distinctions possible. For example, the word "tone" probably means muscle tone to the internist but audio tone to the ear specialist. The occurrence of that word as a key word would establish an entirely different contextual mode, or call in a different subscript, depending on whether it was identified in an internist or an ear specialist script.

Of course, another important advantage of this kind of subscripting is that scripts (sub or otherwise) can presumably be written by specialists in a very narrow field. The fact that scripts now tend to be rather short means that a specialist might actually find the time to produce one as part of a larger cooperative effort.

The conversations reproduced below were governed by a script in the new ELIZA system. This script was designed to illustrate the power of the evaluator to which ELIZA has access. The key word and other such mechanisms are not very different from those described above. The important departure is that expressions can be turned over to the evaluator, evaluated, and the results displayed and stored.

The area of a circle is pi times the radius of the circle squared.
The area of a sphere is pi times the diameter of the sphere squared.
The area of a square is the side of the square squared.
The diameter of an object is twice the radius of the object.

The radius of a ball is 10.
What is the area of the ball.
THE ASSUMPTION THAT BALL IS CIRCLE IS CONSISTENT—SHALL I GO
      ON? no
THE ASSUMPTION THAT BALL IS SPHERE AND OBJECT IS CONSISTENT
      —SHALL I GO ON? yes
IT'S 1256.6359

What is the diameter of the ball.
IT'S 20

The radius of a dish is 10.
What's the area of the dish.
THE ASSUMPTION THAT DISH IS CIRCLE IS CONSISTENT—SHALL I
      GO ON? yes
IT'S 314.15899

The radius of a globe is 10.
A globe is a sphere. A sphere is an object.
What is the area of the globe.
IT'S 1256.6359

The side of a plate is 10.
What is the area of the plate.

THE ASSUMPTION THAT PLATE IS SQUARE IS CONSISTENT—SHALL I
   GO ON? yes
IT'S 100
When I say board I mean plate.
What is 3 times the side of the board.

IT'S 30

Please call that x.
Let f(z) be z squared minus z.
Compute f(x).

IT'S 870
When I say ich sage I mean I say.
When ich sage meine ich I mean I mean.
Wenn ich sage wieviel ist meine ich what is.
Wenn ich sage quadrat meine ich squared.
Nun, sagen sie mir bitte, wieviel is x quadrat.

I DIDN'T UNDERSTAND YOU

Ja, tut mir leid, ich sollte fragen wieviel IST x quadrat.
IT'S 900
Thank you.
YOU'RE QUITE WELCOME, COME AGAIN

The particular example shown here is one in which the system is
asked not merely to entertain but to perform some useful service. The
script is one which establishes a context in which a few terms can be
interpreted as giving directions about the evaluation of certain expressions. The number of keys which actually lead to decomposition rules
is very small. They are as follows:

$$\begin{array}{ll}
\text{I mean} & \\
\text{Is} & (* \text{ a an}) \\
\text{Of} & (* \text{ a an the}) \\
\text{What} & (* \text{ the is}) \\
\text{Where} & \\
\text{Call} & \\
\text{Let} & \\
\text{Define} & \\
\text{Compute} & \\
= & \\
\text{Also} & \\
\text{Thanks} & \\
\end{array}$$

(A key of the form "Is (* a an)" will match either "Is a" or "Is an".) In
addition, there are 1/ substitution keys like "Twice = 2*". The effect of
that particular one is to substitute the symbols "2*" wherever the

word "twice" appeared in the input text. Of course, the evaluator sitting behind ELIZA, so to speak, recognizes words like "SQRT", "LOG", etc. The function of this script is to interpret the user's wishes with respect to the evaluation of expression, perform certain translation functions on these expressions, and control the traffic between the input/output system of ELIZA and that of the evaluator.

Consider the dozen keys shown above. The sentence "*Let* me try to *define what the call of the* sea means" contains five of these keys. It could perhaps be understood by the DOCTOR but not by the program we are now considering. It would reply "I didn't understand you."

I call attention to this contextual matter once more to underline the thesis that, while a computer program that "understands" natural language in the most general sense is for the present beyond our means, the granting of even a quite broad contextual framework allows us to construct practical language recognition procedures.

The present script is designed to *reveal,* as opposed to *conceal,* lack of understanding and misunderstanding. Notice, for example, that when the program is asked to compute the area of the ball, it doesn't yet know that a ball is a sphere and that when the diameter of the ball needs to be computed the fact that a ball is an object has also not yet been established. Appropriate questions are therefore asked. But when, later on, the area of the globe is required, all the parameters are known and no questions are asked. The transcript also makes clear that the program now has memory and, of course, that it can compute.

I can imagine at least two questions that might have arisen in the mind of the reader in response to the above material. First, but least important, is what role the kind of psychiatric program shown here has in serious psychotherapy. My answer to that must be that psychotherapy is not my field and that I have no intention to pursue any therapeutic implications of this work. It is clear that there is considerable psychological material to be exploited here, material that may conceivably lead to some therapeutic developments. There may also be some use in this kind of technique in simulation of the neurotic processes. K. M. Colby, a practicing psychoanalyst, does propose to use conversational programs as psychotherapeutic tools vis-a-vis real patients. I believe the unsolved technical problems in the computer realm alone are so enormous as to guarantee the postponement of the realization of such a goal for yet a very long time.

The second question concerns itself with the implications of this work on so-called teaching machines. Here I feel on much firmer ground. It is my belief that the kind of programmed teaching that is based on multiple choice testing of the student is best done without the use of computers. With the techniques described here, it becomes possible to instruct the student in a corner of some field and then, the contextual framework having been established, to have the student interact with the machine in natural language.

The following conversation, based on a script written by Dr. Edwin Taylor of the Education Research Center of MIT, makes the point very well.

Please consider how we might synchronize two clocks to read the 'same time'. One of these clocks is in San Francisco, the other is in New York. As you think about the problem, ask me any questions that occur to you. When you are ready to propose a synchronization method, type 'ready'. Then I will quiz you about your proposed method
WHAT DO YOU MEAN BY SYNCHRONIZE
For the present make use of the everyday meanings of such phrases as 'same time' and 'synchronize'. Later we will discuss the meaning of these terms more carefully
MAY I USE TELEGRAPH SIGNALS
Certainly, feel free to use telegraph
READY
Now I will quiz you on your synchronization method. Does your method of synchronization involve the propagation of some signal—or material object— from one place to another
YES
What kind of propagating signal or traveling object do you propose to use
A WATCH
Will your watch move at a speed very much smaller than the speed of light
OF COURSE
Good. Traveling clocks can be used to synchronize distant clocks to arbitrarily high accuracy if they travel slowly enough. You may leave the problem by pushing the 'quit' button twice. If you would like to explore further the matters of principle associated with other methods, choose another way to communicate between the distant clocks
What kind of propagating signal or traveling object do you propose to use
LIGHT
Well, of course the light signal will not follow the curvature of the earth. So let us assume that some system of relay towers is used. Now let me ask, will the light signal travel directly between New York and San Francisco or will the light signal travel to or from some intermediate point
IT WILL TRAVEL FROM ST LOUIS IN BOTH DIRECTIONS
Is your intermediate point equidistant from New York and San Francisco
LET'S SAY IT IS, YES
My understanding is that you expect to use two signals and that these signals will either converge on or be sent out from a point equidistant from New York and San Francisco. Is my understanding on this point correct
YES
Will this pair of signals converge on the intermediate point or be sent out from this point
THEY WILL BE SENT FROM THE POINT
Will the two signals leave the intermediate point at the same time
CERTAINLY
Aha, I've got you. You are trying to synchronize the New York and San Francisco clocks to read the 'same time'. How can it be valid to assume a 'same time' for the departure of a pair of signals from the midpoint
BECAUSE THE PAIR OF SIGNALS LEAVE FROM THE SAME POINT
Right
The phrase 'same time' has an unambiguous meaning when applied to events

that occur near the same point in space. Now you are going to continue your argument by saying that the two signals that start from the midpoint at the same time will presumably reach New York and San Francisco at the same time. These signals can thus be used to synchronize the New York and San Francisco clocks. Is this the way your argument will continue
YES
One final question. What assumption are you making about the speeds of the two signals that travel in opposite directions
THAT THESE SPEEDS ARE EQUAL
Very good. You have devised a valid method for synchronizing two clocks, one in New York and one in San Francisco. I am now returning you to the CTSS system

I have chosen to skew this discussion in the direction of "understanding" and have used that difficult word almost as if it were synonymous with "recognition." Actually, recognition is a prerequisite to understanding. The latter provides a test of the former. Even though no test of understanding can be defined with rigor, we do feel we are understood when the person we're talking to asks what we believe to be relevant questions and when he finally answers our question or solves the problem we posed. By such criteria, the conversations displayed above justify the assertion that the programs that produced the responses recognized textual patterns and understood what they were being told.

Finally, I wish to call attention to three pieces of work, two of which predate the programs discussed here and to whose authors I owe a considerable intellectual debt. The last is more recent but nevertheless highly relevant to my own current line of attack.

The SIR program of Raphael is capable of inferential data acquisition in a way analogous to that displayed in the ELIZA ball and sphere conversation displayed above. Notice that in that conversation the program had to infer that a ball was a sphere and an object. Once that inference was affirmed, the program retained the information by, in this case, associating with ball the fact that it is a sphere and an object and with sphere and object that ball is an instance of each, respectively. SIR is a program which specializes in establishing such relationships, remembering and invoking them when required. One of its principal aims was to establish methodology for formalizing a calculus of relations and even relations among relations.

Bobrow's program STUDENT is capable of solving so-called algebra word problems of the kind that are typically given in high school algebra texts. He uses a mechanism not very different from an ELIZA script. Its chief task is to transform the input text, i.e., the natural language statement of an algebra word problem, into a set of simultaneous linear equations that may then be evaluated to produce the desired result. A particular strength of his program is its power to recognize ambiguities and resolve them, often by appeal to inferentially acquired information but sometimes by asking questions.

The work of Quillian is mainly directed toward establishing

data structures capable of searching semantic dictionaries. His system could, for example, decide that the words "work for" in the sentence "John works for Harry." mean "is employed by", while the same words appearing in the sentence "That algorithm works for all even numbers that are not perfect squares." mean "is applicable to."

Each of the computer papers referenced below represents an attack on some component of the machine understanding problem. That problem is not yet solved.

References

1. BOBROW, D. G. Natural language input for a computer problem-solving system. Ph.D. Thesis, MIT, Dept. of Mathematics, Cambridge, Mass. 1964.
2. COLBY, KENNETH MARK. Computer simulation of change in personal belief systems. Paper delivered in Section L_2, The Psychiatric Sciences, General Systems Research, AAAS Berkeley Meeting, December 29, 1965. To appear in *Behav. Sci., 1967.*
3. QUILLIAN, M. R. Semantic memory. Ph.D. Thesis, Carnegie Inst. of Technology, Pittsburgh, Pa., 1966.
4. RAPHAEL, B. SIR: A computer program for Semantic Information Retrieval. Ph.D. Thesis, MIT, Dept. of Mathematics, Cambridge, Mass., 1964.
5. ROGERS, C. *Client Centered Therapy: Current Practice, Implications and Theory.* Houghton Mifflin, Boston, 1951.
6. WEIZENBAUM, JOSEPH. ELIZA — a computer program for the study of natural language communication between man and machine. *Comm. ACM 9,* 1 (Jan. 1966), 36–45.

The essence of rhythm is the fusion of sameness and novelty,
so that the whole never loses the essential unity
of the pattern, while the parts exhibit the contrast
arising from the novelty of their detail.
ALFRED NORTH WHITEHEAD, *An Enquiry Concerning the Principles*
of Natural Knowledge

15 Editing: focus and loading

As we said in Chapter 13, the proposition Agent (*police*), Act (*arrest*), Affected (*my roommate*), Time (*yesterday*) can take several forms. For example, each category in the proposition can function as the grammatical subject of a sentence, yet the sentences developed in this way say roughly the same thing.

1) The police arrested my roommate yesterday.
   (Agent as subject)
2) My roommate was arrested by the police yesterday.
   (Affected as subject)
3) My roommate's arrest by the police was yesterday.
   (Act as subject)
4) Yesterday was when the police arrested my roommate.
   (Time as subject)

Why should there be so many different ways of expressing a proposition? One answer is that we need a means of bringing any one of these categories to the center of our attention, of establishing focus on it. Our chief means of establishing focus on a propositional category is to make it the grammatical subject of the sentence. The English language contains mechanisms that allow us to make any category of a proposition the subject of a sentence. For example, the passive construction used in sentence 2 above establishes focus on the category labeled "Affected." The same means can be used to create somewhat comparable centers of attention in sentence sequences.

Focus in paragraphs

The topic sentence in a paragraph with a single underlying plot (i.e., the generalization that fills the Statement slot in a plot such as Statement-Example or Statement-Restatement) introduces a set of propositional categories, one or more of which recur repeatedly in the subsequent sentences. The result is one or more "chains" of lexical items that run through the sentences and help to bind them together, to give them coherence and unity. Each sentence except the topic sentence thus contains old information (the repeated items) and new information. Or as Alfred North Whitehead expressed it in the epigraph, each contains "sameness" and "novelty." Such repetition is the way one talks on a subject. When we say that someone sticks to the point in his discussion, we are saying that he repeats certain items in a sequence of statements. To break all the chains at once while continuing to talk is to stop the discussion of that subject and begin another.

Notice in the following paragraph how the repetition of the word *process* results in a lexical chain linking all the sentences:

> There is however another process at work in the universe which is creative rather than destructive, which builds up rather than tears down, which makes for diversity rather than uniformity and for the complexity of structure rather than for the simplicity of chaos. It has operated to build structures of higher degrees of organization, that is, of lower and lower probability. In our part of the universe this process reaches its furthest point in man—the most improbable of all structures! This of course is the process to which we give the name of evolution.
>
> KENNETH E. BOULDING, *The Evolutionary Potential of Quakerism*

The function of focus in such structured sequences of sentences is (1) to establish a center of interest and (2) to signal the structural relationships among the sentences. In the paragraph just quoted, *process* is clearly the center of interest; the fact that it is the subject of every sentence is a strong signal that the sentences are all in some way parallel to each other, that the sequence is structurally simple. But this paragraph is unusual, for most paragraphs contain more than one plot. In these more complex structures the focus may shift several times, indicating shifts in center of interest and, sinultaneously, signaling the stages of the paragraph's structure, as in the following paragraph:

> The English Constitution — that indescribable entity — is a living thing, growing with the growth of men, and assuming ever-varying forms in accordance with the subtle and complex laws of human character. It is the child of wisdom and chance. The wise men of 1688 moulded it into the shape we know, but the chance that George I could not speak English gave it one of its essential peculiarities — the system of a Cabinet independent of the Crown and subordinate to the Prime Minister. The wisdom of Lord Grey saved it from petrification and set it upon the path of democracy. Then chance intervened once more. A female sovereign happened to marry an able and pertinacious man, and it seemed likely that an element which had been quiescent within it for years — the element of irresponsible administrative power — was about to become its predominant characteristic and change completely the direction of its growth. But what chance gave, chance took away. The Consort perished in his prime, and the English Constitution, dropping the dead limb with hardly a tremor, continued its mysterious life as if he had never been.
>
> LYTTON STRACHEY, Queen Victoria

This paragraph contains two plots, Statement-Restatement and Statement-Examples. Notice that *English Constitution* is in focus in the first two sentences, the second of which restates the first in metaphorical terms. This restatement in turn functions as the statement in the second plot, providing the categories (*wisdom* and *chance*) that are developed by a series of examples in the following sentences. In this series, the focus shifts back and forth between *wisdom* and *chance* (and related terms); focus on *Constitution* is reestablished in the final clause, which relates back to the first sentence and serves to close the paragraph. Unlike the paragraph by Boulding, this paragraph contains one chain (introduced by the topic sentence) whose domain is the entire paragraph, and other chains (introduced by a subtopic) whose domain is limited to the subplot.

Poor writers sometimes shift from one subject to another unnecessarily, often out of a misguided desire for variety. A series of these false signals makes prose awkward and often hard to understand. For instance, the following paragraph, which although not obscure is rather awkward, arbitrarily shifts focus in the middle:

> A successful disaster organization plan, whether for a single plant, community, or entire state, should have these characteristics. It

should be simple and easy to understand. For functioning at any disaster regardless of size or nature, inclusiveness and yet flexibility are important. And recognition of those constituted authorities of state or local government who have jurisdiction over, or who are affected by, the disaster is a vital part.

Editing out the flaws in this particular paragraph requires establishing a consistent focus, which can be done by moving *plan* to the subject position in each sentence.

A successful disaster organization plan, whether for a single plant, a community, or an entire state, should have these characteristics. It should be simple and easy to understand. It should be inclusive and yet flexible, so that it is functional for any disaster regardless of size or nature. And it should recognize those constituted authorities of state and local government who have jurisdiction over, or who are affected by, the disaster.

Revising paragraphs to eliminate such flaws is yet another variant form of what should by now be a familiar process. Sensing problems in his first draft, the writer develops an alternative version to solve the problems, thus cycling toward a form that is consistent with his notions of good prose.

Loading grammatical patterns

One of the reasons, then, for a writer to select one way of expressing a proposition rather than another is that he wishes to establish and maintain focus on a particular category in a sequence of sentences. As we saw in Chapter 13, another reason is that he wants to avoid overloading his sentences and thereby confusing his reader. In theory, a sentence can be infinitely long; certainly the longest sentence that you can write can always be made longer. There are three general ways in which to expand a simple sentence: by adding to it various optional constituents, by embedding within it one or more subordinate clauses, and by conjoining grammatically similar units (e.g., Agents expressed as subjects, Motions as predicates, Goals as objects).

ADDING

Although a sentence may consist of no more than an unmodified subject and predicate, there are a number of optional constituents (sometimes grouped together under the label *adverbials*) that can be added to it. For instance, the sentence

My brother opened the window.

expresses the underlying categories Agent, Act, Goal. As we have seen, other categories, such as Place, Time, and Cause—categories that are potential parts of the underlying proposition—can also be expressed in the sentence:

> My brother opened the window upstairs yesterday because it was too stuffy.

Still other categories can be added—for example, Manner and Purpose—but notice what happens to the sentence:

> My brother opened the window upstairs yesterday because it was too stuffy carefully in order to get some fresh air.

The sentence is becoming overloaded, and the relationships of the various parts, rather confusing. These relationships, however, can frequently be clarified by reordering the parts of the sentence:

> Because it was too stuffy my brother carefully opened the window upstairs yesterday in order to get some fresh air.

But further additions (e.g., Accompaniment, Instrument, Beneficiary) seriously overload the sentence:

> Because it was too stuffy my brother with my uncle Bill carefully opened the window upstairs yesterday with a crowbar for me in order to get some fresh air.

Instead of relying solely on reordering to make the relationships among the constituents clear, most writers would probably express this in two or more sentences. For example,

> Because it was too stuffy yesterday, my brother with my uncle Bill opened the window upstairs for me in order to get some fresh air. He did it carefully with a crowbar.

EMBEDDING

A sentence can also be expanded by embedding. Two clauses that share a common category can often be embedded one within the other. Thus,

> My brother opened the window. The maid had closed it.

becomes

> My brother opened the window the maid had closed.

But extensive embedding, like adding optional categories, can overload a sentence:

My brother opened the window the maid the janitor Uncle Bill had hired had married had closed.

Once again, most writers would express these propositions in two or more sentences:

My brother opened the window the maid had closed. She was the one who had married the janitor Uncle Bill had hired.

CONJOINING

Finally, a sentence can be expanded by conjoining. Whole sentences can be conjoined:

I tried to understand, but I couldn't follow.

But not all sentences can be linked together:

Close the window and here comes John!

Parts of sentences can also be conjoined, but usually only parts that express the same underlying category. That is, Agents can be conjoined only with Agents, Beneficiaries with Beneficiaries, Goals with Goals:

Henry and Bill and Andy and . . . (etc.) . . . helped
Sue and Sandy and Jean and . . . (etc.) . . . . move
the books and the chairs and the lamps . . . (etc.). . . .

Theoretically, one more item can always be added to each series in a sentence—provided that the addition stands for the appropriate underlying category. In actual practice, however, there is a limit to the complexity that the average reader can reasonably be expected to process in a single sentence. The following sentence—the result of a series of conjoinings—probably overtaxes the reader's capacity for comprehending complexity:

Either John and Bill or John and Sam or Andy or Bill and Andy but not Sam may come with us.

Can you state this clearly in two or more sentences?

Like sentences, paragraphs can be overloaded. An overly long or complex paragraph taxes the reader's understanding and ability to attend to what is said. We seem to be unable to sustain attention for long and need to pause regularly if we are to read without effort. An overloaded paragraph can be made more readable by dividing it between stages in its plot structure.

Guidelines for editing

Editing, a special instance of the process of inquiry, begins when you sense something wrong with the way ideas have been expressed in your own or someone else's writing. In this chapter and the preceding one we have shown that this process need not be a random one, that it can be guided by a series of questions that function as a simple heuristic procedure:

1) *Is the plot of the troublesome passage clear?* If it is not, you should reorganize the passage and mark the plot with proper cues.
2) *Is focus maintained on the center of interest in the troublesome passage and does it signal the relationships among the sentences?* If not, rephrase sentences.
3) *Are parts of the troublesome passage overloaded?* If they are, you should probably divide the overloaded sentences and paragraphs, although you can sometimes clarify an apparently overloaded sentence without disturbing the focus of the passage merely by rearranging its constitutents.

One word of caution, however: Guidelines are not inflexible rules that will inevitably yield good prose. Rather, they are suggestions for dealing with the most common difficulties found in *troublesome* passages written by intelligent writers. There are, of course, a host of other problems that the writer must confront in editing his work — among them, grammatical and spelling errors and problems of diction and ambiguity. Problems of plot, focus, and loading, however, seem to cause the most frequent difficulties to advanced writers and therefore require special instruction and practice to overcome.

Continuity in paragraph sequences

In our discussions of hierarchy and paragraphs in the two preceding chapters we have implicitly adopted particle and field perspectives by emphasizing choice of units to fill slots in grammatical constructions and paragraph plots. As is to be expected, this distorts reality since it implies that units of writing can be — or even, perhaps, should be — sharply segmented. To some extent, such segmentation does occur, and it is important, since it makes the discourse more comprehensible. Graphically separated sentences, paragraphs, and chapters help the reader know where he is in the discourse. Chapter titles and section headings indicate the nature of particular segments in the hierarchy. If the segments are given outline numbers (I, A, 1, for example), as they frequently are in scientific discourse, the hierarchical relationships of the segments are further clarified. As we have implied in our discussion of recurrence and focus, however, discourse has wave features as well. In a sequence of sentences certain elements are continuous; key words are repeated, and tense, number, even syntactic patterns, are often held constant. As a result sentences can be seen as merging and interacting with one another.

But how do paragraphs interact? Participation in higher-level plots establishes relationships among sequences of paragraphs in a discourse; but do we also find indeterminate borders and continuous features in sequences of paragraphs comparable to those in sentence sequences? Consider the following excerpt from Albert Einstein's essay "The Laws of Science and the Laws of Ethics":

> Such cooperation, however, is essential to make human life possible and tolerable. This means that the rule "Thou shalt not lie" has been traced back to the demands: "Human life shall be preserved" and "Pain and sorrow shall be lessened as much as possible."
>
> But what is the origin of such ethical axioms? Are they arbitrary? Are they based on mere authority? Do they stem from experiences of men and are they conditioned indirectly by such experiences?
>
> For pure logic all axioms are arbitrary, including the axioms of ethics. But they are by no means arbitrary from a psychological and genetic point of view. They are derived from our inborn tendencies to avoid pain and annihilation, and from the accumulated emotional reaction of individuals to the behavior of their neighbors.

Notice, first, that the series of questions set off as a paragraph provides a transition between the preceding and following paragraphs; it refers to what has gone before and anticipates what is to follow. Second, *axioms* and equivalent terms recur in each of the paragraphs, although their grammatical function shifts (change in focus being one cue to the reader that the writer is beginning another unit of the discourse). Third, grammatical features such as tense and number are held constant. Finally, the word *such* (in the second paragraph) refers to prior statements and thus emphasizes continuity of topic.

Paragraph indentions have been removed from the following sequence of paragraphs; but by noting what is continuous and what changes (particularly changes in focus), you and your classmates should be able to agree on where indentions could reasonably be placed.

```
1    Grant was, judged by modern standards, the greatest general of the
2    Civil War. He was head and shoulders above any general on either
3    side as an over-all strategist, as a master of what in later wars would
4    be called global strategy. His Operation Crusher plan, the product of
5    a mind which had received little formal instruction in the higher arts
6    of war, would have done credit to the most finished student of a series
7    of modern staff and command schools. He was a brilliant theater strat-
8    egist, as evidenced by the Vicksburg campaign, which was a classic
9    field and seige operation. He was a better than average tactician, al-
10   though like even the best generals of both sides he did not appreciate
11   the destruction that the increasing firepower of modern armies could
12   visit on troops advancing across open spaces. Lee is usually ranked as
13   the greatest Civil War general, but this evaluation has been made
14   without placing Lee and Grant in the perspective of military develop-
15   ments since the war. Lee was interested hardly at all in "global" strat-
16   egy, and what few suggestions he did make to his government about
17   operations in other theaters than his own indicate that he had
18   little aptitude for grand planning. As a theater strategist, Lee often
19   demonstrated more brilliance and apparent originality than Grant, but
20   his most audacious plans were as much the product of the Confed-
21   eracy's inferior military position as of his own fine mind. In war, the
22   weaker side has to improvise brilliantly. It must strike quickly, dar-
23   ingly, and include a dangerous element of risk in its plans. Had Lee
24   been a Northern general with Northern resources behind him, he
25   would have improvised less and seemed less bold. Had Grant been
26   a Southern general, he would have fought as Lee did. Fundamentally
27   Grant was superior to Lee because in a modern total war he had a
28   modern mind, and Lee did not. Lee looked to the past in war as the
29   Confederacy did in spirit. The staffs of the two men illustrate their
30   outlook. It would not be accurate to say that Lee's general staff were
31   glorified clerks, but the statement would not be too wide of the
32   mark . . . .
```

T. HARRY WILLIAMS, *Lincoln and His Generals*

The author indented at lines 12 and 26. He might also have indented at line 21, where there is a shift in focus from *Lee* to *the weaker side*.

Transitional devices such as the ones we have isolated merge one paragraph with another (or one chapter with another, or one part of a book with another). At the end of one paragraph or the start of the next, the reader is given cues that lead him to anticipate what is to come or to recall what has already been said. The task of editing is not complete until such transitions have been supplied. Without them your prose will not "flow," nor will the relationships between the paragraphs be clear.

EXERCISES

1 Read each of the paragraphs below and then do the following: Find the generalized plot (or plots) in each. Find the topic sentence. Isolate the categories that are developed into lexical chains. Isolate those that are brought into focus, and note the relation of focus to plot structure.

a Occasionally, things that we see, or read, or hear, revise our conceptions of space and time, or of relationships. I have recently read, for instance, Vasiliev's *History of the Byzantine Empire*. As a result of reading this book I have considerably revised my image of at least a thousand years of history. I had not given the matter a great deal of thought before, but I suppose if I had been questioned on my view of the period, I would have said that Rome fell in the fifth century and that it was succeeded by a little-known empire centering in Constantinople and a confused medley of tribes, invasions, and successor states. I now see that Rome did not fall, that in a sense it merely faded away, that the history of the Roman Empire and of Byzantium is continuous, and that from the time of its greatest extent the Roman Empire lost one piece after another until Constantinople was left; and then in 1453 that went.

KENNETH E. BOULDING, *The Image*

b Since childhood, I have been enchanted by the fact and the symbolism of the right hand and the left—the one the doer, the other the dreamer. The right is order and lawfulness, *le droit*. Its beauties are those of geometry and taut implication. Reaching for knowledge with the right hand is science. Yet to say only that much of science is to overlook one of its excitements, for the great hypotheses of science are gifts carried in the left hand.

Of the left hand we say that it is awkward and, while it has been proposed that art students can seduce their proper hand to more expressiveness by drawing first with the left, we nonetheless suspect this function. The French speak of the illegitimate descendant as being *à main gauche*, and, though the heart is virtually at the center of the thoracic cavity, we listen for it on the left. Sentiment, intuition, bastardy. And should we say that reaching for knowledge with the left hand is art? Again it is not enough, for as surely as the recital of a daydream differs from the well wrought tale, there is a barrier between undisciplined fantasy and art. To climb the barrier requires a right hand adept at technique and artifice.

JEROME BRUNER, *On Knowing*

c Now what do we do with this rather bright child when he gets to school? In our own way we communicate to him that mathematics is a logical discipline and that it has certain rules, and we often proceed to teach him algorisms that make it seem that what he is doing in arithmetic has no bearing on the way in which he would proceed by nonrigorous means. I am not, mind you, objecting to "social arithmetic" with its interest rates and baseball averages. I am objecting to something far worse, the premature use of the language of mathematics, its end-product formalism, which makes it seem that mathematics is something new rather than something the child already knows. It is forcing the child into the inverse plight of the character in *Le Bourgeois Gentilhomme* who comes to the blazing insight that he has been speaking prose all his life. By interposing formalism, we prevent the child from realizing that he has been thinking mathematics all along. What we do, in essence, is to remove his confidence in his ability to perform the processes of mathematics. At our worst, we offer formal proof (which is necessary for checking) in place of direct intuition. It is good that a student knows how to check the conjecture that $8x$ is equivalent to the expression $3x + 5x$ by such a rigorous statement as the following: "By the commutative principle for multiplication, for every x, $3x + 5x = x3 + x5$. By the distributive principle, for every x, $x3 + x5 = x (3 + 5)$. Again by the commutative principle, for every x, $x (3 + 5) = (3 + 5)x$ or $8x$. So, for every x, $3x + 5x = 8x$." But it is hopeless if the student gets the idea that this and this only is *really* arithmetic or algebra or "math" and that other ways of proceeding are really for nonmathematical dolts. Therefore, "mathematics is not for me."

JEROME BRUNER, *On Knowing*

d For poverty is not a simple concept: a mere absence of wealth. Rather it is a whole complex of debilitating conditions — each reinforcing the other in an ever-tightening web of human impairment. Illiteracy, disease, hunger, and hopelessness are characteristics that of their own momentum spiral human aspirations downward. Poverty begets poverty. It passes from generation to generation in a cruel cycle of near inevitability. It endures until carefully designed outside assistance intervenes and radically redirects its internal dynamics.

ROBERT S. MCNAMARA, Speech before the Veterans of Foreign Wars,
New York, August 23, 1966

2 Rewrite the following paragraphs, correcting problems of plot, focus, and loading.

a The S.S. *Gateway City* is an unusual ship. It has two cranes, each capable of traveling along the deck under the control of a transverse operating bridge. Pan-Atlantic Steamship Corporation, owners of the vessel, wanted the ship to be as independent of shore facilities as possible. This meant she had to carry her own cargo-handling gear. The *Gateway City*, the nation's first ship built to use a lift-on, lift-off container system, carries 226 containers, each 35 feet long, 8 feet wide, and 8 1/2 feet high, weighing 21 tons. The containers are filled with cargo on shore. Then they are hoisted aboard ship where most of them are lowered into the holds where they are stacked within vertical guides. The rest (one layer only) are placed atop the hatch covers after the holds have been filled.

b The stimulus (intense emotion over a bad grade) produces a reaction (running instead of walking to the next class) which provides an acceptable escape from reality while I consider how to cope with this setback. A similar escape might be a cigarette or a drink to relieve the tension caused by the bad grade. This would be the obvious sensation provided by the running, and in the case of a good grade, it would also be an escape similar to shouting or singing out of sheer joy. A less obvious sensation that occurs from time to time is one of punishment. This sensation is closely allied with the one of escape but with a little different slant.

c To intruders, the bark of a dog is a forecast. The tone of bark lets the intruder know whether he is welcome, or whether he should leave without hesitation. A delightful welcome or yip is normally given the master, children who pet and play, or a favored dog. Children who play too rough, however, very often hear an irritated bark. Strangers are more frequently than not issued a signal to leave. This is evident from the ferocious bark resounded at their approach. To prevent being bitten or chased, intruders should always take heed of the type bark man's best friend greets them with.

d Japan and Western Germany have been stepping up their efforts to boost sales of scientific apparatus in America. German instruments are of high quality and could prove a threat. Japanese goods so far have suffered from a lack of adequate inspection, and the inconsistency of the instruments exported to America has prevented the Japanese from taking full advantage of the tremendous difference between labor costs in Japan and in the United States. British manufacturers are being quite businesslike in their approach to the American market, offering such scarce items as electronic test instruments for immediate delivery without priority ratings, and including service agreements as part of their sales package.

e In choosing a power plant for any ship, several important factors must be considered: power requirements, endurance, weight, cost, total ship weight, and desired payload. Obviously, a small submersible requires a light, compact power plant. Endurance is also important in such a vehicle. Submarines cannot utilize systems which require the combustion of a fuel, such as internal combustion engines.

3 In the following passage all paragraph indentions have been removed and all nouns, verbs, adjectives, and adverbs have been replaced by nonsense words. Indicate in the margin where

paragraph breaks would be appropriate. Compare your results with those of your classmates. Can you develop a hypothesis about paragraph signals that accounts for these results? Make a list of the different kinds of signals you use to identify the paragraphs. (The English version is part of the passage that begins on page 98, but don't look at it until you have finished making your list of signals.)

1	Worling still further, I buse our rast the sude as a memon of comlions
2	upon comlions of athors in the Fropoly. Worling still further, I enclivize
3	the Fropoly as one of comlions upon comlions of athors in the versilane.
4	I am not crolly sormated in grome, I am sormated in rale. I spone that I
5	leme to Nornubata about a zen ago, and I am scralling it in about lind
6	ruths. I spone that I have daned in a brandle of climallant hapsens at
7	climallant rales. I spone that about mag zens ago a rass nerg leme to an
8	alb, that about oblant zens ago another rass nerg leme to an alb. Taltion
9	tromes are spregiale: 1776, 1620, 1066. I tair a montle in my drine of the
10	calution of the perg, of the groab pristation of logealical rale, of the prin
11	pristation of creck. The rass lizalibations raspe before my tolemate
12	creal. Many of the boulations are smitt, but Thede rogoles Spath, Tarn
13	rogoles Ossryia. I am not crolly sormated in grome and rale, I am sor-
14	mated in a lide of nalerone sibations. I not only spone where and when
15	I am, I spone to tume grotex who I am. I am a felsorale at a rass tate
16	monicollium. This mares that in Ostriner I shall hibe into a croomscale
17	and expride to drobe tume wollines in it and sothine to labe to them,
18	and nobody will be rispused. I expride what is herabes even more abli-
19	mable, that galatle rattonate reabs will libate from the monicollium. I
20	expride that when I nerpole my thome on taltion cramotions leopons
21	will ristle. I spone, furthermore, that I am a busrate and a thamer, that
22	there are leopons who will replode to me factomially and to whom I
23	will replode in like crisple. I spone, also, that I tair droggs, that there
24	are oshes here, there, and everywhere into which I may hibe and I will
25	be colmeled and maluded and rechumed as a prode. I relote to namy
26	critalations. There are hapsens into which I hibe, and it will be maluded
27	that I am exprided to holdate in a taltion crisple. I may trig down to
28	shorate, I may fose a crone, I may ristle to a rescone, I may do all trags
29	of negs. I am not crolly sormated in grome and in rale and in nalerone
30	sibationates, I am also sormated in the dile of rution, in a dile of how
31	negs peronate. I spone that when I sote my cag there are tume negs
32	I must do to drobe it; tume negs I must do to crish out of the dexling
33	loap: tume negs I must do to vire hown. I spone that if I murp off a
34	grite hap I will norally crope myself. I spone that there are tume negs
35	that would norally not be kume for me to surp or to lish. I spone taltion
36	faciations that are vilabiate to kane to raintle kume leath. I spone that
37	if I neal too laise scwarmate in my chct as I trig here at my cheem, I
38	will norally spint over. I dane, in athor goobs, in a dile of roperably
39	spanal sibationates, a dile of "ifs" and "thens," of "if I do this, then
40	that will mogate." Dantially, I am sormated in the crind of a dile of
41	snoople matilations and amortions. I am tumerales oloted, tumerales

42   a spinkle desponded, tumerales loople, tumerales crabe, tumerales
43   spilate, tumerales profilate. I am osine to snoople matilations of a
44   respode beyond the dile of grome and rale and nert. What I have been
45   labing about is sponedge. Sponedge, perhaps, is not a kume nile for
46   this.

4   One of the functions of an essay's initial paragraph is to establish focus for the essay. Frequently this focus is achieved by
what has been called the "funnel technique"; the writer begins with broad generalizations or with several illustrations
and then narrows his scope down to a more specific aspect of
the generalizations or illustrations, as in the following passage:

> Goering and Hitler displayed an almost maudlin concern for the wel-
> fare of animals; Stalin's favorite work of art was a celluloid musical
> about Old Vienna, called *The Great Waltz*. And it is not only dictators
> who divide their thoughts and feelings into unconnected, logic-tight
> compartments; the whole world lives in a state of chronic and almost
> systematic inconsistency. Every society is a case of multiple personal-
> ity and modulates, without a qualm, without even being aware of
> what it is up to, from Jekyll to Hyde, from the scientist to the magi-
> cian, from the hardheaded man of affairs, to the village idiot . . . .
>
> ALDOUS HUXLEY, *Madness, Badness, Sadness*

Examine the opening paragraphs of several essays in this book
What other techniques for establishing focus can you discover?

5   Writers are often given the advice, "Avoid the passive." Judging from what we have said about focus, do you think this
advice is sound? When is the passive useful? Select an essay in
this book and underline the passive sentences in it. How
many of these sentences are passive in order to maintain focus? Why do you suppose some rhetoricians have formulated
the rule of avoiding the passive? (If you can't answer this
question, look in a few traditional college composition handbooks. What reasons do they cite for the rule?) In what contexts
is the advice valid?

6   Randomly select sequences of two or three paragraphs from
several of the essays included in this book. Isolate the means
by which the writer conjoins the paragraphs. Then make a list
of such means, adding to the one suggested on page 352, which
included the following: transitional paragraphs, lexical repeti-
tions, recurrent grammatical features, and demonstratives
(words like *such*).

By intelligence we mean a style of life,
a way of behaving in various situations,
and particularly in new, strange, and perplexing situations.
JOHN HOLT, *How Children Fail*

16 Conclusion: style as a way of behaving

WHEN people think of a writer's style, they usually think of the distinctive features of his prose—a distinctive lexicon and syntax and, less often, a distinctive subject matter. That is, style is conventionally defined in terms of characteristics of the finished work. While granting that this concept of style is at times useful, we want to offer an alternative that emphasizes instead what one does as he is writing. We propose to view style as a particular way of behaving. Our focus, then, is on characteristics of the process of writing rather than on characteristics of the product.

The conventional concept has its uses, particularly for the literary critic, since he is primarily interested in the study and appreciation of the work itself. The concept is a fundamental one in his discipline. When this concept captures the attention of the rhetorician, however—as it has several times in the past and as it has today—

the result is an excessive emphasis on the work itself, particularly on matters of elegance, clarity, structure, and linguistic propriety. When the discourse itself becomes the principal focus of attention, the activity of creation and the psychological and social functions of the discourse tend to be ignored. But for the student of writing the creation and function of the work are, necessarily, his primary concerns; learning to write is learning to control an extremely complex process in order to bring about social change.

As a writer, he must be concerned with formulating elements of experience and ordering them in coherent and meaningful systems, with formulating his relationship with his readers, and with shaping the notions welling up in his mind into a verbal object that is the best expression of what he has understood and that is at the same time an instrument for inducing activity in other minds. As a creator, then, he must see the art of rhetoric in dynamic terms, as search and choice, as a way of behaving.

Everyone who has written much at all has developed a distinctive way of carrying out these activities. Many of us rely heavily on intuition and habit born of past experience; others work more consciously and analytically; still others, lacking experience or blessed with great energy, depend on trial and error and consequently make numerous false starts and prepare several drafts. Thus everyone has a distinctive style, but not everyone has what might be called an "intelligent" style—a way of proceeding that is efficient and effective.

Much of this book can be seen as one answer to what constitutes an intelligent style. Such a style implies, we believe, an ability to isolate and identify the problems inherent in the activity of writing and to move toward workable solutions deliberately. It also implies an ability to see the problems of the moment as only variants of kinds of problems met and solved before, to view them generically as well as specifically. Unless the writer can do this, he is unable to bring past experience to bear consciously or to use heuristic procedures, for he must have some idea of the problems he is trying to solve before he can know what is relevant. The intelligent stylist, then, behaves in new situations as if he has been there before; and in one important sense he has, since all writing tasks have some features in common. If he regards each new situation as unique he is in danger of being overwhelmed by the particulars of the task; the result is often frustration and mental paralysis.

This view of writing, as a process that can be analyzed and controlled, underlies this book. By conceiving of the process of writing as a search for solutions to an interrelated sequence of problems and by providing heuristic procedures as guides in this search, we have sought to provide the tools necessary to form an intelligent style or reform an unintelligent one.

In taking this approach we have implicitly rejected two popular notions about how one becomes an effective writer: that practice alone is sufficient and that natural talent is essential. As anyone knows who has tried on his own to learn a second language or a sport such as tennis, practice alone will not produce excellence, for it is possible to practice errors and ineffective methods. A clear idea of what is to be practiced is necessary. The same may be said of writing. Furthermore, by attempting to learn only by practice, the would-be writer cuts himself off from an extremely rich store of knowledge about communication that has accumulated over the past 2500 years. Thus he must rediscover what has long been known. By itself practice is, to say the very least, an inefficient way to learn. The second notion is harder to deal with, since talent is difficult to define. We grant that brilliant writers have special capacities, which may well be genetically conditioned. But we are not trying to teach brilliance; we are trying to teach effectiveness in workaday situations. The ability to write effectively can be, and often is, acquired informally; but it can also be taught, at least significant features of the process can be taught. And teaching speeds learning.

The discipline of rhetoric as process

Rhetoric is today undergoing rapid change and development. As a result it is difficult to write a rhetoric textbook, for the very existence of a textbook normally implies the existence of not only an extensive body of knowledge but a relatively stable, well-developed theory. However, there are compensations; the unstable state of the discipline offers us the opportunity to participate in the development of a modern theory of rhetoric rather than merely to write a textbook that carries over into the classroom what is already generally accepted by scholars. We are interested in helping you become effective writers, and this requires that we concern ourselves with helping you become independent inquirers into significant human problems. Hence we invite you to participate in the process of creating a rhetoric adequate to our times. The following exercises, placed within this chapter rather than at the end, are designed to suggest hiatuses in this book and in present-day knowledge about communication. They by no means identify all areas that need exploration; their function is to direct your thinking beyond the book. Eventually you should be able to pose your own problems as well as to solve them.

EXERCISES

1 One subject touched upon in several chapters but not explored in detail is the nature of the particular human personality. If a personality is viewed as a particle, it can be examined for its contrastive features, its range of variation, and its distribution. See if you can answer the following questions, making use of this heuristic procedure. When someone says that he is alienated from his own society or that he does not know his own identity, what does he mean? (In seeking answers, pay particular attention to our discussions of choice in slots and in hierarchical structure.) When someone says he is being treated like a thing, what does he mean?

2 We have discussed writing extensively but have said little about speaking; in particular, we have said little about conversation, even though it is the most common means of communication. As a way of extending your thinking into this area, write a brief essay on "The Use of Transitions in Capturing and Controlling Conversations." To stimulate your imagination, consider this not-too-farfetched episode:

Jones and Brown have been discussing the dangers of driving over snowy mountain passes without chains. Smith joins the group, listens a while, and then says, "You know, it seems to me that risk taking is not confined to physical activity; last year I was writing a book on the colors of birds' wings . . . ," and continues at length.

Describe the events of the capture in terms of a wave perspective, nuclei, and bridges. Can the units of the conversation be seen as parts of a larger, hierarchically structured whole? If so, what are its features?

Listen carefully to what people do with their voices in conversation. How do they signal when it is appropriate to interrupt? Inappropriate? What happens when someone interrupts at an inappropriate moment? What does a speaker do if he wants to continue speaking when others seek to interrupt and seize control? Draw on the earlier discussions of wave and change in formulating your answers.

3 The relationship between form and meaning is a controversial subject among grammarians and rhetoricians. Our discussions in Chapters 2 and 13 by no means exhaust the subject, nor are they likely to still the controversy. As a means of reopening the subject, consider this statement by a young child:

A mother is the only one if she sings your favorite song it stops thundering.

In LEE PARR MCGRATH and JOAN SCOBY, What Is Mother

Restate the sentence, expressing the "same" idea as a mother might, then as a psychologist lecturing on parent-child relationships might, and finally as you yourself might. Is restatement merely a matter of substituting synonymous constructions? If not, what else is involved? How, for example, do the beliefs, knowledge, and experience of each of the three persons affect the way he reformulates the idea? How does each person's awareness of his universe of discourse and of what is appropriate to it affect his restatement? In what sense don't the four statements mean the same thing? Is there a best way of stating the idea? Why?

4 Nowhere have we studied poetry as a form of communication, although it is a powerful one, or examined the characteristics of verse, although the expressive capacities of language are most obvious and most fully exploited in verse. Nor have we examined the relationship of verse and prose. When we read verse, we react to and enjoy language as language, and the constraints imposed on us by our language (e.g., that it has certain vowels and no others) are turned to serve us, as in rhyme.

After noting that "glottal stop" is the technical term for the way we hold our breath by closing the vocal cords, read the following annoyance.

Murder by Phonetician
KENNETH L. PIKE

Preferred sound
in my neighbor:
lengthened
glottal stop.

It stops
for good
all cries
all moans
all boasts.

Silence pours,
reigns alone
where
words as weeds
grew before.

Now the words
grow o'er
the grave
of Dear old Dave
(the knave—
—the bore—
he'll breathe
no more).
Dirt chokes
the joke.

What additional meaning does the term *glottal stop* take on in this context? How is sound used to call attention to meaning? Where is word shape exploited? Vocalic likeness? Where are consonantal relations exploited? What parts of the poem—words, phrases, and so on—are closely associated in your mind (e.g., *glottal stop* and *choke; weeds* and *words*)? By what means are such associations established? What general voice quality is appropriate for reading the poem aloud? What would be ridiculous? Offensive? Ironical? Is there any difference in effect when you read it aloud and when you read it to yourself?

Rewrite the poem in prose. What effects and associations disappear? Why? What is the plot of the poem? What minimum changes will destroy the effect of the original?

5 We have said nothing about graphic communication in this book, although it is a common and important means of communication. When are graphic supplements, such as pictures, charts, and diagrams, useful? The following statement by C. S. Lewis should set your mind going.

Language exists to communicate whatever it can communicate. Some things it communicates so badly that we never attempt to communicate them by words if any other medium is available. Those who think they are testing a boy's 'elementary' command of English by asking him to describe in words how one ties one's tie or what a pair of scissors is like, are far astray. For precisely what language can hardly do at all, and never does well, is to inform us about complex physical shapes and movements. Hence descriptions of such things in the ancient writers are nearly always unintelligible. Hence we never in real life voluntarily use language for this purpose; we draw a diagram or go through pantomimic gestures. The exercises which such examiners set are no more a test of 'elementary' linguistic competence than the most difficult bit of trick-riding from the circus ring is a test of elementary horsemanship.

Another grave limitation of language is that it cannot, like music or gesture, do more than one thing at once. However, the words in a great poet's phrase interinanimate one other and strike the mind as a quasi-instantaneous chord, yet, strictly speaking, each word must be read or heard before the next.

C. S. LEWIS, *Studies in Words*

In what way is the question related to field perspective? Notice that very few graphic devices are used in this book. Where are they and why were they used? Are there kinds of writing in which visual explanation is inappropriate? In which it is conventional? Test your answers by examining examples of each kind of writing.

6 Here is one of Pike's experiments in using graphic design to highlight verbal intent. The story (from Luke 8:22–25) is that of Jesus commanding the waves of the Sea of Galilee when his disciples were frightened. Can you explain the reason for each special shape?

He Walked on the Waves of the Water

He was the one who built the flowing surface.

He Knew (the spoken) for (the tuning)

by voice controlled

till all was

quiet — solid—flat.

I wish I were calm like that.

What conventional graphic devices are available for highlighting verbal intent? What effects can we create with our voices that we cannot achieve in writing using these devices? Can you think of conventional ways of highlighting verbal intent in writing other than by punctuation and spelling? In *The Five Clocks* Martin Joos provides a very subtle example: he points out that the writer can arrange sounds to force a particular way of reading a sequence of words; in the phrase *people preparing,* for example, the four [p] sounds coupled with the [l] force a dipping intonation and a pause between the two words, and as a result the word *people* is emphasized.

7   It is often said — though seldom elaborated on — that using punctuation is an art in itself. Compared with vocal inflections, punctuation marks are, of course, crude indicators of meaning, but they do have more expressive power than we ordinarily make use of. Repunctuate the sentences in Exercise 1, Chapter 13, to show surprise, irony, emphasis, doubt. Find in the essays included in this book several sentences that convey strong emotion. Can you make them go flat by changing the punctuation?

Consider what additional effects you can create by rearranging the parts of a sentence, whole sentences, and paragraphs on the page. That is, consider how space can be used expressively.

8   One subject touched on in Chapters 13 and 14 is the classification of linguistic units. As we read various paragraphs and higher level units of discourse (like informal essays, scientific reports, letters, poems, stories, and plays), we become aware of the existence of kinds, just as we are aware of kinds in the biological world. Biologists have developed elaborate classification systems that are based on essential features of the units classified; but, no well-established system exists for classifying high-level units of discourse into a single, comprehensive system.

Try first to develop a classification system for complete written works. What are the bases for your distinctions? Does your system include non-fiction as well as fiction? Verse as well as prose? Are there types of discourse that do not fit into your system? Are there mixed or ambiguous forms somewhat analogous to bats, whales, and duck-billed platypuses? Can your system handle these? Do not assume that there is a single correct system to be discovered. A classification system is an invention, and inventions are not correct, but useful — some more, some less. If you worry about correctness rather than reasonableness, you will lose much of the profit from the exercise. Try, and learn from trying.

Do the same for paragraphs. If you are not able to develop a coherent system, make a start by labeling a number of paragraphs (e.g., narrative, explanatory, logical, preliminary; or topic-division, topic-illustration, topic-comparison). Again, do not look for right answers. No one knows much about this aspect of paragraphs.

9   Every teacher of rhetoric makes assumptions about how people write, but no extensive study has been made of what people actually do as they write. Using the definition of style given in this chapter, describe your own behavior as you wrote your best essay for this course. The result should be an account of a process, a narrative of how the finished essay was produced.

10 It has been said that a comprehensive philosophy must account for itself. We would like to examine our own rhetoric to see if it has this ability. One nuclear component of our rhetoric is the heuristic procedure presented in Chapter 6, which incorporates the maxims and procedures discussed elsewhere in the book. This procedure might be described metaphorically as a set of windows through which we can examine any unit of experience, including a particular rhetorical theory. What happens when you view this rhetoric "through" the perspectives described in the chart? How, for example, does it contrast with other rhetorics? What is its position in a larger context of human affairs? In a system of values? In a universe of discourse? What is the dominant perspective in this chapter?

Beyond analysis

Becoming an effective writer requires that you develop intelligent habits of proceeding. With sufficient practice in confronting the problems of communication, lessons in theory and technique should become habits of thought, and acts that were at first awkward and self-concious should become normal ways of behaving. Then deliberate and extensive analysis of the writing task is necessary only when habit cannot supply adequate solutions. In time, you should be able to relegate technical and theoretical matters to the margin of your attention and focus your powers on the real business of communication—understanding, and sharing with others what you have understood.

All that has been discussed in this book is clearly apparent in the essay that follows: a mind coming to grips with a problematic experience, an effort to share what has taken form, a clear intention, and a linguistic structure that is the instrument of that intention. We could, of course, supply questions that would direct your attention to specific rhetorical techniques, as we have with other essays in the book. But we omit such questions here to stress an important point often lost sight of in the rhetoric class. Although the essay may illustrate rhetorical techniques, its function is social rather than pedagogical. Rosenthal addresses the reader not as a student of rhetoric but as a student of life and as a member of a community whose coherence is in constant jeopardy. It is important to remember in those moments when we are preoccupied with technical problems and the elegance of the written word that technique and polished discourse are only means to an end, not ends in themselves.

There Is No News from Auschwitz
A. M. ROSENTHAL

The most terrible thing of all, somehow, was that at Brzezinka the sun was bright and warm, the rows of graceful poplars were lovely to look upon and on the grass near the gates children played.

It all seemed frighteningly wrong, as in a nightmare, that at Brzezinka the sun should ever shine or that there should be light and greenness and the sound of young laughter. It would be fitting if at Brzezinka the sun never shone and the grass withered, because this is a place of unutterable terror.

And yet, every day, from all over the world, people come to Brzezinka, quite possibly the most grisly tourist center on earth. They come for a variety of reasons—to see if it could really have been true, to remind themselves not to forget, to pay homage to the dead by the simple act of looking upon their place of suffering.

Brzezinka is a couple of miles from the better-known southern Polish town of Oswiecim. Oswiecim has about 12,000 inhabitants, is situated about 171 miles from Warsaw and lies in a damp, marshy area at the eastern end of the pass called the Moravian Gate. Brzezinka and Oswiecim together formed part of that minutely organized factory of torture and death that the Nazis called Konzentrationslager Auschwitz.

By now, fourteen years after the last batch of prisoners was herded naked into the gas chambers by dogs and guards, the story of Auschwitz has been told a great many times. Some of the inmates have written of those memories of which sane men cannot conceive. Rudolf Franz Ferdinand Hoess, the superintendent of the camp, before he was executed wrote his detailed memoirs of mass exterminations and the experiments on living bodies. Four million people died here, the Poles say.

And so there is no news to report about Auschwitz. There is merely the compulsion to write something about it, a compulsion that grows out of a restless feeling that to have visited Auschwitz and then turned away without having said or written anything would somehow be a most grievous act of discourtesy to those who died here.

Brzezinka and Oswiecim are very quiet places now; the screams can no longer be heard. The tourist walks silently, quickly, at first to get it over with and then, as his mind peoples the barracks and the chambers and the dungeons and flogging posts, he walks draggingly. The guide does not say much either, because there is nothing much for him to say after he has pointed.

For every visitor, there is one particular bit of horror that he knows he will never forget. For some it is seeing the rebuilt gas chamber at Oswiecim and being told that this is the "small one." For others it is the fact that at Brzezinka, in the ruins of the gas chambers and the crematoria the Germans blew up when they retreated, there are daisies growing.

There are visitors who gaze blankly at the gas chambers and the furnaces because their minds simply cannot encompass them, but stand shivering before the great mounds of human hair behind the plate glass window or the piles of babies shoes or the brick cells where men sentenced to death by suffocation were walled up.

One visitor opened his mouth in a silent scream simply at the sight of boxes — great stretches of three-tiered wooden boxes in the women's barracks. They were about six feet wide, about three feet high, and into them from five to ten prisoners were shoved for the night. The guide walks quickly through the barracks. Nothing more to see here.

A brick building where sterilization experiments were carried out on women prisoners. The guide tries the door — it's locked. The visitor is grateful that he does not have to go in, and then flushes with shame.

A long corridor where rows of faces stare from the walls. Thousands of pictures, the photographs of prisoners. They are all dead now, the men and women who stood before the cameras, and they all knew they were to die.

They all stare blank-faced, but one picture, in the middle of a row, seizes the eye and wrenches the mind. A girl 22 years old, plumply pretty, blonde. She is smiling gently, as at a sweet, treasured thought. What was the thought that passed through her young mind and is now her memorial on the wall of the dead at Auschwitz?

Into the suffocation dungeons the visitor is taken for a moment and feels himself strangling. Another visitor goes in, stumbles out and crosses herself. There is no place to pray at Auschwitz.

The visitors look pleadingly at each other and say to the guide, "Enough."

There is nothing new to report about Auschwitz. It was a sunny day and the trees were green and at the gates the children played.

* * *

We have another reason for withholding analysis. Rhetorical problems pale beside the writer's message. Rosenthal presents so powerfully one nightmarish consequence of the differences that separate men that contemplation seems more appropriate than analysis. Yet in contemplating the nightmare, we might remember that one reasonable response to the perception of human differences, no matter how huge and ineradicable they may seem, or be, is a concern for rhetoric.

Rhetoric enables you to enter the battle of the mind, for it supplies the tools necessary for bringing about changes in the way men think—the way you think and the way others think. It thus enables you to work effectively for the good. Style has an ethical dimension; in addition to intellectual and linguistic choices, moral choices must be made. But "good" and "moral" by whose criteria? Yours, we must say, even though your criteria will at times differ from ours. Human differences are inevitable, as are the ills arising from them. However, ills can be ameliorated whenever thoughtful men use the written and spoken word to come closer together. As John Dewey explained, "Not perfection as the final goal, but the ever enduring process of perfecting, maturing, refining, is the aim in living."

Index